Counseling and Spirituality

Integrating Spiritual and Clinical Orientations

Joshua M. Gold

University of South Carolina

Merrill

Upper Saddle River, New Jersey
Columbus, Ohio

Library of Congress Cataloging-in-Publication Data

Gold, Joshua M. (Joshua Mark)
  Counseling and spirituality: integrating spiritual and clinical
orientations/Joshua M. Gold.
    p. cm.
  ISBN-13: 978-0-13-239313-3
  ISBN-10: 0-13-239313-1
  1. Counseling—Religious aspects. 2. Spirituality. I. Title.
  BF636.68.G653 2010
  158'.3—dc22

                                2008046762

Vice President and Executive Publisher: Jeffery W. Johnston
Acquisitions Editor: Meredith Fossel
Editorial Assistant: Nancy Holstein
Senior Managing Editor: Pamela D. Bennett
Senior Art Director: Diane C. Lorenzo
Cover Design: Candace Rowley
Cover Image: © Ferrell McCollough/SuperStock
Operations Specialist: Matt Ottenweller
Director of Marketing: Quinn Perkson
Marketing Manager: Amanda L. Stedke
Marketing Coordinator: Brian Mounts

This book was set in Garamond by 10/12. It was printed and bound by King Printing Co., Inc.
The cover was printed by King Printing Co., Inc.

Pearson® is a registered trademark of Pearson plc
Merrill® is a registered trademark of Pearson Education, Inc.

Pearson Education Ltd., London   Pearson Education North Asia, Ltd., Hong Kong
Pearson Education Singapore Pte. Ltd.   Pearson Educación de Mexico, S.A. de C.V.
Pearson Education Canada, Inc.   Pearson Education Malaysia Pte. Ltd.
Pearson Education—Japan   Pearson Education Upper Saddle River, New Jersey
Pearson Education Australia, Limited

Merrill
is an imprint of

PEARSON

www.pearsonhighered.com

2 3 4 5 6 7 8 9 10 V0CR 16 15 14 13 12
ISBN 13: 978-0-13-239313-3
ISBN 10:   0-13-239313-1

BRIEF CONTENTS

CONTENTS

PREFACE

"Let us watch well our beginnings, and results will manage themselves."
—ALEXANDER CLARK, BROADWAY PERFORMER
(CA. 1866–1932)

INTRODUCTION

The preparation of any work of this length and complexity must reflect an emerging trend within a professional field of study. Although in the popular literature one may be able to create interest and demand by writing a book, scholarly books, by contrast, tend to appear as the result of already existing interest and demand from practitioners and from those in graduate training. In the case of this book, both the interest and demand are based on the expanding importance of issues of religion and spirituality within mental health services.

The emerging area of religion and spirituality in counseling thrusts upon professionals the important issue of which aspects of the subject would be of interest and value to clinicians, clinicians in training, clinical supervisors, and faculty who seek to prepare the coming generations of mental health service providers. As an author, one hopes to identify an approach that honors previous scholarly research and writing, yet extends such research in new directions with added depth or perspective. It is that aim which drove the development and preparation of this book.

The guiding force behind the book is the ever-growing sensitivity to multicultural issues in the provision of mental health services. The ethical commitment to respect those aspects of the self which define identity as part of culture continues to expand and direct both training and clinical service. Attention to issues of culture has brought to the fore a number of explicit and implicit contributors to identity and life functioning. Among the former are those factors which are readily visible, such as gender, age, and ethnicity; the latter consist of those less obvious dynamics such as sexual orientation, socioeconomic status, education, and religious or spiritual orientation. The growing awareness of the diversity of relevant, vital multicultural concerns demands attention to those individually identified contributors to identity. Mental health practitioners are challenged to help individuals, couples, and families honor those aspects of individual and conjoint culture which direct one's sense of self, community connection, and life focus. The decisions made in that regard are meant, not to exclude or diminish the importance of other documented human experiences of culture, but rather to ensure a directed focus of research, writing, and deliberation.

THE THESIS UNDERLYING THIS WORK

The professional focus on multiculturalism in the helping professions, in terms of both the delivery of services and standards for the preparation of future mental health clinicians (Schulte, Skinner & Claiborn, 2002), has provided a consistent direction in respect of opening the perspectives of mental health practitioners to the ways in which culture defines and identifies individuals and groups. Multiple aspects of multiculturalism have been identified and are still being identified for clinical consideration and professional research. One issue arising out of this focus is the need to identify those aspects of culture and identity which are relevant to directed study, clinical preparation, clinical supervision, and professional research. Initially, multiculturalism was seen to include only ethnic and racial differences (Parker, 1988). More recently, Sue, Bingham, Porche-Burke, and Vasquez (1999) and Pate and Hall (2005) identified religion and spirituality as entering into the multicultural mix as well.

All current ethical codes and standards for graduate-level mental health training programs identify cultural concerns as an area in need of therapeutic sensitivity and integration into the delivery of efficacious mental health services, but, as of the date of preparation of this book, none of those codes or standards itemizes cultural concerns or specifies which concerns are of primary importance. (A notable exception was the Curricular Standards of the 2001 Standards in Counselor Education put forth by the Council for Accreditation of Counseling and Related Educational Programs; however, in 2009 it was proposed that these standards be moved to the glossary.) This purposeful omission of itemized cultural concerns may be vital in order to allow the clinician to meet clients without assuming which aspects of culture each client has adopted as a contributor to self-identity. Thus, by understanding that culture is important, but not knowing which aspects of culture are important to a particular client, the clinician can encourage the client to identify for him- or herself those very aspects.

Nonetheless, this omission of specific aspects of culture has two potential drawbacks. First, as regards curricular training, course content in multicultural issues may vary widely with the instructor's priorities, the available texts, and the doctoral preparation that the instructor has received (Knox et al., 2005; Schulte, Skinner, & Claiborn, 2002). Second, an ill-equipped clinician may overlook those defining barometers of culture which are irrelevant to his or her own individual identity. For example, should an individual clinician not have been introduced to the dynamics of socioeconomic status as a variable in self-definition in graduate training, and not have contemplated his or her own values, mores, etc., as a member of a specific social class, then that clinician cannot be expected to consider the client's socioeconomic status as an aspect of self-definition. In effect, the clinician is oblivious to the strengths of these defining aspects of human identity. This may be the challenge regarding the clinician's understanding, or lack thereof, of religion and spirituality as a defining force in the lives of individuals and in the training of culturally sensitive and skilled mental health professionals.

The mounting attention being paid to religion and spirituality in the helping professions stems from three roots: (1) an improved professional receptivity to spirituality, (2) a growing acknowledgment of the importance of spirituality and religion as multicultural variables, and (3) an increasing client demand for secular mental health clinicians to address issues of religion and spirituality within mental health services. I shall briefly discuss each of these causes in turn.

"In psychology as well as anthropology, religious beliefs and values have long been considered among the defining elements of culture, reflecting a culture's shared perspectives on ethical and existential issues" (Schulte, Skinner & Claiborn, 2002, p. 118). Patterson et al. (2000) spoke to the historical overlap among physical, emotional, and spiritual healing, citing the scientific revolution as the initial divisive factor between medicine and, later, psychology, on the one hand, and religion/spirituality, on the other. Miller

(1999) proclaimed that "the spiritual dimension is a necessary and beneficial component in mental health counseling" (p. 498), and a number of researchers have reidentified spiritual beliefs as vital aspects of a multicultural perspective (Hoogestraat & Trammel, 2003; Riemer-Ross, 2003; Souza, 2002). Powers (2005) asserted that "at the beginning of the 21st century, spirituality and counseling seem to go hand in hand" (p. 217) and related that her own clinical training in clinical psychology considered religion a "taboo topic" (p. 220), a trend that she sees being finally redressed. This sentiment was an echo of Weinstein, Parker, and Archer (2002), who attributed their own omission of discussions of religion and spirituality in clinical service to the absence of any such discussions in their training. Put succinctly, spirituality is a meaning-making activity (Sink & Lee, 2004), and because counseling counts meaning-making among the tasks it is charged with attempting to provide insight and resolve problems, religion and spirituality must be broached in clinical sessions, to be acknowledged either as irrelevant by the client or, more likely, as part of an untapped or overlooked reservoir of client resources that are available to respond to and resolve the immediate problem.

One of the conclusions of the UNESCO Conference on Education for the 21st Century was that training on "diversity in religion and spirituality is specifically linked to [a] multicultural and multi-faith context" (Haw & Hughes, 1998, p. 156). With regard to the rationale for the connection to a multifaith perspective, Hoogestraat and Trammel (2003, p. 414) asserted that

- "All humans are spiritual beings;
- Spirituality [affects] mental, physical and emotional health; and,
- It is essential to address spiritual and religious issues in therapy to maintain ethical care"

On the basis of these three assertions, it would seem fit that religion and spirituality have a rightful place in the provision of mental health services in the 21st century.

What appears to be evolving reflects the "interconnectedness of spirituality and the human services" (Riemer-Ross, 2003, p. 73), as reflected in the evolution of the Association for Spiritual, Ethical, and Religious Values in Counseling (ASERVIC) (Powers, 2005), a current division of the American Counseling Association that mirrors the increase in professional interest. (For an informative and succinct review of the development of the organizational aspects of the spiritual focus in counseling, see Miller, 1999).

Additional confirmation of the professional embracing of religious and spiritual concerns within the provision of mental health services appears elsewhere in the professional literature as well. Miller and Thoresen (2003) referenced a special edition of the *American Psychologist* that was dedicated to research on the topic of spirituality and physical and emotional well-being: "[P]sychologists have increasingly recognized that religion and spirituality are relevant aspects of client diversity that psychologists should be able to recognize while treating religious or spiritual clients with sensitivity" (Walker, Gorsuch, & Tan, 2004, p. 69). From such stances comes the corollary that graduate-level training in religion and spirituality in the provision of mental health services is of vital importance (Hall, Dixon & Mauzey, 2004). From the perspective of wellness, spiritual and religious growth must be included as normative aspects of human development (Miller, 1999). In summary of this section on the professional response to this topic, the words of Miller (1999) resound.

The events from the initial inclusion of the National Catholic Guidance Conference in the American Personnel and Guidance Association through the current Phase III of the

Summit on Spirituality speak to a willingness to dialogue with ASERVIC to make the inclusion of spirituality in counseling respectful, compassionate and ethical. (p. 500).

"For many people, spirituality and religion are vital aspects of their lives" (Cashwell & Young, 2004). Knox et al. (2005) proclaimed that, for the vast majority of individuals in American society, and perhaps worldwide, religion or spirituality plays "a central role in their existence" (p. 298). Lukoff, Lun, and Turner (1992) asserted that "the spiritual and religious dimensions of culture [are] among the most important factors influencing human experience, beliefs, values, behaviors and illness patterns" (p. 1320; Patterson et al., 2000, Souza, 2002). In addition, clients and potential clients are increasingly calling for the mental health professional to address their religious or spiritual concerns in session. Rose, Westefeld, and Ansley (2001) spoke to the growing numbers seeking personal religious/spiritual resources outside the bounds of traditional faith institutions and ". . . believing that discussing religious concerns in counseling was appropriate" (p. 68). However, "potential clients have fears and negative expectations about how a therapist might respond to their beliefs and may even avoid secular counseling because of those fears" (p. 68).

HOW THIS BOOK ADDRESSES THIS GOAL

The goal of this text is to "build and apply a body of knowledge and practice that reflects fully the integrity, uniqueness and wholeness of each person" (Burke, et al., 1999, p. 256). The content of the book is designed to foster the connection between the professional literature and the self as spiritual journeyer, as related to the self as clinician. This objective sounds like a complex mission; perhaps it could be more simply stated as a request that present and future mental health professionals contemplate how they see religion and spirituality in their own lives—as a struggle or a fount of resources, as an area of strength or an area for growth, and to appraise how their own spirituality sways who they are as clinicians and what they do in the provision of mental health services for their clients. If any passage in this text sheds light upon any of those questions, then the exercise of writing the book has been worthwhile.

The book offers 15 different topics, making up a semester's length of material and summarized, chapter by chapter, as follows:

Chapter 1: "Religion and Spirituality—Counseling and Psychology" (similarities and differences in definitions of religion and spirituality; historical background to the neglect of spirituality in clinical service; the present re-integration of religion and spirituality within clinical mental health services)

Chapter 2: "The Personal and Professional" (the self as a spiritual being within the delivery of mental health services)

Chapter 3: "Varieties of Spiritual Beliefs" (overview of major world religions; overview of the writings about major counseling theorists; overlap in attention between major world religions and counseling/psychology theory)

Chapter 4: "Developmental Models of Spirituality and Psychosocial Functioning" (integration of existing models of spiritual, psychosocial, moral, and cognitive development)

Chapter 5: "Spirituality Identity and Maturity" (the place and function of religion and spirituality in optimal human functioning for those clinicians who seek to present a strength-based or potential-focused model of treatment)

Chapter 6: "Assessment of Spiritual Functioning" (identification and evaluation of current modes of self and client assessment along differing barometers of spirituality)

Chapter 7: "Guilt and Mental Health" (understanding guilt and the ways in which religion and spiritual practice may contribute to, and provide respite from, human guilt)

Chapter 8: "Evil and Counseling" (reconciling the presence of evil in the world from spiritual and clinical perspectives)

Chapter 9: "Balancing the Concepts of the Divine and the Penitent" (wondering whether one's view of his or her relationship with God, Allah, Yahweh, the Divine, etc., may affect one's view of the role of the clinician as authority figure and the client as penitent)

Chapter 10: "Spirituality and Ethics" (the application of professional ethical standards specific to issues of religion and spirituality in clinical service)

Chapter 11: "Theory-Based Approaches to Wellness in Counseling and Spirituality" (an integration of spiritual wellness into counseling, as presented by differing theoretical models of both)

Chapter 12: "Spirituality and Marginalized Groups" (the experiences of marginalized groups within mainstream religious institutions)

Chapter 13: "Spiritual Strategies for Individual Counseling" (identification and application of spiritual interventions within the repertoire of clinical services for individuals

Chapter 14: "Spiritual Strategies for Couples and Family Counseling" (identification and application of spiritual interventions within the repertoire of clinical services for couples or families)

Chapter 15: "Opportunities for Future Professional and Personal Development" (synopsis of the themes of this book, plus directions for future study; professional development and considerations for oneself as a spiritual journeyer, as offered by authors of previous works on counseling and spirituality)

Each chapter opens with a case example offering a real-life application of the chapter's content to the dilemmas of mental health professionals. Each chapter closes by revisiting that same case example as a mode of reconciling the opening personal and professional challenge. The writing attempts to link issues of religion and spirituality with issues that are of importance to learning, practicing, or supervising mental health service providers. Each chapter also offers sections titled "Self-Understanding Exercises" and "Opportunities for Future Learning," the former focused on knowledge of the self as a spiritual being, the latter on professional development.

FOR WHOM THE TEXT IS INTENDED

"Mental health professionals are beginning to acknowledge the need for competency regarding religion and spirituality issues in the counseling field" (Hall, Dixon, & Mauzey, 2004, p. 507). The question then arises, What is meant by "competency"? Generally speaking, a clinician's competency in the delivery of mental health services is based on (a) skills, (b) knowledge, and, (c) self-awareness. All three components are integral for efficacious and respectful mental health service, and it is their confluence, rather than disparate impacts, which is deeply felt. In other words, a clinician's mastery of each area is vital: skill in one area cannot compensate for inability in any of the other two areas. Skills are grounded in one's abilities of relationship, assessment, and intervention; knowledge regarding theories of development, growth, and pathology; and awareness of the use of the self as the sole medium in clinical service for the expression of both knowledge and skill. This book was designed to utilize the third dynamic (the self of the clinician) as the gathering theme of each chapter, around which specific knowledge or skills are clustered. There are two main reasons for this approach: (1) Clinicians seek to model genuineness or personal authenticity for their clients as a way for clients to legitimize and honor all parts of the self as a function of adopting a biopsychosocial model of human experience (Patterson et al., 2000); and (2) clinicians can help clients no further on their personal life paths than they themselves have yet traveled, so their awareness of themselves as religious or spiritual beings is essential to delivering counseling services.

This book is intended for mental health professionals in the field or in training, including counselors, social workers, psychologists, psychiatrists, and marriage and family therapists. In sum, any individual who provides some sort of mental health service, regardless of professional training or title, may find the book of interest and of value. According to the professional literature, it may be of interest to clinicians to learn that the "spiritual heritage of psychotherapists differs from that of [the] average American" (Walker, Gorsuch, & Tan, 2004, p. 76) and that ". . . they risk alienating clients who present with spiritual issues, particularly if the counselor is unaware of his or her own spirituality" (Souza, 2002, p. 213). So the message is clear that clinicians need to consider their own and their clients' perspectives on how religion and spirituality influence one's life functioning.

ACKNOWLEDGMENTS

Any type of scholarly work may have one author, multiple authors, or editors with multiple contributors listed on the title page; however, all these works are actualized through the support and encouragement of one's personal and professional community. Allow me to begin with acknowledging my personal support system. I would first like to acknowledge my wife, Hope, who was instrumental in guiding my thinking on these topics and for her insights that were of inestimable value. The joy of seeking her feedback extended to the depth of her understanding of each topic, plus her depth of insight into herself as a spiritual being. I also honor the input of my stepchildren, Aia and Della Andonovska, who were kind enough to let me type this book without interrupting and who cared enough not to be too upset at how long it took. I also appreciate the input from my mother, Yhetta, in Winnipeg, and the encouraging comments from Hope's family here in Fort Mill, South Carolina: Bill, her father; Sylvia, her mother; and Cloria Alsup, her aunt.

Any work of any professional sort cannot claim its strengths and relevance without careful input from other professionals who cared enough about the topic to offer their thoughts and perspectives. In that sentiment, I gratefully acknowledge Guerda Nicolas, Boston College; Kimberly N. Frazier, Clemson University; Scott E. Hall, University of Dayton; Randall R. Lyle, St. Mary's University; Reid Stevens, University of Southern Maine; Timothy J. Teague, George Madson and Edward A. Wierzalis, University of North Carolina–Charlotte, all of whom served as reviewers for different parts of this production.

I cannot speak too highly of Meredith Fossel, my editor at Merrill Prentice Hall Publishing, and the rest of the editorial staff. Ms. Fossel first embraced the concept of this book and guided me through its conception, writing, revising, and editing. Her patience and input were consistently dedicated toward strengthening the book while allowing my voice as an author to remain.

I must also acknowledge the contributions of my colleagues at the University of South Carolina. Provost Mark Becker, Dean Les Sternberg of the College of Education, and Educational Studies Department Chair Alan Wieder all supported my request for a sabbatical to be able to dedicate a semester of full-time writing to this project. Their foresight and support in doing so allowed me to immerse myself within the project and proceed toward its publication. In my absence during that sabbatical term, I must thank my faculty colleagues in the Counselor Education Program at the University of South Carolina for taking on my campus-based program responsibilities so that I could concentrate on this work. I also wish to acknowledge the input from several graduate students who were interested in the topic and whose interests I hope are well-served by this book. The book has truly been a team effort. While my name will appear as author, I could not have accomplished this feat without the noted contributions of these individuals so mentioned.

CONCLUSION

Perhaps the field of counseling has arrived full circle regarding the legitimacy of religion and spirituality as topics of relevance. James (1895) stated, more than one hundred years ago, that spiritual experiences are legitimate psychological phenomena. It would seem that the field of mental health services is catching up with James. As the idea of multiculturalism expands to encompass more facets of the human experience, including religion and spirituality, this ending citation may be oft repeated: "Through such exploration, we may learn to acknowledge, and more powerfully honor, pivotal elements of our clients' lives" (Knox et al., 2005, p. 301).

SELF-UNDERSTANDING EXERCISES

1. Before you move farther into this book, identify which of the chapter topics seem more, and which less, appealing to you? How do you account for your choices?
2. As you examine the thesis of this book, how does it resound with your prior notion of what this sort of a course might entail?
3. As you begin this course, identify three "big spiritual questions" to which you hope to find answers or direction through this directed study.

OPPORTUNITIES FOR FURTHER LEARNING

1. Review the table of contents of other texts with titles similar to this one. How do the topics or chapters listed agree or disagree with those presented here? What does that tell you about the status of scholarship on this topic?

2. Ask the instructor in your school who is teaching this course how he or she decided on the syllabus and the choice of this book.

3. Go online to review other graduate-level syllabi in this content area to compare offerings at other graduate schools and the course on religion or spirituality in the helping professions in your graduate program. Which topics do you find are consistent between courses? Which are unique to your course? How do you make sense of those similarities and differences in coverage?

1

Religion and Spirituality—Counseling and Psychology

Religion is the sum of the expansive impulses of a being.

—HAVELOCK ELLIS

CASE EXAMPLE

Terrance was initially interested in becoming a therapist because he had been in counseling and had found a greater acceptance of himself as a result. He was unsure of how to find a good clinical-preparation program and used Web sites to review program mission statements and testimonials from program graduates. He focused on large, state-supported schools that claimed that their students would meet the academic and clinical requirements for licensure in his state. He noticed that some programs required training in religious and spiritual issues in counseling and some did not. Such coursework was not required for his state license, so he was puzzled why one program might insist on such a curriculum whereas another would not.

INTRODUCTION

This chapter explores four themes that define the current status of scholarship directed toward religious and spiritual issues in mental health services. This investigation provides a context in which to better understand past differences between religion and the helping professions as a way to grasp existing professional schisms and to decide to what extent those divisions are warranted and which "turf battles" need to be relegated to the archives.

First, a working vocabulary of the differences and similarities between the terms *religion* and *spirituality* will be supplied because such wording is not used synonymously in current academic discussions. Second, the historical confluence and the rift between religion

1

and psychology will be presented, followed by the third theme, which is the current emergence of issues of spirituality in counseling and the other helping professions. The final theme of relevance to those in the helping professions, either already in practice or in training, revolves around the legitimacy and importance of consideration of the self as a spiritual being in one's professional preparation. These themes echo those espoused by Parsons and Jonte-Pace (2001) in their search for the common ground between psychology and religion, and by Hall, Dixon, and Mauzey (2004) in their advocacy for greater roles for religion and spirituality in counselor education and school counseling.

DEFINING THE TERMS *RELIGION* AND *SPIRITUALITY*

Religion and spirituality dictate the nature of this chapter. By separating these constructs in terms of definition and description, there is an assertion that these concepts are related but not identical. In addition, there is an implied assumption that one can be (a) spiritual without being religious, (b) religious without being spiritual, (c) both religious and spiritual, or (d) neither religious nor spiritual. Your first challenge is to decide to what extent this vision of these two concepts holds merit; the second challenge is to determine in which of the four categories you see yourself. Finally, you need to ponder what placement into that category says about your religious and spiritual strengths and opportunities for ongoing growth in this area of personal and professional development.

Kelly (1995, p. 3) used both terms to offer an affirmation of transcendence, or "otherness," beyond the boundaries of everyday culture, the ordinary, and the tangible. Almost a decade later, Hall, Dixon, and Mauzey (2004) acknowledged that these terms, when used synonymously, encompass an area of concentration grounded in a dimension of reality beyond the boundaries of the strictly empirically perceived material world. In both of these working definitions, there is attention toward an existing phenomenon beyond the ken of everyday life that is implicit within the human scope and worthy of human endeavor. The wording by Hall et al. also suggested some "other way of knowing" in addition to that of empiricism as a means by which to access or experience this phenomenon. This suggestion will be fully explored in the section of this chapter that summarizes the split between science and religion.

Hodges (2002, p. 112) presented a summary of 10 similarities between religion and spirituality. Both offer:

1. meaning in life;
2. intrinsic values as the basis for one's behavior;
3. transcendence (going beyond commonly understood boundaries);
4. a relationship with a Higher Power;
5. a belief in a creative and universal force;
6. a shift of "locus of centricity to humanicentricity, of egocentricity to cosmicentricity";
7. inclusion within a greater collective;
8. guidance through a divine plan;
9. an experience, a sense of awe and wonder when contemplating the universe; and
10. shared values and support within a community (need not be in a building).

You may need to review the preceding list after reading this chapter to evaluate how accurate or complete the itemization presented here may then seem. This suggestion is meant solely to underscore the fluidity in the process of describing these two terms, and to emphasize the responsibility that each individual may assume for struggling with this process of understanding as an aspect of one's ongoing personal and professional evolution as a spiritual/religious being.

Defining Religion

This section will provide a synopsis of the definitions of the term *religion*. The intent is to offer an overview of the commonalities between all religions prior to defining the term *spirituality*. The objective is to educate the reader to the differing operationalizations between the two terms so that each term can be used appropriately.

Kelly (1995, p. 2) cited a description from Albanese (1992, p. 3) to define religion:

> Why is it that so common a feature of human life proves so baffling? Is the inability to define, like the optical illusion, simply caused by staring too long into the religious landscape? Or are there other problems as well, intrinsic to the nature of religion? A definition means an end or a limit, a boundary. A definition tells us where some reality ends; it separates the world into what is and what is not in that reality. Religion cannot be defined very easily because it thrives both within and outside of boundaries. The boundaries of religion are different from the logical boundaries of good definitions. In the end, religion is a feature that encompasses all of human life.

Perhaps the response to this concern voiced by Albanese is identical to that decided on at the 1995 Summit on Spirituality, where the participants concentrated on "definition" versus "description." From *Merriam Webster's Online Dictionary* come the following two entries:

> *definition:* a statement expressing the essential nature of something; a statement of the meaning of a word or word group or a sign or symbol.
> *description:* kind or character especially as determined by salient features.

On the basis of the wording, the descriptions of religion and spirituality will endeavor to offer the salient features common to each term.

Kelly (1995, p. 5) described religion as "creedal, institutional, ritual expressions of spirituality associated with world religions and denominations," and cited Corbett (1990, p. 2):

> A religion is an integrated system of belief, lifestyle, ritual activities, and institutions by which individuals give meaning to (or find meaning in) their lives by orienting them to what is taken to be sacred, holy, or the highest value.

Sperry (2001) described all religion as dedicated to an awareness of the transcendent. Although the form or name of that transcendence is one of the distinguishing aspects of each world religion, the commitment to that figure and ideal remains constant across major world religions. Religion also manifests itself in "conceptual, cultural and social form" (p. 4). There must be an outward presentation of this shared belief system (dogma) and shared ritual practices (liturgy). The learning of the dogma and the practicing of the liturgy are designed to provide the guidance or path toward the facilitation of those experiences identified as transcendent.

Hodges (2002, p. 110) spoke to the behavioral and cognitive aspects of religion by specifying "a set of rituals and creeds [that] may be manifest in the context of a religious institution: Jewish, Catholic, Islamic and so forth." Therefore, religion offers a formalized ritual and tradition, supported by an established belief system to which the affiliate is expected, or hoped, to aspire. The idea of the "institutionalism" of religion offers added weight and formality to this concept. Institutionalism implies a formal organizational structure, a hierarchy, a process of ascending that hierarchy (and perhaps exclusion from that ruling hierarchy), and a way to financially support itself. In addition, the idea of an "institution" brings to mind a specified place of worship. In the example given, these houses of worship would include synagogues, churches, and mosques, and usually well-defined styles and ceremonies of worship. Also, this "agency of God" requires individuals who dedicate their lives to this mission and become learned leaders within their respective religious communities. Therefore, in conjunction with the organizational structure, there must be an administrative structure created to monitor the differing denominations or houses of worship within a specific religion to ensure a constancy of allegiance to the specific religious doctrine.

Faiver, Ingersoll, O'Brien, and McNally (2001, p. 2) described religion as the "outward, public and more conventional form of a spiritual impulse." This statement implies that "less conventional forms" of the same spiritual impulse exist that would not qualify to be labeled a religion. Perhaps the mark of a religion is the establishment of that conventionalism, but there was no mention of the criteria for such a designation. In addition, these four authors spoke to the creeds, rituals, and stated beliefs sculpted by culture and adopted by the individual within each religion. This latter phrase speaks to the expectation that a new member will adhere to pre-existing doctrine; that the initiation process involves taking on the expectations of the religious institution and not having a voice at that time in what those creeds or practices may be. This notion also suggests the potential for an errant or argumentative member to be ousted from that religious community because loyalty and obedience, rather than divergence of opinion, may be much more strongly encouraged and tolerated.

Frame (2003, p. 4) spoke to religions as exemplified by ". . . a set of beliefs and practices of an organized religious institution . . . [It] implies a cosmic or metaphysical backdrop as well as some behavioral expectations." Within that view, the idea of a metaphysical context is added. This aspect rings true of all formalized religions, both in terms of characters (gods, angels, devils, etc.) and places (heaven, hell, etc.). The purpose of the codified beliefs and practices are to promote a specific value system expressed through a specific mode of living that is said to please whatever deity is worshipped and to earn the individual an afterlife blessed by the Creator. There is also a covert warning that adhering to a value system not endorsed by a specific religion and, therefore, living in a manner incongruent with the lifestyle advocated by that religion, will earn the individual the displeasure of the Creator and an afterlife of pain and punishment.

Hall et al. (2004, p. 505) described religion as "the social vehicle to nurture and express spirituality." This wording implies a community of worshippers who adopt the learning and practices of a particular religion toward the individual expression of one's spiritual growth and the communal experience of the congregation. There is an admonition about a shared experience, but whether that sharing is designed to promote a diversity of opinion and expansion of the religion or to ensure ongoing compliance and early recognition of deviance or heresy is not specified.

Religion provides "a particular framework that includes a belief structure, a moral code, and authority structure and a form of worship" (Hayes & Cowie, 2005, p. 31). Religion is also characterized by an "existential certainty—optimism about the future and alleviation from the fear of death and dying" (p. 28)—offering answers to life's most profound questions and "peace of mind." Each religion seems to address the same existential questions and offers its adherents not only answers but also reassurance that those answers are more correct than those offered by any other religion. In addition, religion promotes altruism and helping within one's communities. The "doing of good work" would seem to be a staple of all major religions. The questions that bear further exploration concern the intended groups (Are these members of the same congregation or those who have yet to embrace the "true faith," and what is the expected outcome of this helping?) This expectation applies both to those who go forth to minister to others and those who receive this help.

In summary, Cashwell and Young (2005) described all major world religions as exemplifying seven similar salient features. These religions are characterized by being (a) denominational, (b) external, (c) cognitive, (d) behavioral, (e) ritualistic and public, (f) institutional, and (g) creedal. It is important to apply these tenets to one's chosen religious institution to see in what ways this list may be complete and in what ways it is in need of expansion. However, reference to these salient features of religion may be of help in better understanding the following section that discusses descriptions of "spirituality."

Defining Spirituality

This discussion must first be recognized as characterized by a lack of common definition (Faiver et al., 2001). Cashwell and Young (2005) echoed this sentiment by remarking on the diversity of current attempts at definition. It is of interest that these authors included the comment by Kurtz and Ketcham (1992) stating that this struggle reflects our own limits but not those characteristics of the phenomenon we seek to better capture. Perhaps that assertion reflects the intense personal nature of the spiritual experience and the possibility that the experience itself cannot be fully articulated through words. It may be of value to the development of this theme that the writings be ordered chronologically because later authors may have consulted earlier publications in the formulations of their own thoughts.

It may also be of value to begin with the description of spirituality as authored by the 1995 Summit on Spirituality:

> The animating force in life [is] represented by such images as breath, wind, vigor, and courage. Spirituality is the infusion and drawing out of spirit in one's life. It is experienced as an active and passive process. Spirituality is also described as a capacity and tendency that is innate and unique to all persons. This spiritual tendency moves through the individual toward knowledge, love, meaning, hope, transcendence, connectedness, and compassion. Spirituality includes one's capacity for creativity, growth, and the development of a value system. Spirituality encompasses the religious, spiritual and transpersonal. (p. 30)

Sperry (2001) included terms such as *universal, developmental, ecumenical, internal, affective, spontaneous, private,* and *highly personal* as vital components of spirituality. He cited Chandler, Holden, and Kolander (1992, p. 169)—"[P]ertaining to the innate capacity to, and tendency to seek to, transcend one's current locus of centricity, which transcendence involves increased love and knowledge"—as contributing notions of the innate foundation of spirituality and the two manifested outcomes of spiritual growth. He wrote that spirituality

". . . connotes a direct personal experience of the sacred unmediated by particular belief systems prescribed by dogma or by hierarchical structures of priests, ministers, rabbis, or gurus" (p. 4), and of "one's search for meaning and belonging and the core values that influence one's behavior" (p. 4).

"Whatever is spiritual touches us deeply and can transform suffering into learning, enmity into collaboration, and indifference into love" (Faiver et al., 2001, p. 1), and can be considered a spiritual awakening or experience. Spirituality promotes and is identified by a sense of wholeness, openness to the infinite, and connectedness. Similar to Sperry (2001), Faiver et al. proposed that spirituality is an innate human quality, deeply part of the human condition but transcending the human condition. This quality is not a human-created structure or institution but an inborn instinct to understand and then move beyond a cognitive grasp to an appreciation of what can only be experienced individually yet, at the same time, known in some way to represent both a core human search and catharsis.

Frame (2003) stated that trying to define spirituality is ". . . almost antithetical to the idea itself" (p. 2). As a point of etymology, the roots of this term are founded in the Greek word *pneuma* used in the Pauline letters in the Bible and translated as wind, breath, life, and spirit—synonymous with the Hebrew term *ruach*. From the Latin comes the word *spiritus,* meaning breath, courage, life, or vigor. Transcending mortality, what is implied by these terms is that force which brings meaning and purpose to life, which may or may not include the presence of a Higher Power or God. To aid in the clarification of this term, Frame also cited input from Cervantes and Ramirez (1992), who referred to the spiritual quest as the search for harmony and wholeness in the universe; Tillich (1959), who alleged that searching is related to one's ultimate concern and is the meaning-making dimension of culture; and Booth (1992), who focused on the presence of an inner attitude that emphasizes "energy, creative choice, and a powerful force for living" (p. 25).

Hodges (2002) described spirituality as a worldview that ". . . represents transcendent beliefs and values that may [be] or may not be related to a religious organization" (p. 110). Perhaps a shift from common shared belief, ritual, and worship to individual choice in multicultural, multifaith, and secular contexts is a defining point in the distinction between religion and spirituality. Hodges predicted an emerging fluidity of affiliation based on need and belief rather than adapting need and belief to the prevailing creed of one specific denomination. This description acknowledges the force of the spiritual drive within each individual and places the conscientiousness of spiritual growth on the person rather than existing religious institutions. In contrast to the notion of adherence to the dogma of one religion, the individual is encouraged to carefully adhere to those aspects of many faiths that contribute in positive ways to one's spiritual orientation. There is also an implied question within this focus. Given the individual nature of true spirituality, how feasible is it to consider that one religion may provide all the answers now and for one's entire life? And what does it say about persons who affiliate so totally with one formal religion that they cease searching our faiths for possibly more applicable answers to their life questions?

Spirituality is "broad enough to accommodate the uniqueness of all individuals . . . and indeed the whole of humanity irrespective of beliefs, values, or religious orientation" (Hollins, 2005, p. 22). Hollins explained this conclusion by citing the concept as "a way of being and experiencing that comes through awareness of a transcendent dimension characterized by certain identifiable values in regard to self, others, nature, life and whatever one considers to be the ultimate" (Elkins, Hedstorm, Hughes, Leaf, & Sanders, 1988, p. 10).

Simply put, spirituality is "a universal given" (p. 22), present in both those who claim religious affiliation and those who consider religion to be nonsense.

Hall et al. (2004) reported that spiritual people describe God as loving, forgiving, and nonjudgmental; religious respondents see God as more judgmental. Walker et al. (2004) offered the final comparison for discussion in this chapter by describing religion as more organizational, ritual, and ideological, and spirituality as more personal, affective, and experiential. It is vital to understand that these terms are not to be dichotomized in discussion; spirituality or religion are not to be seen as "all that or never that," but rather as shades of comparison based on individual experience.

HISTORICAL PERSPECTIVES: NEGLECT OF SPIRITUALITY IN MENTAL HEALTH

Given the assertion that spirituality is an innate human characteristic and that religions have merged, disappeared, and existed in various forms through history, how can the neglect of, or hostility toward, spirituality and religion within psychology be understood? This brief chronology and explanation will place the postmodern struggle to revalidate spirituality and religion within the helping professions into a contextual history of centrality, marginalization, and discrimination (these terms are offered merely as possible metaphors of that specific period and are by no means established historical epochs).

"The historical neglect of spiritual issues in psychiatric and psychological theory is well documented" (Hickson et al., 2000, p. 59). Delaney and DiClemente (2005) introduced this observation by stating,

> Throughout most of the 20th century, the idea of taking Judeo-Christian teaching seriously within psychology was generally considered taboo. This taboo was particularly true in regard to religious ideas of sin, guilt, and repentance as being relevant to psychological health. (p. 31)

However valid these remarks may be about the interaction between religion, spirituality, and psychology, such was not always the case, nor may it seem to be the future.

The Period of Centrality

Frame (2005) related the account of religion and psychology being originally linked as the study of human mind, spirit, or soul. In ancient Greece, the later distinctions between *pneuma* (the spiritual aspect of the individual) and the psyche (the soul or mind of the individual) were not clearly articulated. Therefore, "psychology is literally the study of the soul, the very essence of what it means to be human" (Miller & Delaney, 2005, p. 291).

Delaney and DiClemente (2005) traced concern about human nature and behavior back to several Greek writers. Democritus wrote regarding the naturalistic perspective of human behavior, Anaximander and Empedocles on the probabilities of evolution, Aristotle on learning and memory, and Plato on issues of human conduct, with his solution being that the problem is fundamentally based in the acquisition of the knowledge of what is right. Such thoughts in the early Christian era shifted to the struggle of individuals with internal conflicts. The dilemma that emerged was how to explain individual behavior that was inconsistent with societal codes of conduct, even when those codes were known and acknowledged. Beginning with Augustine, issues of sexuality, ambivalence, the unconscious, and guilt were explored. Over his life and writings, Augustine offered multiple thoughts on the human condition, summarized as follows:

1. Certain things must be taken on faith or a scriptural basis.
2. Human nature exists as a function of God as creator and center of life.
3. Individuals hold an interior sense of truth, right, and responsibility.
4. Life is directed by reason, led by faith, and illuminated by revelation.
5. One's motivations and conflicts are an aspect of a personal accountability to God.
6. Basic human motivation is the desire for happiness tempered by personal morality.
7. All people are made in the image of God, and varying degrees of virtue can best be explained by the practice of free will or individuals becoming morally responsible agents of their own lives.

Delaney and DiClemente summarized Augustine's contribution to our understanding of psychology by focusing on internal conflicts, the role of sexuality, the value of dreams in revealing unresolved issues, and the catharsis possible by confronting one's ambivalent feelings.

Aquinas worked from a perspective of joining together the writings of previous thinkers in his work *Summa Theologica,* which served as a treatise on questions of the integration of soul and mind. He opined that experience allows one the intimate knowledge of particulars, but it is reason that places that experience within a universal context. The psychology of knowledge is then truly cognitive psychology. In this view, principles that are created by God are discovered, but not generated, by man. It is one's intellect that offers possible venues for the individual to find happiness and enjoyment in life. However, that choice is led by moral reasoning of one's duty, and refusal to conduct oneself accordingly is a departure from the role of reason. One of Aquinas's most vital contributions to this discussion comes from the admission that there are many truths that can be known through faith and reason, some that can be known by reason alone (such as geometric proofs), and others that can be known by faith alone. One way of knowing is not better than another; each is equally appropriate given what one wishes to study. The end goal is knowledge, regardless of how it is derived.

Frame (2003) spoke about the healers known in all cultures up to and through the Middle Ages. These persons (both male and female) were charged with care of the mental, emotional, and spiritual aspects of the person as a unified whole. Psychology was originally viewed as being closely intertwined with a religious epistemology. Pneumatology had three related fields of study: (a) the study of God, (b) the study of angels and demons, and (c) the study of the human spirit or psyche. The initial use of the term *psychologia* came in 1524, credited to the Croatian poet and Christian humanist Marko Marulić, and defined specific attention to the human spirit.

Period of Marginalization

However, the replacement of the Age of Faith by the Age of Reason during the 18th century Enlightenment led to the growing schism between science and faith as a function of the development of the "scientific" study of psychology. Sperry and Mansager (2004) discussed a salient contest between physician and astrologist Franz Mesmer and exorcist Johann Gassner over the use of psychological tools versus the power of religious exorcism to treat the same client. Gassner's failure to heal the client signaled the need for a split between psychology and religion but also legitimized denigration of religion as a viable healing mechanism.

Within this historical period, as in all periods, dissenting voices were heard. Delaney and DiClemente (2005) cited John Locke, who referred to the importance of "demonstrable knowledge" (p. 38); however, the foremost truth is that an eternal omnipotent Being exists. The argument goes that man knows that he exists and knows that he could not have come from nothing, so something must have existed from eternity to create man and the world, a thesis that is acknowledged by wise men of all nations. In addition, Descartes's modern rational tradition and contribution to cognitive development and language led to the unshakeable truth that God must exist. However, as with most writings, future scholars in both the areas of religion and the merging field of psychology sifted through the extensive prior literature to discover just the phrase that would anchor each point of view.

Period of Discrimination

DiClemente and Delaney (2005) wrote that psychology grew up in the late 19th and early 20th centuries "in the context of a scientific empiricism that was reductionistic and materialistic" (p. 271). Miller and Delaney (2005) offered examples of focused study on memory, reinforcement schedules, behavioral response to specific drugs, and so forth. Frame (2003) offered a succinct description of the emerging polarization of views between traditional religion and the newly burgeoning perspective of psychology. Perhaps it was more the intransigence of both sides that contributed more to the present schism:

Religion	Psychology
Accept the existence of God	Reject God
Freedom of individuals to make choices	Individuals ruled by outside forces
Transcendence makes each individual unique	Individuals as machines with separate parts that worked together
Absolute and encompassing values	No universal moral principles
Transcendence and inspiration	Physical world, senses, and empirical evidence
Based on faith	Based on fact

The core of this emerging division seems to be based on the desire of founding thinkers and writers in psychology to establish the "scientific nature" of the new discipline and also to offer theories of human functioning to replace religious thinking, which was, by nature, not verifiable through empirical means.

The pioneers of psychology (B. F. Skinner, John B. Watson, Sigmund Freud, etc.) sought to bolster the legitimacy of the new discipline as a "science" by disparaging the issue and place of faith. This goal of the societal acceptance of psychology as a science was envisioned as a way to lend credibility and respectability to their newly inked theories of human functioning and human dysfunction. In addition, the founders of this new approach to understanding the human condition and experience sought the approval of other, more established professions such as medicine, law, and philosophy. These other professions had already rejected the place and value of religion in favor of scientific empiricism, and psychologists insisted that their discipline was equally astute in the embracing of the new epistemology of science. Their insistence led to an epistemological conflict between science—physical world, sense, and empirical evidence (*FACT*)—and traditional religion—transcendence and inspiration (*FAITH*).

The role of science in knowledge and psychology reflected an emergence of the cultural and social focus on reductionism: to take things apart to see how they work. Much like a machine, the human psyche began to be explored to identify its prominent parts based on the assertion that recognition of the disparate aspects would lead to isolation and manipulation in order to experimentally determine its impact (Faiver et al., 2001).

Conceptually, the most expeditious way to identify and describe new variables is to differentiate between them to create an atmosphere of opposition rather than overlap (e.g., mind/body/spirit, or in clinical work, affect/behavior/cognition). By doing so, delineation and demarcation are emphasized over similarity and overlap. This attempt to polarize and segregate (objective differentiation) parts of the human experience fostered a loss of any consideration of the connection between the spiritual and the scientific. The impact of Descartes's rationalism *"cognito, ergo sum"* (I think, therefore I am) served to negate much of what is intangible, including the soul.

If one accepts that the purpose of research is to explain phenomena and make predictions (Hall et al., 2004), then the isolated study of variables, given the constancy of all other variables of relevance, is the means by which one may be reasonably certain that the one manipulated variable indeed caused the result. This notion, when applied to the human experience, seems more pure in theory than in practice. Such an approach assumes that (a) the variable in question can be isolated, (b) all other relevant variables can be identified and then can be held constant, and (c) the isolated variable can, in fact, be manipulated. Although such practice may prove achievable in the physical realm, such as heart rate and blood pressure, the challenge becomes far more complex when considering variables such as ego development or affect. However, given the precariousness of the new field of psychology, rigorous attempts were made to replicate as well as possible the scientific approach, because the very legitimacy and future of the field were at stake.

It is of prime importance in this discussion that the reader fully grasp that the practice of science of the late 18th century does not equal the science of the 21st century. So any review of the research of that time must consider the cultural context in which it was conducted. In addition, mental health professionals in the 21st century must always be appreciative of the study done in the beginning of the profession, for that knowledge forms the foundation of modern thinking and clinical practice.

In conjunction with the challenge of religion from the perspective of scientific methods, mental health theorists also confronted the relevance and value of religion. Championed by Freud (1963) and Ellis (1980), religion was viewed "at best, as irrelevant or as a benign neurosis and, at worst, as detrimental to mental health" (Sperry & Mansager, 2004, p. 151).

Freud viewed religion as "potentially so infantile, so foreign to reality . . . it is painful to think that the great majority of mortals will never be able to rise above this view of life" (Freud, 1963, p. 11). From his orientation, religion fostered the view of the father figure as omnipotent and omniscient, as well as caring and protective, a longing for a father god-to-be (Frame, 2003). In addition, religion created a fear-induced repression of the critical examination of belief systems. Freud saw the threat of excommunication or exclusion as a way to stifle dissent within the religious community and to deny to individuals the right to question. He also denigrated religion as a whole as providing defense mechanisms to protect one from the anxiety complicit with acknowledgment of one's own unacceptable or evil impulses. Decried as a form of communal neurosis with rituals and practices that acted as a defense against forbidden desires, Freud relegated religious belief, affiliation, and practices to a form of psychopathology.

Hodges (2002) spoke to the link between Freud's (1954) view of formal religion as an illusion/wish fulfillment/fantasy and Ellis's (1980) statement that religious beliefs are irrational beliefs: "Religiosity is in many respects equivalent to irrational thinking and emotional disturbance" (p. 637). Finding no beneficial purpose for religious practices, Ellis decried religious affiliation as a belief in something that does not exist and a refusal of individuals to assume appropriate responsibility for their own thinking in the world.

Skinner saw religious behavior as a function of reinforced stimuli with clergy, liturgy, and morality as reinforcement contingencies designed to serve individual as well as religious institutional and social order. He criticized the use of negative reinforcement or punishment (threats of hell, damnation, and excommunication), instead of positive reinforcement, as a way to maintain religious community and foster conformity.

Humanists adhered to the Renaissance philosophy of the basic dignity of all persons, who, if in a positive supportive environment, will strive toward self-actualization. These theorists placed human expression as the driving force rather than the Supreme Being. The presence of God, if indeed God exists, was as a bemused bystander who delegated human potential to each individual and then watched, uninvolved, to see what may unfold. Given the focus on positive or supportive environments as critical for human development of this innate potential, serious questions were raised concerning how positive or supportive organized religion may be of individual human growth. The response seemed attuned more toward criticism and dismissal of institutional practices than religion per se. The atmosphere of formal religion seemed stifling, conformity demanding, individuality sacrificing, and bent more toward maintenance of the hierarchy of the institution and the power of the clergy at the expense of human growth, creativity, spontaneity, and potential.

Existentialists saw the belief in God and immortality as immature defenses against anxiety about death. Maturity and growth came from facing this anxiety and coming to resolution rather than relying on an unproven savior with a promise of everlasting joy to alleviate such angst. Following religious codes and behavioral expectations were viewed as avoidance of personal choice and responsibility. Part of the struggle of life was to weigh differing moral codes and own the right and responsibility for arriving at an individual code of aspirational conduct rather than blindly following the crowd and adopting a ready-made list of rules of conduct. Individuality can never be found through joining a crowd. A reliance on God was considered a crutch for those who had not "owned" the possibilities of being fully human.

The reader is to assess how accurately Hollins (2005) summed up the criticisms of traditional religion:

1. All mainstream religion is judgmental in all aspects of life.
2. The practice of traditional religion is ill-equipped to address the emotional and psychological needs of individuals.
3. Traditional religions subsume individuals into faith-based practices and rules, which are confronted only at great individual cost.
4. All religions are associated with conversion toward a pre-established dogma and liturgy into which the individual has no input.
5. The negative association of religion with the "prophet-like" stances of ministers and the "hard sell" by some religious groups is indicative of the exploitation and corruption of religion.

The volume of criticism from "psychologists" may be misleading as to how universal that criticism was among theorists. As in any community of strong-minded individuals, controversy and conflict tend to flourish, and never more so than within the emerging discipline of psychology. Again, it is central to this discussion to remember that most of these individuals had first-hand personal experience of differing major religions in their upbringing, and while many individuals spurned its practice and relevance, others sought to find a place for psychology and religion in harmony.

William James (1890), "America's psychologist," debated whether the essence of man is truly spiritual versus material and argued in *The Principles of Psychology* that the spiritual "me" is the basis of the self:

> The very core and nucleus of our self, as we know it, the very sanctuary of our life, is the sense of activity which certain inner states possess. This sense of activity is often held to be a direct revelation of the living substance of our Soul. Whether this be so or not is an ulterior question. (p. 181)

James envisioned free will as the key to moral responsibility; that the most certain indication of an individual's adherence to a value is when that person freely chooses that value from others and, even in the face of overwhelming dissenting opinion, still acts in accordance with that value. James also advanced the notion that the narrow objectivism of science is shallow and inadequate for many aspects of the person. This "cult of reductionism" seemed to ignore much of what constituted humanity. Although he personally could not accept popular Christianity, he affirmed the reality of a mystical or supernatural realm, stating that each person and God "have business with each other" and that, during experiences of prayer, there is a subjective awareness of the addition of a higher energy that one could account for mustering only through prayer. Whatever that presence, it seemed to provide support for the individual and brought a sense of calm and serenity where there was tension and worry; such a phenomenon was beyond the ability of psychology or science to explain.

Søren Kierkegaard saw himself as a psychologist whose mission was the reintroduction of true Christianity into the monstrous illusion we call Christendom (Delaney & DiClemente, 2005). For Kierkegaard, psychology represented "depth psychology," focusing on anxiety, self-deception, and despair. Sin was equated to prideful attempts to break away from what God wants one to be. The human condition is to face bravely the moral demands to live an ethical life, which one may recognize or fail to recognize. However, it is that choice which defines who one becomes. The highest level of morality is accepting one's own need for grace and making the faith-based leap to be forgiven for one's sins by God.

Erikson (1972) viewed religion as a function of early trust in parent–child relationships. Religion "translates into significant works, images and codes the exceeding darkness which surrounds man's existence and the light which pervades it beyond all desert or comprehension" (p. 19). The value of religion lies in its potential for affirmation of love or terror in the dark unknown (Hayes & Cowie, 2005, p. 30).

Delaney and DiClemente (2005) also cited the comments of Donald Campbell in his 1975 American Psychological Association (APA) presidential address: "Present day psychology and psychiatry in all their major forms are more hostile to the inhibitory message of traditional religious moralizing than is scientifically justified" (p. 1103). Even more than 40 years ago, there was a growing suspicion that psychology, in its fervency to be perceived as scientific and relevant to the 20th century, had gone too far in its dismissal of the place of religion and spirituality.

Miller and Delaney (2005) wrote in favor of the spiritual backlash against the opinion of traditional psychology, questioning the notion that phenomena that could not be empirically observed (observable, quantifiable, and measurable) were nonexistent. They also raised serious concern as to whether the exploration of psychology on solely problematic or pathological functioning oversimplified the importance of the role of religion in the lives of many people and perhaps prejudiced new generations of psychologists against a potentially health-fostering social institution. They concluded that religion creates knowledge in differing ways and those very different styles of seeking answers prove to be a threat to the science of psychology. Miller and Delaney (2005) raised three questions that were intended to facilitate a dialogue aimed at breaching historical professional differences in ways of understanding the world:

1. What evidence can be accepted to support the existence of a phenomenon?
2. What are the newest and best analyses of complex interactive phenomena?
3. Given the "cultural grounding of psychology and religion in metaphysical, historical and philosophical roots," how can new mutual respect be forged, similarities recognized, and differences accepted? (p. 278)

They advised that "[d]ifferences turn into divisions where there is a lack of mutual respect and absence of dialogue" (p. 282), and perhaps the time has come to move forward in this dialogue rather than remain mired in past arguments.

Miller and Delaney (2005) firmly asserted that "psychology is not modeled on the other sciences. . . . To understand the *psych* involves not only the integration of part processes but also consideration of the higher order agentive and meaning processes that distinguish human nature" (p. 294), so the focus on "parts" may be a vital component of contemplating the human condition, but equally important is how the different aspects of human nature relate. What people have in common, plus individual differences, are essential to the diversity of humanity.

Having outlined the historical transitions in the relationship between religion and psychology as moving from centrality to marginalization to discrimination, the next section of this chapter will initiate an exploration of the postmodern movement toward reintegrating spirituality and religion in the helping professions.

CURRENT PERSPECTIVES: THE RE-EMERGENCE OF SPIRITUALITY IN THE HELPING PROFESSIONS

Given the relative brevity of the history of psychology and the formal helping professions in comparison with the historical breadth of spirituality and organized religion, it is of interest to wonder how, at the onset of the 21st century, spirituality is becoming such a force and topic of interest for mental health professionals on both personal and professional levels.

Popular Interest in Spirituality

Faiver et al. (2001) asserted that "all human cultures have a psychological sense of the spiritual" (p. 8), which implies that, even if overlooked or neglected, such an instinct has remained present. It could be argued that this omission of attention to the spiritual and the religious is a contributing factor to the social malaise of the 21st century (Hayes & Cowie, 2005). These authors cited Pook's (2000) research, which reported that 10% of that sample believed that they would be better off dead, with a "high proportion" feeling unappreciated and dissatisfied with work and home life, with a tendency to overlook one's spiritual experiences, whether or not they were connected to religion.

Hickson et al. (2000) stated that almost one third of Americans reported having had a healing experience of physical, emotional, or psychological problems, which they attributed to God, Jesus, or a Higher Power. They professed a belief in God, a belief that religion and spirituality are personally important, and that religion and spirituality can answer all or most contemporary problems. Sperry (2001) reported that 97% of Americans believe that their prayers are answered, and 40% reported a life-altering experience. Cashwell and Young (2005) cited 2000 data findings which state that 96% of Americans believe in God, more than 90% pray, 69% are members of a house of worship, and 43% have attended services in a mosque, church, or synagogue over the past week. In addition, they asserted that these numbers do not include those whose spiritual practices do not involve affiliation with a formalized religious institution and those who may not have a belief in a Higher Power. Miller and Delaney (2005) cited a 1944 study which found that 58% of the population was interested in spirituality and a 1998 survey where that percentage had risen to 82%.

Faiver et al. (2001) reported on a widespread dissatisfaction with organized religion. Referring to the scandals, violence, proliferation of sects, and arguing over miniscule points, these authors questioned whether the proliferation of such issues is diminishing the attractiveness of organized religion. This sentiment was echoed by Sperry and Mansager (2004), who found that Americans were less satisfied with mainstream religions and were, in increasing numbers, beginning to seek answers to questions of wholeness and wellness from sources outside religious traditions.

Sperry (2001, p. 3) cited Lesser (1999) as proclaiming the emergence of the "new American Spirituality." This movement is seeking to replace the traditional religious trappings of hierarchical power and a clearly defined route to spiritual salvation reached through the adherence to prescribed rituals and practices. The new "spirituality" draws on the teachings of Christian tradition, blended with meditative and Eastern practices, feminism, and psychology. Frame (2005) described the 21st century as "ripe for a spiritual revolution" (p. 11). The emerging philosophical focus of postmodernism fosters an ongoing examination and questioning of absolutes, objective truth, and empirical knowledge.

Professional Interest in Spirituality

Delaney and DiClemente (2005) referred to the professional period of psychology from 1900–1930 as characterized by an increasing preoccupation with being scientific. The assertion of logical positivism in which the only meaningful statements are those that can be empirically verified was embraced uncritically by American psychology. This focus on the observable and measurable both fit in with Watson's behaviorism and fostered a professional rejection of spirituality, religion, and introspective methods in favor of animal learning and conditioning studies. Religion was marginalized in mainstream psychology for most of the 20th century. This partition was challenged by theorists such as Jung who stated that Christianity has failed the baptism by fire—the test of reality—and that Christ does not exist outside of the psyche. The most critical spokesperson in favor of integrating spirituality and psychology was Abraham Maslow. He argued that humanism offered the most potential-affirming alternative to the narrow perspective of scientific psychology. He advocated that personal values be derived from psychology rather than from religion and that God is truly an impersonal part of nature, and he also envisioned transpersonal psychology as a religion surrogate. However, more recently, a shift of perspective seems underway.

There appears to be an "increased tolerance for spiritual issues within the psychology profession as a whole" (Sperry & Mansager, 2004, p. 150). This interest is manifested in a "substantial upsurge in the interest in spirituality among helping professionals . . . as evidenced by an increasing number of professional publications over the past 10 years" (Cashwell & Young, 2005, p. 1).

From a different mode of challenge, Hall et al. (2004) questioned the scientific, evidence-based focus of "how to test the truth of spiritual hypotheses" by asking a better question: "Is such an orientation itself passé?" A discussion has emerged about the relative values of qualitative and quantitative ways of knowing; the ongoing creation of new, more complex ways of analyzing data from both schools of research design; and the more in-depth identification of relevant variables specific or common to religion and spirituality that are worthy of investigating in relation to human functioning, in addition to the established dependent variables of pathology. Hodges (2002) found multiple research studies substantiating the value of spirituality to mental health. Hickson, Housley, and Wages (2000) cited 17 studies from 1976 to 1998 documenting the beneficial impact of spirituality and religion on well-being and mental health. Future research may be founded in notions of well-being, focusing on purpose in life and social support, and the development of psychological states/religious issues such as gratitude, forgiveness (Joseph, Linley, & Maltby, 2006), and compassion. In addition, experimental study on spiritual integration in the array of clinical concerns may prove to be a guide for future clinicians answering outcome-oriented questions, such as "Which spiritual interventions work better for whom?" and "How does one know?"

There has been renewed focus on the therapeutic process through the client–counselor relationship as a function of the attention now directed toward ideals of "wellness." Questions have arisen within the process of clinical training as to how adequately attitudes such as empathy, acceptance, and congruence can be reduced to "skill sets" only. Although there is no debate about the necessity for technique building in clinical training, there are concerns about whether such a training approach is sufficient. Attention must be paid to the core beliefs of clinicians-in-training. Topics such as a belief in the value of the therapeutic relationship, an emphasis on the experience of the client, a desire to understand the perspective of the client, and a willingness to further the quality of life of the client are instrumental in the genuineness of the clinician and in promoting the success of the therapeutic endeavor. Specifically, five aspects of the self with other require awareness, evaluation, and consistent effort: (a) working alliance, (b) transference/countertransference, (c) developmental need or reparative, (d) person-to-person or real relationship, and (e) transpersonal relationship (Hayes & Cowie, 2005). Miller and Delaney (2005) directed clinicians to ". . . enlarge and enrich the conception of the human person" (p. 304). As a corollary, it may be of interest within this aspect of the discussion to explore the current status of training in the field of medicine. Within that field, attention is being directed toward broadening the physician-in-training's view of the client beyond the client's presenting physical malady (such as cancer, diabetes, etc.) toward a holistic vision of physiological functioning and translating that approach into new attention to "bedside manner" to interact with the whole patient rather than simply attend to the unhealthy organ or disease. If medical science can evolve in this manner, perhaps the mental health professions can now readily embrace an aspect of clinical work that has always distinguished that profession but, perhaps until recently, was denigrated as unscientific.

Attention to spiritual and religious issues is also becoming more accepted as a function of the assertion that clinicians have become "secular priests" (Sperry, 2001; Sperry & Mansager, 2004, p. 150). This opinion is ventured because of religious institutions' inability to address psychological issues. Given the lessening stigma of seeking professional mental health services, clients bring with them a belief that the clinician will attend to all their concerns and will be sufficiently wise and skilled to interconnect all aspects of their lives both to foster greater understanding of the depth of the presenting problem and to identify previously overlooked strengths or coping mechanisms. Among those potential stressors or resources must be one's religious or spiritual orientations.

Along that line of thinking, Walker, Gorsuch, and Tan (2004) spoke to the need for clinicians to be culturally sensitive and relevant. They stated that "religion and spirituality are relevant aspects of client diversity that psychologists should be able to recognize while treating religious or spiritual clients with sensitivity" (p. 69). The integration of spiritual and religious issues within mental health services adds the positive study of human motivation, strengths, resources, and potential. On a wider scale than the therapeutic encounter, one cannot appreciate distinctions among peoples or nations without appreciation of their religious and spiritual heritages (Miller & Delaney, 2005).

Sperry and Mansager (2004) advocated that professionals adopt a shift to the *monisitic* view of the relationship between spirituality and psychology, with spirituality as a controlling aspect, rather than a pluralistic view, where each aspect carries equal influence on the individual. These authors argued that the religious desires within each person—the common seeking of ultimate answers—is the core motivation of life and that providing clinical service without attention to this core element may be superficial and disrespectful of the guiding force that spirituality and religion offer.

Miller and Delaney (2005) remarked on the growing shift toward holistic health by advising that "focusing on any one link may miss the bigger picture of the chains constraining the person's life" (p. 293). In support of this admonition, they cited the work of William James, for whom the study of psychology was the study of human nature. However, this shift in attention may be more arduous than imagined, given the current discrepancies in religious orientation between mental health professionals and the general population. For example, there may be an underrepresentation of practicing religious people among psychologists. These authors included a recent study which stated that 72% of the American sample endorsed the statement that "my whole approach to life is based on my religion," in comparison with only 33% of psychologists (the lowest percentage among the differing groups of mental health professionals who responded to the survey). This finding echoes a previous finding by Shafranske (1996), who polled 59 different academic disciplines and found psychology to be sixth from the bottom in the percentage of faculty endorsing any religion. One might then raise the issue of whether the helping professions attract individuals with little personal use for religious or spiritual concerns, or whether the current training process demands an abandonment of those concerns as a component of professional education.

Another example of this re-emergence of interest in spirituality is the work by Watts, Dutton, and Gulliford (2006) on positive psychology connected to faith practices—what the authors described as "enacting spiritual practices in secular contexts" (p. 277):

1. ***Forgiveness:*** "the overcoming of negative affect and judgment toward the offender, not by denying ourselves the right to such affect and judgment but by endeavoring to view the offender with compassion, benevolence, and love while recognizing that he/she has abandoned his/her right to them" (p. 278). The process of reframing reflects

social order, contributes to it, and distinguishes between anger that is mature and constructive and that which is immature and destructive, based on Christian Gospels and Jesus's model of constructive anger, conditional versus unconditional forgiveness, and forgiveness as a gift from God enacted through the victim, as transgression is both contrary to the individual harmed and God's laws. Forgiveness is seen as a mark of psychological maturity and as a virtue in itself.

2. *Gratitude:* derived from the Latin root *gratia*, meaning grace, graciousness, or gratefulness. It is directed outward toward others, including recognition of a gain with the understanding that someone else is responsible for that gain (e.g., a Higher Power). Gratitude is a positive emotion fostering social cohesiveness, creativity (a response beyond reciprocity), and psychological resilience. It is the act of purposefully "undoing" a negative act.

3. *Hope:* optimism for the future when all such grounds for positive expectations are no longer present and where the past has not been positive. Hope is an expectation of a more positive future even in the face of despair and pain. One can hope for things one does not expect, hope for what is morally good, and hope for things that are important to the individual. Hoping for something commits one to working to try to make it happen.

In summary, Miller and Delaney (2005) proclaimed that "a psychology that ignores spirituality, however, necessarily promotes an incomplete understanding of the human person" (p. 304).

Case Example Revisited

As Terrance spoke to the faculty, he received a diversity of opinions as to which social and cultural variables were relevant to the understanding of client issues and resources. His one required graduate course which focused on issues of cultural diversity covered gender, ethnicity, socioeconomic status, and sexual orientation issues. He came to understand the complexity of the interaction among these variables and came to the conclusion that, while knowledge was vital, what may prove more directing was his personal exploration of which variables contributed to his own identity and in which way. He accepted the importance of those four variables and also identified his religious upbringing as a defining factor in who he was and how he saw the world around him.

He also began to wonder, within the realm of his religious upbringing, how the discussion between spirituality and religion was relevant to him. He realized that becoming a competent clinician required more than the accumulation and mastery of knowledge and skill; until he could identify which spiritual questions had fostered his own growth, he would feel ill-equipped to work with clients through an integration of their spiritual or religious concerns in his clinical practice. So his driving questions became "What do I know about myself as a religious and spiritual being?" and "How do these answers define me?"

Conclusion

Both psychology and religion purport to ". . . enable people to live their lives with courage and optimism and to strive toward creating conditions that give people the strength to live well and that dispel beliefs and patterns which trap people in lives of misery" (Hayes & Cowie, 2005, p. 32; also Watts, Dutton, & Gulliford, 2006). In addition, "both spirituality and psychotherapy provide methods for exploring, deepening, and expanding consciousness" (Sperry & Mansager, 2004, p. 158) and for ". . . appreciating the mystery and sacred in life" (Hodges, 2002, p. 114). Research studies confirm that ". . . involvement in religion or religious activities may be of bene-

fit to both mental and physical health" and "more mental health professionals are beginning to acknowledge the importance of incorporating a client's religious and spiritual beliefs into mental health assessment and treatment plans" (Hall et al., 2004, p. 507).

Self-Understanding Exercises

1. Hayes and Cowie (2005, p. 32) referred to spirituality as "engagement in God in ourselves." What is your reaction to this statement?
2. Faiver et al. (2001, p. 15) asked, "Do you agree or disagree with the notion of spirituality as an innate human quality? Why or why not?"
3. Frame (2003, p. 32) recommended keeping a "spiritual journal" that allows the author to address issues such as
   • How does the notion of free will fit into your religious/spiritual framework?

• Why do bad things happen to good people?
• What happens to people after they die? Describe it.
• What are the qualities of a Supreme Being if you believe in one?
• Which types of client-involving religious or spiritual issues would be the most challenging for you? Why? Which ones might be the most exciting? Why?

Opportunities for Further Learning

1. Interview senior members of your clinical staff or training faculty about their impressions of the overlap between religion and spirituality.
2. Choose one psychology or counseling theorist of interest to you. Review original source material (i.e., authored by that theorist) about his or her views on clinical work and spirituality, and see how those views may

have changed over the length of that individual's professional life. If no such writing on spirituality can be found, what message do you take from that?
3. At your next professional conference, seek out those colleagues who present on issues of spirituality and clinical work, and ask a presenter how he or she became interested in this topic.

2

• • •

The Personal and Professional

Of all knowledge, the wise and good seek most to know themselves.

—WILLIAM SHAKESPEARE

CASE EXAMPLE

Sandra entered her graduate training program invested in gaining competencies in dealing with her chosen clinical population of teens and young women with body image issues and eating disorders. Having served as a support system for many friends through their challenges around these concerns, she had always worried that she was "incomplete" in her capacity to be of help and looked to her graduate program as the way to become more competent.

However, once admitted to the program and moving through her courses, she felt confirmed by her academic performance and role-play experiences, but confronted by the notion of the self-of-the-therapist as a variable in clinical efficacy. She was deeply concerned that she would not "measure up" and was confronted by peers regarding what they described as her lack of honest self-disclosure in group exercises and the superficiality of her class input. Sandra felt demeaned by this feedback and sought an appointment with her faculty advisor to discuss her withdrawal from the program.

■ ■ ■

INTRODUCTION

The process of the academic and clinical preparation of mental health professionals directs students' attention toward three areas of importance: (a) knowledge about clients, (b) knowledge about counseling, and, (c) knowledge about self in the context of counseling. As other professionals utilize instruments or tools to perform their duties, mental health professionals rely on the three factors just cited, and it is their skills at integrating those three factors that are predictive of their success with clients.

The Discrimination Model of Clinical Supervision (Bernard & Goodyear, 2004) identified these three categories of counselor competence as conceptualization, intervention, and personalization. The third dynamic, which is of relevance to this chapter, was defined as "how the trainee interfaces a personal style with therapy at the same time that he or she attempts to keep therapy uncontaminated by personal issues and countertransference responses" (p. 95). Training and supervision of new mental health clinicians entails experience plus guided reflection, with the latter intended as the growth-producing stimulus (O'Connor, 2004), with attention paid to all three areas. It is the integration of all three areas of knowledge and competence that fosters efficacy of service, and, conversely, the lack of knowledge or competence in one area may negate any efficacy in the other two areas (Nugent & Jones, 2004). In this book, the first two factors are addressed in other chapters, leaving the attention paid to the knowledge of the self of the counselor as the theme for this specific chapter.

In the evolution of a clinician's professional efficacy, one challenge is the integration of professional knowledge through the person of the clinician with what Simmonds (2005, p. 240) described as an "authentic identity." The individuals in Simmonds' sample reported connecting ". . . their spiritual concerns with the decision to pursue the vocation of psychotherapist" (p. 243). Although these individuals related narratives of having to re-author their spiritual versions of the world after discarding the traditional religious teachings of their childhoods, they all avowed the connection between the spiritual and the clinical. Kelly (1995, p. 10) wrote of a "widespread awareness of the importance of religion and spiritually for counselor training." A 2002 survey of programs accredited by the Council for the Accreditation of Counseling and Related Educational Programs (CACREP) reported that only 46% of CACREP liaisons saw themselves as prepared to teach such a course and only 28% saw their colleagues as capable of such a teaching task (Young, Cashwell, Wiggins-Frame, & Belaire, 2002). Compared with, and relevant to, the thesis of this book, "mental health professionals are beginning to acknowledge the need for competency regarding religion and spirituality issues in the counseling field" (Hall, Dixon, & Mauzey, 2004, p. 507). Briggs and Rayle (2005) cited a previous (2000) study of Licensed Professional Counselors (LPCs), the majority of whom (73%) rated spiritual interventions as either "important" or "vitally important." This admonition is echoed by Russell and Yarhouse (2006, p. 430), who challenged psychologists to reconsider their "historical ambivalence" or "open antagonism" toward spirituality and religion and to "engage in the training or experience need[ed] to fully understand this important area of client diversity." Hage (2006, p. 303) stated that "clinical faculty and leaders report minimal competence in spiritual and religious interventions, as well as little actual integration of spiritual and religious themes in their training curricula."

In addition, the shifting religious and spiritual demographics of the country and the demand for cultural sensitivity to these defining characteristics, as a function of awareness of counselor-as-self within this context, require the purposeful development of such insight (Hagedorn, 2005). Richards and Bergin (2000) enumerated more than 160 denominations, mostly Christian, and more than 700 non-Christian groups that constitute the spiritual census of the United States, underscoring the need for mental health professionals to determine their own spiritual community and its meaning in their own lives and lifestyles, as prerequisites for guiding clients through similar religious or spiritual explorations. Such spiritual and religious connections are seen as vital aspects of self-identity and crucial sources of support and strength (Hage, 2006; Mattis, 2002). These connections are also seen as definitional markers of life-span events such as birth, death, adult status, and marriage, and as part of individual coping and healing processes through life's traumas and challenges (Hagedorn, 2005).

The diagram shown on this page offers a conceptualization of the integral aspects of religion and spirituality in responding to daily living and the challenges of life (Gall et al., 2005, p. 89). This visualization of individual response to stress portrays the integration of one's religious or spiritual resources in response to the perceived stress. Of vital importance, and ethical obligation, is the resulting ipsative meaning-making step that is composed of the synthesis of the person factors, spiritual connections, and spiritual coping toward a unified life purpose. The integrity of that unity is then facilitative of individual transformation and growth, rather than stagnation and despair, as an outcome of the experience of stress. Finally, the synthesis of these resolutions is seen to foster a sense of holistic well-being, which includes, but far transcends, resolving the identified stress.

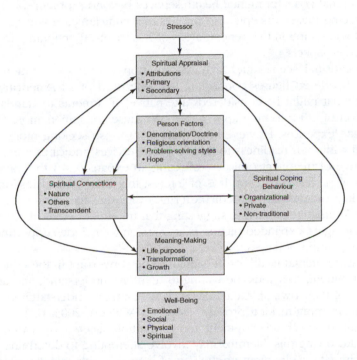

In utilizing such a framework, mental health clinicians must first grasp their own journeys within this matrix before attempting to guide and explore that process with others. Hagedorn (2005, p. 67) questioned, "Can clinicians truly assist clients through the self-exploration process if they themselves (the clinicians) are not committed to the continual exploration of their own feelings, motives and experiences?"

A Rationale for the Spiritual Health of the Clinician

Virtually all models of psychotherapy call for self-awareness and knowledge on the part of mental health practitioners. Hagedorn (2005) referenced the attention paid to possible countertransference in psychoanalysis, to the Jungian admonition that the clinician attend to personal psychological needs prior to engaging clients, and to the calls for authenticity and congruence that characterize Adlerian, existential, person-centered, gestalt, reality, and rational emotive therapies. Across these diverse approaches to the provision of mental health services is the unswerving need for self-awareness on the part of the service provider.

Kelly (1995) reported that counselors seem to value spirituality in their personal lives and in conducting counseling; specifically, 85% responded in a positive way to whether "seeking a spiritual understanding of the universe" was personally relevant. So, even more than a decade ago, counselors were acknowledging an ownership of their spirituality and the value of such an integration of one's spiritual or religious path in the development of a worldview.

Mental health professionals are also beginning to consider alternative paradigms to the biomedical model (Savolaine & Granello, 2002). An emerging focus on salutogenic (health-enhancing) services is demanding that clinicians begin to formulate concepts of well-being and health over and above the absence of illness or dysfunction. Such versions of well-being provide aspirational goals for mental health services beyond problem solving or issue reme-diation. Embracing these concepts also implies that clinicians are willing to attend to their own personal well-being in the general areas of health and functioning, including the spiri-tual and religious aspects.

On the national scene, such a transformation would seem timely. Savolaine and Granello (2002) offered figures confirming that one third of all Americans seeking health services used what might be considered "alternative" treatments to standard medical care. This exploration of other healing approaches cost these consumers more than $13.7 billion in out-of-pocket expenses. However, the number of those seeking more holistic interven-tions, coupled with their readiness to pay for such services, indicates a growing acceptance of a wider range of treatment options, reflecting an expansion of the traditional directions and purposes of professional care. It is of interest that the National Institutes of Health re-named its Office of Alternative Medicine (1992) the National Center for Complementary Medicine and Alternative Medicine, suggesting that traditional medical practice itself is con-sidering embracing an expanded picture of its mission to include supporting health in addi-tion to the remediation of illness.

However, for mental health professionals to be conversant in the notion of salutogenic spiritual development, they must be willing to "explore, understand, and articulate the per-sonal meaning of their own spirituality as well as [gain] an understanding of the individual nature of their meaning-making process" (Myers & Williard, 2003, p. 149). For if they lack personal insight into such development and its multiple facets, how can clinicians hope to guide clients? Resolving this dilemma may involve attempting to determine what constitutes salutogenic spiritual development on the part of mental health professionals—those in prac-tice and those in training programs.

Clinicians' Spiritual Health and the Delivery of Clinical Services

An ever-emerging theme based on recent data confirms that mental health professionals are only "as effective as they are self-aware and able to use themselves as the instruments through which change occurs" (Capuzzi & Gross, 2007, p. 27). On the basis of this assertion, fatigue, lack of knowledge, insufficient skill, personal impairment, and lack of self-awareness pose potential hazards for the delivery of efficacious mental health services. Mental health professionals are, ideally, "open to new experiences, aware of their own motivations, values vulnerabilities, and unmet needs" (Nugent & Jones, 2004, p. 80). Among the nine criteria for psychological health, Nugent and Jones included self-acceptance and self-knowledge. Their review of identified characteristics of effective helpers continually speaks to awareness of self within the context of counseling. This awareness is not seen as a rationale for repressing one's personal growing edges, but instead "ensures that the personal issues do not diminish the capacity to engender personal growth on the part of the client" (p. 29). Each of the articles cited in the following paragraphs offers differing views of the potential impact of the clinician's approach to spirituality in counseling on the delivery of clinical services. The intent in including these materials in Chapter 2 is to present the range of findings and opinions of these scholars so that the reader may choose which concerns are most relevant to his or her personal and professional growth.

Worthington and Sandage (2001) suggested that clinicians must be prepared to respond to inquiries from clients about personal religious or spiritual beliefs. As in any opportunity for self-disclosure, clinicians must first know themselves within the context of those inquiries and then decide which disclosures may be of help to the client and which may impede the client's insight or growth. Clinicians also need to consider that, should their response seem inattentive to the issue raised by the client's question, that very response may diminish the client's sense of the legitimacy of the issue or its place within clinical services. A second recommendation stated that clients may be opposed to religious influences. Any clinician who cannot respect the right of the client to choose his or her own spiritual orientation, including the rejection of all orientations, places himself or herself in jeopardy of damaging the trust and respect valued in the therapeutic relationship by insisting that clients' spirituality be acceptable to the clinician. On a related note, the initial perception of the all-accepting mental health professional may conflict with the expression of implicit counselor beliefs regarding less mainstream religious or spiritual choices (e.g., white supremacy, Satanism, Wicca) later in counseling. This inconsistency may generate subsequent conflict in therapy and may greatly impair the clinician's ability to be of help because the client may see the conflict as embodying an initial expression of clinician dishonesty.

A third area of sensitivity revolves around religion or spirituality as an aspect of culture and may interact with the acculturation efforts of clients. A reconsideration of one's religion of origin may be seen as a rejection of part of one's cultural heritage and the shattering of one's connection to his or her own identity. The importance of religion or spirituality within one's definition of self cannot be overlooked by the clinician. Rather than needing to be changed, such beliefs, if they turn out to be a foundational aspect of self-definition and ego strength, force the clinical agenda to move from one of change to one of compromise regarding cultural values, accommodation (where that is possible), and perhaps acknowledgment of one's alienation from some aspects of the larger societal system. A final caution was raised regarding religion and spirituality as aspects of relational imbalance when spouses hold differing values or are at different places in the development of their faith. Should spouses in conflict try to impose religious beliefs on one another, the clinician must both understand the process issues involved from a systemic perspective and be familiar with the current literature discussing the role of religion and spirituality within family functioning.

Focusing on the needs of the clinician as regards the effective use of the self within the realm of counseling in relation to spiritual issues, Curtis and Glass (2002) identified four qualities of the mental health professional that they viewed as related to the efficacy of the delivery of mental health services: (1) level of confidence in addressing spiritual issues, (2) awareness of how spiritual belief systems are of help to the client, (3) sensitivity to personal reactions to clients with differing belief systems, and (4) the ability to refrain from imposing spiritual beliefs on clients.

Savolaine and Granello (2002) advised mental health clinicians to reexamine the professional literature on the detrimental impact of religion on mental health, with an eye toward viewing those writings within their cultural context and reassessing their applicability to today's cultural context. These authors directed clinicians to embrace a "health" focus emphasizing the maintenance and enhancement of differing aspects of holistic human functioning, rather than continue to focus only on remediation. They also directed clinicians to consider religion and spirituality, again in contrast to received historical professional opinion, as areas of life that provide the foundations for identity and for addressing life's challenges. Finally, Savolaine and Granello challenged clinicians to consider how they would validate transcendent experiences for clients, even if they themselves could not recognize such experiences.

Russell and Yarhouse (2006) stated that 80% of the studies that they reviewed pointed to a connection between the integration of religion or spirituality into participants' lives and greater happiness, life satisfaction, morale, and other measures of well-being. They cautioned clinicians against dismissing the benefits of such practices and affiliations for clients, even if the clinician does not find them relevant. They asked clinicians to identify how religious or spiritual groups provide sources of community and support for them personally and to look for ways that such groups may augment individual therapy. Furthermore, Russell and Yarhouse asked mental health professionals to see if they could envision such community as protection against worldly pressures their clients might experience, even if such institutions did not provide such a function for them personally. This request is echoed by another author's call for "awareness of one's spiritual and religious groups in order to more adequately conceptualize a client's religious and spiritual beliefs and community" (Hage et al., 2006, p. 218).

Hage et al. (2006) reiterated the greater subjective well-being and life satisfaction reported by those who describe themselves as "religious" and "spiritual," and, conversely, how negative religious coping styles (e.g., difficulty forgiving God) were linked to depression, stress, and suicidal behavior. These authors urged (1) greater receptivity on the part of professionals to a client's bringing up religious and spiritual concerns, (2) increased clarity within the therapeutic alliance of the spiritual values of the counselor, and, (3) in closing, questioned the comprehensiveness of clinician preparation in terms of all three domains of conceptual, practical, and knowledge-of-self in order to adequately address religious and spiritual issues in the provision of mental health services.

In sum, it would seem that the spiritual well-being of the mental health professional is predictive of the quality of the services that he or she offers to clients. In the ongoing process of individual development, which then fosters professional growth, attention to one's spiritual genuineness is a crucial aspect of the potential for mental health professionals to be truly responsive to their clients' needs.

Descriptions of Spiritual Genuineness

If medical professionals wish to include a salutogenic orientation in their approach to healing, then they must consider what could be meant by the "optimal functioning" of patients in the differing specialties of medical practice. Such a definition appears to be absent in the literature. However, as mental health professionals know, there exists an admonition that clients cannot be expected to move toward a goal of "optimal functioning" separate from or beyond the level of personal growth and development that the clinician has achieved. It is important to remember that such a challenge in no way requires that mental health clinicians have spiritual answers for clients. Instead, the task before mental health professionals is to be aware of the questions that need to be addressed and the experiences that need to be examined openly and nonjudgmentally on the client's journey toward individual development and the counselor's progression toward spiritual genuineness.

Given the relative novelty of the notion of spiritual health and functioning, the list of opportunities for mental health professionals that follows cannot be viewed as complete, but instead must be seen as a compilation of current thought and as an impetus toward professional discussion and consensus on this topic. Those caveats understood, the 10 facets of mental health professional spiritual genuineness are as follows:

- *Placement of self within a developmental model of spirituality to identify spiritual growth and challenges* (Savolaine & Granello, 2002). By being able to determine at what stage one is currently functioning, the clinician or student may, on the basis of a developmental model of the spirituality of choice, better grasp the strengths of his or her spiritual genuineness and the current limits of his or her personal development. Together, the two qualities may define the ethical boundaries of competence in terms of responding to client need.

- *Openness to examining one's personal spiritual values* (Hall, Dixon, & Mauzey, 2004; Savolaine & Granello, 2002). This receptivity to the invitation to explore one's spiritual values would seem to be a core facet of genuineness. The vulnerability implicit in such an investigation and the personal experience of the process foster an empathy to the client's experiences that can be gained in no other way. Conversely, a reluctance or refusal to examine one's spiritual values could be seen as a caution against broaching such a topic with clients and, consequently, as an area requiring further personal growth for the mental health professional.

- *Connection of one's values with one's beliefs and individual moral code for living* (Savolaine & Granello, 2002). The exploration of personal spiritual values may be a valuable experience in and of itself. However, one application of that genuineness is the utilization of values to guide one's life and everyday actions. Such congruence between values and behavior provides a consistent example of how one goes about meeting life priorities and living authentically.

- *Acknowledgment of one's struggles with, and resolutions of, issues such as forgiveness, transcendence, sin, faith, the afterlife, and one's relationship with a Supreme Being* (Hagedorn, 2005; Briggs & Ryle, 2005). This struggle does not imply an inability to assist clients in their spiritual journey, but instead can be viewed as a statement of honesty and a commitment on the part of the clinician to continue to pay attention to these issues. For the truly genuine individual, each life stage or stress provides a new arena in which to reexplore life issues, including spiritual issues, in order to gain new learning and insight. The intent and follow-through in doing so confirms that one is not satisfied with past answers, but instead consistently reexamines those answers for current relevance and applicability.

- *Acknowledgment of what one knows and what one does not know about diverse spiritual belief systems.* Part of being honest with oneself demands acknowledging what one has yet to learn. This admission would seem to be the starting point for acquiring a new knowledge and understanding. It confirms the clinician's insight into his or her levels of preparation and readiness to respond professionally to clients' spiritual and religious issues. Such acknowledgment may even lead to intentional participation in ongoing professional development specific to this study. Failure to acknowledge what one does not know, perhaps out of a desire to appear perhaps more skilled or competent than another clinician, may eventually harm the client.

- ***Identification of life events that have shaped or developed one's value system and identity*** (Hagedorn, 2005; Savolaine & Granello, 2002). Undertaking a personal life review allows an individual to identify those nodal, identity-defining experiences that come along in life and, more importantly, to examine how the choices made in response to such events shaped one's current values and life priorities. One aspect of this exploration involves tracing one's religious and spiritual roots through one's family of origin, adolescence, and maturation toward the present. Understanding the role of one's spiritual or religious influences prepares the clinician to better understand and honor the role of those influences in the client's life.

- ***Identification of how personal spirituality has contributed to overall wellness and general mental health*** (Myers & Williard, 2003). Although perhaps an oversimplification, it is nonetheless a truism that all influences in one's life either promote greater health or maintain the current level of wellness, which may be seen as retarding further growth. This insight on the part of mental health professionals may provoke a more empathic understanding of how clients' spiritual or religious choices facilitate or impede general health, growth, and functioning.

- ***Attainment of an awareness of any personal spiritual or religious values that may interfere with demonstrating genuine empathy, openness, and acceptance of differing belief systems*** (Briggs & Rayle, 2005; Pargament & Zinnbauer, 2000). Part of the knowledge of self as a spiritual person involves acknowledgment of the limits of acceptance. Although, as individuals, all persons have a right to accept or reject differing religious or spiritual orientations, as mental health professionals they must adhere to ethical standards that demand (1) the identification of those client life choices that may prove beyond the clinician's ability to accept and (2) the development of suitable venues for client referral so that clinician bias will not contaminate the professional delivery of services. Whether the clinician chooses to view such personal biases as statements of individual preference or as material for introspection and perhaps greater acceptance in the future, in the present moment at least, the needs of the client are respected, the welfare of the client is valued above all else, and the reputation of both the professional and the profession remains untarnished.

- ***Attainment of an awareness of one's need for spiritual community*** (Savolaine & Granello, 2002). Mental health professionals also need to reconcile the needs of one's spiritual journey within the context of a spiritual or religious community. The acknowledgment of one's experience within that community and of the supports and stressors that are implicit in affiliation with any formalized institution generates the types of questions with which the client may need to grapple. To what extent does such affiliation confirm one's spiritual direction, and to what extent might one's spiritual individuality be compromised by the institution?

- "Fill[ing in of] the existential vacuum—[the] fundamental uncertainty about the value of one's life, leading to a deficit of meaning and resulting in unfulfilling states ranging from frustration to boredom" (Savolaine & Granello, 2002, p. 182). To avoid filling that void with substitutes such as addictive behaviors, unsatisfying relationships, and so forth, mental health professionals may wish to investigate the personal confluence of spiritual or religious beliefs within that existential quest for value and meaning. The questions that one's choice of religion or spirituality addresses may be of value to the client in that individual's search for these common life answers.

The Status of Graduate Training in the Development of Spiritually Genuine Clinicians

Given a renewed focus on the need for formal training in issues of religion and spirituality in counseling, including the attention to self as a spiritual being, it is vital to explore the current status of graduate training programs in order to ascertain how well that topic has been integrated into current curricula. This section will begin with an overview of current research on the topic, followed by a review of the current training standards as published by the Council for the Accreditation of Counseling and Related Educational Programs (CACREP), the American Association for Marriage and Family Therapy (AAMFT), the American Psychological Association (APA), the National Association of Social Workers (NASW), and the related fields of counseling psychology and rehabilitation psychology.

OVERVIEW OF THE CURRENT LITERATURE Previous exhortations for more attention to spiritual issues in clinical training programs and the dearth of such curricular offerings can be traced to Kelly's 1994 survey, (Kelly, 1995), which found that only 25% of 341 programs surveyed offered some sort of training in responding to clients' religious and spiritual issues in counseling. Pate and High's (1995) subsequent survey of CACREP-accredited programs found that 60% of the programs attended in some manner to this topic under the core curriculum in the Social and Cultural Foundations standard. Kelly's (1997) follow-up study revealed that attention was paid to spiritual issues by more than one half of the 48 programs accredited by CACREP only, as opposed to programs possessing multiple accreditations. In their survey of graduate program offerings, Young et al. (2002, p. 24) utilized Miller's (1999) specification of four relevant knowledge domains as developed by the Summit on Spirituality: "(a) general knowledge of spiritual phenomena, (b) awareness of one's own spiritual perspective, (c) understanding clients' spiritual perspectives, [and] (d) spiritually related interventions and strategies." CACREP liaisons who participated in the survey agreed that spirituality and religion are important training issues. These professors offered moderate to strong agreement regarding the importance of such competencies, but not even one half of the faculty reported feeling prepared to introduce them to training and supervision.

On the basis of the results of behavioral health research linking increased participation in religious or spiritual activities with improved health outcomes (Miller & Thoresen, 2003), awareness of the importance of spirituality and religion in the lives of the general population has expanded. This expansion has taken root in the inclusion of these topics within multicultural competencies in the emerging professional literature and as a foundation advocated for mental health services. However, to date, the expansion of attention seems more philosophical than curricular.

Zinnbauer, Pargament, and Scott (1999) spoke to the recent shift from the historical rationale against the inclusion of these topics in mental health preparation programs to their inclusion in clinical training programs. Surveys of students and faculty seem to support this infusion of the spiritual dimension into clinical theory, practice, education, and research (Yarhouse & Fisher, 2002). However, Young, Cashwell, Wiggins-Frame, and Belaire (2002) found that many counselor education programs do not address these issues due to three main obstacles. First, current faculty pointed to a distinct lack of training in this area in their own clinical programs and doctoral-level faculty-preparation curricula, leaving them feeling unprepared to instruct others. Second, the traditional skepticism put forth by the field of psychology based on "conflict between the scientific, objective perspective of psychology and the transcendent, subjective aspects of religion and spirituality" (p. 22) is set forth as a rationale suggesting that spirituality and religion are best discussed within ecclesiastical settings. The third obstacle was reported to be negative personal experiences with organized religious practices and institutions, resulting in a personal rejection of those practices and institutions. These negative personal experiences may color a clinician's perspective on the value of such affiliations for others. Despite such concerns, it would seem that clinical training programs are headed toward taking account of these topics. A brief review of professional standards from each field may illuminate the current thinking within the different mental health professional training programs.

CACREP Training Standards. In the area of counselor education, the accrediting body, the Council for the Accreditation of Counseling and Related Educational Programs (CACREP, 2009), recently released the latest version of the new accreditation standards. Among the new standards is Section II.F.2, Social and Cultural Diversity studies that provide an understanding of the cultural context of relationships, issues, and trends in a multicultural society, including all of the following:

- "multicultural and pluralistic trends, including characteristics and concerns between and within diverse groups nationally and internationally;
- attitudes, beliefs, understandings, and acculturative experiences, including specific experiential learning activities that are designed to foster students' understanding of self and culturally diverse clients;
- theories of multicultural counseling, identity development, and social justice;
- individual, couple, family, group, and community strategies for working with and advocating for diverse populations, including multicultural competencies;
- counselors' roles in developing cultural self-awareness; promoting cultural social justice, advocacy, and conflict resolution; and other culturally supported behaviors that promote optimal wellness and growth of the human spirit, mind, or body; and
- counselors' roles in eliminating biases, prejudices, [and the] processes of intentional and unintentional oppression and discrimination."

It is of interest that, unlike previous standards in this area of curricular attention, the wording of the current standards omits specific "multicultural and pluralistic trends" relevant to the practice of counseling. Wording in previous standards had included religion and spirituality among a listing of cultural issues; however, such wording, including comments on gender, sexual orientation, ethnicity, and so forth, have been stricken from the latest standards. Although this format gives faculty greater freedom to attend to those issues of social and cultural diversity specific to the context of students' clinical careers, future research may wish to explore the commonalities of curricular coverage among programs once the new standards have been implemented.

It is also of note that whichever issues of social and cultural diversity are addressed, "understanding of self" is specifically mentioned as one of the training standards. This mandate echoes the notion that acknowledgment of oneself as a cultural being, however an individual defines such an identity, is a vital aspect of one's professional competence. This development may be linked to the ongoing mandate for student evaluation throughout training programs. Standard O stated (CACREP, 2009),

The program faculty conducts a developmental, systematic assessment of each student's progress throughout the program, including consideration of the student's academic performance, professional development, and personal development. Consistent with established institutional due process policy and [the] *ACA Code of Ethics*, when evaluations indicate that a student is not appropriate for the program, faculty assist in facilitating the student's transition out of the program and, if possible, into a more appropriate area of study.

So, although relevant social and cultural issues are not identified, there remains an indication of the need for the student to demonstrate appropriate professional and personal development within such contexts in order to progress through his or her graduate training program.

In sum, although the latest edition of the CACREP standards do not specifically mention attention to the religious or spiritual concerns either of clients or of counselors-in-training, there is an expectation that whichever issues of social and cultural diversity are included in the training program, they will entail attention to self-development, as well as an understanding of clients and a consideration of effective therapeutic interventions.

AAMFT Training Standards. The AAMFT Commission on Accreditation for Marriage and Family Therapy Education's latest training standards listed only two relevant standards pertaining to issues of cultural diversity:

I-B. **Educational outcomes** reflect an understanding and respect for **cultural diversity**.

Competence		
5.5.2	Professional	Consult with peers and/or supervisors if personal issues, attitudes, or beliefs threaten to adversely impact clinical work.
5.5.3	Professional	Pursue professional development through self-supervision, collegial consultation, professional reading, and continuing educational activities.

It is of relevance to this chapter's focus that (a) the self-of-the-therapist continues to be a vital issue in the delivery of efficacious clinical services and (b) ongoing professional development is a vital aspect of one's expected post-degree professional activities. Also, it is of interest that these standards omit any specification of facets or definitions of cultural diversity relevant to the 21st-century population.

This current status seems consistent with the only survey of the curriculum of AAMFT programs that appeared in the professional literature. Given the latitude permitted by the absence of a definition of relevant cultural variables, Carlson, Kirkpatrick, Hecker, and Killmer (2002) wondered what percentage of programs attended to issues of religion and spirituality. They found that 76% of their sample reported no coursework or supervision specific either to addressing religious or spiritual issues with clients or in the supervision of new clinicians. At that time, a new inclusion in the 2002 Standards for Accreditation (version 10.3, standard 300.1) called for the infusion of issues of diversity, including spirituality and religion, into marriage and family therapy training programs. However, a more recent study of students indicated "minimal training in spiritual and religious diversity and interventions" (Hage, Hopson, Siegel, Payton, and DeFanti, 2006, p. 307). This finding suggests that the preceding mandate has yet to be fully implemented or realized. The finding was also a disappointment to many students who had chosen training in marriage and family therapy, partly, they reported, as a function of the closeness of this area of practice to pastoral counseling and to their personal affiliation with organized religions.

APA Training Standards. The American Psychological Association develops guidelines and principles for the accreditation of programs in professional psychology. As part of the 2005 document, Standard 3.c speaks to a focus on "cultural and individual diversity" more in terms of clients than psychologists. This code of preparation seems more invested in the clinician-in-training understanding the role of culture in the identity of the client, rather than also in the self-identity of the mental health professional. In addition, and similarly to the two previous codes of professional preparation, this standard does not specify those cultural issues of relevance that the psychologist-in-training needs to be prepared to address.

In terms of clinical preparation, an earlier survey by Shafranske and Malony (1996) reported that only one third of clinicians surveyed felt well prepared to address these issues with clients, although the same clinicians indicated the personal importance of both and acknowledged the relevance of this content to their clinical work. Brawer et al. (2002) found that 17% of clinical training directors of APA programs stated that such content was covered systematically and 16% stated that there was no coverage at all. In addition, only 13% of programs offered a course devoted to spirituality and religion in psychology, but 77% expected such topics to be included in clinical supervision. There was no explanation provided for how supervisors ought to develop competence in these areas when they were not covered in their academic programs.

It is worthy of note that Russell and Yarhouse (2006) found discrepancies between the personal attitudes toward religion held by psychologists and those held by the American public. These researchers found that (a) only 72% of psychologists reported a belief in God, compared with 90% of the general population; (b) 51% of psychologists reported that religion was of little importance, compared with only 11% of the general population; and (c) only 50% of psychologists reported seeing the importance of the exploration of clients' religious beliefs and practices. Among the psychologists who responded to Russell and Yarhouse's survey, 64.7% reported no training in spiritual or religious issues and 21.9% stated that these issues were considered together with other issues of multicultural diversity; however, 90.6% acknowledged that the absence of training in spiritual or religious issues was discussed at least once during supervision. They summed up their findings by stating a concern about the perceptions of psychologists as "a-religious" or anti-religious and about counseling sessions not being a safe venue for clients with spiritual issues to seek help. However, in a study separating affiliation with formal religion and personal spirituality, Bilgrave and Deluty (2002) reported that 71% of psychologists reported a belief in a "higher power which may include God" and 44% believed in "an eternal, universal essence of One" and endorsed private spirituality over organized religion. Smith and Orlinsky's survey of psychotherapists from New Zealand, Canada, and the United States concluded that "therapists may be both secular and religious . . . secular as it is independent of institutional religion yet religious insofar as it tends to focus on matters of 'ultimate concern' to individuals" (2004, p. 151).

In sum, there seems to be an inconsistency between APA training guidelines and APA ethical statements. APA guidelines for training mention religion only once as a demographic factor defining cultural and individual diversity (Domain A5) and spirituality not at all. However, the APA Code of Ethics (2002) and Multicultural Guidelines (2003) urges psychologists to obtain knowledge and training in order to develop competencies to address issues of religious and spiritual diversity. Hage (2006) added sensitivity to, and competence in, personal awareness of one's theoretical orientation regarding religion and spirituality. In addition, psychologists are personally, although not professionally, attuned to issues of spirituality, including religion. More confounding is the notion that this content is not to be covered during one's clinical training but during clinical supervision, raising the question of how a psychologist is expected to attain suitable levels of competence in the area when it is not addressed within the clinical training program.

NASW Training Standards. The National Association for Social Workers spoke to the issue of sensitivity and professional responsiveness to issues of cultural diversity in its 2001 version of the standards for clinical preparation. The text is offered as **Standard 2: Self-Awareness—Social workers shall develop an understanding of their own personal and cultural values and beliefs as a first step in appreciating the importance of multicultural identities in the lives of people.**

Interpretation of the Standards. Cultural competence requires social workers to examine their own cultural backgrounds and identities to increase their awareness of their personal assumptions, values, and biases. Social workers' self-awareness of their own cultural identities is as fundamental to practice as the informed assumptions about clients' cultural backgrounds and experiences in the United States. This awareness of personal values, beliefs, and biases informs their practice and influences their relationships with clients. Cultural competence includes social workers knowing and acknowledging how fears, ignorance, and the "isms" (e.g., racism, sexism, ethnocentrism, heterosexism, ageism, and classism) have influenced their attitudes, beliefs, and feelings.

Social workers need to be able to move from being culturally aware of their own heritage to becoming culturally aware of the heritage of others. They can value and celebrate differences in others rather than maintain an ethnocentric stance, and they can demonstrate comfort with the differences between themselves and others. They have an awareness of personal and professional limitations that may warrant the referral of a client to another social worker or agency that can best meet the client's needs. Self-awareness also helps in understanding the process of cultural identity formation and helps guard against stereotyping. As one develops an understanding of the diversity within one's own group, one can be more open to the diversity within other groups.

Cultural competence also requires social workers to appreciate how they need to move from cultural awareness to cultural sensitivity before achieving cultural competence, and how they need to evaluate their growth and development throughout these different levels of cultural competence in practice.

Self-awareness becomes the basis for professional development and should be supported by supervision and agency administration. Agency administrators and public policy advocates also need to develop strategies to reduce their own biases and expand their self-awareness.

The NASW standards address the need for both professional and personal development around these issues and, while exemplifying six issues, does not include religion or spirituality specifically among that number. The NASW directive specifies the importance of self-awareness, but would seem to delegate the designation of areas of important self-awareness to those who provide the academic training and clinical supervision. Previously cited research regarding supervisors' level of knowledge and comfort with religious and spiritual issues in the delivery of clinical services may prove to be the deciding factor as to whether or not new social workers are introduced to these issues.

COUNSELING PSYCHOLOGY TRAINING STANDARDS   This area of clinical training is being offered separately from that of psychology because the counseling psychology division of the APA represents the more service-oriented, rather than research-focused, aspect of that professional field. Attention to issues of spirituality and religion in clinical work was cited in proceedings from the 1999 Multicultural Conference and Summit: "[P]eople are cultural and spiritual beings . . . and that spirituality is a necessary condition for a psychology of human existence" (Hage, 2006). However, as Hage went on to state, this directive has yet to be translated into training standards and curricula.

In the most recent study of 40 training directors of APA-accredited counseling psychology programs found in the professional literature, Schulte, Skinner, and Claiborn (2002) reported that

- 87% said that they had seen no faculty effort to introduce this religious and spiritual developmental theory into curriculum,
- 73% said that only manifestations of religious or spiritual dysfunction were introduced,
- 65% of faculty opined that these factors were less defining of individual identity or cultural diversity than gender and ethnicity,
- 69% stated that these topics were not included in discussions of issues of diversity,
- 91% of faculty and 76% of supervisors were not expected to be knowledgeable about these issues, and
- 82% of training directors could not identify a course that covered this content.

However, 75% stated a willingness to discuss such topics in class, assignments, and supervision; 90% of faculty said that they would welcome research on these topics; and 83% stated a willingness to supervise student inquiry on such topics.

REHABILITATION PSYCHOLOGY TRAINING STANDARDS   In their survey of rehabilitation psychologists, Yamey and Greenwood (2004) found opinions that spiritual and religious beliefs are integral to views of recovery and sources of resilience and that the incorporation of religious or spiritual interventions or resources into counseling provides confirmation of an additional coping mechanism and supports rehabilitative efforts. That perspective was supported by 79% of the faculty surveyed, yet 82% of rehabilitation psychologists could not identify any attention to these topics in their training. So although the importance and value of knowledge and techniques in utilizing religious and spiritual interventions in rehabilitation psychology are noted by faculty and clinicians alike, intentional action to ensure such competency is still hard to come by.

In sum, this review confirms the variability of the inclusion of attention to spirituality within differing clinical training programs. Given the surge in attention to religious and spiritual issues among the populace as a whole and client populations in particular, clinical training programs across professional disciplines may wish to consider how best to address these topics within their curricula.

The Challenge Ahead

This section traces the emerging attention in the current professional literature to the need for clinical training programs to offer new clinicians systematic preparation in the areas of religion and spirituality. Suggestions for how clinical training programs may accomplish this task follow. While not intended as a training model, the material presented may provide an introductory foundation for how each program, within each distinct helping profession, may incorporate attention to these issues into its unique philosophy.

ATTENTION TO ISSUES OF RELIGION AND SPIRITUALITY IN CLINICAL TRAINING PROGRAMS

Given the purposeful historical neglect of religious and spiritual issues in counseling programs, the presentation of a chronology detailing more recent manifestations of this schism may support the curricular suggestions that follow. This summary of current writings is intended to validate the need for attention to the notion of the self of the professional as a spiritual being as a pre- or corequisite to any accompanying interventions with clients.

"Over the past two decades, the volume and quality of literature on religions and spirituality in psychotherapy have increased" (Worthington & Sandage, 2001, p. 473). This finding, based on a careful review of published articles in professional journals, speaks to the emerging interest in this topic. Hall, Dixon, and Mauzey (2004, p. 506) assert that religious and spiritual training for psychotherapists is "increasing in importance"; however, these authors also question whether that acknowledged importance is being implemented in practice through the development of curriculum and required coursework. They cited a 2002 survey of CACREP programs in which 78% of program representatives reported no specific course addressing religious or spiritual issues. Concluding their study, the authors wondered whether infusing religious and spiritual issues into existing courses was a more viable way to present that material than developing separate courses.

As a response to this recommendation for further research, Cashwell and Young (2004) discovered that more courses that focus on religion and spirituality in counseling are being developed but are usually offered as electives. Their survey of syllabi reported consistent attention to self-exploration (competencies 3 and 4 from the 1995 Summit on Spirituality), encouraged by the inclusion of autobiographical assignments, spiritual genograms, narratives, and spiritual lifelines. O'Connor (2004) utilized focus questions about students' spiritual autobiographies to illuminate the critical experiences one encounters on his or her personal spiritual path. This author mandated the establishment of a weekly support group to explore personal spiritual journeys and provide a safe, supportive environment, on the basis of the supposition that community also offers a challenge to move beyond the "limits of individual perspective" (p. 231).

From a differing perspective, Briggs and Rayle (2005) offered a protocol for injecting attention to religion and spirituality into all eight core curricular areas of clinical psychology as an academic discipline: professional identity, social and cultural diversity, human growth and development, career development, helping relationships, group work, assessment, and research and program evaluation. They proposed that the holistic role played by spiritual beliefs cannot be adequately covered in a stand-alone class. Besides, a stand-alone class may overlook the fact that such belief systems pervade all facets of human functioning.

In sum, the professional literature reveals a growing attempt by professional training programs to expand the minimal preparation of mental health professionals in psychological issues in religion and spirituality, usually through the provision of elective courses. If programs choose to infuse this content into existing courses, the question then arises as to which courses they might be. If programs follow the suggestions made by Briggs and Rayle (2005), then each core class will require revision. If programs choose to include this content in courses dealing specifically with social and cultural issues, then the differing aspects of diversity would need to be weighed in order to decide which to include and which to omit. Also, faculty in those programs which prepare future helping professionals must be open to classroom discussion and to the inclusion of the topic of responsiveness to client needs. One issue for ongoing professional consideration is whether more mental health preparation accrediting agencies should formulate standards of preparation that require attention to religious and spiritual issues.

POSSIBLE DIRECTIONS FOR INFUSING RELIGION AND SPIRITUALITY INTO CLINICAL TRAINING PROGRAMS Myers and Williard (2003) stated that, although the infusion of religion and spirituality into mental health professionals' training may still be a concern, it increasingly is becoming a reality. The initial step in the process of legitimizing study in this area seems to be the acknowledgment of its importance. The next step is an exploration of how best to offer that material in an already crowded curriculum. Setting the issue of curricular priority aside for another discussion, faculty who wish to consider paying attention to the preparation of helping professionals in religious and spiritual issues may do well to heed Myers and Williard's statement that "counselors-in-training should be given opportunities to explore, understand and articulate the personal meaning of their own spirituality as well as an understanding of the individual nature of their meaning-making process" (p. 152), equivalent to recommendation 3 in the following list of those authors' recommendations with regard to clinical training programs:

1. Add developmental wellness base, including spirituality.
2. Teach a constructivist view of spirituality as distinct from religion.
3. Assign learning experiences of differing faiths within developmental and multicultural courses.
4. Learn and practice assessment and intervention techniques congruent with the philosophy of spiritual and holistic wellness research in religion and spirituality.
5. Help students understand their own spiritual issues, on the assumption that faculty can model this process (Myers & Williard, 2003).
6. Ensure that attention is paid to the various aspects of diversity within the multicultural training competency required of programs, included is an examination of one's own personal beliefs and attitudes (Hage et al., 2006).
7. Review one's spiritual and religious heritage.

As a guide to helping faculty, Hagedorn (2005, p. 74) provided a list of 13 relevant questions to pique students' interest in contemplating themselves as religious and spiritual beings:

1. What were the specific religious and spiritual beliefs and values of my parents (or family of origin)?
2. What religious and spiritual beliefs and values was I taught as a child? Who influenced those beliefs and values, outside of my immediate family?
3. How common were those values to my peers, or were they unique to my experience?
4. How have my religious and spiritual beliefs and values changed as I moved through developmental life stages? How has the practice of those beliefs changed?
5. How do I assimilate values and beliefs different from my own into my current beliefs and values?
6. What factors caused me to accept or reject the religious and spiritual values of my family or peer group?
7. What were some of the turning points along the development of my religious and spiritual beliefs and values, and when did they occur?
8. Where am I now on my religious and spiritual journey?
9. How active am I in organized religion?
10. How do I reconcile the ideas of religion and spirituality?
11. How does religion help or restrict my spirituality?
12. What meaning does this period of my life have in the context of my life as a whole?
13. What are my current struggles and challenges as they relate to my religious and spiritual beliefs and values? What is the likely outcome and how will I grow as a result?

In sum, Hage et al. (2006) recapped the challenges facing faculty as (a) what to include, in terms of client issues, counselor values, and counselor willingness to introduce topics in a more comprehensive format in a graduate school mental health training curriculum, and how to include such material; (b) how to prepare a life map with clients; (c) how to explore normative and pathological expressions of spirituality; and (d) how to distinguish spiritual distress from spiritual immaturity or dysfunction. In conclusion, they stated that this academic challenge holds the potential for spiritual awakening and a positive transformation for students through the formality and direction of such a learning experience.

Case Example Revisited

Sandra's visit with her faculty advisor came both as a welcome relief and a challenge. While empathizing with her vulnerability to her peer's opinions, her faculty advisor directed Sandra to personally evaluate her own characteristics that would support, and could impede, her professional growth. Sandra was instructed to attend to her own awareness of her spiritual health and development—not as an overriding concern, but as one aspect of a holistic model of personal well-being. Sandra was left with two puzzling thoughts: How do I define components of my own well-being? and How openly can I assess, through personal evaluation plus input from trusted others, how best to foster my growth as a person and a professional counselor? Sandra felt reassured that a counselor need not be perfect before being ready to assist others on their life journeys, and she felt challenged to weigh which questions pertaining to her spiritual growth, as well as other aspects of her development, were integral to her own life journey, both now and in the future.

Conclusion

"An important part of the spiritual journey was service to others, work with a social justice theme and, for many, this was instrumental in their choice of a therapeutic profession" (Simmonds, 2005, p. 250). If such sentiments are indeed valid, then the confluence of spirituality and professional helping would appear to be natural. Although training standards seem to be slowly addressing issues of spirituality and religion, among other issues of social and cultural identity, the literature review presented in this chapter reveals that more attention is needed to determine how to develop spiritually and religiously competent multicultural counselors. Although knowledge of others' practices, traditions, and beliefs is important, it pales in comparison with attention to the self as a spiritual being. It is this purposeful exploration of self as a spiritual being, both in one's present and toward one's future, that represents an ongoing commitment to one's evolution as a clinician and to the sharing of a spiritual and religious quest with one's clients.

Self-Understanding Exercises

1. Review the curriculum demands for your program as a function of the accreditation standards, and prioritize religion and spirituality within the list of relevant "cultural factors" that you identify. Compare your list with those of your peers, and discuss the implications of these priorities for case conceptualization practices.

2. How do you factor your religious and spiritual orientation into your definition of personal identity on your personal journey of self-understanding?

3. In what ways do your religious and spiritual views of human nature, evil, and so forth overlap with your clinical perspectives? In what ways do the two types of visions diverge? How do you explain the divergence in terms of your potential to be genuine as a clinician?

Opportunities for Further Learning

1. If you are in a graduate training program, survey your faculty about the importance of training in the issues of spirituality and religion.

2. Compare the curricula of programs that offer graduate courses in religion and spirituality as a component of mental health professional training, and explore how similar or distinct the courses are. In your opinion, what may be absent from current teaching content?

3. Ask practicing clinicians in your professional field how they utilize the self as a spiritual being in their delivery of mental health services.

3

...

Varieties of Spiritual Beliefs

The future of religion is connected with the possibility of developing
a faith in the possibilities of human experience and human relationships
that will create a vital sense of the solidarity of human interests and inspire
action to make that sense a reality.

—John Dewey

CASE EXAMPLE

Patricia was a graduate student in a community counseling program with the intent of earning her clinical license and focusing on the issues of substance abuse. Having come from a family system in which alcohol abuse was rampant, she was curious about the etiology of alcoholism and addictive behaviors in general. As part of her personal growth, Patricia had rediscovered Bible study, a weekly experience that had been part of her childhood, but, until recently, had been relegated to that period of her life. She felt confirmed and exhilarated after each week's session and eagerly awaited the next meeting. After one of her counseling classes, she was explaining to her peers her affective responses to her Bible study, and one of her colleagues laughingly suggested that she might be a "Bible addict." Although said in jest, this comment deeply disturbed Patricia, given her personal family history around addictions and her clinical interest. She wondered if she was too invested in her Bible study and should pull back. She also wondered how what she was learning in her counseling classes was relevant to her response to her study group.

■ ■ ■

INTRODUCTION

Counseling and the other helping professions consider their primary focus to be an understanding of the human experience that has its basis in a philosophy of holism, or attention to all facets of the human experience, with a belief that emerging health or dysfunction in one area must affect the interrelated facets of human existence (Tse, Lloyd, Petchovsky, & Manaia, 2005). Accordingly, when focusing on multiple sources of client pain, there is no predetermined starting point because self-understanding and positive change as specific to the presenting issue will generalize to increase functioning in all other aspects of the client's life (Hassed, 2002). This focus on client holism represents a guiding theme of professional helping (Dyson, Cobb, & Forman, 1997).

Within that holistic focus must be included an attention to client spirituality. Spirituality, regardless of practice or dogma, is unified around a search for the sacred (Paragment, Magyar-Russell, & Murray-Swank, 2005). That search may be for some reference to a Higher Power, be it God, ultimacy, transcendence, or a Supreme Being. This "sacred" is the core of life, fundamental to the identity of many individuals (Genia, 2000; Olive, 2004). The need for sanctification (Paragment & Mahoney, 2005) is a universal need. Sanctification refers to the need to imbue roles, attributes, and objects with sacred qualities or see them as manifestations of the Divine. Moreover, spirituality has been identified as a "basic character-istic of humanness" (Dyson, Cobb, & Forman, 1997, p. 1184). On a related note, Carson (1989) saw one's spirituality as the central aspect of individuality. Ellis (1980) stated that spir-itual meaning provides an individual with uniqueness and individuality. In contrast, those lacking such spiritual resolution would be bereft of such identity/certainty and subject to the values and dictates of others.

This chapter will present the basic beliefs of major world religions and practices, ex-plore how the consideration of spirituality and religion has influenced the development of counseling theory, and begin to identify the distinctions and overlaps between spiritual be-lief and clinical belief, described as a "daunting but rewarding task" (Eliason, Hanley, & Leventis, 2001, p. 78).

SPIRITUAL BELIEF SYSTEMS

Central to all spiritual and religious belief systems is the relationship between the self, others, and God (Dyson, Cobb, & Forman, 1997, p. 1184). Inner resources, community connection, and a relationship with a power higher than oneself are common across spiritual traditions. So, too, is a search for meaning, a sense of worth, and a reason for living (Howden, 1992). Frankl (1959) and Bown and Williams (1993) offered that this search for meaning forms the core of identity and is the motivating force behind intellect and emotion. Therefore, this sec-tion will present a very brief overview of the tenets of major world religions so that coun-selors can begin to appreciate how adherence to such beliefs may affect clients' worldviews (Frame, 2003).

BASIC BELIEFS OF MAJOR WORLD RELIGIONS
Major Western Religions

JUDAISM   The basic tenet of Judaism is monotheism—that there is one God of the universe who created and continues to govern. This God is Yahweh, described as "eternal, omnis-cient, omnipotent and holy" (Frame, 2003, p. 63). The second major tenet of Judaism is that the Jews were chosen to receive the law of Yahweh and serve as a model for humanity. The third tenet is that of a covenant that if Jews acknowledged God and kept to his command-ments, and subsequent laws, they would be rewarded. Lack of obedience would result in divine retribution. At some point, God would send the messiah to redeem the Jews and return them to sovereignty in the land of Israel. Last, among some Jews, there is a belief that study of the Torah and fidelity to the commandments might hasten the arrival of the promised messiah.

Jewish law focuses on dietary practices, the Sabbath, and annual festivals. Keeping kosher involves the specification of which animals are clean enough for food; how they are to be slaughtered; which foods may, and may not, be served together; and the use of separate sets of dishes and utensils so that meat, dairy products, and the Passover meal can be separately prepared. For Jews, the Sabbath is observed on Saturday. This is a day when no work is done but the time is spent in prayer, study, rest, and family feasting. The major festivals honor the agricultural cycle as this cycle was uppermost in the lives of historical Jews. The New Year is celebrated through Rosh Hashanah (in early fall) and, eight days later, Yom Kippur marks the annual day of fasting, confession, and atonement.

Among modern Jews, there are three distinct groups. Orthodox Jews are traditionalists who adhere to their traditions in the midst of modern life. The Torah is the supreme religious authority and as the word of God must be taken literally in the face of more modern interpretations. They adhere strictly to the laws of Judaism. Conservative Jews respect the Jewish traditions and practices, yet tend to be more flexible and more inclined to update traditional practices in light of modern life. Reform Jews focus heavily on reason rather than obedience and tend to be liberal and nonauthoritarian. In Reform synagogues, families are seated together rather than by gender, as is the practice in Orthodox congregations; sermons are given in English rather than Hebrew; and women can become rabbis.

CHRISTIANITY   This religion is based on the centrality of Jesus Christ, who was seen not only as a teacher, healer, and example of virtuous living, but also as the means through which salvation and eternal life can be obtained. Raised from the dead after his crucifixion, Jesus lives and rules with God. At the end of time, Jesus will return to earth to inaugurate his eternal reign, which he began during his earthly existence. One major theme of all Christian religions is that Jesus was both human and divine—God in human form. God became human in the form of Jesus to conquer worldly sinfulness; however, he was punished for the sins of the world. One view of this occurrence is that Jesus was sacrificed because of human sin or alienation from God. Jesus's resurrection from the dead gives humans a model by which they, too, can be freed from the punishment of sin if they truly repent and accept Jesus Christ as their salvation.

In addition to the presence of Christ, God offers the Holy Spirit as an ongoing source of comfort and direction. Christians believe that salvation from evil, sin, and death comes not from obedience to law (as do Jews), but by the grace of God. Grace is not earned through good works, serving others, or adherence to a moral code, but rather is granted by God without regard to merit. Christians are urged to model their lives after the example of Christ. For some Christians, the message from Jesus to spread his gospel legitimizes evangelical activities. The concept of the Trinity is also basic to Christian belief. Although God is one, God is also expressed in the Father (creator), the Son (redeemer), and the Holy Spirit (sustainer). Worship for Christians is to take place within a community of believers or church. This becomes the center of practice, study, worship, and service.

Within the framework of Christianity are three major divisions: Catholicism, Eastern Orthodoxy, and Protestantism. Catholicism asserts a primacy among denominations, claiming that the Pope is the latest in an unbroken line of succession from the apostle Peter to the present day. The Church is hierarchically structured and emphasizes the importance of the Liturgy of the Eucharist (Mass). During this ceremony, bread and wine are transformed into the body and blood of Christ.

The Eastern Orthodox Church differed from the Catholic Church more along political lines than religious lines, the main contentions revolving around relationships with the papacy and between clergy. The Eastern Orthodox Church is also conservative and traditional in belief and practice. Humans are believed to be created good and in search of divinization. However, the Church does not see scripture as the sole authority or as being rigid. In addition, the entire Church is seen as fallible.

Protestantism focuses on the Bible and individual faith and rejects the authority of the Pope. In addition, Protestants believe in the "priesthood of believers," implying that individual Christians can directly access God without the need for priests, as is espoused within the Catholic Church. Protestant denominations tend to have five general characteristics in common: (1) a positive view of human nature, (2) freedom to question scripture and church practices, (3) rejection of a literal interpretation of the Bible, (4) openness to scientific discovery and an integration of medical and psychological thought, and (5) minimization of the distinctions among the denominations and a focus on similarities in the belief systems.

Evangelical Christians and Fundamentalist Protestants represent a growing segment within American Christianity. Evangelical Christians tend to be moderately conservative in their theology and socially, while Fundamentalists are very conservative in both areas. Both groups practice converting nonbelievers to Christianity. Fundamentalists hold to a literal interpretation of the Bible and claim that it is the irrefutable word of God. Evangelical Christians tend to want to reform society, with its structure and its institutions, but Fundamentalists often see the very structures of the world as sinful and beyond salvation and withdraw from them as much as possible. Fundamentalists expect a level of personal holiness and that members will refrain from dancing, premarital sex, gambling, smoking, drinking, and swearing, and hold to a strict moral code. Some sects demand modest dress of both male and female members. Both groups share a conservative agenda toward social issues, opposing homosexuality, extramarital sex, abortion, divorce, and substance abuse (Thurston, 2000). Some Fundamentalist groups demand that women be submissive to their husbands and not work outside of the home or seek leadership within the church.

These are only brief overviews of the major aspects of Christianity; there are differences among and within each group. In principle, it is important for counselors to understand the tenets that may distinguish one group from another, but not to presuppose that a client who claims membership in any one specific group adheres to all of the tenets.

ISLAM   This section will offer a brief overview of the tenets of Islam. Given that the universe was created in accordance with the will of God (Allah), the most important aspect of the human psyche is the spiritual heart (*qalb*). The *qalb* is the site of intuition, understanding, and wisdom. Humans share the qualities of animals and of angels, and can sink lower than animals or rise higher than angels. It is awareness of the *qalb* that helps lift the veil between Allah and the individual and that facilitates the actualization of one's true and pure nature. The purpose of spiritual life is to heed the messages of the *qalb* and transcend the written word of doctrine toward transcendent experiences of Allah. Faith is seen to protect against ill health and misfortune, and to manage those problems when they arise. Inayat (2005) cited three recent studies that explain how Muslims understand mental distress as occurring according to the will of God.

The Islamic View of Personality. Islam holds to four aspects of personality: heart (*qalb*), ego (*nafs*), soul (*raf*), and divine potential (*fitra*). The heart (*qalb*) refers to the spiritual heart in which resides deeper wisdom. The goal is to build a heart that also encompasses sincerity, love, and compassion. This knowledge is more central and grounded than rational abstract intelligence because its source is the will of Allah. The ego (*nafs*) offers a continuum of functioning from the lowest levels of negative traits and tendencies to the highest levels of positive attributes and inclinations. The *nafs* is individually controlled by emotions, desires, and the need for gratification. Each level of development of the ego has traits and disorders specific to that stage, as well as methods of healing and transformation. The soul (*raf*) is in direct connection with the Divine, although the individual is unaware of that connection. The soul has multiple levels, and the goal is to develop its strengths and achieve a balance among the differing drives. Divine potential (*fitra*) refers to the natural condition and disposition of humans. Islam holds that the natural state of humankind is positive, good, and incorruptible. The *fitra* holds physical and spiritual tendencies, both seeking gratification and actualization within each life relationship and transaction.

The spiritual drive is directed by an innate state of purity, and the physical drives are directed by the *Shariah* (Islamic code of conduct). Born in a state of natural purity, only man, among all beings, has the ability and choice to leave this pure state of being. To remain pure, man must gain control over his negative tendencies. If emotions are controlled and channeled toward higher spiritual ends, then the psychical nature is disciplined, allowing the transformation of the lower self—one's base needs and drives—into a spiritually higher state so that the individual can be liberated from bondage to the lower self.

The Islamic Self. The developmental self has three levels, referred to as *nafs*. Imbalance is viewed as being "stuck" at one of the lower levels, or *ruh*, of the *nafs*.

1. ***Nafs Ammara (the commanding or lower self):*** The lower self, representing negative drives, is akin to the Freudian id. This stage appears in response to provocation, which Islam teaches must be avoided.
2. ***Nafs Law Wamma (the self-reproaching self):*** This self becomes aware of wrongdoing and feels remorse. The solution is to repent and turn to Allah for guidance. Although governed by an inner voice of conscience, Islam also believes in an external court of justice that is to convene on the Day of Judgment. In this court, truth will prevail and Allah will mete out the appropriate reward or punishment.
3. ***Nafs al-Mutma'inna (the peaceful self):*** This state of the self is characterized by feelings of inner peace and contentment. This state is not about contentment with the external aspects of life, such as wealth, possessions, or achievement, but rather about an inner sense of personal satisfaction. With the lower self controlled and focused toward spiritual ends, and the remorseful self in balance, then one arrives at a belief that all sorrow and joy reflects the will of Allah.

Given the belief that the four elements of the human psyche reside in the region of the physical heart, it can be expected that Muslim clients see the heart as the source of all emotional pain. Therefore, somatic complaints are heard in the initial concerns of counseling. Although the head is the animating principle, it is the Muslim heart that suffers.

Major Eastern Religions

HINDUISM One of the world's oldest religions, Hinduism is a polytheistic religion. There are three major deities: Shiva, Vishnu, and Devi (the goddess). Hinduism holds to four paths toward God as a function of the temperament of each individual (Frame, 2003). Jnana Yoga appeals to the intellectuals and philosophers who will travel the path of knowledge. Their challenge is to shift their focus toward the Divine within, rather than becoming fixated on the ego. Bhakti Yoga draws on the strengths of love and devotion as a path to God and utilizes mantras to alter one's consciousness. There is also the path based on daily work, Karma Yoga, in which God appears through daily activities rather than contemplation. The final path, Raja Yoga, uses psychological experimentation and meditation to lead to one's true nature (Sharma, 2000).

In addition to the four paths toward God, Hinduism holds to four stages in life that resemble rungs on a ladder toward liberation, or *moksha*. The student stage (Brahmacharin) involves studying the scriptures and religion under the guidance of a formal teacher and spans the ages of 8 to 12. The householder stage (Grahasthin) requires the individual to marry, earn a living, produce sons, and give donations or alms to those who have already reached a higher rung. The third stage is characterized by elder males performing ancestor-venerating rituals and is referred to as "the forest dweller" stage, or Vanaprasthin. The final stage is that of preparation to give up the world entirely in search of liberation and is referred to as the ascetic stage, or Sannyasin (Wangu, 1991).

Two concepts are central to Hinduism. The human soul, like human life, comprises developmental stages. Karma involves the notion of effect and consequence across life spans so that every action done in a past life affect one's present life, just as actions in this life will influence an individual in subsequent lives. The circumstances into which one is born reveal the conditions and actions of past lives. This cycle of birth–life–death–rebirth continues until the soul can release itself from all pain and pleasure, all fear and attachment, into a state called *samsara*, or transmigration. Unlike the western notion of sin, Hinduism holds to the innate divinity of humans, requiring that humans "uncover their perfection by removing [the] layers of illusions in which we are wrapped" (Sharma, 2000, p. 345).

The practice of Hinduism centers on the temple, which serves as a cultural center for songs sung aloud, texts read aloud, and rituals that are performed. Every rite of passage, or *samskara*, carries its own rituals. The chanting of mantras, called Vedas, is claimed to have transformative powers through their timeless universal sounds. Icons or sacred images are seen as ways that one gains access to the deity through worship. Daily worship and offerings are important aspects of Hindu practice. In addition, holy shrines are visited through pilgrimages and local shrines are visited during festivals. No longer relegated to India and southern Asia, Hinduism is a growing practice in the United States and is undergoing a transformation in consideration of women's concerns and the caste system.

BUDDHISM   Buddhism has its roots in the Brahman Hindu tradition, but it turned away from Hindu beliefs, the priesthood, the Vedic scriptures, and the attendant cult of sacrifice. In contrast to the strict caste system implicit in Hinduism, Buddha opened the tenets of his practice and faith to all persons regardless of birth.

The story of the Buddha tells of a prince raised in luxury who discovers the emptiness of his life, uncovers the reality of death and suffering, and sets off on a lifelong quest for release from the endless cycle of rebirth (Frame, 2003). Neither extreme pleasure nor the denial of pleasure leads to Nirvana (release from suffering), but instead, "the way" is a middle way of attention to purity of thought and deed. This awareness of this middle way and the guide of virtue is the way to overcome death.

Buddhism is constructed around the Four Noble Truths and the Eightfold Path. The Four Noble Truths are the following:

1. There is suffering.
2. Suffering is caused by desire, attachment, and craving.
3. Suffering can be overcome by ceasing to desire.
4. The way to end desire is to follow the Eightfold Path (Wangu, 1993).

Wangu (1993) listed the Eightfold Path as "right opinion, right intentions, right speech, right conduct, right livelihood, right effort, right mindfulness, and right concentration" (p. 26). These eight focuses are divided among morality, wisdom, and concentration (McDermott, 1993).

Similar to Hinduism, karma is a major aspect of Buddhism. Again, in Buddhist thought, karma speaks to one's actions and ethical outcomes. Simply, good deeds are rewarded and bad deeds are punished. Rather than viewing karma as divine judgment, Buddhists view karma as a universal, natural moral law. Karma determines one's rebirth and the state in which one is reborn—as a human, insect, devil, or god (McDermott, 1993). Buddhism tends to overlook the presence or importance of god(s), either as creators of the universe or arbiters of the human condition, in favor of the psychological and ethical aspects of life (Finn & Rubin, 2000).

CONFUCIANISM   One of the major schools of thought in China, Confucianism was utilized as the "official ideology of China but was never a religion per se" (Frame, 2003, p. 75). Confucianism espouses five main concepts:

1. *Jen* is best understood as love, human-heartedness, and goodness—what Smith (1958) described as "a feeling of humanity toward others and respect for oneself" (p. 159). In addition, righteousness, propriety, integrity, and filial piety are desirable traits and actions (Liu, 1993).
2. *Chung-tzu* is a state of centeredness in self such that one would exemplify the Confucian virtues without the need for monitoring oneself and would make the following of these virtues seem effortless. In this way, the individual could wholly attend to others.
3. *Li* is a sense of propriety or order within life, within social convention, in such a way that grace characterizes all interactions regardless of the circumstances.
4. *Te* is a reference to the appropriate use of power by all in society. Those entrusted with authority as leaders ought to be wise and benevolent, and those who are being led need to respond with respect and obedience.
5. *Wen* is the cultivation of those arts which honor and display the beauty within a culture.

TAOISM   "The Way," or Tao, arose as an individually focused Chinese philosophy to offset what its adherents decried as the conformist agenda of Confucianism. Within the *tao* are three meanings:

1. As "the ultimate reality, this 'way' is unspeakable and transcendent, the ground of ultimate existence" (Frame, 2003, p. 76).
2. The cycles of nature and constant change are the principles of reality and evidence of the universal force.
3. The way to serenity is to arrange one's life in accordance with the natural rhythms, both in nature and in oneself (Hartz, 1993).

Taoism is atheistic in that its adherents do not worship a god-figure, but instead work on aligning their lives with the natural forces and rhythms, both personal and cosmic. For Taoists, physical health, spiritual health, and emotional health are interconnected. Pain in one area must infect the other areas of functioning. Accordingly, diet, exercise, and meditation are used to seek balance and harmony in life, to reconcile the yin and yang (opposite forces) implicit in any situation or event.

SHINTO   With its basis in the ancient history of Japan, its members tend overwhelmingly to see themselves also as Buddhist. Shinto teaches that all things in the world are imbued with spirit(s) (*kami*, singular and plural). Therefore, nature, in all its forms, is to be respected. Shinto focuses on "simplicity and cleanliness as signs of inner goodness" (Frame, 2003, p. 77). Purity, in both physical and spiritual forms, is venerated. Adherents are taught to be grateful for all blessings that come their way (Hartz, 1997), although how that gratitude is expressed is left to each believer. Often this gratitude is expressed in the offering of coins or food when visiting Shinto shrines. The visit also entails writing prayers on slips of paper for nearby *kami* to find. The spiritual roots of Shinto are in its pervasiveness of the sacred in all of nature and the expectation of gratitude.

New Age Spirituality

The New Age movement in spirituality cannot be assumed to be a coherent code of beliefs or practices, as in the religious traditions previously discussed. Its guiding force could be a "holistic worldview wherein the sciences are considered sources of unity within the physical reality" (Frost, 1992, p. 1). Rather than rely on the mechanistic and reductionist approach of science, New Age spirituality seeks to expand consciousness (Frame, 2003). Sensing that the spirit of the whole pervades all of life, the quest is to access and focus that energy. To that end, practices such as meditation, biofeedback, acupuncture, reflexology, yoga, and so forth allow the participant to free clogged energy within the body and to be open to new energy sources from without.

Drawn to a common theme of mystery, New Age spirituality reacquainted practitioners with the older forms of spiritual and mystical expressions found in Christianity, Kabbalah, Shinto, Taoism, Zen Buddhism, and other traditions. Explanations for life events are also sought in astrology, magic, palmistry, and so forth (Guiley, 1991). In his 1998 survey of practitioners, Bloch identified seven common themes that may serve as linkages among the diverse practices:

1. an emphasis on the self, self-autonomy, and the self-as-expert;
2. a belief that one is "born different" spiritually;
3. moral and spiritual conflict with traditional religious institutions;
4. a personal sense of spiritual empowerment;
5. a resistance to traditional societal labels and roles;
6. the value of alternative spiritual communities; and
7. a resignation that traditional social institutions are no longer viable choices.

Guiley (1991) summarized the difficulty of categorizing such a movement:

> *New Age* is a controversial term applied to a spiritual and social movement encompassing a broad range of interests in religion, philosophy, mysticism, health, psychology, parapsychology, ecology and [the] occult. . . . It is virtually

impossible to define precisely what constitutes "New Age" . . . and much of what is called "New Age" is not new, but a renewed cycle of interest and discovery. (p. 403)

WICCA   Wicca, stemming from an early Anglo-Saxon word for witchcraft (Frame, 2003), may be considered one of those practices that is not "new" as in recently discovered, but instead newly rediscovered. Its history can be traced through many centuries, probably back before the dawn of written records and communicated over time through oral history. It is only with the advent of the Catholic Church that Wicca became notorious for its association with the Devil, which justified its persecution in the eyes of the Church. Wicca is a nature-based religion, in tune with its rhythms and cycles. Its emphasis is on respect for life, a celebration of the magical, and on personal experiences (Grist & Grist, 2000, as cited by Frame, 2003). There is no focus on casting spells, but there is a belief that all actions that one does will return in kind. Kindness begets kindness; evil begets evil. Becoming a Wiccan reflects a personal openness to mystery and self-searching.

The practice of Wicca is as diverse as its adherents. Although they are offered a connection to a Higher Power, Wiccans may see themselves as New Age practitioners or as members of other religions. Helping professionals may be challenged to suspend their personal incredulity about these practices and principles in order to convey the appropriate respect for individual spiritual choices and to develop the trust necessary for counseling to proceed.

SUMMARY   This section of Chapter 3 has presented only brief overviews of major world religions. The "fleshing out" of these frameworks is the ethical responsibility of all helping professionals who wish to be able to speak the same spiritual "language" as their clients and who may be interested in expanding their own personal spiritual world. With the backdrop of spiritual and religious practices provided in this section, the next section will offer some insight into the integration of spirituality and religion in the thinking and writings of leaders in the field of psychology, counseling, and professional helping.

COUNSELING THEORY AND SPIRITUALITY

Genia (2000) claimed that the belief that traditional psychology-oriented professions overlooked religious beliefs and practices was inaccurate. Attention to the relationship of spirituality and psychology is as historically rooted in the discipline as the emergence of psychological theory. Durkheim (1915) described religion as an expression of social need: "[T]he idea of society is the soul of religion" (p. 433). Each religion offers a specific representation of society and brings together adherents around that vision. This belief was reflected in the initial works of Parsons (1909) and Davis (1911) and represents quite a contrast to the negative perspectives offered by Freud (Kelly, 1995). This section will present an overview of the opinions of the psychology-oriented theorists on the place and function of religion in their own lives and in their theories—a reflection of the central thesis of this book.

Frank Parsons

Parsons spoke positively of the potential contribution of religion and spirituality to personal development. For Parsons, religious affiliation was less an observance of ritual at Sunday services than a week long life-guiding practice. Parsons associated such practices with those character traits that facilitate personal industry, social responsibility, and tolerance of religious differences. He further advocated the guiding factor of religion in moral and ethical decision making and religion as an aspiration toward a higher level of functioning. Kelly (1995) likened this thinking to Allport's (1950) notions of "mature religion." Parsons' main focus was explaining the conscious processes that went into informed career decision making. However, his comments on superficial religiosity suggest that he did not completely overlook both the potentially negative and positive aspects of religion as a guiding force.

Jesse Davis

Davis (1914) spoke more explicitly than Parsons about the connection between the moral qualities of good works and positive religious influences (Kelly, 1995). He wrote that guidance was to help the student develop a "better understanding of his own character . . . [and] an awakening of moral consciousness" (p. 18). Vocational guidance was secondarily about career choices and primarily about counseling students to "seek out those elements of character— habits, virtues, faith—which stand out prominently as the very foundation of success" (p. 49). Davis was aware of the mistaken propensity for religion to serve as morality, with the consequences of intolerance, oppression, and persecution (Kelly, 1995). He wrote in a critical voice of "religious thought . . . dominated by self motives," "religious dogmas dominating the actions of men," and social interests being limited by issues of caste or class systems (p. 99).

In summary, Kelly (1995) linked the writings of Parsons and Davis because they both saw religion as "a viable human possibility squarely in the context of enlightened self-knowledge and personally clarified decision making, deep and active concern for the good of others and a forthright and energetic sense of social interest and reform" (p. 49). Each of these pioneers in the field of counseling envisioned a positive contribution for religion as personally humanizing forces. However, they also shared a deep concern based on a knowledge of human history and keen observation of how religion can be used to oppose human empowerment, freedom, and justice.

Sigmund Freud

Freud's writings represent one of the initial comprehensive, systematic interpretations of the psychology of religion and spirituality, and continue to influence psychology, counseling, and all helping professions (Kelly, 1995). This body of work, together with that of Carl Jung, claims to explain how spirituality functions psychologically and discusses its effect on human development and mental health.

It has been suggested that Freud's secularly based theory was a resolution of his inner conflict over having been raised in a Hasidic Jewish home, guided by the teachings of an affectionate, yet harsh, father and nurtured by a Roman Catholic nanny. Jacobs and Capps (1997) noted similarities between the practice of Jewish mysticism (Kabbalah) and psychoanalysis in that both place great emphasis on dream interpretation and human sexuality. Freud proposed and elaborated on these two issues as explanations for guilt-ridden neuroses. Freud opined that God and Satan represent the two polarities of a fixed father/God image. Although later challenged by developmental models of spirituality, this vision exemplified the role of the unconscious and a child's immature attempts to reconcile the issues of love and annihilation. In addition, Freud's attention to the exploration of the unconscious and its contribution to a client's presenting situation had a direct parallel in the exploration of a client's spirituality and its relationship to the presenting issue. Lastly, Freud's attention to a client's history, less in terms of events than in meaning, bore a direct connection to helping a client understand the etiology of his or her spiritual belief system.

Freud saw religion as an illusion, an obsession with neurotic wishes expressed in ritualistic compulsions. To Freud, the human needs expressed through religious practices, especially dogmatic religious practices, represent the deep-seated childish need for reassurance of one's specialness in an uncaring world.

Freud considered participation in formal religion to be indicative of moral weakness in confronting life's basic challenges and drives and in resolving them in an ego-conscious manner. He saw religion as playing to these human insecurities by purporting to offer "knowing answers" to unanswerable questions. To Freud, issues such as the purpose of life, the existence of God, one's purpose in being, and the issue of life/salvation after death formed the content of religion. And each religion claimed to hold the one "true" set of responses.

God, Freud claimed, represents one's unresolved infantile wishes rooted in the father complex and expressed as a projection of those unresolved father issues. Freud claimed that these unresolved issues fulfill the "oldest, strongest and most urgent wishes of mankind" (Freud, 1927/1964, p. 47). However, Freud's views on religion have been constantly reviewed and a synopsis of positive and negative comments can sum up his position (Kung, 1981):

1. Historical data suggest that Freud's atheism, which reflected the then-popular focus on scientific materialism, preceded, rather than was drawn from, his clinical studies.
2. There is an inconclusive connection between psychoanalytic theory and his explanations of religion.
3. Freud correctly identified the destructive practices of religion and their detrimental psychological impacts, such as self-deception, escapism, and religious legalism and ritual that constricts one's range of thinking.
4. Freud explained how the "childish" version of God reflects a culturally determined stereotype and a wish-fulfilling stage of childhood development that healthy developmental demands be transcended.
5. Freud also criticized the history of religion, its misuse and exploitation of power, and its intolerance and persecution of differences.
6. Freud further condemned the exploitation of the dependence and vulnerability of the psychologically or spiritually immature.
7. Freud chastised organized religion for its ongoing negative obsession with, and suppression of, human sexuality.

In summary, Freud is neither the first nor the last critic of religion. However, his preeminence in the history of psychology and his attention to the force of the unconscious in religious beliefs and practices contributed to our present understanding of the potentially negative impact of religion on mental health. For those who value the positive potential of religion, Jones (1991) wrote that Freud's ideas were generalized "toward a psychoanalysis of the sacred" (p. 1111) and they facilitated "a connection to the self-sustaining universal matrix" (p. 135).

Carl Jung

Jung was raised as the only son of a Reformed Church pastor. Said to be disenchanted with the experience of Communion as a child, Jung spent much of his career in search of alternative spiritual answers. Through his exploration of psychology, religion, myth, and the occult,

Jung crossed many religious boundaries, including Christianity, Judaism, and Buddhism (Jung, 1965). Although originally applied to dream work and ritual theory, Jung's concepts of myth, metaphor, and archetype (a collective unconscious) offer insight for both helping professionals and spiritual exploration. In both fields of study, Jung asserted that archetypal images found in all societies of God, hero, man, woman, child, and so forth form the foundation of the societal units and the relationships among those units as defining forces for the individual and for each unique society as a whole.

Jung's ideas of human development also incorporated a positive model of religion and he wove a spiritual dimension into his notion of individuation (Jung, 1954/1977). He wrote (p. 23):

[M]any neuroses are caused primarily by the fact that people blind themselves to their own religious promptings because of [a] childish passion for rational enlightenment. It is high time the psychologist of today recognized that we are no longer dealing with dogma and creeds but with the religious attitude per se whose importance as a psychic function can hardly be overrated.

Although Jung wrote in support of the contribution of spirituality to overall functioning, he cautioned against the codified and institutionalized creeds and structures of denominational religion (Kelly, 1995).

Jung saw religion as a function of the movement toward individuation, seen as the emergence of the true self through integration of conscious and unconscious factors. Religious faith was seen to give legitimate voice to the archetypal images found in the collective unconscious. Jung wrote of its vitality in helping individuals resolve the interplay of intrapsychic forces such as the ego, persona, personal unconscious, anima/animus, and collective unconscious. The emerging true self then becomes an infusion of the resolution of these tensions and "this self is an inner spiritual reality, an inner psychological expression of God" (Kelly, 1995, p. 54).

Jung never entered the controversy as to the objective reality of religion or God but instead claimed them as important and positive psychological realities. On three occasions, he spoke to this issue:

It is not for psychology, as a science, to demand a hypostatization [i.e., to make an actual real person] of the God-image. But, the facts being what they are, it does have to reckon with the existence of a God-image. (1960/1981, p. 278)

There are unfortunately many feeble minds who thoughtlessly imagine [that the problem of God] is a question of truth, whereas it is really a question of psychological necessity. (1968, p. 3)

A new Weltanschauung [philosophy of life] will have to abandon the superstitious belief of its [i.e., the self in its likeness to God] objective validity and admit that it is only a picture that we paint to please our minds, and not a magical name with which we conjure up real things. (1960/1981, p. 379)

Although Jung refused to claim that a psychological affirmation of the spiritual dimension must equate to an objective validation, he cautioned spiritually believing helping professionals that one's personal convictions cannot legitimize a personal imposition of these beliefs within the therapeutic relationship. Helping professionals are challenged to maintain professional boundaries between what is the most personal of belief systems and what may be incongruent with the client's belief system around the same issues.

Gordon Allport

Like William James, and in contrast to Freud, Allport (1950) held an optimistic view of religion. Consistent with the tenets of modern counseling, Allport espoused a developmental focus, understanding the richness and complexity of human functioning and a strength-based, rather than pathology-oriented, focus. He wrote succinctly: "I am seeking to trace the full course of religious development with the normally mature and productive personality. I am dealing with the psychology, not the psychopathology, of religion" (p. viii). He acknowledged the neurotic and escapist uses of religion, but disagreed with those who decried these maladaptive uses as either the sole or dominant use of religion.

Allport saw the origins of religion as based on the common need for companionship, value, intelligibility, and meaning. He viewed religion as a purposeful move toward, rather than away from, reality. He challenged those who would denigrate religion as a guiding life principle to recognize that all humans choose such a principle as a life guide, religion being one choice among many (Kelly, 1995). As an evolution of the religious self, Allport coined the phrase "religion of maturity," which results from the doubt, experimentation, and testing of institutions and traditions (pp. 52–53). Individuals functioning within this epitome of religious development are characterized as

1. *differentiated:* They are a product of increasingly complex distinctions among belief systems based on knowledge and experience, which culminates in a personally organized and relevant pattern of religious understanding and living.
2. *functionally autonomous:* This belief system is based not on fear, self-justification, guilt, or self-glory, but rather as a motivating force for humanistic personal and social development.
3. *consistently moral:* There is an obvious and overt congruence between the individual's religious beliefs and practices and active social concern with, and attention to, the well-being of others.
4. *comprehensive:* In addition to guiding interactions, this belief system addresses all of the larger questions of life that require resolution in order to develop a philosophy of life.
5. *integrally related:* This ability marks the consideration and meshing of scientific knowledge, one's belief system, and actions on the part of those holding differing belief systems against the betterment of humanity.
6. *heuristic:* The belief system is open to new experiences, knowledge, and input in order to remain an evolving entity rather than a static system with the implicit risks of stagnation and dogmatism.

By providing such a model, Allport directly confronted the prevailing scientific notion of religion as either irrelevant or detrimental to mental health and offered an optimistic view of religious development as a strong balance to other, more pessimistic voices.

Viktor Frankl

As an existential thinker, Frankl insisted that the process of living—the search for meaning and personal dignity in the presence of dehumanizing experiences—becomes the focus of one's existence. Maintaining a belief that humans have freedom of choice, self-reflection allows an individual "to identify options that might provide meaning in his or her life" (Eliason et al., 2001, p. 82). The word *existere* means "to exist," "to stand out," and "to emerge," speaking to the emergent quality of the human experience and the impetus toward growth (Frankl, 1959). The absence of such abilities and their substitution by direct seeking of pleasure, self-gratification, and the control of others form the roots of neuroses and antisocial behaviors.

Frankl's life philosophy was deeply shaped by his experiences in the Nazi death camps of Auschwitz and Dachau. On the basis of his experiences with those who abandoned the will to survive and those who struggled to live, he posited that the "will to meaning" is the guiding human motivational force (Meier, Minirth, Wichern, & Ratcliff, 1997).

In addition to the search for meaning, Frankl's concept of love is as one of the most meaningful aspirations of humanity. Within this experience, one becomes aware of the innermost essences of another human being and, moreover, becomes aware of the individual's potential, which the individual him- or herself may be, as of yet, unaware. By helping the individual become aware of any unrealized potential, the individual is being helped to achieve such potential. To Frankl, this theme was the crux of all intimate human relationships, including the therapeutic relationship and the relationship of each individual with a supreme power.

For Frankl, the search for meaning entailed a spiritual consciousness (the locus of human freedom), a religious unconscious (an implicit need for transcendence), and the unconscious God (man's search for the God who is, in turn, hidden). The God in the search also serves as the exemplar for the transcending I–thou relationship, seen as being the ultimate connection in human existence.

Abraham Maslow

To Maslow (1968/1980), the plateau experience, which is more enduring and more cognitively aware than the peak experience, was a reflection of authentic religiosity. Although Maslow claimed that there was no connection between this experience and God, the supernatural, or religious practices (Kelly, 1995), it was described as a transcendence of one's ego and an experience colored by wonder and awe of both personal integration and universal connection (Maslow, 1968/1980). Such experiences characterize highly actualized individuals, the state of which epitomizes maturity in personal and social potential. Such experiences are not limited to a certain theology or practice, but instead represent a common core of religious experience that transcends all religious institutions. In common is held a focus on self-actualization instead of a focus on human pathology, deficit, or weakness.

Carl Rogers

Rogers was raised in a close family, with a judgmental mother and an atmosphere of strict religious standards. Rogers attended a seminary, but transferred to the Teachers College of Columbia University after finding that he could not subscribe to any of the sets of beliefs offered in the seminary. Instead of adhering to pre-established sets of beliefs and meanings, Rogers followed constructivist orientations that led him to focus on each client's experiences and his or her phenomenological interpretations of the events. It was his intention to create a therapeutic relationship based on unconditional positive regard during which the client could explore his or her subjective experience of life issues in such a way as to feel honored and supported toward individual meaningful change. Rogers moved away from the child-hood experience of conformity based on the judgments of others and toward a belief in the inherent potential of each person to grow in meaningful ways, serving as a powerful foun-dation for a belief in the innate human capacity and potential for positive growth.

Frederick Perls

Perls was born into a Jewish home in Berlin and his early life was characterized by difficulty with authority figures. However, he completed his medical training and served as a medic in the German army. In working with brain-damaged soldiers, he recognized the need for all parts of each individual to function as a unified whole, or gestalt. Dysfunction in any one area of life must affect the individual in all other areas and lead to a general lack of life sat-isfaction. The purpose of counseling is to help the individual rediscover unresolved neu-roses and verbally express the attached anxiety in order to reintegrate those aspects of life into one's gestalt. This process of discovery demands a more personally aware and expres-sive helping professional who can help the client reach behind social roles and expectations toward an I–thou encounter. It is in the mutuality of this I–thou encounter that both, or all, parties grow as the aspects of self-discovery by one participant apply to all. This encounter, as also described by Buber (1970), is a synthesis of the spiritual notion of self, human rela-tionships, and a relationship with the Divine.

John Watson and B. F. Skinner

The contributions of these two behaviorists are considered conjointly as both eschewed at-tention to the notion of religion. Both elevated attention to observable, measurable human behavior over such undefinable, and therefore unusable, concepts such as the unconscious (Eliason et al., 2001). Watson (1925) saw "old psychology" as using the term *unconscious* as a version of "the soul" and suggested that the old psychology is dominated by a type of re-ligious philosophy. Skinner rejected the notion of free choice and self-determinism and con-centrated on societal control and manipulation of human behavior through reinforcement patterns. This focus on behavior has also evolved into a "newer psychology" of individual learning theory and cognitive psychology, which promotes an understanding of how behav-ior is learned and unlearned. This understanding can be used by helping professionals to empower clients rather than control their actions.

William Glasser

Although Glasser's model of counseling incorporated elements of cognitive, existential, person-centered, and Gestalt theories into reality or control theory, he made little specific mention of religion or spirituality. Meier at al. (1997) claimed that Glasser's model mirrors many of the tenets of humanistic psychology by focusing on meeting basic needs. Meier et al. also found elements of the I–thou experience in Glasser's writings. Glasser (1965) based his model on two core needs: (1) the need to love and be loved, and (2) the need to feel that we are worthwhile to ourselves and others.

This approach examines one's perception of a personal framework of reality in com-parison to external reality frameworks. Assuming that one can deliberately select one's thoughts and feelings in addition to one's actions, Glasser asked the client to consider the rationality of his or her choice, given personal experiences with feedback/response from others and the client's own personal affective state while exhibiting the specific behavior. Given the basic need to connect with others who share common worldviews and an orientation toward spiritual issues, Glasser's reality therapy allows the individual to explore how his or her spiritual environment is meeting personal needs.

Albert Ellis

The rational emotive therapy developed by Ellis reflected his personal battle to overcome poor health and personal anxieties (Eliason et al., 2001). Ellis saw humans as possessing both rational and irrational beliefs. Although he did not concentrate on the role of spirituality, Ellis identified irrational beliefs such as *others must approve of us* and countered them with the rational notions of self-acceptance and the acceptance of others. Part of being "rational" involves a skepticism or resistance to being suggestible or amenable to the dictates of others. In the practice of religion, Ellis questioned the "rationality" of the absolute, judgmental qualities of sin and redemption plus the pressure to conform based on affiliation.

In summary, it is worthy of note that all of the pioneers of counseling and psychology recognized the power of religion, albeit for good or evil, and spoke to its presence in society. The diversity of their opinions spans the range of possible considerations. Although no concrete answer is provided, it is hoped that their attention to this topic will serve to legitimize ongoing attention by 21st-century helping professionals and that their writings will support the individual struggle faced by each of those professionals to connect their spiritual and religious belief systems with their clinical orientations.

INTEGRATING BELIEF SYSTEMS

In comparison to the two potentially divisive issues of religion and spirituality, a review of the professional literature has identified 12 salient issues addressed by both religion/spirituality and counseling/psychology theories. The commonalities in these areas provide topics for discussion between the client and the helping professional, and for reflection by each helping professional as he or she seeks to create a congruent gestalt between personally held spiritual and clinical views. These 12 issues are as follows:

1. *An individual's sense of meaning and purpose* (Tse et al., 2005). Both belief systems offer answers as to the purpose of life. Whether those responses are to live a "Christian life" or to seek self-actualization, perhaps for a specific individual, the first response serves as a personal definition of the second goal.

2. *An explanation for life's struggles* (Graham, Furr, Flowers, & Burke, 2001). Both belief systems explain how one's life has evolved in the manner in which it has to date. For clients who seek an answer to the question "Why?," both frameworks offer answers.

3. *Statements of cultural identity* (McColl, 2003; McLennan, Rochow, & Arthur, 2001). Both belief systems acknowledge the importance of connection and human interdependence as promoting a sense of security and belonging in life. Perhaps it is easier to identify those who subscribe to specific religious practices by their participation in "church"; however, helping professionals committed to advocating for social justice also support the right of people to be "as they are" and to take pride in cultural affiliation and identity. Although the choice of spiritual or religious affiliation may be one important aspect of cultural identity, it is the client's task to prioritize how the differing cultural components of life contribute to a personal sense of identity.

4. *A sense of control over one's life situations* (Graham, Furr, Flowers, & Burke, 2001). Both belief systems, as discussed within the previous section of this chapter, designate which aspects of life that one has control to influence or change. Given the idea that "belief of ownership" leads to acceptance of responsibility and possible change, or no change (acceptance or coping), then all religious and spiritual traditions and all theories of counseling and psychology address this issue. The main question is not so much whether answers exist, but, more crucially, what the choice of specific answers says about any one individual.

5. *Answers as to the origins and destiny of humanity* (Frame, 2003). "What does it mean to be human?" is a question that has challenged all philosophers, religious thinkers, and psychological theorists throughout the ages. Although religions have provided answers as to the origins of humanity, both belief systems offer notions of aspiration for the betterment of the human condition. If one were all one could be, what might one become? From a holistic perspective, that response must include one's spiritual self, but not be limited to that aspect alone.

6. *Values orientation* (Frame, 2003). Both sets of belief systems offer a wider range of values about self-conduct, relationships with others, and obligations to society. Although religious or spiritual traditions may also speak about a relationship with a Divine Power, psychological theory does not speak to this concern, even to historically dismiss its validity.

7. *Human nature* (Ibrahim, 1996). Once again, both belief systems address this idea. Barring unshakeable proof, this one issue will continue to challenge spiritual and clinical thinkers alike. The response forms the foundation of beliefs about change, individual will or lack thereof, and the efficacy of intervention, be that intervention therapeutic or prayer.

8. *Personhood and nature* (Tse et al., 2005). This issue refers to believing in the power of nature, living in harmony with nature, or seeking to control nature, which may seem to be most relevant to the Eastern spiritual traditions discussed previously, but at the heart of this matter lays the issue of free will, and on whom or which force does one have the right to exercise that will. In addition, the notion of the role of science is introduced. Science seeks to explain, predict, and control nature, but our lives are still a function of life cycles (birth, death, aging, etc.), so the question could be posed as to how one acknowledges the power of both science and nature, as well as the spirit and psyche.

9. *Activity* (McLennan, Rochow, & Arthur, 2001). If a purpose in life must be devised by each individual, so, too, must be the priority on spontaneity or actualization. Which seems more applicable: "to go with the flow" or to have a plan, which implies the power to carry that plan to fruition—in essence, to create one's own future along a blueprint of one's own making? The second component of this exploration revolves around the evaluation of moral and spiritual success through internal or external standards. On what basis does one decide the "rightness" of one's activity? Which seems preferable, an individually owned evaluation schema that may place one at odds with society, or adoption of a ready-made societal barometer guaranteed to meet with the approval of others but at what cost to personal integrity?

10. *Social relations* (McColl, 2003). This issue speaks to how individuals connect and exist in relationships. Seen as a crucial element of counseling through the multiple discussions of rapport and the therapeutic relationship, this issue permeates family relationships, church relationships, and one's relationship with the Divine.

11. *Hope and optimism* (Worthington et al., 1996). Both belief systems offer the potential for a brighter future. Although the definitive characteristics of this future vary widely on the basis of the choice of spiritual orientation or clinical theory, both approaches to life share a commitment to human growth and an alleviation of personal pain and human misery.

12. *Possible solutions* (McLennan, Rochow, & Arthur, 2001). Consistent with the previous item, both religious practices and clinical interventions are very clear about what one needs to do to improve one's situation. Once again, although the processes of remediation or growth are vastly different, anyone seeking answers within either modality will be certain of the direction that he or she must take to move forward in life.

In summary, given the great number of issues in common, perhaps it is the banality of the issues themselves, rather than a client's or helping professional's answer, that provides the opening for exploration. If any of these issues is a possible entry into the client's epistemology, then there is an acknowledgment that client and counselor share common life questions, and only the answers provide a sense of individuality. All questions are legitimate; however, the therapeutic agenda may ask how well the client is served by the answers chosen.

Case Example Revisited

Patricia wondered whether she could faithfully practice her religion and still become a professional counselor. She approached one of the faculty members in her training program about this question. That professor offered several perspectives or ideas for her to contemplate. She was directed to explore the initial schism between religion and counseling, and to try to make sense of it given its historical and societal context. She was then directed to the professional literature to investigate more up-to-date references on the integration of the two fields. Finally, she was told that "like counseling, faith traditions offer questions to which their practices are observable answers. Explore those questions in common whose answers seem confusing."

Patricia discovered that instead of focusing on the practices of each part of her life, she needed to better understand the belief systems on which each aspect of her life was based and to try to establish the commonalities. On the basis of that mandate, she met with her Bible teacher to explore three questions that were of concern to her and then met with her peers in the counseling program to discuss the same three issues. Next, she referenced original source material from the counseling theorists who seemed to be most influential in her clinical vision.

However, her learning experience became more personal when she chose to first be clear on her values and then determine which of the external sources supported that vision rather than trying to conform her personal beliefs to differing traditions. This process was disturbing to her because no one belief system matched hers, and she questioned the validity of her own emerging congruence of religion and counseling. She found relief in an offhand comment by a professor who asked, "Who said only one was to suffice?" That statement seemed to validate her desire to integrate the best of both traditions into her personal orientation, and to acknowledge the areas of dispute as personal growing edges that would become clearer with time, learning, self-reflection, and clinical experience.

Conclusion

One can assert that "building competencies for integrating religion and spirituality into counseling is a crucial direction for working with a culturally diverse population" (McLennan, Rochow, & Arthur, 2001, p. 138). Although an understanding of differing spiritual orientations is a component of this process, the key to its success lies in the mental health professional's willingness to erase historical divisions between religion/spirituality and psychology and move toward a model of holistic mental health.

Self-Understanding Exercises

1. Which aspects of your personal spiritual view and clinical view are most closely aligned?
2. Which aspects of your personal spiritual view and clinical view are most discrepant?
3. From which of the identified spiritual practices might a client prove to be the most challenging for you? What tenets of his or her spiritual belief system might be a challenge for you?
4. How do you relate intense religious experiences with mental health or psychopathology? (Pieper, 2004)

Opportunities for Further Learning

1. Interview a leader from a religious or spiritual tradition about which you have little firsthand knowledge. Ask about the essence of that spiritual or religious tradition, its strengths, its position on social issues, its view on counseling and mental health services, and what a counselor might need to know in order to be competent to respond to the needs of adherents (Frame, 2003).
2. Invite a faculty member from the Religious Studies program on campus to speak to your class and ask class members to prepare questions.
3. Invite a practicing clinician whom you know holds a specific religious or spiritual orientation to class and discuss how he or she has integrated spiritual and clinical beliefs into a cogent model of counseling.

4

■ ■ ■

Developmental Models of Spirituality and Psychosocial Functioning

CASE EXAMPLE

Cassandra presented at a college counseling center complaining of a sense of lethargy and a lack of direction. A clinical intake did not confirm symptoms of depression, but rather the reporting of a sense of malaise and uncertainty about a "sense of identity." This issue was of great concern to Cassandra because, according to her, all of her peers knew exactly what they wanted out of school, life, and "everything else," and there must have been something terribly amiss with her that she couldn't figure it out for herself.

A session exploring her family relationships, romantic connections, choice of major, and living arrangements in a coed dormitory consistently revealed what might be considered the age-appropriate developmental struggles of a new college student. However, her affect seemed blunted around the discussion of these issues, so the counselor asked for permission to explore aspects related to her spiritual development. This question seemed to shock Cassandra because the idea of spiritual development was foreign to her. In response, she began to relate the narrative of growing up in a specific church from childhood, attending the required religious education classes, participating in rituals, and "enduring" confirmation.

However, she began to weep when she related that her church did not feel like home anymore and she was terrified that her questioning the sanctity of her practices would lead to terrible consequences from family, friends, church members, and God. She tried to convince herself to attend church, but could not, as though she thought that her religious side had died. She had even dabbled in attending the services of other faiths and had met someone who described herself as a Wiccan. She was certain that these activities were known to a God who knew all and that she would be severely punished for her actions. Moreover, she assumed that she had to be "wicked" because a "good person" would not question one's religious traditions.

■ ■ ■

INTRODUCTION

The objective of this chapter is the exploration of spiritual growth, both from a unique developmental perspective and anchored within a holistic model of human growth and development. This orientation toward a developmental perspective will help the clinician and the client identify normative challenges and triumphs throughout the client's path in life. From this viewpoint, clients' issues represent a sense of being "stuck" within one specific set of life's challenges that are characteristic of all people, rather than being "sick" or mentally ill. This knowledge is crucial if the helping professional wishes to "normalize," rather than pathologize, the client's issues. In addition, this orientation provides a framework from which the client can identify past successes and recognize present challenges.

In principle, adherence to a developmental perspective assumes a commitment to focusing on a series of identifiable normative and predictable stages and tasks through which individuals become different from what they were prior to the onset of that specific stage's experiences. Beginning at birth and lasting until death, people are challenged to become more and more "actualized" over a range of interrelated aspects of human functioning. Formulated through observation, interview, and assessment of individuals at different ages, each model of development helps clinicians to better grasp the commonalities of the human journey, in addition to appreciating the uniqueness and diversity of individual responses to each opportunity for personal growth. Growth through the developmental stages does not imply that a later stage is inherently better than an earlier stage, but that perhaps it is more complex. For the purposes of discussion in this chapter, the idea of stage "complexity" reflects an increased personal challenge in terms of the depth of self-understanding, coupled with responsibility for self, in a specific area of human processing and existence.

However, the concern about those in later stages being "better" than those in the earlier, more formative stages remains a constant criticism of developmental models. These models are depicted as linear in nature and hierarchical in arrangement (Frame, 2003), so such an assumption would seem logical. If stage 4 follows stage 3, how can it not be deduced that those individuals in stage 4 are somehow superior to those in stage 3?

Mitroff (2003) responded to this issue by delineating "facilitative hierarchies" and "rigid or authoritarian hierarchies" (p. 490). Models in the first category, such as the ones described in this chapter, provide a description of present functioning and future growth opportunities. Models in the second category, such as rigid caste systems or social "pecking orders" or prejudices, are designed to place groups and individuals into rigid boxes from which escape is impossible, thereby stifling human development. If helping professionals see that stage and task characteristics are descriptive rather than comparative, they can then ask the following questions about their clients:

1. Which tasks has this individual successfully or unsuccessfully faced?
2. Which tasks currently confront this individual?
3. For which tasks is this individual preparing by paying attention to current stage demands? Or is the individual failing to prepare?

The possibility of a successful resolution of each stage is a function of successes in the previous stages. From the perspective of spiritual development, Kornfield (1993) believed that each new stage provides opportunities for active living, service to others, and contemplative living. Success in resolving tasks from earlier stages implies a stronger foundation for equal success in later stages, and, conversely, failure or weakness in resolving tasks in an earlier stage must have a negative impact on tasks in later stages. There is also an assumption that tasks in earlier stages can be resolved later in life if previous experiences have not provided the strong foundation necessary for further growth. Thus, models of development cannot be considered "one-chance-only" propositions, because individuals can revisit earlier stages to attend to unfinished business that may be hampering current functioning. Adherents of this perspective would advocate such attempts at remediation because they believe that even great success in later stages cannot truly compensate for earlier disappointments.

The focus of this chapter is on taking a "holistic approach" to spiritual development because such development cannot be examined or understood outside of the context of an individual's cognitive, psychosocial, and moral development (Frame, 2003; Kelly, 1995). How individuals think about the world in general, how they relate to others, and how each person decides what is right and wrong are reflections of, and contributions to, their spiritual development. To attempt a reductionist approach by attending to one process of development without consideration of its recursive influence on the other processes of development may ignore human complexity and the rich mosaic of the thinking, feeling, behaving, and "meaning-making" processes (Worthington, 1989).

In that spirit, this chapter provides an overview of the models of spiritual development espoused by James Fowler (1991), Fritz Oser (1991), Vicky Genia (1990), Ana-Maria Rizzuto (1991), and Moshe Spero (1992). Also included in the chapter is a synopsis of Jean Piaget's model of cognitive development, Erik Erikson's model of psychosocial functioning, and Piaget's, Lawrence Kohlberg's, and Carol Gilligan's models of moral development. Consideration of these other models of facets of human development will place the idea of spiritual development within the context of emerging abilities in thinking, relating, and moral reasoning. Growth or stagnation in one of these models must have an impact on other areas of functioning. For example, a young child's thinking style is less complex than that of an adolescent or an adult, and a child's ability to make "spiritual sense" must occur on a level commensurate with that of his or her general cognitive prowess.

Next, the chapter presents some of the emerging developmental trends by offering summaries of developmental psychopathology (Kazdin, 1989), optimal development (Chu & Powers, 1995; Wagner, 1996), resiliency (Rak & Patterson, 1996), and emotional intelligence (Goleman, 1997; Mayer & Geher, 1996). Finally, we attempt to link the two schemas to challenge clinicians to create holistic models of human development that encompass all of these factors of the human condition. This comprehensive focus fosters the multiple interconnected processes of experiencing, thinking, and relating, and offers multiple venues for intervention. From the perspective of the clients, such knowledge creates a more comprehensive picture of their presenting struggles and places their issues within a context for promoting increased functioning and satisfaction in all aspects of life.

AN OVERVIEW OF CURRENT MODELS OF SPIRITUAL DEVELOPMENT

James Fowler: Faith Development

Fowler's theory has been lauded as "the most comprehensive theory on faith development" (Frame, 2003, p. 39). For Fowler, *faith* was defined more as a dynamic, positively oriented focus toward others, life, and a Supreme Being, and less as the clinging to a set of beliefs (Fowler, 1996). Fowler presented a six-stage model of spiritual development, with the ages of 1 through 3 characterized by a "pre-faith" stage that is dedicated to the development of trust in caregivers as a precursor to faith building.

***Stage 1: Intuitive-projective faith* (ages 3–7):** In this stage, the child is prone to fantasies of angels (protective figures) or a punitive God (a dangerous figure) and is deeply directed by his or her relationships with primary adult figures.

***Stage 2: Mythical-literal faith* (ages 7 to puberty):** At this stage, the child begins to internalize the stories, beliefs, and observances that are symbolic of belonging to a specific spiritual community. The child believes the stories literally, and the stories are the major vehicle for the interpretation and conveyance of spiritual themes and content. There is a tendency to believe that the Supreme Being is a cosmic ruler who rules fairly and expects/demands moral behavior. There is an assumption that the Supreme Being rewards goodness and punishes evil. These beliefs may be manifested in an attempt to move toward perfection in expectation of reward or, conversely, toward self-abasement if one has been maltreated by significant others and expects punishment.

***Stage 3: Synthetic-conventional faith* (puberty to adulthood):** During this stage, spirituality is understood in relational terms, but mostly in terms of relationships with authority figures and the idea of conformity. Although beliefs and values specific to a spiritual orientation are strongly held, these tenets are largely unexamined. Fowler asserted that this stage is typical of adolescents and is the norm for adults.

***Stage 4: Individualistic-reflective faith* (beginning in early adulthood):** In this stage, the individual begins to develop a phenomenological system of meaning to which he or she is personally committed. Although symbols may be transformed into concepts for personal examination, the majority of the tenets of one's spiritual belief system have yet to be critically evaluated. It is during this stage that the decision to retain previous beliefs becomes a conscious one rather than an automatic acceptance.

***Stage 5: Conjunctive faith* (midlife and beyond):** This stage is characterized by a personal examination of the concepts left unexplored in stage 4 during which the individual self-challenges to consider what may appear paradoxical or opposite in belief, and to establish a personally meaningful inclusion of these seemingly inconsistent elements. Myths, stories, and legends are evaluated on the basis of personal meaning versus conformity to imposed meaning. Individuals who have reached this stage stand ready to publicly declare their individual belief systems. However, most adults do not reach this stage; in fact, Lownsdale (1997) approximated that only 1 in 6 individuals actually move into stage 5.

Stage 6: Universalizing faith: This is a stage in which the individual is challenged to transcend the paradoxes and content of one's belief system in order to develop a level of interaction with others, not on the basis of shared content, but on the foundation of a shared commitment to justice and kindness to others. Fowler characterized these rare individuals as unconcerned with self-preservation, attentive to moral actualization, devoted to universal compassion, and holding an expanded vision of universal community. He cited as examples Martin Luther King Jr., Mahatma Ghandi, and Mother Teresa.

Fritz Oser: Development of Religious Judgment

Oser (1991) offered a series of "transformations in the way in which individuals understand their relationships with God or a Supreme Power" (p. 5). According to cognitive models of development, times of crisis provide the context in which to explore this relationship. Because of the disequilibrium present in a crisis, the individual may recognize that "something is not right" within this relationship and may be more open both to the awkwardness of uncertainty and to the opportunity to reconceptualize the dynamics of this relationship. Oser also interviewed individuals at different stages in life and identified seven polarities through which individuals make spiritual sense of situations:

1. freedom versus dependence,
2. transcendence versus immanence,
3. hope versus absurdity,
4. faith (trust) versus fear (mistrust),
5. holy versus profane,
6. eternity versus ephemerality, and
7. transparency versus opacity (a quality of the understanding of God's will). (Oser, 1991, p. 9–10)

Within the five stages of a relationship with the Divine, Oser offered the following:

1. The Supreme Being is seen as active, powerful, and effective, with the person being reactive.
2. The Supreme Being is still viewed as external to the individual and all-powerful, but susceptible to the influence of the individual through observed rituals and the performance of good deeds.
3. The Supreme Being (if such is acknowledged as existing) is placed within a realm of covert influence separate from human autonomy and responsibility.
4. The Supreme Being and the individual work in concert toward the individual's self-defined meaning or plan for life.
5. The individual's understanding of the Supreme Being now coordinates all seemingly polar opposites of life and is imbued in each moment and commitment.

Vicky Genia: Development of Growth

Genia's model was founded in psychoanalytic theory, beginning in egocentric faith and progressing toward spiritual commitment. However, in times of crisis, individuals may regress to more comfortable styles of practicing one's faith, and, in times of little spiritual challenge, they may plateau, maintaining the characteristics of one stage. Genia's stages of faith are as follows:

Egocentric Faith: In this stage, one's religion is based "in fear and [the] need for comfort" (Genia, 1995, p. 19). Although comforted by a connection with a Supreme Being, in instances of disappointment or emotional pain, individuals may feel tormented by the Supreme Being. Individuals in this stage try to be perfect in order to retain the favor of the Supreme Being, and they utilize prayer as a way to manipulate the Supreme Being into protecting them. Adults found in this stage have usually suffered abuse or neglect.

Dogmatic Faith: In this stage, individuals apply themselves ceaselessly to earning the love and approval of the Supreme Being. Their effort is usually expressed through strict adherence to religious codes. They desperately want to be assured of reward and eternal blessing, and no cost or self-denial is too great. These individuals also believe that religious affiliation and participation are critical elements toward earning the approval of the Supreme Being.

Transitional Faith: In this stage, individuals are daring to critically examine their religious beliefs. Open to exploring new spiritual paths, they tend to rely more on personal conscience than on religious dogma. However, this period of searching may leave individuals feeling alone and disconnected. During this time, if they do not revert to the strict adherence of the previous stage, they may explore different ideologies and spiritual affiliations.

Reconstructed Internalized Faith: In this stage, individuals have chosen a spiritual path that provides individual meaning and purpose. Driven by self-defined morals and ideals, they relate to the Divine as a caring, reliable person who offers sustenance. In prayer, they offer thanks and praise, acknowledge their human frailty, seek forgiveness, and make restitution for wrongdoing whenever possible. However, they are still challenged by the ambiguity and paradoxes implicit in spirituality.

Transcendent Faith: Although achieving this stage is rare, individuals who do reach it are dedicated to universal ideals, are devoted to truth and goodness, and can experience community with others from diverse spiritual paths. They have a transcendent relationship with some form of a Supreme Being. Their lifestyle is consistent with their spiritual values. They can be committed to an ideal or tenet and still retain healthy doubt. They can accept the paradox of the existence of evil and suffering, yet celebrate life and promote tolerance.

Ana-Maria Rizzuto: Development of Representations of God

Rizzuto (1991) based this model of development on psychoanalytic and object relations theory, asserting that one's version of a Supreme Being is initially founded in the child's internalizations of significant adults and the child's relationship with these individuals. The author wrote,

> In summary, then, throughout life God remains a transitional object at the service of gaining leverage with oneself, with others and with life itself. This is so, not because God is God, but because, like the teddy bear, he has obtained a good half of his stuffing from the primary objects the child has "found" in his life. The other half of God's stuffing comes from the child's capacity to "create" a God according to his needs. (1979, p. 179)

Children are seen as passing through the initial five years of life developmentally unable to grasp what religion has to offer. Although the songs, games, and stories of religious practices are enjoyable to children in this age span, the messages behind these activities are beyond their cognitive abilities. However, they are having the formative experiences in everyday life that facilitate an ever-emerging individual sense of self, of others, and of interpreting personal events in a unique way in order to provide cognitive schemas of self, of others, and of the relationship between self and others in the context of a particular event. These private interpretations could be construed as a proto-religion, complete with a child-created private sense of God, private rituals that guide interactions with this God figure, and a series of complex beliefs about the world, God, and one's place in relationship to both.

These beliefs are all formed bereft of actual experience, yet they carry the conviction of emotionally lived experiences.

The earliest sense of God is as a representational object created by the child, who infuses the affect-laden experiences of his or her interactions with the mother and father. The feelings present in this self–God relationship reflect the child's beliefs about the dynamics of that relationship. For example, if the child creates a God who is seen as loving and protective, the child feels trust and joy; if the child creates a God who is seen as judgmental, the child may respond with avoidance based on fear. In either case, the prototype of this image is the child's sense of the relationship with his or her primary caregiver(s). The traits ascribed to God do not come directly from the parent(s), but rather from the child's version of his or her interactions with the parent(s) and the child's interpretation of adult behavior.

Rizzuto (1991) offered a seven-step "ideal" evolution of the relationship with God as composed of seven perspectives that evolve from one into the other:

1. "God as a fully trustworthy being;
2. God as a good, tolerant companion;
3. God as a lovable and loving (even if a bit frightening) being;
4. God as a knowledgeable, good protector;
5. God as a being that can tolerate questioning and doubt while believers face the contradictions of life and evil in the world;
6. God as a being who is there and lets believers be themselves; and
7. God as a trustworthy being whose mysterious existence is not challenged" (p. 56).

There is also a sense of compromise within this development between the self-created vision of God (a private source) and the vision of God espoused by the consensus of the community in which one worships (a public source). The private source provides the intense affective experience with the divine figure. This affect is founded in one's lived feelings connected to the experience of the divine figure and defines the type of exchange between the individual and his or her God. Rizzuto defined public belief as "a collective act of attribution of religious meaning to the world" (p. 55). The public source represents the indispensable confirmation of God's capacity to intervene in human affairs as reported through other congregation members and clergy. In the concrete moment of the experience, the contributions of the private and public sources complement each other in the reality of the perceived interventions that arise from God.

Moshe Spero: Development of Religious Transformations

Also having its basis in the object relations adaptation of psychoanalytic theory, Spero's (1992) model addressed the issue of God as objectively real. Linked to the process of individuation, especially from the mother figure, the relationship with God also undergoes a series of transformations over time. The following schema contains two parallel themes: the quality of the God concept and the quality of the relationship with one's religious community, both of which evolve over a four-step process of symbiosis, differentiation, practicing, and rapprochement.

The symbiosis stage is characterized by a state of fusion in which the child expects total fulfillment of his or her needs. There is a longing for a reduction of tension in the child's life and a search for a constant object to fulfill that function. In terms of the relationship with one's religious community, the young child seeks to attempt a state of "oneness" with the group by fusing his or her sense of identity with the group's norms, coupled with a belief (hope) that group membership will solve all of one's problems and inhibit all troubling urges. The quality of the God concept can be described as a protective, all-good figure whose sole duty is to respond to the narcissistic needs of the child. There is a strong belief in a union with God in which speech and prayer are unnecessary as means of communication because God hears all thoughts, being directly attuned and sensitive to this one person's needs. Conversely, there is an intense fear of sinning and being found out, because such a discovery may lead to annihilation. Spero wrote that an implicit danger in this stage is a too sudden shift toward individuation, which may promote feelings of abandonment. This potential exists within the group setting as well, should that setting prove to be incapable of support and nurturance.

The differentiation stage is characterized by an emerging interest in other viewpoints, but with the familiar view safely at hand. Individuals in this stage relate to those holding other views with curiosity and interest, and not just the anxiety of encountering a stranger. In terms of the relationship with one's religious community, the individual begins to acknowledge the religious traditions and lore, but also senses differences between the self and the group. Within this struggle to be part of a whole and a whole unto oneself, the individual may either seek greater knowledge or immerse him- or herself completely within the group doctrine and become afraid of learning new material. The individual comes to realize the demands of the community in which he or she worships, and either manifests empathic cooperative relationships or a resentment of the intrusion of the community's needs over personal needs. The quality of the God concept changes as the individual realizes that God is not an aspect of the self. He or she may begin to see God as less "all good" or "all bad," but still, as mysterious.

The practicing stage is characterized by increased exploration of the familiar belief system out of curiosity and without guidance. In addition, there may be increased exploration of alternative belief systems under the benign approval of the parent figure(s). There is a concurrent sense of escape from the confinement of one's parochial belief system and anxiety caused by the separation, both of which may be eased by a belief in the "blessing at the end of the road" (Anthony, 1971). In terms of the relationship with one's religious community, there seems to be an increased interest in one's spiritual history and past, and in religious symbolism in general. If this search is satisfying, it could lead to the development of confidence in one's choice of belief system; dissatisfaction could lead to thoughts of alternative spiritual systems. The quality of the God concept may be seen as reflecting this heightened awareness of symbolism and of aspects or explanations of God. There also may be a tendency to fantasize about God's acceptance and approval, and the idea of divine guidance on one's path in life. God may be seen as a more benevolent, ever-present figure, offering a less threatening presence for the "spiritual explorer."

The rapprochement stage is characterized by the balancing of unity with the powerful figure and the newfound skills and pleasures derived from independence. There is an evolution toward increasingly complex relationships founded on mutual definitions of need and response. In terms of the relationship with one's religious community, these relationships seem to deepen and become less need-dominated. The earlier idealization of religious leaders is replaced by more stable and complete identifications, and the issues of guilt and shame within a religious community are addressed. The quality of the God concept can be described as internally created, and the relationship with God becomes more reciprocal. Expectations of magical help are replaced by a more complex ideology with a greater emphasis on the role of the behavior of the individual. With an increased sense of self-worth, the individual is more capable of separating self-image and "divine judgment." The individual is now on a path toward developing a relationship with God that is not based wholly on anthropocentric experiences.

In summary, these five models offer related, yet distinct, perceptions of the spiritual evolutionary process. Tables 4.1 and 4.2 offer a synopsis of the three models of spiritual development and the two models of the relationship with the Divine.

TABLE 4.1 A Summary of Models of Spiritual Development

Life Stage	Fowler's Model	Genia's Model	Spero's Model
Childhood	Stages 1 and 2: A focus on religious stories; absolute good and evil; reward and punishment are based on following church rules	Stage 1: Religious obedience is based on fear; religious adherence is seen as a comfort against the uncertainties and anxieties of life; the use of prayer and adherence to ritual are ways of seeking favor from God	Symbiosis: A sense of being one with God; God exists to meet the narcissistic needs of the child
Adolescence	Stage 3: Religious practices are based on adherence to church rules as a form of seeking the blessing of the authorities	Stage 2: The purposeful use of obedience to church rules as a way to earn the love and approval of the congregation and elders; based on a desperate need for reward and blessing	Differentiation: Acknowledgment of an affiliation with a church, but an interest in other views; an attempt to fit in, yet remain unique
Adulthood	Stages 4 and 5: Examination of one's spiritual path and religious affiliation and practices; emergence of individual spiritual meaning	Stage 3: Individual exploration of spiritual options; use of one's spiritual conscience over religious dogma	Practicing: An emerging interest in one's personal spiritual history and religious symbolism
Transcendence	Stage 6: Actions guided by principles such as justice and kindness to others; a devotion to universal compassion; an expanded vision of universal community	Stage 4: Individual meaning and purpose; self-defined morals and ideals; working with universal ideals (truth and goodness); lifestyle consistent with spiritual values	Rapproachement: Unity with God balanced with acceptance of human responsibility; separation of self-image and divine judgment

TABLE 4.2 A Summary of Models Describing a Relationship with the Divine		
Life Stages	**Oser's Model**	**Rizzuto's Model**
Childhood	The Divine as the all-powerful being, exists separate and apart from the individual	Development of a proto-religion to define a personal sense of God based on experiences with authority figures
Adolescence	A susceptibility to ritual and the practice of good deeds as the way to curry favor and approval from God	God as a personal protector, whose task is to respond to prayer
Adulthood	God is now seen as having a covert influence on the actions of each person	God can tolerate doubt and questioning as vehicles on the road to an emerging sense of a "real" relationship between the individual and the Divine
Transcendence	God and the individual work collaboratively toward the emergence of a personally defined spirituality; the individual lives each moment through the personal connection with God	God and the individual reach an accord of mutual respect and practice that honors the ideals of each

It is also important to integrate the evolution of cognitive, psychosocial, and moral processes with an understanding of spiritual development because the growth-facilitating changes within those three processes enhance and support the increased insight, knowledge, sense of self, and morality that seem to provide a foundation for the differing theories of spiritual growth.

In summary, Mitroff (2003, p. 487) expanded on Wilber's Fourfold Framework of Development:

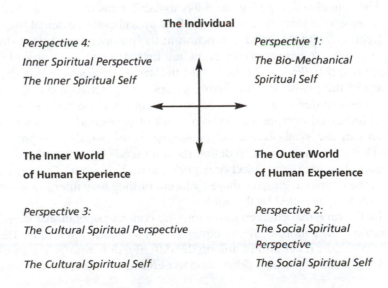

The Individual

Perspective 4:   *Perspective 1:*

Inner Spiritual Perspective   *The Bio-Mechanical*

The Inner Spiritual Self   *Spiritual Self*

The Inner World   **The Outer World**

of Human Experience   **of Human Experience**

Perspective 3:   *Perspective 2:*

The Cultural Spiritual Perspective   *The Social Spiritual Perspective*

The Cultural Spiritual Self   *The Social Spiritual Self*

THE GROUP, ORGANIZATIONS, AND SOCIETY

In the preceding figure, the horizontal axis indicates the extent to which what one experiences spiritually comes from personal experiences, values, and emotions, and the extent to which that experience comes from outside the individual—from institutions such as family, church, and society in general. The vertical axis represents the extent to which one owns a personal spiritual experience and to what extent one may borrow a spiritual experience from others and from societal institutions.

AN OVERVIEW OF CURRENT DEVELOPMENTAL MODELS

> *Whosoever says he has religion must derive a faith from it which is transmitted to infants in the form of basic trust; whoever claims he does not need religion must derive such basic faith from elsewhere.*
> —ERIK ERIKSON (1959, p. 65)

This section provides a brief review of the developmental schemas that explain how individuals change over time. Although intended solely as a summary of these models, it is important to keep these processes in mind in order to better understand the evolution of one's spiritual growth. Readers who seek a deeper understanding of the models should refer to the works of each theorist cited. This content also expands the rest of the developmental picture (by including attention to religious and spiritual models of development) and facilitates a subsequent discussion of the two categories of developmental theory.

Models of Cognitive Development

It is appropriate to begin with a review of the constructs put forth by Piaget (1952, 1965). Since Piaget posited that more complex thinking characterizes each subsequent stage, understanding how individuals think about their worlds, including their spirituality, is vital to both their acceptance of their individual worlds and nurturance within those worlds. Prior to age 2, children are developing the ability to recognize familiar objects and to associate objects with specific emotions. They are also developing the ability to recall items or situations and are beginning to develop a sense of agency (to act in a specific way without an external trigger or command).

By age 2, children tend to function in the preoperational stage. In this stage, children focus on only one experience or event at a time. Piaget argued that children of this age are egocentric and believe that others hold the same perspectives that they do. They are also unaware of the possibility of differing perspectives. Between the ages of 4 and 5, children begin to realize that others know different things, and the children coupled this realization with an increased perspective that is a result of experiences with social interactions. These children can use symbols and are beginning to use words as representations of everyday items. However, their ability to define the item tends to be one dimensional, ascribing only one salient feature to any object or experience in their world. Complex concepts seem to be beyond the cognitive grasp of these children, or they may interpret a concept in a way other than what was intended by the adult.

By the time that children move into the concrete operational stage (6–12 years of age), they can consider more than one dimension of a situation at a time. This ability allows children to construct relationships among the differing dimensions of a situation and to infer the underlying realities. These children tend to perform concrete, rather than abstract, tasks better.

For example, they are better at responding to a question such as "Do you like math?" than "How's school?" because the second question is far too abstract and unfocused for a child of this age. They still tend to confuse their own ideas and assumptions with objective fact. The development of their thinking skills tends to be domain specific, whereby the amount of knowledge of a specific subject tends to influence the complexity of the thinking about that one subject; however, such cognitive complexity cannot be generalized across subjects. As the child's knowledge grows, so, too, does the capacity for the retrieval of knowledge such as facts, events, and experiences. Language development helps children store memories in coherent verbal form and improves their retrieval.

In Piaget's final stage (formal operational thinking, age 12+), the development of abstract thinking facilitates responses to open-ended questions. The increased ability to think logically about abstract concepts and to discover multiple relationships among events and experiences allow for the emergence of a multifaceted perspective on one's life. Children at this stage of cognitive development are starting to generate and evaluate multiple possibilities. In addition, the ability to construct "ideals," such as the ideal political system or the ideal person, seems to emerge at this stage; however, the ability to accept the fact that the "real" always falls short of the ideal emerges at a later time, contributing to the angst of adolescents who are therefore critical of anything that is, in their eyes, less than perfect or ideal, including the self. In addition, the skills of metacognition (thinking about one's own thinking) and of being able to anticipate the consequences of one's actions are beginning to emerge.

Elkind (1984) expanded Piaget's original thesis to include adolescent egocentrism. This idea suggests that adolescent thinking tends to be self-centered, which interferes with communication processes and psychological functioning. For example, as a function of seeing things from their own viewpoint only, adolescents tend to argue with anyone holding a divergent view, especially adults. Adolescents, according to Elkind, also function under the notion of an imaginary audience, which is related to the adolescent's tendency to be self-conscious. They think that everyone's eyes are on them, criticizing their actions or performance. Adolescents also develop what Elkind referred to as a personal fable of invulnerability through which they believe that no harm can come to them because what they do is so special. This accounts for the risk-taking behavior of adolescents and their surprise when the outcome is negative or harmful.

In summary, it seems that thinking processes change in both quantity (the amount of information and knowledge that one can absorb, retain, and retrieve) and quality (how one thinks about what one knows) over the life span. Although controversy exists about the extent to which this growth is a function of innate capacity or social influence, the reality is that humans mature within a social environment that must, in some way, interact with one's innate capacities. Therefore, helping professionals must also understand both psychosocial development and the development of notions of right and wrong in order to fully understand the maturation process.

Models of Psychosocial Development

The works of Erikson (1959, 1968) provide a framework for understanding the interaction between the individual and the environment by specifying eight stages and their attendant tasks:

> ***Stage 1: Oral-Sensory (infancy, birth to 1 year), Conflict: Trust versus Mistrust:***
> The child is first confronted with the task of developing trust, an inner certainty that primary caregivers will provide nurturance and support and that he or she can trust himself or herself. These tasks seem to form the basis for social trust and identity.

Stage 2: Muscular-Anal (toddler, 1 to 2 years), Conflict: Autonomy versus Doubt: The child begins to explore his or her personal power in becoming an autonomous, competent adult.

Stage 3: Locomotor (early childhood, 2 to 6 years), Conflict: Initiative versus Guilt: The child develops the necessary motor skills to explore his or her surroundings, to practice being an adult in play and fantasy, and to develop a conscience. Failure in this stage is experienced less as a loss of parental love and more as a loss of self-esteem.

Stage 4: Latency (elementary and middle school, 6 to 12 years), Conflict: Industry versus Inferiority: During the next six or seven years, the child learns the values of the culture in which he or she is raised through school, church, and so forth. All children receive formal instruction as a way of fostering self-discipline, imparting the values and goals of the society in which the child lives and promoting satisfaction in one's accomplishments.

Stage 5: Adolescence (12 to 18 years), Conflict: Identity versus Role Confusion: Adolescence confronts the teen with the end of childhood and the proximity of the responsibilities of adulthood. The adolescent begins to question the personal feelings and beliefs that together developed the sense of self in childhood. There begins a comparison between a personal image and the way in which one is seen by others, a role at home and a role with peers. The challenge of this stage is to create a sense of inner continuity, an identity.

Stage 6: Young Adulthood (19 to 40 years), Conflict: Intimacy versus Isolation: This stage is based on the successes of the previous stage in which the young adult has achieved a firm sense of identity that can now be shared with others. Individuals in this stage commit to relationships and affiliations, and maintain those commitments. One must balance both the personally derived sense of self and the expectations of others within those voluntary committed relationships and attend to both sets of needs so that one remains secure in oneself and with one's relationships.

Stage 7: Middle Adulthood (40 to 65 years), Conflict: Generativity versus Stagnation: Adulthood is characterized by an expansion of interests and concerns. Erikson described this stage as one in which the individual provides guidance for the next generation, both directly and indirectly. The focus is on raising one's children, working to improve the world, and contributing to society.

Stage 8: Maturity (65 years to death), Conflict: Integrity versus Despair: The final stage deals with the actualization of one's ego integrity as a result of the fruition of the tasks of the previous stages. It is a realization of self-fulfillment.

In adolescence and adulthood, Erikson's tasks can be viewed in relation to the schemas of adult development proposed by George Vaillant (1993), Jane Loevinger (1978), and Mark Gould (1976). (See Table 4.3.)

However, the development of cognitive skills and of psychosocial relationships must be augmented by an understanding of the process of deciding what is right and what is wrong. Since every spiritual practice seems to be concerned with issues of correct and incorrect actions, clinicians must consider how individuals make such decisions. This discussion does not detail specific behaviors or actions, but, consistent with the thesis of this chapter, it provides maturational maps of how an individual's concept of morality evolves.

TABLE 4.3 A Summary of Models of Adult Psychosocial Development

Approximate Age Period	Erikson	Vaillant	Loevinger	Gould
Adolescence	Identity vs. identity diffusion	(like Erikson)	Conscientious, conformist	Separating from parents; becoming independent
Young Adulthood	Intimacy vs. isolation		Individualistic	"Nobody's baby"; becoming a competent, self-maintaining adult
Middle Adulthood (Early)	Generativity vs. stagnation	Generativity–Identity consolidation to include significant others (vs. self-absorption); producing	Autonomous	Opening up; exploring inner consciousness; coming to a deeper understanding of self and needs
Middle Adulthood (Late)		Generativity–Openness to the expansion of personal life meaning (vs. rigidity); giving, mentoring		Midlife: Finding the courage and resourcefulness to act on deeper feelings; awareness of the pressure of time
Late Adulthood	Ego integrity (vs. despair)		Integrated	Beyond midlife: Establishing true autonomy; becoming self-directed rather than governed by roles; "I own myself."

Models of Moral Development

The study of moral development seeks to identify the guiding principles that underlie moral choices. The two most often cited models of moral development are those proposed by Piaget (1965) and Kohlberg (1981). Table 4.4 presents a summary of the approximate ages, stages, and tasks of each model.

In essence, this progression reflects an initial concern solely about the self, which is then balanced by attention to the social order, and then transcendence of both guiding factors in favor of principle as the moral barometer.

Gilligan (1993) was critical of this schema, stating that it did not take into account the gender issues associated with moral development. She suggested that female moral reasoning is more concerned with the needs of others than with equity; she also argued that the development of moral reasoning is related to the social context because significant others play a large role in influencing the development of one's moral reasoning. She outlined three stages of moral development. The first is a selfish stage, the second is a belief in conventional morality, and the third is post-conventional. This is a progression from selfish, to social, to principled morality. Female children start out with a selfish orientation. They then

TABLE 4.4 A Summary of Models of Moral Development

Approximate Age	Piaget's Stages	Kohlberg's Stages
Pre-school	Premoral stage: Child is unconcerned about rules; makes up his or her own rules	
5 to 8 or 9 years	Heteronomous morality: Child is a moral realist; rules are determined by the authorities and are unalterable, moral absolutes; must be obeyed; violations are always punished	Preconventional Level Stage 1: Punishment and obedience orientation: Child obeys to avoid punishment and because the authority is assumed to be superior or right; rules are interpreted literally; no judgment is involved
8 or 9 to 11 or 12 years	Autonomous morality: Social rules are arbitrary and promote cooperation, equality, and reciprocity; therefore, they serve justice; can be changed by agreement or violated for a higher purpose	Stage 2: Concrete, individualistic orientation: Child follows rules to serve own interests; others' interests may also need to be served, so the principle of fair exchange is followed (i.e., "You scratch my back, I'll scratch yours.")
13 to 16 years		Conventional Level Stage 3: Social-relational perspective: Shared feelings and needs are more important than self-interest; helpfulness, generosity, and forgiveness are idealized
Late adolescence/ young adulthood		Stage 4: Member-of-society perspective: The social order is most important; behaviors that contribute to the functioning of social systems are most valued (e.g., obeying laws, working hard)
Some adults		Post-Conventional Level Stage 5: Basic individual rights and social contract: The social contract is most valued; specific laws are not valued, but the ideas that they serve are (e.g., democratic principles, individual rights)
Some adults		Stage 6: Universal ethical principles: Certain abstract moral principles are valued above all else, including specific laws; the social order is also highly valued, unless it violates the highest moral principles

learn to care for others and that selfishness is wrong. So in their second stage, conventional morality, women typically feel that it is wrong to act in their own interests and that they should value instead the interests of others. They equate concern for themselves with self-ishness. In the third stage, post-conventional, they learn that it is just as wrong to ignore their own interests as it is to ignore the interests of others. One way of achieving this under-standing is through their concern with connecting with others. A connection, or relationship, involves two people, and if either one is slighted, it harms the relationship.

EMERGING MODELS OF HUMAN DEVELOPMENT

Recently, researchers in the field have endeavored to see psychopathology in a develop-mental light. Kazdin (1989) defined this approach as "the study of clinical dysfunction in the context of maturational and developmental processes" (p. 180). This line of inquiry seeks to build on the idea that developmental challenges and failures in achieving developmental tasks must result in the emergence of some display of pathology. Given the current growth in the number of identified disorders in children, the relative paucity of disorders in adoles-cents, and the differing descriptions of mental disorders between child and adult sympto-mology, one might wonder whether mental illness can be traced throughout the life span.

Perhaps, conversely, helping professionals need to identify barometers of optimal de-velopment (Chu & Powers, 1995; Wagner, 1996); such an endeavor would be congruent with the strengths-focused model of mental health. Emphasizing health and wellness over pathology, this approach would specify age/stage competencies. (See Wagner, 1996, for the characteristics of optimal development in adolescents.)

Chu and Powers (1995) emphasized the impact of the person–environment fit on fos-tering personal independence, self-determination, and decision making. Although the actual cultural definitions and behavioral expressions of these constructs must be age appropriate, their attraction is clear.

Another area of strengths-focused research is the topic of resilience. Defined as a ten-dency to be able to overcome adverse conditions, resilience is seen as a moderating factor between experience and the impact of that experience on the growth and functioning of in-dividuals. Rak and Patterson (1996) traced the development of seven factors that are charac-teristic of resilient individuals, and they are exploring their development over the life span. These factors are (a) a positive self-concept, (b) an optimistic outlook, (c) good interper-sonal skills, (d) good decision-making skills, (e) a well-developed sense of personal autonomy, (f) an environmental support system, and (g) a significant other who can provide mentoring. This field of study has also been linked to the study of spiritual health.

A final area to consider is that of emotional intelligence (Goleman, 1997; Mayer & Geher, 1996). Defined as

> an ability to recognize the meanings of emotions and their relationships and to reason and problem-solve on the basis of them . . . [e]motional intelligence is in-volved with the capacity to perceive emotions, assimilate emotion-related feel-ings, understand the information of these emotions, and mange them. (Mayer, Caruso, & Salovey, 1999, p. 267)

Related to, but independent of, standard intelligence, emotional intelligence is hypothesized to develop along a similar framework; however, the study of emotional intelligence has not yet evolved sufficiently to provide concrete ages, stages, and tasks. In spite of this, its definition confirms its applicability to the study of spirituality, since more advanced levels of spiritual functioning, as presented earlier in this chapter, tend to move from the cognitive and behavioral realms toward a transcendent experience that seems affective in nature, and it may follow that the more emotionally mature an individual may be, the more readily, and perhaps easily, this experience is accessed.

INTEGRATING DEVELOPMENTAL SCHEMAS

Although the multiple models of development are presented separately, their interconnectedness may be illustrated by visualizing the models as a series of recursive domains of growth in which success within one area of development has a "ripple effect" when dealing with the challenges in other spheres of development. The situation is presented visually in the following figure from Peterson & Nisenholz, 1999 (p. 314):

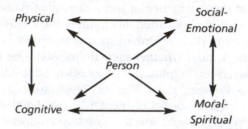

For example, all of the models describe the tasks from the earliest stage as learning to trust that authority figures will provide security as one begins to tentatively explore one's world. If this stage is cognitively, psychosocially, and morally well achieved, then the child trusts those from whom the child can learn about different aspects of his or her world and is encouraged to experiment with new ways of being, is secure in the support of the authority figure, and is prepared to move into the conventional institutions (school and church) of society as part of that ongoing growth. Conversely, frustration within one sphere of development must negatively affect growth within the other spheres. In this case, the child's lack of trust in authority may be expressed in a stand-alone approach, in which the child becomes wary of all adult figures, resentful of adult guidance, and ill-equipped to become one of a group within a school or church due to a residual fear of not getting one's needs for reassurance and approval met.

A second example concerns the final developmental stage of life. A review of all of the models implies that the final stage is the culmination of the individual's ability to function from the perspective of personal aspiration. Individuals in this stage have a solid sense of self, which includes being able to honor, yet not brag about, one's strengths, and to honor, yet not feel belittled, by one's limitations. They have a conscious awareness of the demands of others and society, yet are able to meet those demands while meeting their own personal needs as well. These individuals are guided by values and positive contributions to society that transcend the banality of legal obligation, and they are secure in their own spiritual orientation, which approximates a sense of integrity. However, if an individual is still resolving issues of trust, balancing the needs of others with personal needs, and having yet to develop a solid sense of self, unaware of personal values, or resentfully compromising such values for the sake of inclusion in some group, then one approaches the end of one's life desperate for more time or convinced that life is truly a misery and happiness only an illusion.

The work by Rak and Peterson (1996) linking resilience and spiritual health provides further substantiation of the interaction among these spheres of human functioning. It could be reasoned that, in times of stress or crisis, individuals with a strong spiritual orientation would seek support and direction from the spiritual realm, and, recursively, that they have explicitly chosen that community and/or spiritual tradition on the basis of the comfort that such adherence provides. From another perspective, the emerging study of emotional intelligence may offer a better description of the brain functioning of those who can, and cannot, relate a transcendent spiritual experience. Perhaps future studies can explore the nature–nurture controversy and address a question such as "Are our brains hard-wired to the notion of God and religion, or are such beliefs merely a product of our environment?" Such a study would be especially interesting if it could be conducted from a worldwide, cross-cultural view, seeking to explore how an individual's "spiritual" brain may be similar or different based on one's religious culture.

For a more recent view on this potential integration, the conceptualization by Murgatroyd (2003, p. 98), who proposed a link between Erikson's developmental tasks and Buddhist spiritual needs and tasks, may prove to be of interest:

Life Stage	Developmental Task	Spiritual Needs	Spiritual Tasks
Infancy	Trust	Connectedness	
School Age	Autonomy, initiative, industry	Belonging, acceptance	Active living
Adolescence	Identity	Search for personal truth	Active living
Early and Middle Adulthood	Intimacy, generativity	Connectedness, compassion, awareness of impermanence	Service to others
Old Age	Integrity	Wisdom, meaning of life, unity	Contemplative living

The reader is also referred to Spero (1992, p. 64) for that author's conceptualization of the integration of stages and levels of faith development between his model and the theories of Freud, Erikson, and Meissner. Fowler (1991) firmly acknowledged the influence of other developmental theorists, such as Erikson, John Dewey, Piaget, and Kohlberg, on his work. The fact that at least three of the sources for this chapter would devote scholarly attention to ascertaining the connections among the developmental theories from different aspects of the human condition may convince professional helpers to dedicate equal attention to this challenge, both for professional understanding and for the benefit of our clients.

With regard to the vitality of an integrative approach to developmental theory, Erikson (1968) specified four important contributions of spirituality to overall human functioning:

1. the development of a faith that fosters and supports a child's sense of trust and hope, in contrast to a religious systems that instills fear;
2. the generation of a value system to support the adolescent's search for identity;
3. the emergence of a sense of universalism to support the adult's search for generativity; and
4. the fostering of the older adult's sense of integrity and meaning in life.

Case Example Revisited

From a developmental perspective, the counselor helped Cassandra to understand the evolving nature of her spiritual dilemma. On the basis of the typologies of theories of spiritual development, Cassandra was experiencing an age-appropriate inquiry into personally relevant spiritual and religious traditions. However, on the basis of the models describing one's relationship with God, she seemed to be working from an age-inappropriate view of God as punishing and demanding of strict obedience to church teachings. Comparing these two developmental stages enabled Cassandra to become cognizant of the incongruence in the two stances and, consequently, of the need to revise one set of beliefs to a more age-appropriate level. She gratefully accepted the appropriateness of her spiritual quest and, in counseling, set out to explore her perspective of her relationship with God and her belief that her search in some way jeopardized that relationship. In addition, the development of personal insights helped to confirm for Cassandra that her experiences were not atypical. She was also told that she could return to her church of origin, but that she might feel more satisfied when she became more convinced of her own spiritual values. That way, her choice of religious affiliation would be directed by her own spiritual values rather than the spiritual values being imposed on her by her choice of affiliation.

Her cognitive development allowed her to accept a multiplicity of views, some more familiar and some less so. Her psychosocial development and search for identity confronted her with the issue of how to explain her search to family and friends. However, in doing so, she discovered an unseen personal strength: the ability to speak in her own voice, whether related to her choice of academic major or her spiritual path.

In this case, a college student's search for identity was centered on her spiritual issues. The introduction of developmental theory helped place her struggle within the context of age-appropriate spiritual challenges. This realization was a great relief, in itself, for the student. This knowledge served to "normalize" her struggles and provide a foundation for her spiritual evolution to date and for the challenges yet to come.

Conclusion

After reading this chapter, the reader should have an understanding of the differing current models of spiritual development. In addition, it is hoped that the reader has gained a contextual framework for the integration of spiritual growth within an overall developmental schema. If, as a professional helper, one intends for therapy to focus on the healthy development of the whole person as a vehicle for problem remediation, then one must pay attention to all aspects of the human experience. In that way, clinical insights and knowledge can be offered to the client so that the client can choose what will promote individual healing and growth and also come to appreciate both the rich complexity and the potential of the human spiritual and religious experience (Kelly, 1995).

Self-Understanding Exercises

1. Consider your own view of your spiritual development. What do you see as your greatest accomplishment? What do you see as your greatest challenge?

2. Which of the models of spiritual develop-ment resonate with you? In what ways?

3. Can you recall a life crisis or a crisis of faith that generated spiritual growth on your part? How do you describe yourself and your spir-itual differences before and after that spe-cific event?

4. What are some of the self-defining benefits of advanced spiritual development? What may be some of the relational drawbacks of such growth?

Opportunities for Further Learning

1. Consider reading one of the earlier authors on this topic by reviewing *The Individual and His Religion* (Allport, 1950). As one of the foundational works linking psychology and religion, the reader is treated to a cogent discourse on the belief in the positive power of religion in life.

2. Obtain the text of sermons or other shared religious or spiritual tracts from your place of worship, and utilize one or more of the models of spiritual development to deter-mine both the spiritual growth of the leader of that group and what that leader sees as the needs of the congregants.

5

■ ■ ■

Spirituality Identity
and Maturity

The idea of God brings us face to face with our own laziness.

—M. Scott Peck (1978, p. 271)

CASE EXAMPLE

Sam spent his childhood in an Orthodox Jewish household and community, defined by adherence to traditional worship and practices. Most of his social connections revolved around his belief system and faith tradition, and he attended a Jewish elementary school. He attended public secondary schools and then was admitted to a local state university so that he could remain close to his home and faith during his undergraduate college career. During one of his undergraduate courses in psychology, a class discussion on the debate between Freud and Jung on the importance of religion in the 21st century surfaced. One of the arguments put forth centered on the possibility that the traditional wisdoms have outlived their applicability or relevance. This point of view startled him. From his viewpoint and life experiences, relevance was never questioned and his core values stemmed from a tradition that now, the other students offered, may be irrelevant. On a personal level, he was outraged by such sentiments, but from an academic perspective, he was intrigued.

He brought this conflict to his rabbi, who listened carefully and confirmed that there was indeed a paradox. The rabbi also spoke to the need for one to come to God not through habit or upbringing, but as a conscious choice in which one option must be the refutation of the existence or power of God. This suggestion stunned Sam as he had expected a traditional lecture on obedience in faith. His rabbi suggested that Sam's answers were less likely to be found in reading and prayer and perhaps more likely to be found in insight and contemplation, and suggested that he enter counseling for this dilemma. The rabbi stated, "Even if you end up back where you started, at least you will have endured the journey."

■ ■ ■

INTRODUCTION

A description of the human experience can be viewed as composed of "several dimensions . . . including the spiritual or religious, moral, social, somatic and psychological" (Sperry, 2001,

p. 23). Of these five facets of human experience and functioning, a diagram representing the connections among these five dimensions might place the spiritual facet at the heart, or core, of the interaction among all five components (Wilber, 1999). Sperry claimed that ". . . it [the spiritual facet] may not involve any formal affiliation with a religious tradition, but it reflects the beliefs, effects and behaviors associated with the basic spiritual hunger or desire for self-transcendence that all individuals experience" (p. 25). Those beliefs and behaviors, then, affect the psychological, moral, social, and somatic functioning of each individual. From that perspective, all purposes and goals stem from that spiritual center and resonate throughout the other components. Although the feedback system is reciprocal, with each aspect exerting an influence on the other features, this outlook places spirituality at the heart of the process. Furthermore, it could be suggested that all impetus for growth originates within the spiritual dimension and that this growth impetus can entail both *deficiency* goals and *growth* goals.

DEFICIENCY AND GROWTH GOALS

In this context, a *deficiency* goal addresses those basic needs in life that must be fulfilled to sustain the individual (Maslow, 1986, 1998). When one set of needs in a particular stage is fulfilled, a person naturally moves to the next stage. The physiological needs—food, shelter, and sex—take precedence. Physiological needs can control thoughts and behaviors, and can cause people to feel sickness, pain, and discomfort. For example, an individual may perform poorly on an exam because, having missed breakfast, he or she is thinking more about a grumbling empty stomach than the exam questions.

When physiological needs are met, the need for safety will emerge. This includes personal protection from crime, economic and vocational security, health and well-being, and a safety net against accidents, illnesses, and their adverse impacts. For example, in late 2008, financial concerns might generate a great deal of anxiety about the security of one's job, the ability to pay one's bills, and one's retirement accounts.

After physiological and safety needs are fulfilled, the third level of human needs is social. This level of Maslow's hierarchy of needs involves emotionally based relationships in general, such as friendships, sexual intimacy, and having a supportive and communicative family. Humans need to feel a sense of belonging and acceptance, whether it comes from a large social group (e.g., clubs, office culture, religious groups, professional organizations, sports teams, gangs) or from small social connections (e.g., family members, intimate partners, mentors, close colleagues, confidants). They need to love and be loved (sexually and nonsexually) by others. In the absence of these elements, many people become susceptible to loneliness, social anxiety, and depression. For example, one of the proactive interventions commonly used by elementary school counselors is a "newcomers' group" to welcome late arrivals to the school and foster a sense of community among these children. The need to belong can often overpower physiological and security needs, depending on the degree of peer pressure (e.g., an anorexic ignores the need to eat and the security of health in order to belong to an appearance-focused peer group).

The belonging needs are followed by esteem needs. All humans have a need to be respected; to have self-esteem and self-respect; and to respect others. People need to engage themselves in order to gain recognition, and they need to have one or more activities that give them a sense of making a contribution in order to feel accepted and valued, be it in a profession or a hobby. Imbalances at this level can result in low self-esteem and inferiority complexes. People with low self-esteem need respect from others. They may seek fame or glory, which, again, is dependent on others. However, confidence, competence, and achievement need to be recognized only by one person—the individual himself or herself. Everyone else is inconsequential to one's self-esteem. It must be noted, however, that many people with low self-esteem will not be able to improve their view of themselves simply by receiving fame, respect, and glory externally, but must first accept themselves internally. For example, professional athletes may have a hard time contemplating the end of their athletic careers as that endeavor has delivered so much attention and praise. They may have a hard time imagining life, and self-identity, without that status. Psychological imbalances such as depression can also prevent one from obtaining self-esteem from both internal and external sources.

Maslow also believed that humans have a need to increase their intelligence through the pursuit of knowledge. Cognitive needs are the expression of the natural human need to learn, explore, discover, and create in order to gain a better understanding of the world.

The *deficiency* needs may be seen as basic, and can be met and neutralized (i.e., they stop being motivators in one's life). In comparison, self-actualization and transcendence are "being" or growth needs (also termed "B-needs"); that is, they are enduring motivators, or drivers, of behavior. Self-actualization is the instinctual need of humans to make the most of their abilities and to strive to be the best they can be. Self-actualization is the intrinsic growth of what is already in the organism, or, more accurately, the expression of all the true characteristics of the organism. Unlike deficiency needs, there is no ultimate conclusion to "being" needs. Although one may eat until one feels full and need not eat again until hungry, there is no equivalent limit to intrinsic growth. It may be suggested semantically that the reframing of growth needs into being needs better illustrates the evolving nature of this need as being in a state of ongoing transition and development. The question of an absolute or upper limit to growth can best be relegated to future study, but there seems to exist a consistent motivation for seeking more from oneself.

Maslow wrote the following description of self-actualizing people:

- They embrace the facts and realities of the world (including themselves) rather than denying or avoiding them.
- They are spontaneous in their ideas and actions.
- They are creative.
- They are interested in solving problems; this often includes the problems of others. Solving these problems is often a key focus in their lives.
- They feel close to other people.
- They generally appreciate life.
- They have a system of morality that is fully internalized and independent of external authority.
- They are discerning and are able to view all things in an objective manner.

In short, self-actualization is reaching one's fullest potential. Maslow later divided the top tier of his hierarchy of needs to add self-transcendence, which is also sometimes referred to as spiritual needs. Spiritual needs are a little different from other needs because they are accessible from many levels. This distinction of the permeability of the needs hierarchy to spiritual needs is an important exception to its hierarchical arrangement. The singularity of spiritual flow throughout the other needs may reflect its vitality and essential nature in directing need fulfillment in the other levels. If so, then this designation further corroborates the focal point played by one's spirituality in directing one's life.

Bauer and McAdams (2004) agreed with Brandtstader (1999) in the belief that individuals can intentionally utilize personal goals as a pathway toward personal development. Identifying *growth goals* also identifies an individual's perception of "the good life" and, equally important, the values that will guide his or her conduct in progressing toward that goal. These outcomes were categorized into "social-cognitive maturity (how complexly one thinks about the self and others) and social-emotional well-being (how good one feels in a world of others)" (p. 114). Social-cognitive maturity speaks to "an increasing ability to understand the self and others" (Bauer & McAdams, 2004, p. 115). Although Damon and Hart (1988) were cited as detailing four stages through childhood and adolescence, Loevinger (1976) extended social-cognitive development into adulthood.

Moving from the lowest level of impulsive and self-protective ego functioning, the self then moves into the middle stage, epitomized by traits such as conformity, self-awareness, and conscientiousness. The highest stage is that of individualistic, autonomous, and integrated ego development. Recent studies have correlated social-cognitive maturity with greater adaptive abilities, levels of responsibility, tolerance, and achievement. Social-emotional well-being speaks to the individual's ability to "adjust to the social and emotional demands of everyday life" (Bauer & McAdams, 2004, p. 115). Such well-being is the outcome of a growth orientation based on eudaimonistic values, rather than a safety orientation. These values encompass a greater commitment to personal growth, happiness, meaningful relationships, and contributions to society, in contrast to extrinsic values such as money, status, and physical appearance.

These traits seem to mirror those exhibited by individuals who function at higher levels of differentiation (Bowen, 1978). From that perspective, there is a conscious awareness of the definitions of the self as learned from the role expectations within the family of origin. The process of differentiation demands the application of cognitive reasoning to evaluate which aspects and qualities of which roles will be retained as the individual seeks to develop a solid self—a self-created, yet multiply influenced identity. Moreover, both of these stages of maturation, or identity formation, also require "explicit expression of intentions to conceptually explore, integrate, deepen or otherwise learn about new perspectives on the individual's life" (Bauer & McAdams, 2004, p. 116).

IDENTITY FORMATION

"Identity formation is central to development across the lifespan . . ." (McLean & Pratt, 2006, p. 714). Identity, although founded in childhood, blossoms in adolescence and young adulthood, and then may or may not be revised during adulthood on the basis of an individual's openness to self-reflection, responsibility, and response to life events. It would be impossible not to have an identity; it is very possible to have an identity not of one's making or choice. Influences such as family legacy, gender role expectations, societal injunctions, cultural mores, and so forth all provide differing characterizations. These social institutions also carry the power of social acceptance and approval, or rejection and exclusion. However, it is important to bear in mind that social institutions enjoy no more power than the individual bestows. However, whatever identity decisions are made by an individual do not function in a social vacuum: There is a constant and natural tension between self-directedness and influence by others in this evolution. A possible solution is to seek a conscious awareness of both preferred sets of beliefs and actions, on the one hand, and work, on the other, to select those which exemplify one's strengths as guided by one's spiritual directives. Within that process, part of the conscious awareness must involve how identity is formed.

Two approaches to understanding identity formation are postulated: the status approach and the narrative approach. The status approach focuses first on the exploration and commitment of the self in the context of life's challenges and then on congruence or consistency among decisions of the self in context. Marcia (1987; Marcia et al., 1993) spoke to issues of identity diffusion and foreclosure as the least advanced. These stages are characterized by apathy toward school and relationships, strained family relationships (diffusion), and authoritarian values and rigid family roles (foreclosure). Moratorium is characterized by anxiety, sensitivity to moral issues, and uncertain family relationships, while identity formation is shown through advanced openness to intimate relationships, psychological flexibility and resistance to emotional reactivity, and the manipulation of one's self-esteem, or peer pressure.

However, adopting a more fluid orientation, the narrative understanding of identity emerged from Erikson's (1968) ideas on identity as a direct product of a person's responses to crises, life development, and psychobiography. This perspective suggests that "humans have a narrative mode of thought . . . in which experiences and the self are storied into culturally acceptable and valued narratives that hold currency in one's community and society" (McLean & Pratt, 2006, p. 715). This narrative characteristic is synonymous with processes such as meaning making, integrative memories (or integration), exploratory processing, and accommodation. It is the emergence of autobiographical reasoning to make sense of life. Therefore, life events are essentially colorless until the individual applies color (interpretation, value, importance, etc.) through the attachment of adjectives and meaning about the event itself, the individual, and others within that context. For example, on a school exam, two students receive the identical grade of "B". One student leaps into the air rejoicing, and the other student lowers her head to her desk in tears. Given that the grades are alike, only the individual student's interpretation of that grade can account for the two differing reactions.

McLean and Thorne (2003) proposed that meaning making is composed of lessons and insights. Lessons are the more rudimentary process of the two because personal learning seems to be limited to like situations and events, while insight involves the generalization of the lesson to all of one's life. Lessons deal with amendments to behavior, while insight deals with amendments to one's self-story. Both lessons and insight emerge from conflicting or tension-filled events. The potential for meaning within an event is in direct proportion to its emotionality. More negative or conflicting events generate the potential for more meaning making. Pals and McAdams (2004) explained this phenomenon by ascribing the negativity of the event to a need to conceptually rework that narrative to reduce cognitive dissonance; coping with, and resolution of, that event will be in the form of narrative construction. When the "bad turns to good" in a life story, the more redemptive the experience has been for that individual and the greater will be the emergence of ego strength. In addition, the amount of optimism (leading to perseverance and more active problem-solving strategies) and commitment (characterized by a personal ideology) that evolve are indicative of greater well-being and personal adjustment.

For example, an adolescent, in the beginning stages of identity formation, who receives detention at school for not bringing his or her math homework, might learn the lesson that the math teacher is a stickler for homework and that there is no room for excuses. That lesson may motivate the student to attend to math homework only and may not prompt any consideration of either the student's responsibility for other assignments or the self as a learner in school. In the first instance, the scope of that lesson is limited to the relationship between the student and the math teacher, and then it needs to be repeated with each teacher for the message to be accommodated. In the second instance, the one experience leads to what can be defined as a turning point in one's identity as a high school student if that learning is generalized to the adolescent's responsibility in his or her relationships with all teachers and for all subject matter.

Within this turning point, it is the narrative that emerges that is more important than the event itself as the message transcends the immediacy of the single event to a redefinition of the self within and across life contexts. Although the events that prompted a new understanding about oneself or the facing of different life paths, each with decidedly different potential outcomes, are important, the emphasis on self-reflection becomes one's barometer of personal truth. The event itself may pass into memory as each individual lives from day to day. Retelling the details of a story cannot change its occurrence or lessons, but reflection on the meaning derived from that story can foster the insight necessary to consider different ways of being in order to both resolve the presenting issue and prevent its reoccurrence. For example, the friend who repeatedly calls and bemoans another failed relationship is seeing neither the lesson nor the insight in the pain of rejection. However, finding neither a lesson nor an insight will ensure that the next relationship will suffer the same catastrophic results as the one that came before it.

One life directive, as a pathway toward self-actualization, may then be to build consistent value themes bridging all five areas (spiritual or religious, moral, social, somatic, and psychological), with the genesis founded in the spiritual area. Ego strength and consistency speak to the virtues that an individual has consciously adopted to guide and define his or her life. Those values or virtues then guide all beliefs, thoughts, feelings, interactions with others, and the evaluation of the self within the multiple roles and contexts of life. Favorable self-evaluation may be seen as a function of the degree of individual congruence and genuineness (i.e., the extent to which one's values are consistently exemplified through action across contexts and are manifestations of the "true self" living toward its highest potential). Negative self-evaluation has its basis in either inconsistent value expressions based on context and social pressures—virtues in one area that lack resonance with values in the other(s)—or lack of clarity of one's virtues within one of the five areas of functioning. For example, if one's spiritual guidance speaks to honesty as a virtue or value, yet an individual lies to a parent about a grade, then the person is presenting a level of value/action incongruence. As a second example, if an individual acknowledges the potential dangers of tobacco use to one's health, yet persists in smoking when out with friends, there is a lack of resonance in values between the somatic and social domains. As a third example, if one is confronted with a moral dilemma, such as whether or not to take credit for a successful project at work even though the idea and effort were put forth by another, who is a subordinate, and one cannot decide what is the right course of action when praised by the employer, then there may be a lack of value clarity within that moral dimension. The theme of the arrangement of the virtue connection presented by Sperry (2001) implies that spirituality lies at the heart of the virtue–action confusion. This depiction can be read as an intent to place spiritual virtue at the core of the decision-making process as to suitable actions in any situation.

If the centrality of spirituality in the definition and emergence of the true self can be accepted, at least for the duration of this chapter, then its very position as the axis of moral, social, psychological, and somatic identity elements directs an attempt to better grasp the idea and features of spiritual identity and maturity. Spiritual maturity would then filter and direct how growth or stagnation in the other four domains might be expressed, and would also serve as the initial focus for insight and intervention to affect the moral, social, psychological, and somatic realms of functioning. Intentional self-development would then be both a precursor and a result of this focus on growth goals because "coherent goal hierarchies are essential to intentional self-development" (Sperry, 2001, p. 124). Regardless of their content, such goals embrace exploration, learning new things, self-challenge, and contributions to society—the very terms utilized by Maslow (1986, 1998) to describe "self-actualizing" individuals. Individuals with any type of growth goals were found to be "more mature and report greater well-being" (Bauer & McAdams, 2004, p. 123).

SPIRITUAL IDENTITY

"Since time immemorial, it is believed that spiritual experiences and practices are significant in life and play an important part in establishing an integrated personality" (Van Dierendonck & Mohan, 2006, p. 227). Spirituality underlies personal growth impulses toward healing and personal development, and cultural and social activities. So the health of the spiritual identity affects both the individual and his or her social milieu. For the purposes of this discussion, the term *spiritual identity* refers to a point in the growth of spiritual maturity. Identity may be construed as the foundation on which maturity surfaces through the confirmation or refinement of the components and expressions of identity. It must be assumed that spiritual identity and maturity remain a lifelong process of evolution for as long as an individual wishes to direct attention and energy toward their emergence. On the basis of the innate nature of the spiritual drive—that such potential is an integral part of a human—this capacity lies dormant until awakened and energized. The following material is intended to offer working definitions and descriptions of spiritual maturity and spiritual identity so that personal assessment can be made of the extent to which one is exercising and expressing one's true spiritual self.

Thoresen, Oman, and Harris (2005) affirmed that spiritual maturity can be explained as the extent to which "spiritual practices based on beliefs, codes, rules and attitudes about how and why one can live one's [faith] in daily life" (p. 206) provide ongoing direction in the life choices made by each individual. Thus, spirituality cannot be just a visit to a synagogue, mosque, or church, to be experienced on a particular day of worship and then disregarded after the services. The transition from participating in religion to living religion begins with an independent preference for the teachings of one or multiple religious and spiritual traditions. Even the claim of general adherence to a faith tradition (e.g., Catholicism, Hinduism, Wicca, etc.) carries the supplementary demand for ownership of its attendant creeds and dictates. The path toward spiritual maturity deals not only with the wisdom and guidance that one's spiritual tradition imparts, but also one's awareness of how that wisdom directs one's multiple daily choices. In addition, this guidance must be consciously reevaluated during challenging or stressful times in order to monitor its application and to consider the next step in one's growth.

The materialization of spiritual identity also involves reconciliation of the mystical, personal, meditative-contemplative, or experiential expressions of faith with the dogmatic and liturgical guidelines offered by each formal religion. It would seem to be simpler to accept totally the certainty of the teachings and rules of any religion rather than consider on a personal level their resonance with that which one wishes to become. Each spiritual tradition provides answers, but each answer does not necessarily fit each person. Adherence to a particular faith may mean, perhaps, accepting the majority of its answers, but then the question arises, What about those items of faith with which one disagrees with the answers neatly provided by the selected faith tradition? Overlooking these items generates the spiritual vacuum of a question with no answer. If the question is central to the spiritual value of a faith, the question must be answered for the faith to be whole or complete. Is there an expectation that joining a faith means accepting all of the answers, even if some "do not fit," or does such dissonance between religious creed and individual spiritual conscience provide the motivation to contemplate alternative answers, perhaps from other faith traditions? A related question arising from the first issue involves the observance of faith. To what extent is one bound or limited to institutionally sanctioned expressions of faith, and to what extent is one free to experiment with expressions of faith from other traditions or to create one's own celebrations? There seems to be an implicit paradox between a desire to live one's faith in immediacy, on a moment-by-moment basis, and being directed to delay ceremony or celebration until pre-established, prescribed times and then being instructed to celebrate only in the time-honored ways. This clash of religious tradition and spiritual spontaneity can be easily resolved by opting to do both instead of trying to choose needlessly between the expressions. Furthermore, if that choice is made, the individual may take comfort in the participation in traditional ceremony, but may still express spiritual spontaneity in his or her life.

In addition, spiritual identity and maturity involve confronting issues such as the presence of God, perceived as being "out there" or "up there" by formal religions, rather than being "in here" (Roof, 1999, p. 60) by a growing number of spirituality seekers. One basic issue is one's belief in God, a supreme force, a universal constant, or whatever the title may be. The question of "knowing" is relevant only so far as the limits of knowledge are accepted. If a working definition of knowing revolves around fact and measurable, observable phenomena, then knowledge is essential in making one's way in the world. Knowledge is necessary and Maslow (1986, 1998) asserted that it is a basic human drive. Humans seem to posses a desire to understand that which seems to be a puzzle or is challenging. However, knowledge is not sufficient for spiritual growth. Spiritual growth depends on a conscious choice to accept the idea that the boundaries of knowledge fall far short of the boundaries of human experience. Human experience also encompasses the mystical and unknowable but felt to be true—the question of believing. Believing necessitates a certainty not based on rational discourse, learned tomes, or direction from clergy, but a sincere, heartfelt certainty of truth. Explored and experienced more deeply, this certainty cannot be identical for each person because each person's characteristics and experience of the same phenomenon must differ slightly due to the person's inherent uniqueness. If knowledge deals with the areas of common agreement, perhaps belief deals with the areas of individual definition. The commonality of agreement creates communities of spiritual agents, but it is the individual's responsibility to contribute both to the spiritual health of the community and to his or her own spiritual health, which must, by the nature of organizational dynamics, become a singular journey.

Finally, spiritual identity and maturity refer to how one's everyday actions, thoughts, and interactions are spiritually influenced. The entire discussion of the development of a spiritual identity may blossom over time toward a sense of spiritual maturity. Perhaps one way to describe "spiritual maturity" is the extent to which one's way of being in the world reflects one's spiritual identity. The key variable in this supposition is that of constancy. The reading of sacred texts is a strong foundation, but it is meaningless if the words and messages remain fixed on the page instead of being translated into worldly action. Inherent within this enactment is the realization that human beings cannot hold perfection, epiphany, or catharsis for long periods of time. What sets those peak experiences of spiritual identity apart is that they are in contrast to the majority of one's day spent in the more mundane, yet necessary, aspects of life. In the instances where one may fail at performing to one's spiritual best, the opportunity for self-questioning arises. One may ask, "What do my actions in this situation say about me and about my spiritual identity?" or "How did I make sense of this circumstance in such a way as to justify an action that is inconsistent with my 'spiritual aspirations for myself'?" The intent of such questioning is not self-punishment, but to gain a deeper understanding of the self in the face of challenges and struggles. It is this personal commitment to one's ongoing development that bodes well for one's spiritual future and the ongoing emergence of psychological well-being as a function of that spiritual evolution.

This linkage of spiritually based action to positive psychological outcome can be refined by distinguishing between hedonic well-being (experiencing joy and avoiding pain and discomfort) and eudaimonistic well-being, which exceeds the hedonistic view by being guided by individual principle rather than self-gratification. Eudaimonistic well-being focuses on those actions that "are an expression of the best within us" (Roof, 1999, p. 232). Aristotle claimed that every person has unique talents and it is their expression that brings true joy. In that moment, one is truly living in accordance with one's true self. Ryff (1989) identified components of eudaimonistic well-being as self-acceptance (self-respect), belonging, autonomy (whether or not to conform to social norms), environmental mastery (mastery, competence, and trust in handling one's environment), purpose in life (directedness and meaningfulness), and personal growth (realizing one's potential).

According to Van Dierendonck and Mohan (2006), spiritual maturity and eudaimonistic well-being are intertwined. Mature spirituality serves as an expression of the inner self and a sense of being part of a deeper dimension. It provides the road to personal significance in life on the pathway to the development of a consistently referenced framework defining how an individual interprets any given life event. Spiritual maturity offers strength in times of crisis, support, and guidance through prayer or contemplation. Spiritual maturity has also been hypothesized to help an individual better relate with others as the growth toward this maturity helps individuals recognize their own projections as a source of relational conflict. Spiritual maturity also provides a sense of optimism or acceptance of the limits of one's power in any given situation and the ability to add a spiritual perspective on any life events in addition to the multiple other viewpoints one may assume.

Beck (2006) linked the spiritual growth orientation to the concept of God as an attachment figure. Before this discussion can proceed, it is important to acknowledge Beck's statement on the limitations of his treatise because the previous literature has focused entirely on persons of the Christian faith. Therefore, although these assertions are founded within this line of scholarly inquiry, their application, relevance, or utility to other faith traditions has yet to be explored, much less corroborated. That limitation noted, Beck addressed the idea of "spiritual searching." The model for this search for spiritual identity is connected to that provided by Batson, Schoenrade, and Ventis (1993), who defined spiritually mature individuals as those who (a) accept the complexity of religion, (b) are ready to face doubt, (c) are open to self-examination and self-criticism, (d) know the implicit incompleteness of their searching, (e) are tentative in their knowing, and (f) are willing to embark in an ongoing search for truth. Gibson (2004) declared that the task of any church is to lead persons toward "deeper levels of spirituality" (p. 295). Such a declaration instigates an exploration of the idea of spiritual levels. Hill, Pargament, Hood et al. (2000) expressed this process as follows:

> Spirituality involves the feelings, thoughts, experiences, and behaviors that arise from a search for the sacred. The term *search* refers to attempts to identify, articulate, maintain or transform. The term *sacred* refers to a divine being, divine object, Ultimate Reality or Ultimate Truth as perceived by the individual. (p. 66)

This exploration can be seen as being based on the works of Kolberg (1974, 1984) and Gilligan (1982). Kolberg identified justice as the key principle in morality. The understanding and application of justice is a reflection of the moral reasoning utilized by individuals at differing stages. "Moral judgment is essentially a way of seeing and resolving moral conflicts. To know whether an action is moral or not, we must know how the person judges the situation with which he or she is confronted" (1984, p. 516). The highest level involves decision making based on the highest principle of justice—"the sanctity of human life and a regard for individuals as ends in themselves rather than means for some other [personal] end" (Gibson, 2004, p. 295). Gilligan (1982) confronted Kohlberg's (1974) ethics of justice by claiming that the principle indicated a male bias in his research and proposed that women base moral judgments instead on caring for others as the key principle. Stonehouse (1998) wrote about more recent efforts to integrate both the ethos of justice and caring by stating that "with our understanding of justice we choose what we believe to be the right or moral solution. With our understanding of care, we decide what our responsibility is in the solution" (p. 296). From that unity of intent and action comes the ideal that moral decision making must be reflected in moral behavior.

As applied to spiritual development and identity, Gibson (2004) identified *agape*, or godly love, as the epitome of moral reasoning. Citing biblical scholars who claim that biblical justice is more like relational responsibility than equality of treatment, agape, according to Stonehouse (1998) ". . . does not compete with justice principles; rather it inspires one to go beyond the demands of justice" (p. 71). Gibson's visualization offered a four-level developmental schema toward what was described as "Christian spiritual maturity" (2004, p. 298):

Level 1	Level 2	Level 3	Level 4
Accommodation to God's Law out of fear of punishment and hope for reward	Imitation of godly exemplars with growing respect for, and obedience to, the Ten Commandments	Personal, principle-centered commitment to a Christian worldview	Movement beyond a focus on individual piety to the active promotion of corporate piety and the redemption of creation's sin-stained creatures
Source of Authority: Self-centered	Source of Authority: Other-centered	Source of Authority: Principle-centered	Source of Authority: Kingdom-centered

For Gibson, spiritual maturity deals with an evolution of perspective away from oneself and toward others, from self-service to service to others, guided not by selfish principles but by selfless imperatives. The first stage reflects a series of experiments in life within the boundaries of one's faith, much like in the family system, where rules are externally imposed and two possible outcomes (reward or punishment) are experienced. The second stage involves carrying on a dialogue with a spiritual mentor who seems to "model an obedient life to God's standards" (2004, p. 300). The function of the mentor is to offer to the searcher the questions through which the mentor has found life meaning and then guide the searcher toward individually relevant truths. The third stage speaks to the growing individualization, or identity formation, of adolescents or young adults and the internalization of personal values and commitments.

As a result of seeking answers to personal spiritual questions, the conclusions reached make up the individual's spiritual identity. However, the crucible for those beliefs is challenge. When one has the option of abandoning one's beliefs in the face of persecution, ridicule, or peer pressure, lacking the reinforcement of church or community, and yet steadfastly chooses to adhere to those beliefs, then that person is well on the way to crystallizing a spiritual identity. The third stage is seen as the foundation for continual questioning and dialogue about matters of faith. To foreclose this exploration, having arrived at the initial answers, is the error that will eventually lead to spiritual stagnation. Because as individuals age, mature, learn, and experience differing life challenges, those questions must be revisited and perhaps the original answers reconsidered in light of new perspectives and understanding. Gibson acknowledged that, for many people, the third stage would seem to be the epitome of spiritual development, but suggested that such a view is a function of the extreme individualism of our society and must be transcended toward "corporate piety," or social advocacy and action. Capturing the principles of love, care, and justice, each individual acts on those principles which reflect the interest of God.

Although founded in Christian theology, especially regarding the nature of the human condition as "sin-stained," this matrix may provide a framework for understanding and promoting spiritual maturity as a reflection of personal responsibility. Working from a model of increased complexity, each subsequent stage may be seen to add sources of authority to that of the previous stage as a function of increased personal insight, cognitive competency, and tolerance for ambiguity within the moral perspective. For example, within the second stage, the individual is both focusing on personal need (avoiding punishment and seeking reward) *and* aspiring to emulate the spiritual mentor in obedience to godly law. How that tension is resolved by each person speaks to the growth in spiritual maturity. The issue of sin within this framework may be construed to encompass all human foibles and errors, and how each person confronts those incidences when his or her behavior falls short of a spiritual ideal. It is in those moments, not of dialogue with another, but of monologue with the self that the truth is told and the self is faced. Whether one welcomes such opportunities for self-understanding, acceptance, remorse, and dedication, or avoids such incidences speaks loudly as to one's potential for spiritual growth. Perhaps spiritual maturity is moments of spiritual bliss surrounded by a lifetime of spiritual struggle, with each person enjoying the former and being faithful to the latter.

Faiver, Ingersoll, O'Brien, and McNally (2001) identified nine common themes related to spiritual growth and identity. The purpose of this listing exceeds a mere checklist of competencies by intending to focus one's contemplation of the self on one's spirituality and then on the world to see how one makes personal sense of these constructs and the extent to which one deems one's actions toward others congruent with such depictions. So the emerging questions focus on two issues: (a) How does one define each term in one's "spiritual dictionary"? and (b) How does one epitomize that spiritual definition in action? Faiver et al.'s nine themes are as follows:

1. ***Hope***   It can be supposed that clients seek therapy due to the "push of despair and [the] pull of hope" (Faiver et al., 2001, p. 21). Hope provides the belief that suffering and the experiencing of setbacks are not in vain. Hope allows an individual to endure, and it serves as a motivator for action and achievement in anticipation of a possible brighter future. Hope serves as the counterweight to possible depression and despair—the fear that life will never get any better and that there is no use in trying. Might loss of hope equate to a loss of faith in God, or in the divine plan for one's existence?

2. ***Virtue***   Defined as the "power to live as genuine a life as is possible" (Faiver et al., 2001, p. 22), virtue transcends religious creed or legal statute and instead admonishes one to live out of, and toward, one's uniqueness—to live with a commitment to truth. That truth can be classified as the capacity to make decisions with maximum consciousness versus loss of contact with the differing parts of the self. For example, to only pay heed to one's intellect and disregard one's affect or somatic responses provides an incomplete and inauthentic appraisal of the self in context. Such selective attention can only lead to partially informed choices and decisions, resulting in illegitimate courses of action and negative outcomes.

   Sperry (2001) defined virtue in action as morality; however, he decried the emphasis within individual psychology that shifted the focus from a collective imperative to an individual imperative, and entitlement to personal fulfillment, perhaps at the expense of the social collective. He cited Frankl (1978), who saw this shift as being at the expense of traditional values such as the power of suffering, the acceptance of one's lot in life, adherence to tradition, moderation, and self-restraint.

   The role of character is played out in one's self-identity and self-regulation as individuals conduct themselves in interpersonal and organizational situations (Sperry, 2001). The following adjectives serve as facets of character: "responsible, trustworthy, respectful, fair, caring, cooperative and rule-obliging" (p. 30). By thus being character motivated in contrast to relying on situation-specific ethical decision making, the individual must aspire not to see what one can "get away with," but rather to envision what one might become. Virtue speaks to both a sense of indebtedness and obligation to the social context *and* personal entitlement to one's own needs.

3. ***Sacred Ground***   Faiver et al. (2001) offered a vivid picture of counseling as fostering the "free flight of a client's soul" (p. 24). The mystery of the future, especially of change in the future without a guarantee that change will be an improvement over familiar misery, takes faith because there is no other basis for action.

   The idea of sacred ground involves not a place, but an attitude—a receptivity to what gradually emerges as one discusses with others, learns, and then quietly weighs the wisdom of what has been learned in light of who and how one wishes to become. Sperry (2001) spoke to the search for the sacred as the emergence of parts of spiritual truths about human consciousness that come out of the psychological search. The intent of both the spiritual and psychological searches for wholeness center on the exploration of consciousness and the contents of that consciousness. The fully conscious individual is aware of blind spots, defenses, symptoms, and self-defeating patterns. In short, sacred ground is that time when one avails oneself of the opportunity to observe one's own ego. If one can accept the maxim that God, or the Holy, or the Divine Spirit lives within each individual, the search of the self for those sparks of divinity would seem to place one in appropriate awe to that which one might become.

4. **Polarities**   Spiritual identity and maturity involve the acceptance of duality and ambiguity in the world (ambiguity itself presents a polarity with certainty). Reconciling the existence of good and evil, happiness and sorrow, and growth and death allows the mature acceptance of each in its place without one's being overwhelmed. On a more personal level, the balance of activity and receptivity, and contemplation and action, prepares the individual to determine when is the time to ponder and when is the time to produce. Pertaining to the spiritual search, themes of lost and found, self-forgetting, and self-discovery merge with the peculiar notions that one cannot be found until one admits that one is lost and that the discovery of the self reveals only that which one has forgotten that one already has.

5. **Facing Oneself**   A spiritual journey entails an inevitable confrontation between the real self and the ideal self, with the self sometimes being seen [as a] spiritual disappointment or failure. The real self is consistent with the Jungian shadow (the parts of the self that we prefer not to accept). However, honesty with others and of others must commence with honesty to the self. Sperry (2001) referred to this idea as self-directedness—the self-determination to "control, regulate and adapt behavior in accord with [one's] chosen goals and values" (p. 31). This self-understanding can then be amended to be manifested in an internal locus of control, purposefulness, resourcefulness, and self-efficacy. If one were to consider those aspects of the "shadow" as a possibility for growth, then the effort expended in hiding or denying their existence could be much better spent alleviating their torment. As a closing word on this topic, it must be remembered that a common human characteristic is the presence of these shadow sides. Bidden or not, they exist. The challenge is deciding whether to face them squarely or "dance around them."

6. **Compassion**   With its basis in an acceptance of common humanness, compassion encompasses a suffering *with*, a solidarity with the other in the pain of the human journey. Pity, for purposes of comparison, emphasizes the differences between the individual being pitied and the one offering the pity. In the first instance, compassion is a spiritual stance that unites; in the second instance, pity is a stance of distance that divides. Compassion can also be seen as a cry for justice: What is the right way to be with others? Social action and advocacy (adding a voice for those whose voices have yet to be heard) are compassionate calls for those in the helping professions on behalf of "quiet" clients.

   Compassion also plays a vital role in forgiveness—the willful process of giving and receiving forgiveness, not just forgetting and not allowing one's life, identity, or interactions to be governed by a past experience. Sperry (2001) described compassionate individuals as those who are socially tolerant, empathic, and helpful; who show unconditional acceptance of others; and who have empathy with others' feelings and a willingness to help others achieve their goals without selfish domination. Compassion—the attention to the potential and actual pain of others—is also manifested in seeking win–win solutions to problems and conflicts while still giving heed to one's own needs in that situation.

7. **Love**   Love can only be experienced rather than defined. Love deepens relationships and expands humanity. Love entails the will to extend oneself to nurture another without an expectation of return, even if that nurturance fosters an eventual departure

by the other (Sperry, 2001, p. 320). The act of loving is based on identification with, and acceptance of, other people. Moreover, its expression is probably the most hopeful indication of how an individual would like to be treated. It may be suggested that love is first an attitude and then an action. To love those who have professed love for one is simple compared with loving those who have not made such a heart-felt declaration, or attempting to act in loving ways to all people regardless of how they respond or act.

8. *Meaning*   The process of developing spiritual meaning in life fosters a sense of emerging peace. In philosophy, theology, and psychology, meaning making is a linking theme (Faiver et al., 2001), a connection among three disciplines. In its barest essence, meaning is the articulation of the sense of what makes life worth living for an individual.

Frankl (1965) suggested that humans possess an innate will to generate meaning and personal meaning cannot be found, borrowed, or explained, but must be individually created. The logical ancillary question to the answer of "yes" to the initial question "Is life worth living?" must be "Why?" A possible answer may be found, not in a cause or for other people, but in terms of the capabilities and potential that one hopes that one has and that may be expressed within those connections and actions. The exploration of meaning with an individual within one event will uncover more personal truths than the iteration of all of that individual's life stories. Until the individual discovers that the path to personal fulfillment rests within his or her capacity to find meaning in any situation, the search will continue unabated, as that meaning exists separate from the person rather than residing within.

9. *Transcendence*   Spirituality, in its ultimate sense, must involve going beyond ordinary or personal limits. Transcendence demands surpassing or exceeding what has been and exemplifies the farther reaches of human development. Within this discovery, the spiritual self must become comfortable with the unknown, but proceed nevertheless in the face of uncertainty. If the process of transcendence is to unfold new elements of the self, then one cannot anticipate what will be found; one can only marvel at the findings.

Perhaps the path to such discovery is rooted in the ability to laugh at oneself—a confirmation of the kind, observing ego; a capacity for play; and a true openness to give oneself over to something greater than oneself. Sperry (2001) spoke to the transcendent using phrases such as feeling a sense of spiritual union, self-forgetfulness, and total absorption and fascination in one thing.

These characteristics can be considered as "ever-developing, trans-cultural themes, universal to human existence" (Faiver et al., 2001, p. 18). From this viewpoint, the challenge is not whether one is in possession of such drives or capacities, but whether one chooses to explore and exercise their pre-existing spiritual potential. The words used, by necessity, are brief, but the declaration of intent is as wide as humankind. However, this is a challenge and a joy for each to undertake in his or her own time and style.

SPIRITUAL MATURITY AND WELL-BEING

The contemplation of spiritual identity and maturity gains credibility for those in the mental health professions if their values or contribution toward psychological functioning and mental health can be substantiated. As a transition to that verification, Worthington, Kurusu,

McCullough, and Sandage (1996) put forth seven salient explanations as to why spiritual maturity is related to psychological well-being:

1. Spirituality provides not only a set of answers to what life is worth living for, but also what it is worth dying for.
2. Spirituality stimulates a sense of optimism and hope in any dire situation.
3. In situations in which one has lost personal control of one's environment, spiritual connection provides a transcendent sense of control to replace the temporal one.
4. Spiritual paths offer a lifestyle that promotes better mental and physical health.
5. Spiritual wisdom offers positive social norms that promote approval, acceptance, and nurturance from others.
6. Spiritual community offers support in times of need and questioning.
7. Spiritual maturity provides the anchor of belief in the transcendent, around which other values are formulated.

INTEGRATION TOWARD A HOLISTIC MODEL OF CLINICAL HEALTH

Given the previous discussion, this section returns, as do the other chapters, to consideration of what meaning or implication such an exploration holds for both clinicians in practice and student-therapists in training. When terms such as *empowerment, actualization, human potential, growth,* and *strength-focused services* are found in the professional literature, there is the implication that mental health service providers see their objectives as including, even exceeding, problem solving. It may be imagined that by stopping at problem solving, clinical intervention ameliorates the current pain, but does little to prevent similar problems from occurring in the future. When the other goals are integrated within the therapeutic process, there seems to be a commitment to assisting clients in taking better charge of their lives in order to prevent the reoccurrence of the same issues that prompted access to services in the first place, and, should a similar issue emerge, clients would then feel more confident and competent to respond more effectively. The debate may then encourage clinicians to integrate the ideas of spiritual identity and maturity within their clinical "growth agendas."

Although the debate between Freud and Jung on the legitimacy of religion in terms of psychological health provides historical insight into their divergences of opinion, the views of Jung seem to be more congruent with the emerging professional integration of spirituality/religion and mental health services. In favor of such integration, Jung remarked,

> Religions are psychotherapeutic systems in the truest sense of the word, and on the grandest scale. They express the whole range of the psychic problem in mighty images; they are the avowal and recognition of the soul, and at the same time the revelation of the soul's nature. (1978, p. 336)
>
> The ideas of the moral order and of God belong to the ineradicable substrate of the human soul. That is why any honest psychology, which is not blinded by garish conceits of enlightenment, must come to terms with these facts. They cannot be explained away or killed with irony. In physics we do without a god-image, but in psychology it is a definite fact that has to be reckoned with, just as we have to reckon with "affect," "instinct," "mother," etc. (1978, p. 339)
>
> A psychoneurosis must be understood, ultimately, as the suffering of a soul which has not discovered its meaning. . . . [T]he cause of suffering is spiritual stagnation, or psychic sterility. (1978, p. 252)

These citations confirm Jung's vision of religion and spirituality as being "fundamental to human experience and psychic evolution" (Zinnbauer & Pargament, 2000, p. 164). Of particular interest in this chapter is the commitment to human evolution. Kelly (1995) directed clinicians to be prepared to explore

> (a) personal client meaning on religious and spiritual dimensions in life, (b) cultural, traditional and institutional context with which meaning is associated, (c) symbolizations in which meaning is dressed, (d) [the] developmental process which has led to this meaning evolution, [and] (e) [the] connections of religious and spiritual areas to other areas of client functioning. (p. 85)

The preponderance of sample respondents in multiple national surveys who identified religious/spiritual practices as key aspects of their definition of the self and coping resources in times of stress or life challenges, plus their preferences that attention to religious and spiritual issues be included in clinical services, confirm the need for clinicians to be prepared to introduce these topics.

Accordingly, as Pargament (1997) directed, clinicians must understand how their personal religious and spiritual beliefs affect the process of providing mental health services. In addition, the knowledge of religious and spiritual evolution that clinicians bring to sessions may serve to support client growth in these areas. However guided mental health professionals claim to be by knowledge, it is now widely recognized that it is their value system that dictates which topics will, and will not, be introduced in sessions.

Zinnbauer and Pargament (2000) spoke in contradiction to the idea of counseling as a value-free undertaking. In fact, they cited multiple studies conducted over 30 years which indicated that clients in fact adopt the values of their counselors. Clinicians' values direct how they see the world, clients, and the process of helping. Values power decisions about therapeutic goals, measures of treatment success, the content of the sessions, what is defined as suffering, and, on a basic level, the decision itself to become a mental health professional (Patterson, 1989). Clinicians are therefore challenged to address their own spiritual identity and maturity, for they can take clients no further along the journey of spiritual growth than they themselves have been able to go. Additionally, or perhaps more basically, mental health professionals are invited to consider their orientation toward the inclusion of spiritual and religious issues in counseling.

In their article in the *Journal of Counseling & Development*, Zinnbauer and Pargament (2000) argued in favor of what they categorized as *constructivist* and *pluralist* clinical stances toward religion and spirituality in counseling. Each outlook will be summarized to assist the reader in clarifying his or her individual stance. The *constructivist* focuses on individuals' ability to generate their own realities, while dismissing the existence of absolute reality. Reality then becomes a function of the experiences, beliefs, and achievements of each person. As applied to religion and spirituality, this stance absolves the clinician of sharing a value system with the client and requires that the clinician accept the client's right to create a reality of choice. It is the quality of that reality which becomes the purview of clinical work. Quality is defined as the coherence, adaptability, and efficacy of that reality in terms of responding to the outside world and other individuals. The advantages of the constructivist stance regarding religion and spirituality in counseling include (a) a more accepting stance on the diversity of religious perspectives that one can expect to find in the general client population, (b) a greater appreciation for client diversity, (c) support for clients' pursuit of individual belief systems, and (d) the empowerment of clients to evaluate the ramifi-cations of their belief systems on their everyday functioning and dysfunction.

The *pluralist* attitude is founded in "the existence of a religious or spiritual absolute re-ality but allows for multiple interpretations and paths toward it" (Zinnbauer & Pargament, 2000, p. 170). This existence is experienced by all people, but is expressed differently in dif-ferent cultures and in different ways.

To cite Pargament (1997), each system holds a different and incomplete slant on the truth. From this orientation, although the clinician is clear about his or her personal beliefs, there is an assumption that the client's belief system and mode of expression must be dis-tinct from that of the clinician, even if both the client and the clinician are affiliated with the same religious institution or denomination, or claim to follow similar spiritual paths. The benefits of such a point of reference include (a) a respectful acknowledgment of the client's chosen religious or spiritual paths and expressions, (b) an admonition that clinicians must be very clear on their own spiritual belief systems, (c) a further admonition that therapists must exhibit true comfort with ambiguity, and (d) empowerment of the client to live through his or her own belief system.

Next, Zinnbauer and Pargament's (2000) two approaches (*rejectionist* and *exclusivist*) will offer similar descriptions, coupled with apprehension regarding the distress that either stance may bring upon the inclusion of religious or spiritual issues in therapeutic services. The *rejectionist*, as the term implies, accounts for religion as a defense mechanism or an indication of psychopathology. The goal, congruent with that value statement, is to confront the defenses and, once defeated, replace religious or spiritual direction with a rational approach to life. There seem to be three serious objections to such a stance among mental health clinicians:

1. Such belief systems interfere with the development of constructive working relation-ships between clinicians and clients, most of whom, according to the data, wish that their religious and spiritual concerns would be included in clinical services.
2. The rejection of all religious practices as inherently psychopathological is not supported by the professional literature.
3. Such a dismissal of religion or spirituality, regardless of the clinician's own practices, is contrary to all current ethical codes of professional conduct on respecting a client's cul-tural diversity.

The *exclusivist* believes in religion, but only in one religion, which must be shared by the client and the mental health services provider. Although the client may present with dif-fering religious or spiritual belief systems, it is the clinician's responsibility to help the client see the "error of his or her ways" and be placed on the only one right track to God. This stance also has its limitations:

1. There seems to be a fundamental absence of clinician flexibility and respect for client epistemology unless such a belief system explicitly matches that held by the clinician. The very idea of empathy presupposes a willingness to see the world through the client's eyes, rather than insist that the client see it through the perspective of the clinician.
2. The potential for a clash of values between the clinician and the client may subvert the creation of any meaningful therapeutic alliance.
3. In instances where the client and the therapist claim to share the same religion, the dis-tinctions between denominations and individual enactments of that faith may be over-looked in light of assumed similarities.

4. Such a stance seems to negate both the efficacy of nonreligious coping strategies and the validity of the coping resources found within the differing wisdom traditions. Such a constricted view would seem to be inconsistent with the professional literature confirming the variability and diversity of effective coping mechanisms from multiple religious and secular orientations.

It would appear to be understandable that stances of *pluralism* or *constructivism* would be the most efficacious, ethical, and preferred stances for therapists who intend to address clients' spiritual issues in clinical services. Both stances, according to Zinnbauer and Pargament (2000), "recognize the validity of searches for significance in ways related to the sacred" (p. 172). Both challenge therapists to identify their own perceptions of mental health/pathology and spiritual health/pathology. The inclusion of these four descriptions (*rejectionist and exclusivist*, and *pluralist and constructivist*) is intended to assist clinicians—those in practice and those in training—to more closely examine their own stances toward spirituality in clinical services. In essence, the clinician's "own consciousness, presence, and inner clarity [serve] as the guiding light for the therapeutic journey" (Corright, 1997, p. 238).

Perhaps Jung (1978) summed up the fundamental role of spiritual maturity when he avowed that "everything to do with religion, everything it is and asserts, touches the human soul so closely that psychology least of all can afford to overlook it" (p. 337).

Case Example Revisited

Sam decided to dedicate a year to exploring several related themes that he had not previously questioned. His first theme involved how "being Jewish" was different in everyday life than being of any other faith. His second theme asked how practicing Orthodox Judaism was different than practicing Conservative or Reform Judaism. His third theme revolved not around behavior, but around belief, and Sam followed his rabbi's advice and initiated counseling with a non-Jewish counselor to begin to explore those existential questions to which he had previously been given the answers found in Orthodox Judaism, but that, as Sam admitted, were answers that he was no longer certain that he wanted to keep. At the time of the completion of this chapter, Sam could not provide a conclusion to his search. He felt that he was "getting somewhere" and he was trying hard to focus solely on the journey of self-exploration, allowing that he would know the end when he felt a sense of solidarity and comfort with his results.

Conclusion

This chapter included spiritual identity and maturity among the *growth goals* common to the human experience and therefore the therapeutic endeavor. The idea of growth entails an understanding of the point of origin, facilitative experiences, and an embryonic template of the desired outcome. This template is hypothesized to be based in one's spiritual/religious values as the conduit through which life decisions are made. In the practice of mental health services, often the specifics of that outcome are yet to be mutually defined by the clinician and the client. This indistinctness of spiritual identity and maturity is one area that requires ongoing clarification. Toward that end, ". . . psychology and religion might form a more collaborative and constructive partnership, each helping to bring out the best in the other" (Thoresen, Oman, & Harris, 2005, p. 221), and, by doing so, they may bring out the best in ourselves and our clients.

Self-Understanding Exercises

1. How do your religious/spiritual views of optimal functioning and your psychological notions of self-actualization intersect? How do they diverge?
2. Define the concept of *virtue* in your religious/spiritual faith and in your everyday life. To what extent do you believe that you lead a virtuous life? How is doing so important for you?
3. If virtue is the path toward heaven, describe what *heaven* means to you. How does one gain entrance to heaven and what happens after one enters?

Opportunities for Further Learning

1. From the perspective of cross-cultural counseling, how do faiths other than your own describe "the good and just life"? How similar are those characteristics to the faith-based tenets by which you live your life? In what ways are they different?
2. Visit the Web site of the Association for Spiritual, Ethical, and Religious Values in Counseling, and explore the topics that interest you. In what ways are these professional discussions echoing your own religious and spiritual searches?
3. Choose one philosopher, one clinical theorist, and one author who are of your faith. Compare and contrast how each one depicts "the good life." What are the similarities? What are the differences?

6

■ ■ ■

Assessment of Spiritual Functioning

CASE EXAMPLE

Kris had recently completed her undergraduate degree in psychology and wanted to earn her master's in mental health counseling on her way to her doctoral degree in counselor education. She was fascinated, on an academic level, by the study of "appraisal" and was amazed by the long and arduous task of creating valid and reliable psychological assessment instruments. She felt that she had been adequately introduced to both standardized and interpretative measures through her undergraduate program and felt confident as she approached her graduate-level course in testing and measurement.

One of the tasks assigned in that course was to create a fictional "client," and then, on the basis of the intake interview, choose and review two psychometric instruments, offering an opinion as to which instrument, if either, would be suitable for use with that specific client. Although many of her classmates chose clients who presented with career issues or depression, and found multiple instruments and reviews for consideration, Kris wanted to explore an area of assessment about which she knew very little. She chose a client who presented to her agency with spiritual concerns, and then she embarked on a mission to learn what she could about the current status of standardized assessment of spiritual and religious issues in counseling.

■ ■ ■

INTRODUCTION

The purpose of this chapter is to acquaint the reader with differing opportunities for counselors to help clients assess their current "spiritual functioning." This statement raises an immediate question: What is meant by *assess?* Harper and Gill (2005) cited the *Oxford English Dictionary Online* as defining *assess* as "determining the importance, size or value of." For the purposes of this chapter, *assessment* means "gaining a better understanding of oneself within a specific aspect of life (Nystul, 2006), determining whether a spiritual orientation is healthy or unhealthy, and ascertaining whether the client's presenting issues are related to spiritual issues" (Richards & Bergin, 1997). This gain in self-understanding can lead to more valid treatment planning and a better choice of therapeutic interventions through a more accurate representation of the client's sense of self in the area of spiritual functioning (Hodge,

2005a). However, treatment planning and intervention must be founded in an accurate picture of "where the client is now," prior to anticipating the client's future. The Association for Spiritual, Ethical and Religious Values in Counseling (ASERVIC) identified this competency on the part of the mental health practitioner as an integral component of effective practice (Miller, 1999). One means through which to foster this insight is the use of standardized tests.

The expansion of testing in society has been phenomenal in the latter half of the 20th century, and the integration of testing and technology has increased the accuracy and decreased the scoring time for testing, quickly providing counselors and clients with more reliable information to assist in all facets of life understanding and decision making (Clark, Madaus, Horn, & Ramos, 2001). However, Hodge (2005b) mentioned a "professional hunger" for more and better information on the availability of assessment options, as supported by Prest, Russel, and D'Souza's (1999) survey of graduate students and Carlson, Kirkpatrick, Hecker, and Killmer's (2002) study of American Association for Marriage and Family Therapy (AAMFT) members. The process of test selection must consider the data on the relative psychometric strengths and limitations of available assessment tools. This data speaks to the validity, reliability, utility, and scoring and norm development of each measure.

The majority of the widely used measures have met some of the criteria of a standardized test (Aiken, 2003), providing reliable and valid assessment of the construct under study. In addition, there are less formal methods of assessment, and this chapter will provide an overview of the multiple choices within each category. The process of test creation must originate with a working definition of a concept or construct. This definition provides the foundation from which questions are formulated, designed, and refined. This process of definition can be pathology based or strength based.

There is currently no model of "spiritual pathology," either in the professional literature or in the *Diagnostic and Statistical Manual of Mental Disorders* (*DSM-IV-TR*; APA, 1995). The *DSM-IV* includes V62.89, Religious or spiritual problem. The text of this diagnostic category reads:

> This category can be used when the focus of clinical attention is a religious or spiritual problem. Examples include distressing experiences that involve loss or questioning of faith, problems associated with conversion to a new faith, or questioning of spiritual values that may not necessarily be related to an organized church or religious institution. (p. 741)

Although this definition and its inclusion exemplify the recognition by the authors of the *DSM-IV* of the importance of spiritual functioning, there is an obvious dearth of information as to how an individual in the throes of such a problem might be different from what he or she was in healthier times. In addition, this brief description has yet to list those criteria through which a trained observer or interviewer could distinguish between individuals who are experiencing a religious or spiritual problem and those who are not.

There also is no agreed-upon definition of spiritual health or the dynamics that make up spiritual functioning. Maslow (1971) stated that the ultimate level of human spirituality encompassed the appreciation of beauty, truth, unity, and the sacred in life. Benner (1991) opined that the degree of spirituality is a function of an individual's awareness of, and striving for, transcendence, surrender, integration, and identity. Cervantes and Ramirez (1992) delineated the quest for meaning and mission in life, the search for harmony and wholeness in the universe, and a belief in an all-loving presence as appropriate spiritual aims. Everts and Agee (1995) offered the following dimensions of spirituality: (a) accuracy, (b) universality, (c) affirmation, (d) a universal life source or divine presence, and (e) an operationalization of transcendence.

The process of assessing personal or psychological qualities is more onerous than it sounds because these traits cannot be directly observed, but instead must be inferred through responses or reports of actions, thoughts, or feelings provided by the client (APA, 2000). Thus, this chapter will adhere strictly to examining those instruments which offer a phenomenological perspective on spiritual functioning.

This approach, which relies on information provided by the client, merits a separate discussion because it seeks to establish the individual as honestly and accurately presenting his or her own experiences. Thus, these instruments provide different ways to ask respondents to comment on their own spiritual identity, growth, obstacles, and so forth. This approach to assessment is in direct contrast to that of observation or diagnosis, where the onus for interpretation of the individual's world rests with a highly trained, supposedly objective professional. Most helping professionals are at least equally interested in the client's sense of his or her own world because that personal understanding, or lack thereof, governs the client's sense of self, of others, and of his or her own self in the world. Therefore, this chapter will present only those measurement tools which ask the client to report on his or her spirituality.

The term *spirituality* is worthy of contemplation. The diversity of the meanings attached to this word reflects its vitality and importance, but also proves to be a challenge in its measurement. The initial step in developing any measure is some statement of what one is actually measuring. In the case of human physical properties, such conditions as weight, temperature, and so forth would seem to be easily measured. However, even in the case of weight, the definition of which seems obvious, there are two viable scales: metric and English measurements. One must be certain as to which scale is being used in order to correctly assess the weight of an object. In the study of nonphysical properties, the issue becomes even more open to interpretation. For example, when we think of the study of intelligence, to which many years of careful research have already been dedicated, we can find differing subscales on differing tests, all purporting to offer a measure of intelligence. If this is the case with such a well-studied concept, how much more complex is the definition of *spirituality* and its component parts, the study of which is in its relative infancy (Richards & Bergin, 1997)?

THE PURPOSE OF STANDARDIZED ASSESSMENT OF SPIRITUALITY

The content of this chapter is based on the assumption that the reader has had at least a graduate-level course in testing or assessment, because a review of the protocols and criteria for effective testing is beyond the scope of this chapter. The information presented for each instrument will discuss the construct, content, criterion and predictive validity, test–retest, parallel or alternative form, and internal consistency analysis of each testing measure, as well as any other relevant literature-based information that may guide the decision as to whether a particular instrument would be a sound choice for use with a specific client or issue. The main reference for this information was the *Buros Mental Measurement Yearbook* series, which provides scholarly test reviews. If a specific test does not appear in *Buros,* this lack of review is not a condemnation of the test, but a reflection of the overwhelming number of tests waiting to be reviewed. However, should such test reviews not be available, there will be distinctly less psychometric data on a specific test. This discrepancy can only be interpreted as a relative lack of current information regarding its psychometric properties, rather than a statement about the weakness of a specific instrument.

OPTIONS IN THE QUANTITATIVE ASSESSMENT OF SPIRITUAL FUNCTIONING

This section will provide the available psychometric data on identified standardized tests. The inclusion of these measures is not intended to be an endorsement of their use, nor is the omission of other measures intended to be a condemnation of the instrument. Rather, the helping professional can best weigh the merits of each instrument relative to the clinical need and the population, and make tentative choices to be presented to the client for discussion.

The Spiritual Assessment Inventory (SAI; Hall & Edwards, 1996)

This measure reflects a Judeo-Christian perspective of spiritual maturity. Forty-three items assesses the awareness and quality of one's relationship with God. With its basis in object relations theory, the construct validity was demonstrated through correlation with the Bell Object Relations Inventory. Although the correlations were acceptable, the relationship with the grandiosity subscale was not acceptable.

The "quality" focus was further specified as instability, grandiosity, awareness, and realistic acceptance. A fifth subscale (defensiveness/disappointment) was added later. Each item is scored on a 5-point scale from "not true of me" to "true of me." All internal consistency measures were good (instability, .88; defensiveness, .91; awareness, .90; and realistic, .76), except for grandiosity (.52). Hall and Edwards also reported acceptable 2-week test–retest reliability (.83–.94) for three of the factors, excluding realistic acceptance and grandiosity.

On the basis of the available data, one can see that this scale is in the developmental stage. The grandiosity subscale needs to be adjusted because its correlations with other measures are inconsistent. In addition, convergent, discriminant, and criterion validity need to be established. Stanard, Sandhu, and Painter (2000) suggested that "in its current form it may be useful as a research tool and to measure client spiritual strengths and weaknesses from a Judeo-Christian perspective" (p. 206).

The Index of Core Spiritual Experiences (INSPIRIT; Kass, Friedman, Leserman, Zutterneister, & Benson, 1991)

This brief instrument (seven items) attempts to measure experiences that convince the respondent of the existence of God and of the perception that God lives within each individual. The first six items offer four different responses for each item, while the seventh question has 13 parts, with the first 12 parts scored on a scale of 1 to 4, from "I have never had this experience" to "This experience convinces me of God's existence." The thirteenth part is an open-ended question in which the respondent may cite other salient experiences.

Internal consistency was established as .90 (Kass et al., 1991). Concurrent validity was established through the correlation of INSPIRIT scores with the Intrinsic scale of the Religious Orientation Inventory. INSPIRIT was also able to discriminate among groups with differing core spiritual experiences. Given the brevity of this test, it could be easily administered. The utility of this measure is limited to those professing a belief in a Higher Power, or God, or for those who are concerned about a lack of such experiences.

The Spiritual Well-Being Scale (SWS; Ellison, 1983)

Stanard, Sandhu, and Painter (2000) described the SWS as "the most researched instrument to date" (p. 207). Ellison (1983), in his definition of *spirituality*, added a fourth need (the need for transcendence) to the core human needs of having, relating, and being. The idea of transcendence involves a commitment to a purpose that is related to the ultimate meaning of life. Ellison based the evolution of the SWS on the 1975 definition of spiritual well-being offered by the National Interfaith Coalition on Aging: "[S]piritual well-being is the affirmation of life in a relationship with God, self, community and environment that nurtures and celebrates wholeness" (Ellison, 1983).

In this instrument, the client rates 20 items, utilizing a 6-point scale (from *strongly agree* to *strongly disagree*). Ten items measure religious well-being (RWB) and 10 items measure existential well-being (EWB); the totals for the two sets of items are summed to provide a measure of overall spiritual well-being (SWB). It was Ellison's intent to avoid specific theological issues or barometers of well-being that might differ among religious belief systems or denominations.

The initial confirmation of content validity was provided by a factor analysis that confirmed the loading of all items on the Religious Well-Being Scale and divided the existential scales into two factors: life direction and life satisfaction. The initial test of internal consistency produced coefficient alphas of .89 (SWB), .87 (RWB), and .78 (EWB). Ellison also confirmed the expected concurrent validity with significant negative correlations ($p < .01$ to $p < .001$) with scores on the UCLA Loneliness Scale and significant positive correlations with scores on the Purpose-in-Life Inventory ($p = .001$ to $p < .001$), the Intrinsic Religious Orientation Scale ($p < .01$ to $p < .001$), and the Extrinsic Religious Orientation Scale ($p < 5$ to $p = .01$).

Ellison also reported multiple studies with men and women, housewives, college students, young adults, senior citizens, high school students, married and single persons, religious and nonreligious persons, and individuals from large and small cities and rural areas. Correlations were also confirmed in the expected positive direction with measures of self-esteem, the quality of the parent–child relationship, family togetherness, and social skills. Stanard, Sandhu, and Painter added test–retest reliability figures of .93 (SWB), .96 (RWB), and .86 (EWB).

A serious concern with the SWS is the possibility of ceiling effects. Ledbetter, Smith, Vosler-Hunter, and Fischer (1991) discovered that the instrument's utility is limited to low SWS scores. They found that the test could not identify high-scoring respondents or discriminate between average and high scores. In summary, the brevity of the test and its easy administration must be weighed against its lack of norms, the ceiling effect, and its application only to a population that professes an acceptance of the concept of God.

The Spiritual Health Inventory (SHI; Veach & Chappel, 1992)

Veach and Chappel acknowledged the work of Ellison (1982) in their conceptualization of spiritual health. They then developed an 18-item instrument that measures four factors that influence spiritual health: (a) personal spiritual experience, (b) spiritual well-being, (c) a sense of harmony, and (d) personal helplessness.

The Personal Spiritual Experience Scale focuses on belief in God and experiences with God, and the experience of a spiritual awakening or spiritual health. The Spiritual Well-Being Scale measures the benefits of an active relationship with a Supreme Being. These purported benefits include a sense of meaning and purpose, acceptance, and internal support. This scale was reported to correlate with an absence of depression, positive psychological health, and general well-being. The Sense of Harmony Scale deals with issues such as optimism and gratitude. The fourth scale, the Personal Helplessness Scale, assesses a lack of self-efficacy. The first three scales have five items each; the fourth scale has three items. Each item has six possible responses, ranging from "strongly agree" to "strongly disagree." The final scale is cited as measuring an inner experience of self-denigration or condemnation; however, this scale's meaning may become better clarified with the addition of more items.

In terms of internal consistency, the Personal Spiritual Experience Scale was found to have a Cronbach's alpha of .90; the Spiritual Well-Being Scale, .85; the Sense of Harmony Scale, .71; and the Personal Helplessness Scale, .49. The first three scales correlated in the expected positive directions with measures of general well-being and negative directions with depression. In further testing, the factors did not generate significant correlations with measures of physical or mental health, leaving one to ponder whether belief itself is sufficient to generate a change in health status (Stanard, Sandhu, & Painter, 2000).

In summary, Veach and Chappel (1992) suggested that there is a relationship between spiritual well-being and psychological health, but insisted that the two are different constructs. Initial validation studies were encouraging with regard to the continued development of this measure. The authors also suggested further scale development and the testing of diverse populations, as well as the testing of persons who have addictions and chronic disorders. This recommendation was echoed by Stanard, Sandhu, and Painter (2000).

The Spirituality Scale (Jagers & Smith, 1996)

A unique feature of this instrument is that it was designed to measure spirituality from an Afrocultural social orientation. The working definition used to generate the original item pool focused on the notion that spirituality is a fundamental organizing principle in African cultures that transcends church affiliation and moves toward a sense of community with one's ancestors (Jagers & Smith, 1996). The eventual 10-item inventory has a 6-point scale ("completely false" to "completely true").

Internal consistency figures on this test yield coefficient alphas of .84 and .87. Test–retest reliability has been reported to be .88. Jagers and Smith utilized constructs such as religious motivation, personal agency, and spiritual well-being in their item construction. The success of this instrument in discriminating between African American and European American respondents lends credence to the aims of the authors. An evaluation of the test also found that women, regardless of ethnicity, scored higher than male respondents— a finding that has yet to be explained. In summary, Stanard, Sandhu, and Painter (2000) described this tool as being valid for the group for whom it was intended, but requiring further validation with older adults.

The Spirituality Assessment Scale (SAS; Howden, 1992)

Howden (1992) reviewed definitions of spirituality found in professional literature from the fields of philosophy, psychology, sociology, theology, and nursing, seeking any common threads in the differing views. From that search, he found four concepts in common: (a) unifying interconnectedness, (b) purpose and meaning in life, (c) innerness or inner resources, and (d) transcendence. The final version of this measurement was culled to 28 positively worded items rated from 1 to 6 ("strongly disagree" to "strongly agree"). The alpha coefficients for the entire survey were found to be .92; for the Purpose and Meaning in Life subscale, .91; Innerness, .79; Interconnectedness, .80; and Transcendence, .71.

Sandard, Sandhu, and Painter (2000) regarded the cross-disciplinary process of construct creation as a strength of the SAS. Its avoidance of any specific religious orientation allows it to be used with a wider variety of individuals. The findings of the factor analysis support Howden's conceptual framework. There may be some concerns about the social desirability or "response set" tendencies of test-takers, given the absence of negatively worded items. In addition, although the initial evaluations are encouraging, they have been conducted solely by the authors, and independent affirmation of the psychometric qualities of the SAS would greatly contribute to its credibility.

The Spirituality Index of Well-Being (SIWB; Frey, Daaleman, & Peyton, 2005)

Among the instruments reviewed, the SIWB was the first to identify a target client population for its assessment: medical patients. This measure was expressly developed to assess "two dimensions of spirituality linked to subjective well-being" (p. 558). Using focus groups of patients, and supported by an exhaustive review of definitions of spirituality in the social and nursing sciences, Frey, Daaleman, and Peyton devised two scales measuring "life scheme" and "self-efficacy," respectively. Life scheme is a cognitive sense of one's world that provides a sense of order and purpose, which lends elements of comprehensibility, management, and meaningfulness to one's life. Self-efficacy is defined as an individual's belief in his or her ability to set a prescribed goal, organize resources toward that aim, and direct efforts to overcome individual problems.

Frey, Daaleman, and Peyton then undertook to establish the validity of these two scales and the total scores by testing 500 older adults and 577 Roman Catholic high school students. Among the older adults, the SIWB scores significantly predicted self-rated good health, whereas age and depression levels did not. Analysis of the data from this group also confirmed a significant correlation with scores from the Religious Well-Being Scale of the SWB. Among school children, moderate correlations were reported between the SIWB scores and the Children's Hope Scale. The SIWB scale and its subscales were also correlated positively with existential well-being, general well-being, spiritual well-being, hope, and quality of life, and significantly negatively correlated with barometers of depression, fear of death, and poor health.

The authors also sought to establish the reliability of the SIWB. Two-week test–retest reliability figures of .79 (full scale), .86 (Life Schema scale), and .86 (Self-Efficacy scale) were found for the older adults. Coefficient alpha estimates of internal reliability ranged from .80 to .92 among the older adults and high school students.

Although Frey, Daaleman, and Peyton feel optimistic about the status and future of the SIWB, they offer three comments regarding its use. First, they are aware that the absence of any religious component may be of concern, but argue that a secular and social constructivist view of spirituality is an emerging force in the process of understanding this dynamic. Second, the use of the tests is limited to the two populations tested so far with the SIWB. Third, the negative wording of the SIWB items may be a concern in terms of allowing a "response set" among test-takers.

The Spiritual Wellness Inventory (SWI; Ingersoll, 2001)

Ingersoll (2001) sought to develop a cross-spiritual model of spiritual wellness through interviews with leaders in 11 different spiritual traditions. The author determined how spiritual wellness would be manifested by a practitioner of each specific tradition and used this information to create an 88-item instrument that measured 10 dimensions of spiritual wellness. This inventory was tested on 515 subjects, and then, on the basis of factor analysis, the inventory was reduced to 55 items, with each construct represented by five items, which included the addition of a scale that offered five items that measured social desirability. Scale items are rated from 1 to 8 ("strongly disagree" to "strongly agree"), with odd-numbered items negatively worded to try to prevent response-set answering. Scores can range from 5 to 40 on each scale.

The SWI presents the 10 dimensions of spiritual wellness as

1. a conception of the Absolute/Divine—the individual's image or experience of divinity;
2. meaning—a sense that life has purpose and is worth living;
3. connectedness—a sense of spiritual belonging with other people, the Divine, or elements in the environment;
4. mystery—a capacity for awe and wonder as one deals with ambiguity, the unexplained, and uncertainty in life;
5. spiritual freedom—a capacity for play, immersing oneself in life, and losing oneself in the moment;
6. experience/ritual—the experience of a proactive practice that promotes present-centeredness, connection with others or the Divine, and the forging of meaning in the face of life's circumstances;
7. forgiveness—one's willingness to give and accept forgiveness;
8. hope—a sense of optimism that allows one to cope with setbacks or misfortune;
9. knowledge/learning—an interest in building the knowledge of one's self and of things perceived as external to the self, which may or may not include academic pursuits; and
10. present-centeredness—a capacity to remain in the moment without worrying about the past or the future.

In terms of interpreting the scoring system, Ingersoll insisted that the scores were a "starting point to discuss spiritual issues" (p. 188). However, revised means are provided for each of the 10 scales, with no mean for the Social Desirability Scale. It is important to note that these means are not subdivided by age, spiritual tradition, cultural background, level of education, and so forth because it would necessitate a much larger sample to determine such group-specific norms. Keeping in mind that the scores range from 5 to 40, it is interesting to note that the norms range from a low of 16 (Spiritual Freedom) to a high of 22 (Mystery), so if they are seen as a true norm, we do not know yet how normally distributed the scores may be or whether the determination of a standard deviation and error of measurement would clarify differing areas of spiritual functioning.

Lacking any external reviews of the SWI, a potential test adopter may be impressed with the construct and content validity of the instrument. The next stage in its evolution would be the confirmation of the instrument's reliability and other forms of validity. Ingersoll may wish to wrestle with the dilemma of whether the SWI was intended as only a qualitative measure of spiritual functioning or whether its standardization would be a more efficacious future development.

In summary, the diversity of the working definitions of spirituality and the relative lack of psychometric data for this category of standardized testing must be noted, especially when compared with other categories of tests, such as measures of intelligence or depression. However, this shortcoming may reflect the relative newness of measures of spiritual wellness, which are awaiting confirmation of psychometric strength. Although perhaps of use to practicing clinicians, care must be taken to attend to the unique definitions and aspects of each scale to ensure congruence with clients' definitions of aspects of spirituality and the interpretation of the results to ensure adherence to the protocols of test interpretation.

OPTIONS IN THE QUALITATIVE ASSESSMENT OF SPIRITUAL FUNCTIONING

One of the distinguishing features among the previously reviewed assessment tools and those to be presented in this section is the philosophy behind their design. In theory, quantitative tools seek to ascertain how much of a certain quality or characteristic is present as reported by the test-taker. Usually, this score can be compared with that of a normative sample to determine one's relative level of functioning. Assuming that everyone must have some of every human characteristic and that there may be a cutoff score that denotes too much of a trait or a point at which its presence interferes in a significant manner in everyday tasks and growth, this approach underlies the process of assessment and diagnosis. Although still less of a science than diagnosticians would like us to believe because of the lack of a diverse normative group, plus the "convenient" application of cutoff scores without regard to multiple contributing factors, this approach to assessment predominates current practice. However, by assuming a qualitative approach, one is less concerned about scores and comparison, and more concerned about the depth of understanding, both of one's past and of the impact of one's past on current functioning. Seeking to establish themes and patterns, rather than categorizations, this model may help counselors guide their clients' spiritual exploration free from the concern of identification of pathology.

To acquaint helping professionals with the current choice of assessment instruments, Hodge (2005b) summarized five options:

1. *Spiritual History*   A spiritual history is the verbal narrative of a client that presents their spiritual journey from childhood to the present (Hodge, 2005a). This tale is related in response to three leading questions:

   a. "Describe the religious/spiritual tradition in which you grew up. How did your family express its spiritual beliefs? How important was spirituality to your family? Extended family?

   b. What sort of personal experiences (practices) stand out to you during your years at home? What made these experiences noteworthy? How have they informed your later life?

   c. How have you changed or matured from these experiences? How would you describe your current spiritual or religious orientation? Is spirituality currently a personal strength? If so, how?" (p. 345).

Hodge (2005b) recommended the identification of six themes in the narrative, citing Nee's (1968) anthropological understanding of spirituality as comprising the following elements:

   • *Affect,* aspects of one's spiritual life that bring pleasure, support, a means of coping, and hope;

   • *Behavior,* rituals and practices, involvement in church, or the role of supportive individuals;

   • *Cognition,* current belief systems, their personal meaning, their utility in overcoming life's challenges, and their impact on health practices;

- *Communion,* the relationship with the Divine, the impact of this relationship, and its helpfulness in facing life's obstacles;
- *Conscience,* values, the presence of guilt in one's life, and the role of forgiveness; and
- *Intuition,* the experience of creative insights or premonitions in one's life and their contributing strengths.

In terms of assessing the use of the spiritual history, Hodge (2005a) stated the four strengths of this assessment: (a) an appeal to verbally oriented persons, (b) an unstructured format that allows for freer expression, (c) ease of conduct, and (d) conduciveness to building a therapeutic relationship with the client. Hodge also offered some cautions in its use. First, not all clients are verbally oriented, and those who may be nervous about sharing such intimate details may be better served by a diagrammatic approach that allows a focus on the diagram rather than the self. Second, some clients may prefer a structured format around which to organize their thoughts and presentation. Finally, some clients may require immediate symptom relief—an immediate goal that is incongruent with the aim of the spiritual history.

2. *Spiritual Lifemap* Hodge (2005b) referred to the spiritual lifemap as a "diagrammatic alternative to verbally based spiritual histories" (p. 344). Drawn from similar interventions that traced career paths or educational experiences, the client's spiritual life is depicted on a lifeline. The client is provided with a large piece of paper, collage materials, crayons, glue sticks, and so forth in order to allow free expression of the meaningful spiritual experiences in his or her life. With their spiritual lives depicted on a single lifeline, clients are offered great freedom of creative expression, and family members can lay their individual lifelines alongside each other to illustrate common themes and/or individual growth. This exercise would appeal to those who are visual learners and those who have a sense of artistic expression.

One of the strengths of the lifemap is that it is client-centered (Hodge, 2005a). With little specification of life events beforehand, clients are free to designate salient and trivial life occurrences and events. Hodge claimed that participation in such an exercise alleviates the helping professional from creating a specific direction, allowing the client to lead and the counselor to follow. The lifemap also provides a unique opportunity for the counselor to remain in the questioning mode, with the client serving as the "expert" on his or her personal spiritual experiences. For very sensitive clients, this exercise offers a subtle shifting of attention from the individual to what appears on the paper, reducing the emotionality and potential explosiveness of the situation. Finally, given the client-directed focus of the lifemap, the project could be assigned as an out-of-session task, reserving in-session time for other tasks, but also extending therapy into a homework assignment.

Hodge also offered three cautions about the use of the lifemap. First, the attention paid by the client to the drawing process may result in his or her feeling alienated from the exercise and uncertain about how to proceed. Second, obviously, not all clients are comfortable with drawing, as a means of either expression or learning. Finally, given the individual nature of a lifemap, clients may seek or need a broader perspective of their spiritual journey, either between individuals in a relationship or over a lifetime.

3. *Spiritual Genogram* Frame (2000) discussed the evolution of the genogram exercise beyond a strictly Bowenian orientation. The genogram is described as a "blueprint of multiple generations of a family" (p. 211). Including family structure, relationships,

and nodal events, the genogram's utility lies in its illustration of the transmission of patterns and themes across generations. It is intended to place current functioning within the historical context of the spirituality of the unique family system in which one was reared (Hodge, 2005b).

Frame offered concise guidelines that will assist the helping professional in the creation of such a genogram (see 2000, pp. 212–213). The creation of the genogram is only the information-presentation stage of counseling. The next step revolves around "information processing" as clients discover the link between their presenting clinical issues and spiritual beliefs, practices, and orientations. The genogram may reveal spiritually meaningful events and how the events might have transformed the faith of the individual. It is also possible to denote the strength and direction of spiritual relationships within the genogram. For example, the shading of a line may indicate the level of commitment or dedication, while the direction of an arrow may illustrate whether the relationship was equal or more hierarchical, demanding obedience or sacrifice. The genogram also provides the vehicle for reconnection with one's family of origin around spiritual issues, especially in cases of emotional detachment around such issues. Frame (2000) described one benefit of this process as ". . . clients often develop a greater objectivity and appreciation for the ways in which they have been shaped (consciously or not) by the role of religion and spirituality in their families" (p. 214).

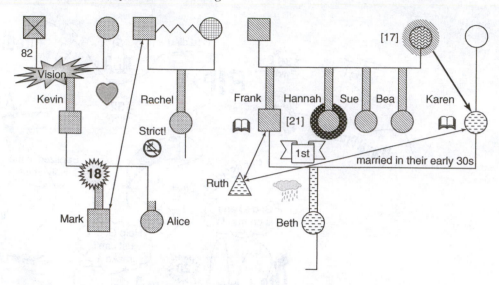

Hodge (2005a) indicated the client populations that were most likely to benefit from the spiritual genogram exercise: (a) clients with whom the family system is a salient aspect of life, (b) clients with a respect for tradition and the extended family, (c) clients who prefer a very structured exercise, and (d) clients who need to compare the similarities and differences in their spiritual journeys with those of spouses or significant others. In terms of the limitations of spiritual genograms, Hodge (2005a) saw the exercise as time consuming, as demanding skillful explanation and interpretation by the practitioner, and as inappropriate for clients who do not connect past spiritual events with current life difficulties.

4. *Spiritual Ecomap* Hodge distinguished between the genogram and the ecomap by emphasizing history with the former and current existential spiritual relationships with the latter. Designed to emphasize current relationships with "spiritual assets" (2005b, p. 347), the family unit is represented by a circle in the middle of a piece of paper surrounded by significant spiritual systems or domains. Hodge suggested that domains such as God, transcendence, rituals, faith communities, and transpersonal encounters are common among faith traditions and could be represented on all ecomaps. One's relationship with God may be seen as a core support, as well as a possible comfort by way of rituals or practices. Faith communities may include, but are not limited to, churches, mosques, synagogues, fellowship groups, weekly Bible study groups, youth groups, and so forth. Transpersonal encounters include the individual's experiences with demons, angels, and other spiritual visitors. The main point of the ecomap is for the client(s) to identify areas of strength and support, and conflict or estrangement as related to the presenting clinical issue(s).

Hodge (2005a) offered the following as the strengths of the ecomap exercise: (a) easy to grasp conceptually, (b) quick to construct, and (c) focuses on clients' current spiritual strengths. The ecomap may also defuse some of the emotionality of the session by allowing the client to focus on the environmental system rather than the client's story. Once again, the ecomap may be less advisable for highly verbal clients and those who are uncomfortable with drawing. In such cases, there is the risk that the drawing

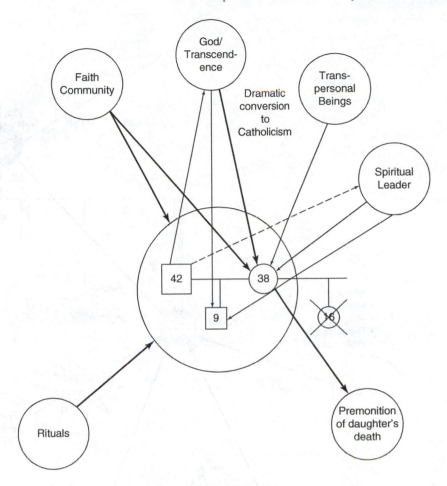

process itself may prove to be more anxiety provoking for the client than the story that the exercise is intended to tell. In addition, this assessment may overlook important historical factors.

5. *Spiritual Ecogram*   Hodge (2005b) suggested that the ecogram provides a bridge between the genogram and the ecomap. Intended to integrate the past and the present into a single visualization, the ecogram "depict[s] the connection between past and present with historical influences" (p. 348). With the current client(s) placed in the center of the drawing, the family-of-origin influences are indicated at the top, with the current spiritual systems or domains indicated at the bottom.

In the figure shown next, the family history is also viewed within the context of a spiritual system. Lines can be drawn that depict the relationship between the family of origin and the current spiritual systems, indicating connections that were once present but are now disrupted, as well as new practices that are unique to the individual in the present but perhaps were absent from his or her early experiences.

One strength of the ecogram is that it encompasses historical and present functioning in one diagram. For cultures in which the past is vital to the present, such a connec-

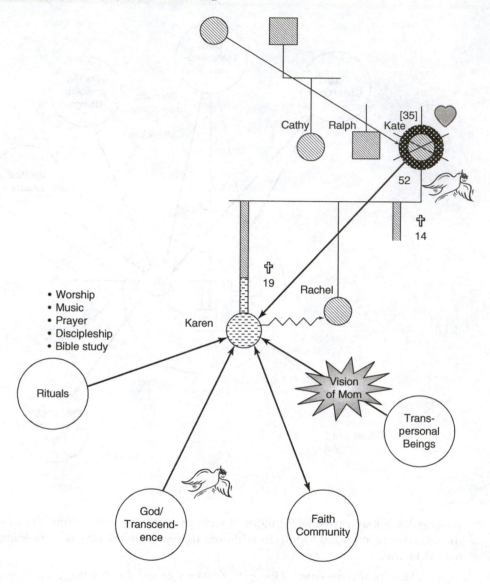

tion may be therapeutic. However, its complexity may be a turnoff to some clients and some helpers.

Hodge (2005b) offered the following considerations for selecting an assessment procedure:

1. How insightful is the client? If the client is more invested in immediate problem solving, this type of exploration may seem tangential.
2. In terms of time orientation, is the client more focused on the past or the present? This preference would be of assistance in deciding on a suitable style of exploration.
3. How can the exercise be explained as being relevant to the client's presenting issue(s)?

Harper and Gill (2005, p. 40) indicated the relative strengths and limitations of the quantitative measure and the qualitative exploration tool in the following table:

	Benefits	**Limitations**
Quantitative Assessment	• Quantifiable results • Comparable results • Preset coverage of themes • Time efficient	• Focus limited by the instrument • Predetermined terminology • Search for deficits
Qualitative Assessment	• Flexible terminology • Flexible exploration • Focus on strengths • Assessment can be an intervention	• Focus limited by the assessor and the client • Not quantifiable • Limited comparability • Time intensive

Both of these assessment modalities imply that a client is interested in some exploration of spirituality, whether seen as part of the presenting problem or as a possible aspect of the solution. In such cases, the exploration process is conjoint and is seen as being mutually beneficial. However, in adhering to the ethical principles of client welfare, a counselor may be required to conduct an assessment of spiritual practices that may be of harm to the client, such as membership in a cult. In these cases, the knowledgeable counselor may utilize the following description of unhealthy spirituality as a way to help a client understand the potentially harmful characteristics of the spiritual community in which he and she is involved.

ASSESSING PATHOLOGY IN SPIRITUAL FUNCTIONING

What is Unhealthy Spirituality?

Although there is no one cogent definition of spiritual pathology, there has been robust discussion of unhealthy spiritual practices. However, it is probably best to define unhealthy spirituality by first describing the elements of healthy spirituality and then recognizing that the absence of these elements indicates the presence of spiritual pathology.

From my perspective, one of the barometers of healthy spirituality is a series of beliefs and practices that enrich the individual and the group to which that individual has chosen to belong. Within this framework, I wish to clarify what I mean by *enrich:* Enrichment of the individual is the process of growth that assists one in developing a deeper awareness of one's spiritual self, one's relationship with the Divine if that is a component of the belief system, and one's relationship with others of like faith; the individual enriches the group by voluntarily contributing time, energy, and perhaps financial resources, given willingly and open to renegotiation as the circumstances of the individual change.

I have purposely omitted within this definition of healthy spirituality the role of a powerful leader because I see this presence as perhaps being the least vital component of a healthy spiritual existence. If a leader does exist, I would view that role as being one of guidance and direction for the spiritual group, where the leader adds specialized knowledge and skills, but remains in a subservient position to both the healthy growth of the congregation and the tenets to which the congregants choose to adhere.

The final aspect of this definition that I believe needs elaboration is that of "choosing to belong." A healthy spiritual group welcomes members and welcomes their transcendence from the group. Members are free to come and go, each according to need, with the absolute absence of malice or coercion to remain or emotional sanctions for thinking of departing. Within the group process, as little pressure as possible exists for conformity or blind obedience to any authority other than one's spiritual growth.

Although this is by no means intended as a complete definition of "healthy" spirituality, I believe that its utility will become clear on comparison with the discussion of cults and their characteristics. Cults can be described as being characterized by "unhealthy spiritual group practices."

What Is a Cult?

Richmond (2004) defined a cult as a group "whose worship practices, adoration and beliefs are outside the doctrines and dogmas of mainstream religions" (p. 368). Cults have seven general characteristics in common (Frame, 2003; Robinson, Frye, & Bradley, 1997):

1. Cults are organized around one core leader to whom all matters are referred. This leader claims some special knowledge that will be imparted only to "true" cult members who, by virtue of their membership in the cult, are "special" or "chosen" apart from the majority of society.
2. Cult leaders proclaim their own divinity.
3. Cult members are expected to conform to all group norms. The leader has the right to intimately scrutinize all aspects of the everyday lives of the members to ensure that there is total conformity to group standards. These aspects may include appearance, financial matters, food practices, child-rearing, and so forth.
4. Cult members share beliefs, experiences, and practices. All members must conform and all members must demonstrate unwavering allegiance to the group identity.
5. Many members live in communal societies. The formation of a strong boundary between the members and people outside of the group furthers the process of indoctrination into one style of thinking and increases the bonds of group cohesion.
6. Many cults demand that members renounce the outside world as evil, corrupt, or inferior to the group's belief system. Such renunciation serves to strengthen the purity of the cult and to support a single-minded focus on the cult's goals.
7. Many cults utilize persuasion and thought control to control members (Gesey, 1993). Applying techniques such as the threat of physical harm for leaving, spiritual isolation for questioning belief systems, and isolation from family members all serve to bind fearful members to the group and the leader.

Berk (2001) and Erikson (1994) spoke to the connection between identity formation and culture, and vulnerability to recruitment into a cult, specifying that those who are struggling with the former are more susceptible to the latter. Accordingly, most cult members are between 18 and 25 years of age—a time when issues of identity and acceptance may prove to be developmentally challenging. Parker (1985) also related cult involvement to a stage of faith development during which individuals may break from the faith traditions of their families, but then may feel lost and uncertain about where they belong. Being assured of a place of welcome, with a ready set of beliefs that will set one apart (confirming one's specialness), and being assured of a strong leader who has ready-made answers to life's challenges will drawn in such individuals. Cults are also attractive to those in search of a cause (Richmond, 2004), especially a cause with a strong leader, often a role model, who offers rescue from uncertainty.

Sirkin (1990) specified five stages in the process of attracting new cult members:

1. *Hooking* is the introduction given by a cult member to a potential recruit with the specific agenda of creating a relationship in which the potential recruit feels singled out and valued.
2. *Joining* is the involvement of the recruit in the group philosophy and practices. Often meetings are scripted to recognize the new recruit and increase that sense of "special welcome."
3. *Intensification* is the polarization of a world view. In this process, cult beliefs and activities are seen as good and all noncult activities (including former relationships, lifestyles, etc.) are seen as evil or corrupt.
4. *Social disengagement* is the isolation of the recruit from the familiar social systems that will be replaced with the closed system of the cult.
5. *Realignment* is the development of a new sense of identity founded solely on cult membership.

In summary, it is intended that this brief description of cults accurately portrays their functioning and, more importantly, the ways in which cults are different from practices of "healthy spirituality." The objective of its inclusion in this chapter is to serve as a blueprint for assessing the relative healthfulness of a spiritual group to which a helping professional may be introduced.

Case Example Revisited

Kris had originally believed that her task would be an easy, albeit interesting, one. How hard could it be to measure something that everyone seemed to possess? She was astounded at the number of differing definitions of spirituality that generated such diverse assessment tools. She realized that she would have to exercise great care and demonstrate a clear understanding of psychometric principles in order to evaluate each measure. Although she completed the course assignment, she felt awakened to what she saw to be an emerging area of study and began to seriously consider following this line of intellectual inquiry into her doctoral studies program.

Conclusion

In 2000, Stanard, Sandhu, and Painter recognized the formative status of assessment in spirituality. They reported on the tendency for assessment instruments to be based either on a Judeo-Christian perspective or on the assumption that a belief in God limits their utility. In addition, as of the date of their review, there was a general absence of normative data for the instruments that they reviewed.

The review in this chapter adds little psychometric data, but does offer a qualitative assessment piece that may be considered by helping profes-sionals. Coverage of this topic generated an obligation to offer what currently is available in the professional literature in order to foster informed decision making among helping professionals. Clinicians may also elect not to use any of the measures. However, creating an awareness of these options was the sole purpose of this chapter. It must be remembered that the confirmation of the efficacy of any measure lies in its use, so perhaps the byword is still merely one of caution.

It is also important to recognize the complexity of defining a construct as vast and multifaceted as spirituality and the rigor to which one must adhere to devise and establish worthwhile assessment tools. However, perhaps the most optimistic view would place this endeavor merely at one stage of evolution—off to a good start and striving to provide refinement and status in order to join the other credible measures of human functioning, dynamics, and interactions.

Self-Understanding Exercises

1. What might you hope to learn by completing a spiritual assessment instrument? Predict how you might score on its constructs prior to taking the test. How closely did your actual score match your prediction? What might any discrepancy tell you about the quality of the measure?

2. What is your definition of spiritual pathology? What is your definition of spiritual health?

3. How might participation in a spiritual assessment exercise be harmful to a client?

Opportunities for Further Learning

1. Speak to helping professionals who conduct "spiritual counseling." Ask them which standardized measure(s) they use and why. According to these professionals, what are the benefits of using such an assessment in the counseling process?

2. Speak to your clergy or spiritual advisor about the idea of spiritual assessment. What does he or she think of such an endeavor?

3. Monitor the listings and reviews in the *Buros Mental Measurement Yearbook* to see if more recent test reviews are presented. How does a review of this new data influence your choice of assessment options?

7

Guilt and Mental Health

The consequences of our crimes long survive their commission, and like the ghosts of the murdered, forever haunt the steps of the malefactor.

—Sir Walter Scott

CASE EXAMPLE

Ted chose to become a school counselor because of his experiences as a classroom teacher of elementary school children. He felt limited in his role as a teacher because of the need to focus on the curriculum at the expense of the emotional needs of the children. He felt strongly that children could not adequately learn when they were distracted by unresolved emotional challenges and disruptive outside forces such as family problems.

He also drew on his experiences as a Sunday School teacher, reflecting on children's concepts of right and wrong, and the enormous burden that they carry when they misbehave despite knowing that what they are doing is wrong. Ted became fascinated by the development of conscience among young children and their experience of guilt.

INTRODUCTION

This chapter begins with a bold assertion: Addressing guilt is the principle mission of both the helping professions and the spiritual traditions. Both of these areas hold multiple views on guilt in common. First, from both perspectives, there is an assumption that human frailty and lack of constant self-monitoring, and perhaps lack of self-control, may result in an individual failing to live up to the standards of conduct set by the individual or by others. Failing in this way may invoke an emotional response (feelings of remorse, shame, regret, or guilt) as a function of the behavior, whether or not anyone else witnesses it. This assumption presupposes that the individual is aware of these codes of conduct (Van Kleef, De Drue, & Manstead, 2006) and of how either the omission or commission of a specific behavior is in contradiction to these tenets. The assumption also demands that the individual either be willing to self-evaluate or be open to the evaluation of his or her behavior by significant others (Faiver, O'Brien, & Ingersoll, 2000).

Second, both the helping professions and the spiritual traditions recognize the individual's obligation to society and the need for the individual to take personal responsibility for his or her actions. It is central to the thesis of this work that the presence of a Divine or Supreme Being be considered both an internal force and an external force.

Finally, there is a common view of the need for the individual to make restitution for any harm that he or she has caused to others through his or her conduct or misconduct.

CONGRUENCE IN SPIRITUAL AND CLINICAL PERSPECTIVES ON GUILT

Whether one confesses to a member of the clergy, directly to a divine source, or to one's counselor, one is developing a conscience. From a religious perspective, this conscience will encourage adherence to the moral precepts and congruent behaviors of the specific doctrine. From a clinical perspective, conscience is the moral imperative that guides an individual in balancing personal desires with societal and relational obligations. The ultimate goal, from both perspectives, is for this code of conduct to transcend the legal and spiritual demands of appropriate conduct, which emphasize the cessation or control of negative behaviors. Instead, what is advocated is an aspirational model of conduct, which Bennett (2005) referred to as a "ripening into maturity" (p. 38).

The difference between the religious and the legal perspectives, on the one hand, and the clinical perspective, on the other, is that the former rely on the fear of punishment as the control mechanism, whereas the latter relies on personal integrity to be the guide. For example, both religious doctrine and legal statute forbid stealing. One considers this action a sin; the other deems it a crime. Both systems demand acknowledgment of one's guilt and both demand repentance. A religious doctrine might impose a series of prayers or good works to atone for this misdeed. The legal system might impose a sentence of incarceration and perhaps monetary restitution. However, the development of a conscience would demand that one not commit the act, less out of fear of being caught and punished and more out of a personal recognition of one's social obligation to respect the property of other people.

A similar case could be made for running a stop sign. Is one hesitant to do so out of the fear of being caught by a policeman lurking in a patrol car, or does one's social contract with other drivers and a voluntary adherence to driving protocol bring one to a complete stop? This distinction is important because the former process relies on constant external vigilance of each individual by the forces of social control, with the attendant notion that if one is not caught, one is not guilty. The second type of aspirational ethics delegates the task of self-monitoring to the individual, with the responsibility for judgment resting solely on each person. In both instances, the emergence of guilt follows the transgression, be that action in opposition to social, legal, or religious codes of conduct, along with the accompanying notion of how to respond to this guilt.

In summary, it has been suggested that "guilt is the state in which religion and psychology meet" (Faiver et al., 2001, p. 76) and that morality is the province of both disciplines because both religion and psychology are fascinated by why some people seem to sin with impunity and some people refuse to do so regardless of the impossibility of being identified or regardless of the circumstances.

MORAL EMOTIONS AND GUILT

Kroll and Egan (2004) noted the emergence of the study of "moral emotions" (p. 352) among helping professionals. Including guilt, shame, regret, and remorse, these emotions are labeled as "moral" because they are said to carry the power to motivate an individual either to take action or to refrain from taking action as a function of one's moral compass and because they foster a sense of self-awareness about one's role in relevant events. This moral code and the resulting behaviors are important factors in the definition of an individual's character.

Bush (2005) considered guilt to be "an exemplar of a pro-social emotion" (p. 46) on the basis of (a) its foundation in an empathic understanding of the suffering of another and the feeling of responsibility for being the agent of that distress and (b) its inhibition of aggression and its promotion of behaviors designed to reestablish communal connections. Therefore, to feel guilty for harming another is a positive response because such a reaction would confront the actor with the results of the action and demand some behavior to acknowledge the pain of the other to restore a balance of trust and kindness in their relationship.

This notion of balance in relationships is an important consideration because its presence acknowledges the concept of relational ethics that is usually founded in mutual trust and respect, and which may be damaged or threatened by the types of behaviors that might facilitate feelings of guilt among one member of the relationship. For example, if one failed to honor a commitment to join a friend for dinner and did not call the friend, then the friend might begin to question the motives or honesty of the other person. In that case, the friend might be hesitant to commit to future plans until a satisfactory explanation was offered. It would be hoped that the simple act of not honoring this social commitment would motivate the offending party to offer such an explanation and perhaps an apology as a function of the individual's guilt over his or her conduct in this situation.

Guilt can also be seen as a function of culture. Since its basis rests on the norms and values that provide the foundation and characteristics of a culture, it can be surmised that guilt is an expression of "culturally transmitted beliefs about personal relationships, social expectations and moral values" (Albertsen et al., 2006, p. 69). For example, in many cultures and religious doctrines, age is to be venerated and one's parents and other elders are to be respected. Although it is not in any legal code, this tenet would dictate the types of behaviors that would be acceptable from the younger members toward their elders. These expectations would also define those behaviors which would be deemed disrespectful, with the resulting expectation of guilt and then apology. However, certain practices, such as polygamy, may be consistent with one's religious doctrine yet contravene legal statute, leaving the individual trapped between cultural norms and society's expectations.

It is important to recognize that modern-day individuals belong to many cultures, so there is the potential for multiple conflicts in values and social expectations. For example, one's university peers may use alcohol on Saturday night, but one's church may preach against its harmful effects on Sunday morning. Wanting to be accepted by both the peer culture and the religious community, the individual feels guilty no matter what behavior he or she chooses.

Smith (1988) also asserted that guilt is a function of indeterminism. By *indeterminism,* Smith was referring to free will and the responsibility that comes with the freedom to choose one's actions. Once an individual acknowledges that he or she *could* have behaved differently, this notion assumes that the person *should* have acted differently. This insight is based on a willingness and an ability to be aware of oneself. Although such a perspective is an aspect of developmental achievements in cognitive and moral reasoning, it is also an indication of an awareness of the impact of one's actions on another and the harm inflicted. In addition, guilt may reflect the violation of a personal moral code. These two explanations for the emergence of guilty feelings are best seen as integrated because such a view then may lead to the two related tasks of atonement to others and forgiveness of the self. The path toward this redemption may be prescribed by religious practice or jointly developed through the counseling process.

A further examination of guilt across cultures hypothesizes that individuals from collectivistic cultures (such as Asian Americans or Latin Americans) would be more susceptible to guilt than individuals from individualistic cultures, such as European Americans. Studies in this area could not support this hypothesis, but they did explain the absence of a difference as being a function of the growing cultural homogeneity of the world.

Another issue with regard to this cultural perspective may be the question whether religiosity and guilt are related. Albertsen et al. (2006) referred to the meta-analysis conducted by Gartner, Larson, and Allen (1991), who reviewed more than 200 studies and found that low levels of religiosity are predictive of impulse-control disorders, drug and alcohol use, suicide, and anti-social behavior, while elevated levels of religiosity are predictive of disorders of overcontrol, such as excessive guilt.

Few studies have been conducted that compare samples across religious traditions to see how membership in one tradition or another may have a significant effect on guilt. Albertson et al (2006) discovered three relevant studies from which the following results were summarized. One 1964 study of Midwestern Americans found higher levels of guilt among Protestants and Roman Catholics, compared with guilt in a Jewish population. A study in 2000 found that Dutch Roman Catholics reported higher levels of guilt than did Calvinists or people who did not belong to a church. A third study in 2002 found higher levels of guilt among Roman Catholics and Lutherans than among Episcopalians and Buddhists in the United States. This background research, as a foundation for the study by Albertsen et al. (2006), implies that culture may play a role in the development, expression, and level of guilt in individuals, and the authors urged clinicians to consider these factors in their work.

GUILT AND SHAME

It is important to distinguish guilt from shame (Faiver et al., 2001). Guilt is seen to result from a particular act or transgression (Pineles, Street, & Koenen, 2006). Guilt can be construed as a reactive attitude (Tollefsen, 2005), an emotion that arises only in reaction to behaviors and their consequences. Moreover, guilt is a function of the "quasi-evaluative stance of holding someone to a demand" (p. 225) or a specific standard of conduct (Ashby et al., 1997). The behavior in question is evaluated negatively and often results in feelings of tension, remorse, and/or regret, and a desire to make reparations or to atone for the behavior.

Shame is seen as a broader, or even total, condemnation of the self (Tangey & Fischer, 1995). Although one specific behavior may instigate feelings of shame, that behavior is viewed as being indicative of a "bad self" (Pineles, Street, & Koenen, 2006, p. 689), which prompts feelings of worthlessness, humiliation, and disgrace, as well as a belief in public disapproval and a desire to hide or disappear. Ashby et al. (1997) summarized the five feelings states of shame as "(1) shame, feeling inferior; (2) embarrassment, feeling undone and uncomfortably visible; (3) humiliation, feeling forced into a debased position; (4) self-consciousness, feeling constantly aware of [the] self-in-action; and (5) guilt, feeling [that] one has violated a standard"

(p. 59). Ashby et al. (1997) differentiated between guilt and shame by stating, "for guilt the antidote is forgiveness; shame tends to seek the healing response of acceptance—acceptance of the self despite its weaknesses, defects and failures" (p. 580).

One action might foster both guilt and shame, in which case the individual's response might indicate how self-accepting or self-condemning he or she may be. For example, if one were to break a lamp, the individual might inform the owner about the mishap. He or she would feel guilty and attempt to make restitution to the owner by apologizing and by offering to replace the item. The individual might feel bad about embarrassing him- or herself in this way and might vow to take greater care in the future. However, were that individual to then describe him- or herself as "always thoughtless" or "purposefully destructive," such adjectives would reflect a degree of self-evaluation that was inappropriate to the situation. Furthermore, in the first scenario, once restitution was agreed on and made, the issue would be closed. In the second scenario, these self-descriptions would be held by the individual until they were disputed. This accumulation of negative self-evaluation holds the potential for such adjectives to become imbedded into one's sense of self and character-definition.

Schmader and Lickel (2006) conceptualized the disparity between guilt and shame as being differentially predictive of the approach or avoidance behaviors. Guilt is seen as an approach behavior, with the intent of remedying the harm caused by the guilt-producing event. These authors see feelings of guilt as motivating acknowledgment of the action, both to the self and to others, with the intent of owning up to one's actions and remedying their consequences.

Shame, on the other hand, is seen as avoidance, with the intent of "insulat[ing] oneself from [the] negative evaluation" (p. 44). Thus, feelings of shame may provoke exactly the opposite response from concealment and may spur the individual on to lie about what happened in order to avoid any responsibility.

These tendencies have been extrapolated to situations in which the individual is a member of a group but holds no individual responsibility for the group's conduct. Thus, as a function of social relationships, individuals might feel guilt or shame for the actions of other group members or might feel that the actions of one member could tarnish the reputation or status of the group as a whole. In their study, Schmader and Lickel found a clear distinction between guilt (I am sorry for what I did) and shame (I am sorry for who I am) with regard to collective behavior, but they found less of a distinction if the actions were self-caused.

In summary, the authors suggest that an individual might conclude, "If I am ashamed of who I am, I probably also feel guilty about what I do. However, I can feel ashamed of the actions of others without necessarily feeling guilty or responsible for their behaviors" (p. 54).

Moreover, guilt can be categorized as "one of the emotions [that is] related to appeasement" (Van Kleef, De Dreu, & Manstead, 2006, p. 124). These authors distinguish between mood and affect, with the former described as being situation-specific, of high intensity and short duration, intentional, and focused on a specific person or event and the latter described as being more of a character trait exhibited throughout different contexts and situations but still consistent in that individual. Guilt is closely linked to regret, self-reproach, repentance, and remorse and tends to provoke behaviors that lessen the damage caused by an action. Guilt tends to prompt behaviors that are aimed at repairing relationships and subsequent helping and cooperation. Guilt also tends to foster a need to apologize and make amends.

Models that explain learned helplessness and hopelessness indicate that individuals who are shame-prone offer internal, stable, and global attributions for negative experiences. When such events are experienced, these individuals are more likely to blame themselves (internal attribution), to see the cause as being consistent over time (stable attribution), and to generalize the situation across contexts (global attribution). For example, were a shame-prone individual to lose another person's possession, he or she might condemn him- or herself as being clumsy, thoughtless, or inconsiderate and then apply those adjectives to him- or herself in all situations and consider such a view of the self as unalterable. It is as though one is cursed by clumsiness and this hex can never be exorcised. In comparison, guilt-prone individuals apply more specific and unstable attributions. In the same example, a guilt-prone person would feel remorse about the loss and perhaps about the impact that the loss might have on the relationship with the owner of the possession, but would view him- or herself as having been irresponsible in that situation only. Kroll and Egan (2004) distinguished between guilty fear, which they described not as guilt, but rather as a fear of being detected at wrongdoing, and true guilt, which they saw as being a more honest struggle with self-derstanding and acceptance.

Shame and guilt also differ with regard to concealment. Shame-prone persons sense the "critical gaze of another," whether that "other [is] an observing parent, a peer group or an internalized super-ego" (Kroll & Egan, 2004, p. 353). This idea would also apply to one's relationship with God, a Supreme Being, or a divine force as a function of how one conceptualized that relationship. If the relationship is seen as being characterized by an expectation of imposed obedience to strict God-given laws with the presence of sanctions for transgressions, one might be very cautious about admitting one's own wrongdoings, however slight. On the other hand, if the relationship between the worshipper and the worshipped is characterized by an acceptance that failure is a natural part of experimenting with growth and change in life, and this lapse is seen as an opportunity to better understand oneself and to grow beyond this conduct, then there may be more openness toward acknowledging one's mistakes.

In response to the first type of relationship, either with the divine or with other authority figures, shame-prone individuals tend to hide or to avoid exposure to others. This tendency may manifest itself in a withholding of personally distressing information from others, which may result in increased physical and psychological symptomology on the part of the withholder (Pineles et al., 2006). Lack of disclosure has been found to be significantly predictive of poor physical and psychological functioning. In contrast, disclosure has been found to be predictive of increased psychological well-being, better reported health, and increased physiological functioning and general functioning in studies cited by Pineles et al. (2006). These researchers found similar results in their study of female undergraduate students.

Sensitivity to guilt is also seen as being a stable trait (Albertsen, O'Connor, & Berry, 2006). In fact, the notion of shame-free guilt—guilt separated from critical self-judgment—is adaptive and not linked to pathology. Such guilt results from a belief that one has hurt or might hurt another and fosters empathy for the aggrieved, leading to either reparation or a conscious intent to avoid harming others in the future.

With regard to the notions of collective guilt and collective shame, Forrest (2006) asked, How am I responsible for the actions of a group to which I belong, which committed actions in which I did not individually participate? One possible explanation may answer the question of responsibility and is based on the assumption that the group does not hold social deviance as its central norm or reason for being. For example, gang mores may include actions that are illegal and force members to choose between referent groups—either the gang itself or society as a whole. In this case, if one's primary allegiance is to the gang, one can act in illegal ways and yet experience no feelings of guilt, shame, or remorse. In such cases, one may take pride in what others deem as shameful acts and exhibit no signs of guilt in deference to group ideals. However, in other cases, where a group does not advocate deviance from the overarching social norms, each aware individual is caught in a conflict of values. To which does one owe a greater allegiance, one's code of moral conduct or the group's mores (should these two orientations be in conflict)?

With either decision, there is a sense of loss and disappointment. Also, there is the risk of censure by the group for choosing individual norms or the risk of individual self-rebuke for choosing group norms. For example, with regard to the Vietnam war, how did an American citizen reconcile seeing him- or herself as a patriot, yet still oppose the war? Or, perhaps even more deeply felt, how does a soldier come to terms with fighting in a war that he or she personally feels is immoral or illegal?

Forrest raises the issue of appropriate shame for choosing to belong to communities that foster or condone wrongdoing or whose past actions are presently judged as atrocious (Tollefsen, 2006). Although guilt may be an inappropriate response unless one was the actual transgressor, shame would be appropriate with regard to one's choice of community because of the impact of the community's actions. For example, with regard to the issue of the rights of Native Americans and the demand by African Americans for reparations, to what extent is the majority culture in the 21st century responsible for the actions of the majority culture 200 years ago? Tollefson (2006) claimed that

> the capacity for collective emotions, specifically collective guilt, further justifies our practice of holding groups morally responsible. If groups are subject to guilt feelings (via their members) then they are capable of engaging in the self-assessment that is characteristic of beings whose actions give rise to reactive attitudes. (p. 223)

One challenging question that arises from the issue of collective guilt is whether leaving a group to enact its agenda of wrongdoing—taking into consideration present and future victims—causes an individual to feel more guilt than that felt for deciding to remain in a group (Tollefsen, 2006) and not being able to divert the group's intent to do harm (Kroll & Egan, 2004). For example, were one to work for a company whose products caused harm to consumers and whose own research confirmed that fact, how does one reconcile the desire to resign in protest, knowing that one's departure will in no way affect company practices, with the desire to stay with the company in order to try to change the company's practices, knowing that one may fail and, if the information in question is released, one's reputation will suffer along with that of the company? Forrest advocates conscious awareness of this dilemma as we consider our affiliations.

GUILT FROM SPIRITUAL PERSPECTIVES

This initial exploration of guilt will be based on the Judeo-Christian perspective. The Old Testament sees guilt as a collective response to practices such as the worship of idols or interfaith marriages. Public confession was viewed as the appropriate response to such conduct, and guilt was seen as motivating self-correction. It is with the New Testament that individual guilt appears. From this perspective, awareness of sin leads to a responsibility for one's conduct with an attendant expectation that guilt comprises varying amounts of remorse. There are frequent reminders of a "heavenly accounting" of one's transgressions, with the implication that even if we try to ignore our misdeeds on earth, we will be held accountable in heaven. This message implies the unseen presence of a "watcher" who notices not only the misdeed, but also whether the transgressor acknowledges and sufficiently atones for the misdeed, or whether he or she is equally guilty of the sin of pride, as manifested in an unwillingness to admit one's wrongdoing and take appropriate corrective measures with regard to the harmed party, one's God, and one's future conduct.

The New Testament also offers clearer standards against which to measure one's behavior. Narramore's (1974b) translation of three Greek words found in biblical translations—*hupodikos, opheilo,* and *enoches*—described guilt as "a specifically social condition, where one is liable to judgment, guilty of an offense, or indebted to someone" (Faiver et al., 2001, p. 80). The New Testament authors spoke to the positive ramifications of guilt acting as motivation to redeem oneself. In the most positive light, guilt prompts an individual to feel an appropriate loss of self-esteem, a need to atone or make amends, and a desire for forgiveness. Should an individual act on these feelings, the individual feels a sense of relief and freedom (Donnelly, 1993). However, should such actions not be taken, the accumulated guilt about the misdeed and the lack of attention to its resolution results in self-punishment and is expressed somatically, emotionally, behaviorally, and even in the language of dreams. In such cases, the unresolved issues of the individual's past interfere with the addressing of the guilt-inducing experience in the present, making future atonement and relief impossible.

McNish (2004), however, claimed that shame is central to Christ's message and that shame is a natural byproduct of the human experience. She disputed previous definitions of guilt and shame by describing shame as the more positive of the two emotions. McNish claimed that it is shame which provokes the introspection necessary for changing the self. It is the experiencing of shame that fosters human growth, interrelatedness, and the creative life force. She asserted that guilt is more outwardly focused, demanding righteousness, lawfulness, and stagnation within the societal rules.

Bynum (1994) referred to a desire for forgiveness in response to guilt as a universal dynamic. Tracing the Sacrament of Reconciliation to the Second Epistle to the Corinthians, authored by Clement of Rome, Bynum held that formal confession was conceived as a second method of repentance for those who sinned after the initial sacrament of baptism. Eventually, the clergy took full control of this ritual, which then emerged as the modern practice of confession. As a causal factor of the Reformation, this cycle of sin and atonement, especially on behalf of the Church, galled some churchmen, who decried this selling of indulgences, which supposedly wiped clean a slate of behavior, only to permit or encourage the repetition of the acts.

In summary, the role of guilt in Western religion seems to be a byproduct of a failure to heed the laws of God. Whether or not those laws are internalized into an individual's moral code may be overlooked in favor of obedience. However, Eastern practices such as Buddhism and Taoism seem to advocate an internal barometer of what is appropriate conduct on the basis of universal humanism. Guilt is simply a byproduct of ignoring human nature, which would lead one in positive ways if not for the artificial rule of social institutions. These institutions, such as churches and governments, exist not for the betterment of their constituents, as they claim, but rather to maintain and enhance the power, status, and repute of the institution.

From this Eastern viewpoint, breaking these laws in favor of following one's nature or "the Way" is the true path to fulfillment. Guilt is a byproduct of abandoning "the Way" in favor of adherence to these artificial and socially created mores. This mistake is easily remedied by turning one's back on such conventions in favor of one's nature. Within this literature, *integrity* often denotes this aspirational path, not in terms of a point of comparison of which one may fall short, but as an unshakeable belief in the human power of growth.

This topic recently formed the thesis of a sermon delivered to a Unitarian Universalist congregation:

"Religion and Guilt: The Unholy Alliance"
A Sermon by the Rev. Dr. Patrick T. O'Neill
Delivered on Sunday, October 15, 2006,
at the Unitarian Fellowship of West Chester, Pennsylvania

. . . This morning I wish to share some thoughts with you about a topic which we religious liberals are often accused of soft-soaping or ignoring completely— namely, the troublesome, seemingly universal condition of human guilt.

The fact is, like it or not, for better or worse, in Western Civilization for thousands of years now, religion and guilt have been powerfully associated in a kind of unholy alliance. So ancient is this association, so ingrained is this linkage of religion and guilt in our culture that we have almost come to take it for granted that the two necessarily go hand-in-hand.

One result is that something basically beautiful and noble in human nature— namely, the religious impulse, the search for meaning, the inclination to give praise and celebration for life—has been somewhat sullied and tainted, if not terribly distorted. Many of us in the liberal church tradition are almost embarrassed to call ourselves religious in some circles, because frankly, a lot of us feel that religion has a bad name.

Religion, of course, has itself largely to thank for this negative image, and the preachers of religion (who for centuries have used the power of this unholy alliance as part of their stock-in-trade) have themselves largely to thank for their poor standing with the public. Of course, philosophy and psychology have been taking well-aimed potshots at organized religion for centuries. Particularly in the nineteenth and twentieth centuries, critics from Karl Marx to James Joyce have had a fieldday feasting on the misdirected emphases of overzealous religionists.

Marxist critique called Western religion an "opiate" that keeps the unwashed masses politically in line. Freud labeled it "infantile projection" that sets up unrealistic and unhealthy expectations for [the] surcease of sorrows in this life and the promise of eternal bliss in the next. Religion, as it has been preached and practiced in Western Culture for upwards of two millennia, has oftentimes trafficked in the most vulnerable human insecurity and superstition, darkening the dreams of children with visions of an angry God; reinforcing in the human psyche a sense of basic inherent unworthiness, a sense of sinful libido; [and] underlining more than anything else an abiding sense of unremitting guilt and shame.

It is this negative starting point—emphasizing and dwelling upon human guilt and shame—that has determined the negative course that much of Western religion—which is to say, [the] Judeo-Christian religion—has taken for itself.

Given all the good things that we know healthy religion has to offer the human community—given the "Good News" of religion's power to lead us to discover what is Godly in our lives, to inspire lives of Godly character and goodly service, genuine inspiration to works of art and works of charity—how did it ever come to be, what happened along the way in the dark, turning corridors of history, that this noble notion of religion is now seen so negatively by so many?

It is my thought that, however well-intentioned such a theology might be, a religion that begins with a negative view of human nature is bound from the beginning for a negative fate. For built into the premise of such [a] religion, a priori, is a concept of humanity as being inherently sinful, ignoble, and unworthy; a humanity in need of "salvation" from its own nature.

It is the starting point of all such theology, its focus on human fallibility and the feelings of guilt and shame that accompany that fallibility, that ultimately allows religion to be manipulated and twisted into a force that separates and divides people rather than uniting them. It is the starting point of such [a] religion that is key, for "[a]s the twig is bent, so grows the branch."

I make bold to suggest this morning that religion need not be "shame-based" or "guilt-based" at all, in spite of what the street corner prophets and television pulpit-pounders may wish us to believe. In fact, this has been the positive claim of [the] Unitarian Universalist tradition since the early days of the Reformation, and this may well be the principle distinction between those who hold religion as a joyful and creative expression of the human soul versus those whose religion is born, driven, and ultimately defined by [a] constant appeal to human fear and inadequacy.

I further suggest that it is a gross misreading and misappropriation of Judeo-Christian tradition itself to leave it captive and unchallenged in the hands of fundamentalist misanthropes who see every human fallibility as evil and sinful, who take the joy out of religion, and who constantly seek to separate the world into obscene definitions of the "saved" versus the "unsaved." . . . .

When religion fails to distinguish between appropriate and inappropriate feelings of guilt and shame, I can't help but feel that such preaching is a great disservice to those whom religion ought to uplift and comfort and encourage. And yet, this is precisely how religion is so often preached and packaged and sold.

It doesn't take a close reading of church history to see that the greatest salespeople of Western religion down through the centuries (like Paul, and Augustine, Aquinas, Luther, [and] Calvin) were successful for the same reasons that all great salespeople succeed: First, they had a great product, and second, they knew their market; they understood human nature.

They understood the basic truth that human beings are hungry for wholeness, and we often fall short of the mark. They understood that most people at one time or another experience the shattered quality of human existence; that most of us do indeed experience appropriate and proportional feelings of guilt or shame for things we should not have done; or for being less than honest or charitable or virtuous in our dealings with others. And yes, sometimes we do harbor that sneaking suspicion that we are "not good enough" ourselves.

Long before Freud and Jung and the modern articulation of psychology, these salesmen of Western religion recognized the basic human struggle for wholeness, for completion, for fulfillment. But these feelings should not, do not define us as human beings; they are simply part of being human.

Nevertheless, they knew, these ecclesiastic salespeople, that human existence is buffeted and subject every day to the sheer centrifugal force of daily living. Our daily struggle—to imbue our lives with a sense of unity and meaning, to keep love alive, to keep our relationships intact, to find work that is meaningful, to build a society that is just and honest and compassionate—our daily struggle to hold it all together, to keep the pieces from flying apart, sometimes takes all the energy we've got.

And the truth is that even the most accomplished life is a hopelessly flawed construction, riddled with imperfections and compromises, not because we are sinners, but because we are human and fallible and mortal. We are, alas, imperfect creatures, and we know it.

And the great salespeople and preachers of religion have always known it, too. The shattered quality of human life, the "not good enough" sense that comes with it all, the sense of existential guilt; that is simply part of being human.

Good salespeople, of course, always look for the "hook," the grabber that will solidify their hold on the customer and help to close the deal. And when it comes to religion, there's no doubt about it, there is no more effective hook than that sense of shame and guilt—just plain universal existential guilt that is inherent in all human beings—we've all got it, it matters not how smart we are, how bright, how educated, how sophisticated we think we are—we can be hooked in a minute by the shiny appeal to our brokenness and by the bright promise of deliverance from the trials and tribulations of this wounded sinful world. By their hook shall you know them!

We find ourselves living now in a time of increasingly strident pressures coming from fundamentalist religions of every stripe in the world. Principles dear to liberal religion are being challenged and tested strenuously in our time, but it is a challenge we should welcome, for it is a challenge we are well equipped to meet.

The witness and mission of liberal religion (and here I use the term as opposed to fundamentalist religion) remains what it has always been—we seek the liberation of the human spirit, as the words of the hymn say it, from "the bonds of narrow thought and lifeless creed." And we stand willing to testify for a religious approach grounded in possibility rather than in pathology; our starting place is the exaltation of the human spirit, rather than its denigration; and with the poet we reject a divinity whose love must be bought by an infant's fear or by a sinner's guilt.

This is what Unitarian Universalism holds. Religion without appeal to shame and guilt; rather a religion that announces life as an Original Blessing calling for praise and thanksgiving, not Original Sin calling for penance and punishment. Religion as the search for wholeness and meaning in community, for a way of living that offers value and hope and vision to the world. A religion that takes seriously the ancient prescription of Micah that first and last we must love justice, do kindness, and walk humbly with God as we discover God in the midst of life. A religion as basic as Faith and Hope and Charity, as profound as the Sermon on the Mount, as open as the Prayer of Serenity.

We do not require people to be "born again." We take them as they were born the first time, in all their imperfection, and we make appeal to what is highest and deepest in each one of us. And we say that the unholy alliance of religion with guilt is a distortion of the true end of religion.

In summary, it seems that guilt plays a part in all spiritual traditions. These traditions may differ in terms of the importance placed on the role of the deity, the power of the human race to transcend itself, and the process of recognition and forgiveness; however, it can be stressed that the presence or emergence of guilt serves as a reminder of the need for self-correction.

GUILT FROM CLINICAL PERSPECTIVES

The study of guilt also appears in the clinical literature. Helping professionals wonder about its impact and its etiology because feelings of guilt are an issue for many clients and they interfere with the attainment of mental health. Faiver et al. (2000, p. 156) utilized Wilber's (1997) definition of mental health as "a state of balance that allows one to grow while maintaining contact with consensual reality." Guilt either maintains or loosens this connection, depending on the type of guilt and the intensity of the feeling. Moreover, guilt can be seen as "a function of the trade-offs and conflicts in life that bear upon the resolution or exacerbation of mental illness" (Kroll & Egan, 2004, p. 354).

Freud originally saw guilt as stemming from a negotiation of incestuous desires. This stance was later modified to focus more on the activation of an internalized superego in response to personal violations of social injunctions that may or may not be rooted in religious doctrine or directives. Narramore (1974) agreed with this basic psychodynamic perspective on guilt and expanded the view of the superego into three aspects: (a) the ideal self, (b) the corrective self, and (c) the punitive self.

The ideal self contains our standards, values, and aspirations. Although the ideal self functions as a barometer of comparison between our actions and our intent, the origin of these standards is less important than the notion that the individual has freely chosen to adopt them. It is this freedom of choice that is seen as promoting ownership of, and responsibility for, one's actions.

In such cases, it is the individual, not an external judge, who determines the appropriateness of a specific behavior. This is a vital distinction because of the potential for the concealment of an action. If an individual assumes the task of self-evaluation, then his or her behavior can truly be concealed. Even if the individual does not acknowledge the behavior, the memory of the act will weigh on one's conscience. However, if one's guilt is dependent on an evaluation by another person, then it is easier to rationalize the correctness of an act on the basis of its not having been sanctioned by this other person. The fact that one concealed the behavior seems to be absent from this equation, and the individual states that "If it was really bad, he (or she) would have told me" or "No one stopped me, so it must be OK."

In general, these standards may comprise individual personality traits and childhood schemas that may integrate religious themes or experiences. According to this model of guilt, every socializing institution (family, school, and church) provides distinct guidelines on appropriate behavior and appropriate responses should one contravene these guidelines. What seems to make a crucial difference in the amount of guilt experienced is the mechanism by which children are taught to adhere to the codes. If developing a moral code or a code of behavior is presented as a medium of growth, exhibiting one's potential as a person and fostering healthy experimentation in life situations, then guilt may be proportional to the severity of the deviance from that code, but anchored to that one specific act. The guilt is then seen as episodic, from which the individual can learn and mature, rather than as a negative comment on the individual's moral fiber. If the teaching process utilizes fear and shame as motivating forces, then it can be expected that the experienced guilt will be disproportional to the activating event. The more intensely these behaviors were imposed and adopted on the basis of fear, the greater is the potential for the individual to contrive methods and rationalizations for subverting them.

The corrective self and the punitive self serve as measures of self-revisal, albeit through distinctly different processes. The corrective self seems to be more understanding of our tendency to make mistakes either through lack of awareness of the self or lack of anticipation of the outcome of our actions. Therefore, the corrective self provides a "healthy guilt" by allowing the comparison between the action and desired behavior to become a learning experience through which the individual understands the error of the behavior and commits him- or herself to improvement.

In comparison, the punitive self, which is seen as the root of "unhealthy guilt," reawakens all of the internalized messages of punishment, rejection, and shame. These messages may be too extreme for the situation and too condemning of the individual given the error of judgment or action; however, their impact is felt nevertheless. In such instances, there may be a tendency to try to hide the offending action, which then compounds the level of guilt. The guilt is experienced for both the initial behavior and then the attempt to conceal it. The longer the attempt to conceal the initial behavior, and perhaps the more deceptions and lies needed to maintain that concealment, the greater the guilt becomes.

Reared in the Lutheran faith as the son of a Lutheran pastor, Jung argued that confession is a vital part of growth for the psyche, which, in its development toward self-awareness, also develops the capacity for harboring secrets. The need to harbor such secrets produces additional guilt, adding the weight of secrecy to the weight of the consequence of the initial action. The longer the time span between the initial action and the resolution, the greater is the tendency for the weight of the guilt to multiply.

Jung states that acceptance is a precursor to change. The individual must accept responsibility for the initial action that is at the root of all the guilt; however, that task can be accomplished only by working with a trained professional whose nonjudgmental attitude models self-acceptance for the client. Given that the client is being overly harsh in his or her self-condemnation, additional condemnation by others (parents, clergy, authority figures, friends, etc.) would generate even greater amounts of guilt, until the individual might bemoan ever being able to extricate him- or herself. However, facing the guilt of the initial action with a nonjudgmental individual allows the individual to become less secretive and more self-accepting (Jung, 1958; Rogers, 1957). It is also this relationship between the counselor and the client that allows the client to face those "demons of the past" that interfere with present-day acceptance of appropriate guilt and its resolution.

Bennett (2005) spoke of his personal journey toward maturity by relating tales of his youth in which he experimented with the internalized standards of his family and conventional existence. He related a sense of both curiosity at transcending these codes and a painful awareness of a "lack of mooring" (p. 39). He wrote, "[G]uilt belongs to our experiences of deviation, to the sense of being off, failing, being unable to relate or connect, recognizing a separation and an alienation from God, community and oneself" (p. 39).

Bennett referred to the "call of guilt" as the voice of our unrealized values. He described this experience as "the painful side of innocence, that sense of deficiency, a not-yetness that might as well be nothingness" (p. 39). He cited Michael Gleven as stating that this reality confronts us with ". . . the means to see one's own existence as that at which one can fail or be inadequate, and that this failure is one's own." It is within this awareness that we experience the birth of conscience to respond to the pain of guilt. It is this voice which activates the "innermost possibilities of our being" (p. 40) and challenges us to become responsible for the fulfillment of our potential. Seen as a call to action to individually confront our instincts, cowardice, egotism, and violence, guilt introduces us to the conscious willingness to become, toward a maturation of the self and the spirit in which one can heed the call of desire, temptation, conscience, and the will of the divine.

In contrast, Bennett bemoaned the current fascination with advanced rationality, which allows us to attribute any emotional arousal to irrationality, and the attitude that being affectively driven is in some way a less mature way of responding. He stated that this belief is grounded in the "assumption that the human soul is best guided by rationality" (p. 42). He labeled Freud's superego as "the representation of all the critical and brutal moral, social and religious authorities that one has encountered" (p. 42) and considered natural guilt to be a "bad" feeling that one must either medicate, rationalize, or deny rather than benefit from. According to Bennett, it is this tendency that cheats us of the inner silence where there is time and space to confront our own limitations and deliver ourselves to something beyond ourselves.

From an existential perspective, guilt is a natural byproduct of (a) forfeiting our potential, (b) never fully knowing others because of our limitations with regard to connecting on such levels, and (c) separating from nature (Yalom, 1980). These challenges exist within the banality of our life choices. Each individual is challenged to make, and then make peace with, personal life choices. We cannot be good at everything, nor can we endlessly experiment at life. We must, at some point, choose a career, a lifestyle, a relational framework (a spouse, children, etc.), and a place to live, and in doing so, we relinquish the desire to choose otherwise, or else we sabotage our chance at satisfaction in life. Yalom also bemoaned our tendency to know others solely through their roles (husband and wife, mother and father, teacher and student, etc.), and even if we could transcend those roles, there is insufficient time in our lives to truly come into deep psychological contact with many people. Yalom acknowledged that we have lost contact with nature, be that human nature or the nature of the outdoors. We may try to control nature (for example, we air condition our homes), but we seem to have entered into a battle with nature rather than living in accord with it.

Frankl (1967) ascribed guilt to "man's fallibility" (p. 29), which is inherent in the human condition. As a function of mortality and the time-limited nature of life, guilt is a byproduct of our brief time on earth and our imperfections as a people. However, Frankl warned that the avoidance of guilt is indicative of the inability to comprehend the message in the suffering of the moment and of the human condition. It is not the suffering that must define one's life, but rather the message gleaned from one's experiences within that suffering that links all people and offers a sense of meaning in life.

Ellis (1980) described guilt as a destructive and unnecessary result of religion. This type of guilt is a function of excessive, unrealistic, or irrational worry about others and the belief that others know what is best, however unrealistic those standards may be. One common irrational belief is that being awarded something good means that someone else did not receive that "prize" and that the winner is directly responsible for the other person's loss. Another belief might be that outperforming others will do harm to them. In that vein, the outcome is that the individual abrogates both developmental and personal goals for the welfare of others. This maladaptive interpersonal guilt has been found to be predictive of somatization, obsessive-compulsive symptoms, interpersonal sensitivity, depression, anxiety, hostility, phobic anxiety, paranoid ideation, psychosis, addiction, pessimism, low self-esteem, jealousy, introversion, and neuroticism (Albertsen et al., 2006). Although maladaptive interpersonal guilt is linked to shame, it has been established that such guilt has an even greater predictive power for psychopathology. (Faiver et al., 2001).

In a more positive light, the emergence of guilt can also be seen as being indicative of "perspective-taking" (Konstam, Chernoff, & Deveney, 2001, p. 26), which is viewed as an integral component of close relationships and the potential to adapt one's actions in light of their impact. Building on the work of Tangey (1991), these authors viewed guilt as being a reflection of empathic awareness and a response to the distress of another person. In addition, there is an awareness of having been either the cause of or a contributor to that distress. Although shame-prone individuals react defensively when faced with their actions, guilt-prone individuals seem to develop better coping strategies for making restitution for their actions. However, Konstam, Chernoff, and Deveney made a distinction between "adaptive guilt" and "maladaptive guilt" by describing the former as a reflection of an appropriate acceptance of responsibility for the outcome of one's actions and the latter as a reflection of grandiose notions of responsibility for others (2001, p. 34). These authors also suggested a further exploration of gender differences with regard to guilt-inducing events and criteria. They based this recommendation on a review of the professional literature on the recognition of the emotional needs of others in relationships.

ABNORMAL GUILT AND PSYCHOPATHOLOGY

The identification of guilt does not, by itself, constitute a formal diagnostic category. However, guilt seems to figure prominently in many diagnostic categories of mental illness. For example, neurotic guilt is described as growth-retarding because of its link to "emotional baggage" (a function of the oversocialized superego) and may appear in major depressive disorder and post-traumatic stress disorders (Kroll & Egan, 2004; Pineles, Street, & Koenen, 2006).

The issue of neurotic guilt confronts both mental health professionals and clients with the question "How good must I be to be an acceptable person?" followed by "To what extent do my mistakes define me, encourage greater growth, or consign me to a life of regret and worry?" The last question revolves around the process of releasing past guilt and then forgiving oneself for carrying that guilt for so long a time. However, in their literature review, Pineles et al (2006) found that a tendency to be prone to shame is more predictive of pathology (psychological distress, anxiety, depression, and post-traumatic stress disorder than a tendency to be prone to guilt. In addition, they cited a 2004 study which found that being prone to shame was responsible for elevations in pre-inflammatory cytokine activity, an immunological effect that is potentially detrimental to physical health.

Ashby et al. (1997) found that guilt was related to poor self-esteem, addictive behavior, and perfectionism. These authors saw the need for perfectionism as an inappropriate coping strategy to try to offset feelings of low self-esteem. There seems to be a notion that good deeds can compensate for poor feelings about oneself.

Faiver et al. (2001) saw guilt as being a function of the emotional distress of supposedly irresolvable or unatonable actions, and they saw addictive behaviors as being a maladaptive coping strategy. This finding also provides an insight into the escalating pattern of addictive behaviors. Over time, more and more of the behavior is needed to mask the effects of the guilt. However, the increased reliance on the addictive behavior may, in itself, become a source of guilt. If this is the case, then the pattern of increased guilt and increased reliance on the masking behavior becomes a continual cycle, moving the individual further and further from mental health.

Bush (2005) spoke to the negative impact of unconscious guilt, especially among children. Bush suggested that irresolvable guilt results in its repression or defense. Common defenses include (a) denying responsibility; (b) blaming, or avoiding, the victim; (c) engaging in self-destructive behaviors; (d) developing an exaggerated sense of entitlement; or (e) self-sacrificing behaviors. In addition, unrelieved guilt may be dangerous in its need to incur punishment and therefore makes the sufferer susceptible to exploitation by others who can promise such relief.

Bush cited the control–mastery theory as an explanation of childhood guilt. This guilt is founded in the child's empathy and concern for family members. The maladaptive guilt stems from the child's mistaken belief that he or she is responsible for the happiness and misfortune of family members. This mistaken belief is a function of the young child's view of his or her place in the world, which is based on egocentrism, omnipotence, and magical thinking.

Children often make erroneous connections between their actions and any harm that befalls them or others. So they believe either that something they have done has caused the pain that their parents feel or that they have failed in their duty to make their parents happy and proud of them. On the basis of this false sense of importance, children cannot conceive of other factors that might affect their parents. Given that they see their parents as central in their lives, they naturally assume that they, as children, are the central focus of their parents' lives. Since they are central to their parents' lives, anything that affects their parents must originate with them. The developmental process that takes children from this central position to one that is more suitable is hindered by parents who, on the basis of their own pathology, blame their misfortune on their children.

Keks and D'Souza (2003) spoke to the role of guilt in the emergence and maintenance of psychosis. Described as a delusional state, psychosis can be linked to maladaptive guilt. The belief that one is being punished for an imagined transgression may contribute to the onset of psychosis.

These authors cautioned clinicians about the role that religious belief may play in the imposition of unrealistic expectations on the self or the imposition of an impossibly strict moral code. In addition, the authors warned about the perceived exclusion that a psychotic client may fear from one's religious community. Convinced of one's unatonable evil, a psychotic individual may feel unworthy of seeking support from his or her religious group and further suffer the pain of isolation and alienation.

Kroll and Egan (2004) cited the absence of remorse as a contributing factor to antisocial personality disorder and as a marker for narcissism. Antisocial personality disorder (also referred to as psychopathy, sociopathy, or dissocial personality disorder) describes individuals who "frequently lack empathy and tend to be callous, cynical and contemptuous of the feelings, rights and sufferings of others" (APA, 2000, p. 703). These individuals tend to be exploitative in their relationships with others, caring little for the needs of others in their lives.

Similarly, individuals with narcissistic personality disorder tend to "have a lack of empathy and have difficulty recognizing the desires, subjective experiences and feelings of others" (APA, 2000, p. 715). These individuals see the world as existing to meet their needs, and they feel that they are so important that the needs of others are a secondary concern. In addition, such individuals combine a sense of personal entitlement with a lack of interpersonal sensitivity, which together may result in the exploitation of others.

In both of these diagnostic categories, it seems evident that too little guilt plays a large role in personal and interpersonal dysfunction. There would seem to be an established curvilinear relationship between guilt and mental health. Excessive guilt would seem to be debilitating and insufficient guilt would seem to be delusional.

Case Example Revisited

Ted began to grasp the complexity of the development of morality from psychosocial and spiritual perspectives. Furthermore, he came to appreciate the redemptive potential of admitting guilt and the emotional dangers of hiding guilt. His study of the issue helped him to balance what he described as "healthy" and "unhealthy" guilt. Finally, Ted came to two vital conclusions that were significant to his growth as a school counselor. First, he became aware of the complexity of guilt, an emotion that he had previously decried as being a "simple emotion." Second, as a counselor-in-training, he began to value the interaction of the differing facets of his own life and belief systems toward his integrated identity as a school counselor.

Conclusion

Guilt would appear to be a natural byproduct of an examined life. The message of this chapter may revolve round two central questions. First, do we live in our guilt, learn from our guilt, or try to avoid our guilt? Second, to what extent do our spiritual traditions and practices contribute to our guilty feelings and to what extent are our spiritual practices and traditions a source of healing and acceptance through our guilt? Both questions are the province of counseling and of spiritual exploration, and in the integrated answers to each question, we might find, and help our clients find, the acceptance of who we are and a desire to fully experience who we might become.

Self-Understanding Exercises

1. Describe the lessons that you learned about guilt in your childhood. From whom did you learn about guilt and with what consequences?
2. Where do you see yourself in the development of a personal moral imperative?
3. To what extent is your punitive self unique to you, and to what extent is it an offshoot of a common punitive self from your family or spiritual tradition?

Opportunities for Further Learning

1. Interview clergy from differing denominations about their views on guilt, and conduct similar interviews with practicing helping professionals. How do their perspectives differ? How are they the same?
2. Compare two treatises on guilt from Eastern and Western theological perspectives, and ascertain how these differing traditions overlap and diverge. Which perspective is closer to your own?
3. Identify any spiritual or religious faith traditions that are "guilt free." If such do not exist, what does that discovery reveal about the shared human experience?

8

Evil and Counseling

Whence evil—if there be a God?

—Epicurus (c. 300 BCE)

CASE EXAMPLE

Alden was a pastoral counselor who was conducting group counseling for the Victim Assistance Program in his city. Part of his approach to working with both the victims and the perpetrators of violent crime included a narrative approach to gain an understanding of how members of each group viewed their circumstances. He believed that these beliefs and attitudes contributed to personally devised stories that explained the circumstances of how one came to be either a victim or a perpetrator and that this exploration was a valid starting point for developing an empathic relationship with members of both groups.

He felt especially challenged when he attempted to connect with perpetrators who claimed to be religiously devout and yet were violent criminals. He saw such behaviors as being in direct opposition to his practice of his faith, and he was deeply troubled that others who claimed such devotion could behave in such socially deviant ways. As Alden prepared to meet the two groups for the first time, he began to wonder about the diverse ways in which individuals make sense of evil in their lives.

INTRODUCTION

This chapter is concerned with coming to terms with the presence of evil in the modern world. For the purposes of the discussion that follows, "the challenge of coming to terms with evil" refers to the development of a cognitive understanding of the phenomenon of evil and of the diverse explanations of its etiology.

The history of humanity is checkered with numerous examples of evil perpetrated by nation against nation and within nations by the more powerful against the less powerful. In the 20th century alone, the deeds of the Nazi extermination squads in Eastern Europe and the cold-blooded executions of millions of concentration camp inmates, the systematic "ethnic cleansing" in the Balkans, and the systematic extermination of opposition to Joseph Stalin are sadly only a few examples of such evil. Evil cannot be explained solely as a function of warring nations because individuals throughout history have performed acts of evil. Names of individuals such as Vlad the Impaler, Lizzie Borden, "Son of Sam," and so forth fascinate both the general public and clinicians, and present the challenge of trying to understand how these individuals came to be the way they were.

Attending to the topic of evil is characteristic of all religious and spiritual traditions, and of many counseling theories, each of which is based on a specific view of human nature. The view of human nature to which a counselor or other helping professional subscribes provides answers to questions about the etiology of client distress, what factors maintain that distress, and the potential for the remediation of the distress. For example, if one believes that an individual is "born bad," counseling or therapy might have little impact on his or her behavior. To change one's behavior would be to work against one's basic nature, a challenge that would appear to be insurmountable. In comparison, if one believes that an individual can rise above his or her circumstances with the aid of better understanding and support, then counseling becomes a viable intervention to provide both experiences to that individual.

Views of human nature range from pessimism (we are born in sin), through neutrality (the mind is *tabula rasa*—a blank slate), to the optimism of the humanists (we are imbued with the potential to achieve our own level of actualization). However, although the counseling and spiritual traditions may differ in their views, they share the goal of trying to make sense of evil.

MAKING SENSE OF EVIL

The exploration of the roots and purposes of evil is of the utmost value because it aids in the development of a foundation on which clinicians can come to understand the reasons that evil is perpetrated and the meaning of the unpleasantness, pain, and suffering in our own lives and in the lives of our clients. It is on the basis of this foundation that counselors develop a clinical conceptualization of the issues presented by the client. That conceptualization provides a framework within which to make sense of the client's presenting issue(s), to focus the search for client insight, to set goals, to take action, to select the appropriate therapeutic interventions, and to define the markers, or benchmarks, of successful counseling.

The presence of evil can be understood through a multiplicity of views. One perspective works from an assumption of random chance: There is no reasonable explanation for the presence of evil in life because the universe operates by means of some sort of "cosmic lotto," and the victim's "number came up."

Consistent with this perspective is the belief that the evil which causes one to suffer could not have been prevented or avoided. Although this is possible, the notion that humans exist because of a fluke of nature is relatively unpalatable to most 21st-century persons. Instead, they find more acceptable the belief that how one's life is conducted and how it unfolds is influenced by a Higher Power. The debate over whether humans are subject to God's will or whether they possess free will still must be reconciled in order to create a sense of existential peace; however, this debate is tangential to the theme of this chapter.

The subsequent questions that then arise include "How much influence does one have on one's own life actions and decisions?" and "What instances or life events are subject to one's own influence?" A related question is "For which of one's actions is one accountable, or are one's actions a function of a force or drive of an ego-alien nature and simply beyond one's power to resist?" One's answers to these questions serve as part of one's narrative for making sense of both aggression and victimization. Since both of these roles, and the multiple expressions of each role that clients bring to counseling, make up the occurrence of evil, it is a personally constructed understanding of each dynamic that directs the counselor's therapeutic conceptualization and subsequent interventions.

CAUSES OF SUFFERING

Some spiritual orientations claim that suffering is a function of the choices that one has made in this life or in previous lives. Had one lived a more virtuous life, one would not be so afflicted now. The amount of pain in one's life may be in direct proportion to the severity of one's evil. From this perspective, humans generate their own suffering as a natural consequence of forsaking God's laws. Because every formal spiritual belief system delineates both correct and sinful actions, disobedience of specific laws results in suffering and punishment. It is assumed in this perspective that an individual had prior knowledge of correct living and deliberately chose to forsake such a course.

Although such a view might explain the punishment of the wicked or a transgressor, questions remain about the suffering of victims. If victims' actions were congruent with doctrine-specific codes of behavior, how does one make sense of victims' suffering? What possible rule of law might they have broken or overlooked that would justify their being victimized by purposeful evil? If their suffering is not a function of "guilt by association" with the transgressor, then how is their plight explained?

Another option is to view life's challenges from a developmental perspective. From this perspective, pain and suffering can be expected at "growth" junctions throughout life and the presence of such angst could be viewed as an impetus for growth. These growth junctions may be an age-related event, such as leaving home, or an event related to out-of-self influences, such as the loss of a job or the premature death of a loved one.

In the first example—leaving home—an individual is faced with the task of developing a separate identity and forging one's way in a generally uncaring world. Experimentation in school, career, relationships, self-definition, and so forth occurs, sometimes succeeding (meeting one's personal goals and expectations and for the experience) and sometimes failing. In addition to the pain of not achieving one's goals, there is even more pain when one is forced to come to terms with one's personal shortcomings or limitations, or acknowledge that one's aspirations may exceed one's personal abilities.

The way in which the individual deals with failures and successes is indicative of, and a defining force in, one's identity. For example, does the individual learn from mistakes and move forward in life, or does the individual dwell on the pain and become defined by it? On an interpersonal level, until an individual can rejoice in one's own triumphs without becoming condescending toward others and accept one's failures without becoming bitter, one cannot be genuinely present for the joys and sorrows of others.

In the second example—the loss of a job or the premature death of a loved one—one is confronted with one's own relative impotence in the world because any sense of control and predictability is shattered by these events. Oftentimes, one is left to wonder aloud, "Why me?" From the objective viewpoint, designating these events as "character building" may serve to promise a brighter future, but does little to legitimize or ease the pain in the present. The unanswerable question—"I am a good person; why did this have to happen to me?"—still creates a struggle for us as thinking beings.

As a consequence of such life challenges, individuals also struggle, implicitly, with notions of free will ("To what extent am I causing my own pain and suffering?"), responsibility ("If I am being punished for sinning, should I accept the punishment or rail against it?" and "Do I atone for my actions, and if so, how do I account for the repetition of a behavior that I have already acknowledged through my atonement as evil?"), and individual power ("Over how much of my life do I exercise authority?" "How much authority do I have?" and "How much of my life is at the mercy of fate, the divine, or karma?"). As stated in the first chapter, religious teachings have formed the core of personal notions about morality and notions about human potential. Thus, explanations of human suffering that are learned by a counselor or other helping professional in his or her studies may confound that individual's perceptions of clients and their presenting and underlying issues.

EXPLORING EVIL

This chapter does not purport to offer "the answer" to all of the questions about evil; rather, it will offer insight into the diverse views of evil by exploring evil from a multiplicity of spiritual orientations, and then it will expand on those views by presenting the conceptualization of evil as espoused by counseling theories. The objective of this discussion is to direct counselors to carefully evaluate the congruence and dissonance between their spiritual and clinical perceptions of evil. Assuming that both genuineness and congruence are characteristics of optimal helping professionals, it would seem to follow that counselors must reconcile discrepant or perhaps competing belief systems regarding this topic.

METAPHYSICAL EVIL, NATURAL EVIL, AND MORAL EVIL

This discussion must originate in the acceptance of a common working definition of evil. For the purposes of this chapter, the definition that will be provided can serve as a common basis for an understanding of evil. Although not the sole definition, it affords a framework for a common understanding of the term. Russell (1988) categories evil as (a) metaphysical evil, (b) natural evil, and (c) moral evil.

Metaphysical Evil

Metaphysical evil is defined as a lack of perfection. From this definition, what is truly holy is that which is perfect and ideal. Any deviation from this ideal must inherently be flawed or "evil." However, the possibility of this ideal is, at best, fleeting and perhaps more of an aspiration than a reality. Although an individual may experience "peak moments" of bliss, joy, and satisfaction, this ideal remains an aim rather than an ongoing event. In that manner, life becomes a constant striving toward a goal that can seldom be met, but its pursuit can never be abandoned. Adhering to such a belief, one is challenged to define and honor the remainder of the personal experience in less-than-ideal terms. On an existential level, individuals are challenged to accept the notion that, although their lives may not be perfect, those lives still contain sufficient instances of the ideal or the transcendence of the mundane to provide confirmation of one's personal worth.

Moreover, the absence or lack of prevalence of the ideal does not imply the prevalence of evil. One is challenged to question the personal concept of good and evil as polarities on a continuum of morality or as absolute opposites with little or no room for nuance or consideration of individual circumstances. Strict adherence to such a dichotomy may be applicable in extreme situations (such as child abuse, etc.). In such an extreme case, individuals tend to be equally horrified by the abuser and shocked by anyone who would speak in the abuser's defense. However, adherence to such a dichotomous view may oversimplify the relativity of many of life's choices and events. (For example, is the removal of life support from an aging and infirm patient "honoring his or her wishes in the absence of quality of life," or is such an action murderous in intent?) If one answers yes to both questions, thereby legitimizing the concerns inherent in each issue, how does the decision get made and by what justification? At some point, one value must take precedence over the other for the actions congruent with that value to be enacted.

Natural Evil

Natural evil can be understood as those calamities of nature, such as tornados, hurricanes, and so forth, whose cause can be explained scientifically and whose impact is felt indiscriminately by those in its path. A recent example is Hurricane Katrina, which devastated New Orleans and the Gulf Coast. Natural evil can also be explained in terms of those who remained unscathed. Updrafts may move a tornado away from a densely populated area, only for the funnel to touch down in a relatively less-populated area.

In a lesser sense, one might see toothaches, illness, and death as natural evils. Such life events can be scientifically explained, although perhaps not with the certainty that one may crave. For example, although information on the health risks of cigarette smoking is widely disseminated, how can one explain that some who smoke tobacco contract fatal diseases and others seem to smoke with impunity well into their nineties? Natural evil seems to be an unavoidable part of life, but one may feel guilty about feeling relief when another person feels the brunt of evil.

Moral Evil

Moral evil is described as a conscious behavior designed to inflict suffering on others when one knows what impact that behavior will have on those others. Spinelli (2001) echoed this perspective by stating that moral evil is characterized by "deliberate, thoughtful yet morally indefensible acts of violence directed toward others" (p. 1). Staten (2005) argued that the notion of "voluntary wickedness" (p. 15), as ascribed to Kant, marks a radical departure in the thinking of our civilization. The notion that an individual or an entire nation might forsake what is commonly held to be "good" in favor of what is commonly understood as an embodiment of "evil" was a radical idea. This type of evil is mystifying on both the professional and personal levels.

Implicit in these actions of moral evil is a deliberate choice, coupled with the ability to justify such actions, with full anticipation of their effect on another individual or group of persons. This type of evil fascinates clinicians because its enactment implies that the individual empathizes with the victim because he or she is able to predict the suffering that the behavior will cause, yet proceeds to inflict the pain and suffering regardless of that outcome or, perhaps more frighteningly, in eager anticipation of such an outcome. One might be astonished that another human being could be so coldly calculating as to accurately determine how to hurt another person and then callously proceed to do so. One might be even more alarmed by the repetition of such actions, whether they are against groups of individuals or against nations. Sadly, human history is replete with such examples. The question is how to determine an etiology or source of evil.

SPIRITUAL EXPLANATIONS OF EVIL

This discussion is intended only as an overview, identifying key themes within the explanations of evil taken from spiritual traditions.

Judeo-Christian Perspectives on Evil

The Judeo-Christian notion of evil seems to be tied to the existence of Satan, or the Greek equivalent, *devil*. The very word *satan*, in Hebrew, merely connotes an adversary, with no implication that the entity is an enemy of God. The evolution of Satan to the status of a second god with a malevolent nature seems to have occurred during the Babylonian captivity of the Jews in the period 597–537 BCE. As opposed to monotheistic Judaism, some religions posited the existence of two opposing gods in an effort to explain the presence of evil. Zoroastrianism provided one explanation by asserting that there is an evil power that opposes God. This explanation seemed to be acceptable both to Judaism, which borrowed it from Zoroastrianism, and to Christianity, which adopted the same notion from Judaism. By the time of the New Testament, this opposing figure had his own realm of fire in which to receive guilty souls (Matthew 25:41). He could enter the heart of a human to create evil (Matthew 13:19). As evidence of his power, Satan caused Judas to betray Jesus (Luke 22:3; John 13:2) (Sanders, 1993).

Carlton (2005) cited the Book of Job, advising that "humans are puny creatures with tiny intellects who should not presume to question the divine order of things" (p. 99). Consistent with that belief, it must be accepted that "suffering and [the] human response to suffering [have] an important character-building potential" (p. 102). Therefore those so afflicted need not wonder about why they are suffering, but instead view such life challenges as some aspect of a "grand design" whose intent is to provoke some character evolution as a result or function of one having faced these life circumstances or events. In addition, since we are not privy to God's plan for each individual or the world in general, either in the present or in the future, one has no right to question the timing or extent of personal suffering. The notion of "cosmic time" transcends one's brief life span, so an individual cannot always anticipate the eventual ramifications of suffering. All this having been said, one is still asked to "bear up" under those burdens, dreaming ever-hopefully for a brighter future, either in this life or in the afterlife.

Perspectives on Sin

One can also ask, "Do humans lack 'the will to reject sin' (Carlton, 2005, p. 85) or do they simply have an inclination to sin that remains dormant until acted upon?" An acceptance of the former premise reinforces a belief in the inherent weakness of human nature—humans, unless somehow controlled or restrained, are likely to transgress societal or religious codes of conduct. In congruence with this belief, one must then identify those social or religious sanctions that will serve to keep members of society on the path of righteous behavior, and one must make the sanctions so severe for transgressions that a potential sinner will think twice before acting. In every religious tradition, this belief seems to form the basis for the mechanisms in place that are intended to inform believers of the consequences of sin, both in this world and after death.

With regard to an "inclination to sin," it is notable that there is no identification of a balancing "inclination *not* to sin." However, the notion of an "inclination" begs the question

"Under which circumstances is this inclination activated, and under which circumstances is it repressed?" This perspective places an emphasis on environmental factors, either chosen or imposed. These external factors may be living conditions, societal oppression, lack of access to resources, or issues such as family system dynamics or legacy. It is from this view that the identification of "social ills" arose as a way to specify and then remediate those social conditions which are seen to foster such inclinations.

God and Evil

Crenshaw (2005) advocated a connection between the justice meted out by a deity and humans' deep psychological need for order. As a corollary, Crenshaw viewed random instances of evil as evidence that "chaos" has the upper hand and that no human society can survive in such an environment. Adherence to a religion's tenets (regardless of the choice of religion) provides the structure, order, predictability, and code of conduct necessary for the creation and maintenance of society. In contrast, abandoning or ignoring such moral guidelines leaves both society and individuals bereft of a sound source of moral guidance and provides an opportunity for the emergence of evil and chaos. It is vital for humans both to grasp the dire consequences of disobeying religious teachings and to feel reassured of the continued beneficence of the deity. For example, the rainbow was seen as representing a covenant between God and Noah that the universe would be stable henceforth, and never again would the deity lash out in such a destructive manner that the survival of humankind would be threatened.

Schwarz (1995) equated evil with actions that are intentionally "god-opposing" (p. 38). This definition must rest on the foundation that one knows the will or law of God and chooses to ignore that knowledge. By doing so, the individual is implicitly claiming equality with God by assuming that his or her desires and God's law are equal choices and that acting on personal desire can take precedence over the law of God.

The story of the Garden of Eden in Genesis provides an example of the application of such a belief. Adam and Eve are specifically directed not to eat from the Tree of Knowledge. However, according to the story, Eve is tempted and succumbs, and then Adam follows suit. Thus, the "first act of evil was an act of disobedience" (Connolly, 2005, p. 134). Within this story are six powerful statements about the nature of evil:

1. The rule of God is to be viewed as absolute, with strict obedience expected and severe sanctions for disobedience.
2. Evil comes as external temptation (in the form of the serpent), emphasizing that when we choose to ignore or question God's law, we make ourselves susceptible to the influence of evil and we may not be strong enough to resist evil's pull.
3. The consequence of transgressing is banishment from the presence of God. (In the case of the Garden of Eden, this also included actual physical banishment from the garden.)
4. There is the perception of nature as a thing to be possessed (controlled or manipulated) by humans for their own use, in contrast to the idea of humans being expected to live in harmony with nature.
5. This story also speaks of the break in the harmonious relationship between God and man as being indicative of the schism between man and nature and between man and woman.
6. The destruction of these harmonies results in an ongoing competition to get one's needs met and in the demand that one constituency be subjugated to the needs of the other.

This story shows the destruction of the harmony between God and humankind and introduces the inherent fall from grace of humankind, as well as the ever-present need to be vigilant in the face of external evil forces.

Crenshaw expanded the roots of evil to include the sin of pride (Job 35:12). In this case, pride represents an expression of arrogance that one can become the equal of God. Such an arrogance may be founded in an insufficient fear of God (Proverbs 8:13), allowing individuals to imagine themselves as being beyond both the law of God and the consequences of breaking that law. In such instances, morality ceases to exist because the individual is no longer bound to any code of moral conduct and need not fear heavenly judgment or sanction. Such an occurrence could be described as "desire run amok," lacking consideration of any force other than one's desires and will. From this perspective, humankind, being without a moral compass, is bound to do all sorts of evil and does not possess the capacity to self-monitor, self-evaluate, or self-discipline.

NON-WESTERN VIEWS OF EVIL

The discussion to this point focuses on Western spiritual traditions; however, non-Western schools of thought have much to offer on the topic of evil.

Hinduism

Hinduism advocates that growth is the way to transcend both good and evil and that this transcendence relegates both good and evil to the concerns of the earthly world and frees the soul from that eternal battle which interferes with its evolution. Hinduism advises that one flee evil and the senselessness of the world. Morality is advocated as a way to live a happy life, not through obedience to the will of God, but rather by appealing to the decency of humankind, almost as a "social contract" between equals. Hinduism ignores speculation about the causes of evil and advocates peace in union with God.

Buddhism

Buddhism sees individuals as being ensnared in an unending chain of evil as a function of living in the world. From that viewpoint, confrontation with evil or the opportunity to do evil is an unavoidable aspect of life. Using Mara (the evil demon who tempted Gautama Buddha by having beautiful women try to seduce him) as the embodiment of evil (passion, angst, self-doubt, and self-delusion), Buddhism seeks to promote the search for a personal Nirvana (complete detachment from this world). This detachment is not seen as isolation from the day-to-day world, but as more of a moral compass in the face of life's challenges. What is advocated is self-monitoring to ensure that one's actions are motivated by noble intent rather than by the base motivations of selfish need and personal gratification. If the intent is pure, the outcome must be commendable, even if not wholly successful. Should the outcome be successful and the motive be self-serving or self-aggrandizing, then the intent contaminates the effort or outcome. Within the tenets of Buddhism, the adage that "the end justifies the means" holds no merit.

In the face of the unavoidable battle between good and evil, Buddhists believe that individuals are imbued with sufficient power to make moral decisions in the presence of evil. One must recognize the evil nature of one's actions through learning and voluntary self-reflection. This process of self-analysis fosters a sense of guilt that is seen to lead to the confession of wrongdoing and the eventual restoration of the condition of goodness. There is concern about how often one can repeat the same experience of evildoing and still expect restoration of the state of goodness. If the first experience of self-reflection is truly meaningful and self-driven (rather than imposed by societal figures of authority), then the change in the individual will prevent a reoccurrence. However, should guilt be imposed from societal structures (parents, family, church, or the legal system), the individual learns, not self-guilt, but rather fear and distrust of the very structures trying to remediate the behavior. As a corollary, the individual is spared the growth experience of self-analysis and final self-acceptance, setting the stage for more evil acts and more impotent interventions by society's institutions.

Islam

Islam sees sin as a manifestation of pride and self-determined arrogance. When one's actions are motivated by these drives, the tendency to sin is greater than when one listens to the word of God. "Although the human heart tends towards evil" (Sura 12:53), individuals are capable of changing their ways and therefore can be held accountable for their actions. The Faithful will be forgiven and infidels (those who do not accept the word of God) will be punished. From an inherent view, man is not evil, but rather weak and susceptible to sin and evil. Therefore, the act of sin is of secondary importance to the susceptibility that must precede the behavior.

CLINICAL EXPLANATIONS OF EVIL

As the discussion moves from the spiritual understandings of evil toward those frameworks espoused by counseling theories, the transition may be facilitated by the examination of a brief synopsis of the existential philosophies that sought to address this concern. Tillich (1973) described evil as (a) "the abyss of meaning" (p. 86), (b) "[a] breakthrough in the direction of the destructive" (p. 86), and (c) "possible only in contradiction to the universal ideal" (p. 87). Congruent with the tenets of existential thought, personal meaning provides each individual with ballast against evil intent in the world, and its absence allows a philosophy of evil to fill that existential void. In addition, evil can only be imagined as the direct opposite of universal goodness.

Evil and the Potential for Annihilation

Peck (1983) spoke in awe of evil due to its implicit potential for annihilation. Evil, taken to the extreme, threatens the very existence of human societies and the notion of the continuity of life. Peck ascribed evildoing to the projection of evil from the transgressor onto the world. If successful, the transgressor can justify any act that has the intent of eradicating evil. However, their energies are misdirected. The evil exists within them, not in those whom they are trying to destroy in the name of "goodness." According to Peck, this projection reflects the individual's need for the protection of an illusion of perfection. Thus, because of an inability to honor common human limitations, someone must become the scapegoat for the very existence of vice or sin because the individual thinks of him- or herself as being totally pure.

The Human Propensity Toward Evil

Rouner (1997) described the human condition as one that is "curiously bent toward doing bad things" (p. 183), in contrast to the "inherent goodness of humankind" (p. 183). The most puzzling aspect of this description is its reference to the idea of a human proclivity toward evil as being "curious." Such a modifier may imply that humankind's innate nature is toward "good," but somehow this nature has either been lost or corrupted. Rouner seemed to prefer the notion of corruption, and he considered evil to be the result of external causes (poverty, unemployment, lack of education, and lack of equal opportunity and resources, etc.). It then follows that external conditions create an internal condition of immorality in individuals that could be remediated or prevented by attending to those facilitating conditions.

Evil as a Function of Human Anxiety

From another perspective, sin could be seen as "a universal phenomenon resulting from our dread or anxiety in the face of freedom" (Rouner, 1997, p. 184). Confronted by "free exercise of finite choices" (p. 190), one becomes overwhelmed in the face of so many choices and feels constrained by one brief lifetime in which to choose.

Choice can be viewed as an act of self-establishment and self-preservation, and also as a repudiation of all of the other options that are available at that moment. There must be a conscious awareness of not choosing. One's life cannot embrace all possible attempts at self-fulfillment, and each individual must choose in spite of not being secure in the outcome of the choice. Such a process is sufficiently daunting in itself, but the challenge becomes more dangerous the less one knows about one's own values and the more susceptible one is to the opinions of others, including those opinions which advocate the choice of evil. Individuals can also be fooled by the seeming absence of sanctions for evildoing, because one cannot seem to ascertain the personal impact of evil on the transgressor. From an exterior view, it seems that there is no downside to such evil and therefore it becomes a viable option.

Evil as a Function of Lack of Fulfillment

Individuals are also confronted with, and perhaps terrified by, an inner sense of unfulfillment. It would seem to be easier, or perhaps it has just become more common, to try to borrow others' vehicles to self-fulfillment.

The media superbly bombard society with messages and celebrity examples of routes to personal happiness, and consumers of these messages seem to be awed both by the seeming ease with which they advance along the pathway and then by how quickly they fall off. Personally, individuals may chuckle about the foibles of those whose lives are paraded before a societal audience, seemingly as a positive example, and then overlook or excuse wrongdoings. These days, it seems like a contrite apology on national television absolves one of a multitude of transgressions.

The irony of this process is that, as one searches wildly and copies the behaviors of others, one may lose sight of one's own unique needs and values, thereby further alienating the individual from the true source of personal contentment and growth.

Ericson (1968) stated that the adherence to any spiritual orientation provides the "qualities of reverence, adoration and a consecrated devotion to life's sacred character" (p. 77). "Religion rests on human foundations, not on any particular metaphysical or theological structure" (p. 78). Rather, religion is a function of the psychosocial need for the permanence and immutability of awe, reverence, and a sense of the sacred. On the basis of these assertions, attending to that need not only meets the personal need for meaning, but also facilitates a sense of community around a common mission. Although particular practices may vary, it is the adherence to spiritual tenets that provides the codes of conduct that are relevant to the organization of society. Conversely, the absence of such qualities or the absence of membership in a spiritual tradition and/or organization leaves the individual at risk for a loss of guidance and direction in making choices and deciding his or her behaviors.

Mental Health Professionals' Theories of Evil

As much as the contemplation of evil and its etiology has fascinated theologians and philosophers, this contemplation is also key to the mental health professions because its explanations form the roots of clinical perceptions of human nature. Such clinical perceptions indicate whether a helping professional works to "save clients from themselves" or to aspire to a higher realm of being. These explanations help clinicians to determine which aspects of the human condition clients may deliberately or inadvertently cause and of which aspects they may be the blameless victim. This decision leads logically to a clinical understanding of which aspects of the human condition are within, and which are beyond, clinical intervention and the potential for the client to change.

This discussion is intended merely to synthesize the thoughts and orientations of some of the leading thinkers in the field of counseling and psychology. They are presented in chronological order because it can be expected that later theorists scrutinized the work of those who came before them. This material is intended to present the main points of the perceptions of key theorists to show the variance in opinion within one field and, hopefully, to identify unifying themes among these theorists.

Freud on Evil

Although Freud seemed to be more interested in the study of human neuroses, he offered important glimpses into his explanations for the evil within society. Freud hypothesized the presence of two instinctual drives: Eros and Thanatos (respectively, sexual love and the death instinct, in which one has an unconscious drive toward self-destruction). The development of the ego was to serve as a mediating force between these two instincts, on the one hand, and the superego, on the other, which was imposed by social institutions. According to Freud, this balance was of prime importance in the expression of aggression. If demonstrated in socially appropriate ways, aggression manifested itself in a competition with oneself to develop one's talents to the utmost and to the benefit of society. Conversely, if manifested in socially inappropriate ways, aggression was expressed in mastery and control over others.

On the basis of whichever defense mechanism was being employed, the transgressor could convince him- or herself that the victims were to be despised for their very weakness in not being able to defend themselves against the aggression. This inability to defend oneself was sufficient justification for their exploitation and manipulation. For example, an individual who utilized the defense mechanism of projection could justify behaviors by ascribing personal motives to others and feeling the need to protect oneself. An individual who utilized the mechanism of rationalization could devise a sound reason for his or her specific aggressive behaviors. For example, "confidence men" who seek to swindle people through the promotion of "can't miss" stock deals believe that those who are foolish enough to respond to their sales pitch with funding are "too stupid" to hold onto their money anyway. From this perspective, it is the victim's fault that he or she is being swindled.

However, the messages of society are effective only if they are received. The impermeability of strong defense mechanisms would interfere with or prevent the acceptance of such messages, leaving the individual lacking societal guidance. In such cases, Freud postulated that the individual relies on narcissism as the guiding force for his or her choice of actions (Seligman, 2006). Given the guidance of self-interest, any action can be justified in terms of self-gratification. In dealing with children ages 3 to 4 years, a caregiver will be told by a child that the child knew that it was wrong to take the toy from another child, but that he or she felt justified in the action because, according to the child, "I really wanted it."

Jung on Evil

Jung viewed evil as the manifestation of the "mask and shadow" (the undeveloped, inferior, and suppressed aspects of the self). The shadow comprises morally objectionable traits and instincts, generating the potential for actions that are socially unacceptable, shameful, and evil. These facets of the shadow are less a function of the individual and more a representation of ancestral archetypes that are manifested in the collective and personal unconscious. These archetypes cannot be directly accessed, but can be manifested in the behavior demonstrated by each individual specific to the archetype. The collective unconscious contains typical images that seem to exist at nodal life events across cultures. These nodal life events include birth and death, triumph over a natural obstacle, and transitional life events such as childbearing. Each culture provides history, ritual, and meaning for these common events. Each culture also manifests typical roles, including the hero, the child, the earth mother, and the demon. Each role has an affective script and specific behaviors.

The personal unconscious is formed from repressed infantile impulses and wishes, subliminal perceptions, and countless forgotten experiences, such as personal conflicts, unresolved moral concerns, and emotionally charged thoughts, all of which may be manifested together as a *complex* if the need of the complex (power) cannot be satisfied. A positive complex may turn into a negative complex, Jung may argue, as evil emerges and becomes part of the personal consciousness as a function of a need not met through socially approved means.

Individuation (the archetype of the self) necessitates an integration of the shadow self into the emerging personality, but not its dominance. It is this sense of holism that guides one to recognize the temptation to do evil that is part of the human condition. On the basis of the acceptance of that part of human nature, professional helpers must understand how one recognizes such an opportunity, yet chooses to reject that path. Through this aspect of personal growth, helping professionals can acknowledge, from personal as well as clinical experience, the seduction of evil and the struggle to remain consistent with one's moral pathway.

Adler on Evil

Adler (1933, pp. 2–4) offered the following comments related to the emergence of evil:

1. "The striving for personal power is a disastrous delusion and poisons man's living together. Whoever desires the human community must renounce the striving for power over others."

2. "It would be a gross deception to admit power intoxication only for the individual psyche. The masses also [are] guided by this goal and the effect of this is the more devastating as in the mass psyche the feeling of personal responsibility is essentially reduced."

3. "Modern psychology has shown us that the traits of craving for power, ambition, and striving for power over others, with their numerous ugly concomitants, are not innate and unalterable. Rather they are inoculated into the child at an early age; the child receives them involuntarily from an atmosphere saturated by the titillation of power. In our blood is still the desire for the intoxication with power and our souls are playthings of the craving for power."

4. "One thing can save us: the mistrust of any form of predominance. Our strength lies in conviction, in organizing strength, in a world view, not in the violence of armament and not in emergency laws. With such means other strong forces before us have fought in vain for their existence."

Adler saw evil as a result of one's attempts to resolve the natural feelings of inferiority. Personal biology and environment limit and direct one's capacity to choose or to take the actions that will solve the problem of an individual's feelings of inferiority. On the basis of the degree of success, the person may feel the need to compensate for what is still seen to be lacking in order to create a "success identity." However, Adler postulated that most people must develop a "success identity," even if its components seem like failures to others. For example, one might consider an alcoholic a success identity in that it seems to organize the individual's life and provide a sense of comfort in times of stress. Although perhaps not the healthiest example of a success identity, addiction provides many satisfactions for those so afflicted.

Adler stated that the inability to resolve personal feelings of inferiority may be a function of pampering or neglect. In the case of pampering in early childhood, the child winds up being unable to care for him- or herself or become a competent adult by the very experience of having every wish answered in the absence of any expectations. In the case of the neglected child, the child may doubt his or her sense of worth. From a child's perspective, the question may arise, albeit unconsciously, "How could I be so defective a child as to lose the affection and attention of my primary caregivers?" followed by the notion "If my parents consider me undeserving of care or attention, I must truly be inferior." In the one case, the pampered child takes the view that he or she is the center of the universe and expects others to care for him or her. In the case of the neglected child, there is a constant unresolved striving to demonstrate one's worthiness, coupled by an inability to trust the very people from whom one seeks confirmation.

However, the process of maturation demands that individuals become both more self-reliant and more able to have healthy interdependent relationships with others. For the pampered child, such self-reliance is a huge challenge, because the child was ill prepared in childhood to develop this ability to trust him- or herself. For the neglected child, the challenge is equally daunting, because the adult he or she has become has no experience with trusting, supportive relationships.

The emergence of evil represents the lack of success in resolving either child-based concern. In both instances, one might seek to control and manipulate others to meet one's needs without respect for the needs of others. Much like Freud's discussion of narcissism as a driving force, Adler sees the practice of evil as a manifestation of a childhood that did not prepare the individual for adult living.

Rogers on Evil

Rogers asserted that humans have a core tendency to actualize their inherent potentialities. This potential exists in all living organisms, even plants. Humans possess an additional form—the potential to actualize the self—known as self-actualization. Potential self-actualization is a function of four core characteristics:

1. *The self* is a person's conscious sense of who and what he or she is. This sense may be in one's conscious awareness, or one may not be aware of it. This self-portrait gradually emerges through experiences with verbal labels such as "I" or "Me."
2. *Phenomenological reality* is a person's private perception of reality (whether or not it agrees with objective reality). Experience is the highest authority. If an individual considers him- or herself to be unattractive or lacking intelligence, this is part of the personal self-concept regardless of any external input.
3. *A need for positive regard* represents the universal need for acceptance, love, and approval from others. Attending to this need is particularly important during infancy.
4. *A need for positive self-regard* is fulfilled when acceptance and approval come from within the individual and from significant others and that positive self-regard forms part of the individual's self-concept. People who have come this far have faith in their worth and value as a function of who they are, in contrast to what they do.

The human being also has personal power, or "vast resources for self-understanding, for altering self-concept, his attitudes, and his self-directed behavior" (Rogers, 1978, p. 7). Problems arise in people for whom this personal power is diminished or restricted due to domination by others, either overt (such as martial law) or covert (such as finding one's self in a manipulative relationship). The implication of placing so much power squarely upon the individual is great, including the potential for personal, social, and political change if all persons are granted the innate ability to move toward self-actualization.

In addition to the problems that arise when personal power is diminished, discrepancies between a perceived Ideal Self and a Real Self may lead to psychological distress. The Ideal Self is a self-concept held by an individual that may or may not accurately reflect reality and one's actual abilities or potential. If one's Ideal Self and Real Self are in alignment, psychological congruence is present. If the Ideal Self is out of alignment with the Real Self, incongruence occurs and is generally expressed through psychological distress. If the individual dimly perceives such incongruence in him- or herself, then a state of tension occurs, which is known as anxiety. The incongruence need not be sharply perceived. It is enough that it is subceived—that is, discriminated as threatening to the self without any awareness of the content of the threat. Such anxiety is often seen in therapy as the individual approaches awareness of some element of his or her experience that contradicts the individual's self-concept (Rogers, 1989, p. 223).

Spinelli (2001) described Rogers' perspective on the etiology of evil as "cultural influences." However, by "culture," Rogers was referring to the culture of the family and the community in which the child was raised. Each family and community imposes standards of conduct and ways of being that may negate aspects of the basic humanness of the child. There exists a tacit contract between the authority and the child: If you wish to have our confirmation of your worth and worthiness, you must adhere to these conditions. Should you violate the rules set down for you, you will be sanctioned. Given the relative physical weakness and emotional dependency implicit in the state of childhood in comparison with the power of adulthood, the child has little recourse but to comply. In addition, these rules are often conveyed as being in the best interests of the child. The child does not question, nor is the child given permission by the authority to question, whether these rules may actually be serving the best interests of the authority only. For example, one rule may address how anger is expressed. The rule, in fact, may convey that only "bad" children get angry. In that case, the child is faced with the dilemma of an experience of genuine affect that cannot be expressed. In addition to the negation of the anger, the child never observes healthy expressions of anger and grows up being fearful of his or her own anger.

The emergence of evil can best be seen as experimentation with the expression of denied affect. Having no models from whom to learn how to express unacceptable emotions, individuals are left to master these skills alone. Given the lack of such guidance, what may emerge are patterns of interaction that provide immediate release from building affective tension, but that perpetuate an unhealthy pattern of expression. For example, temper tantrums serve the need for immediate release, but tend, over time, to manifest a relational pattern of escalation and explosion that makes relationships short lived. Although the underlying emotion (e.g., frustration) may be justified given the context of its emergence, the individual's expression is so vehement that the very expression overwhelms the appropriate emotion and generates attention, not to addressing the frustration, but to controlling the outburst.

From another perspective, the squelching of the primary emotion then generates secondary emotional residue that amplifies the eventual expression of the primary emotion. For example, to return to the example of anger, if one has internalized messages forbidding the feeling or expression of anger in instances when one's anger is a most legitimate and honest emotion, the individual not only is terrified of the consequences of "getting mad," but also is perhaps ashamed of the anger, embarrassed by the anger, or fearful of the anger. In this case, rather than dealing with the expression of one strong emotion (anger), the person is confronted and probably confused by the need to express three other strong emotions (shame, embarrassment, and fear) for which that individual probably has no sound vehicle of expression. Therefore, when the anger finally erupts, it is out of proportion to the context and it tends to frighten all involved. Over time, this becomes simply "That's how I get mad," because there is no knowledge of any other way.

Evil also emerges as a logical consequence of one's personal experience. If, as a child, one was, for example, abused or neglected, but was told that he or she was loved, that individual would have grown up with a skewed sense of what "loving" means. It would then make sense that in future relationships that individual might treat others whom one claims to love in the same manner in which those who claimed to love the child expressed that love.

Kazdin on Evil

According to the tenets of behaviorism, a behavior is both the producer and the product of environment (Kazdin, 2001). Any action that is accepted within an environment then becomes part of its definition. In essence, any behavior that is not supported or reinforced by its environment must be extinguished. Therefore, it is the environment, rather than the individual, that could be labeled as "evil." Once part of the defining factors of an environment, the behavior can be expunged only through purposeful intervention. In opposition, the environment serves as a self-regulating function, seemingly resistant, or at least reluctant, to change.

Once evil becomes imbued in the environment, be that environment a society, a school, a family, or any other group, evil becomes spread through the impact of social learning (Bandura, 1986). According to this process, one need not directly experience the reinforcement of a behavior; instead, one can observe others in the same situation. In this manner, evil becomes contagious and then becomes an epidemic. Having found momentum, the majority quickly works to eradicate any voice of opposition and to firmly entrench that specific evil in that specific society at that specific time. In this way, society becomes subject to mob rule. The best example of such a social phenomenon was the rise to power of the National Socialist Party in Germany after World War I. A small group of followers of one man began to recruit and reinforce others who would ascribe to their beliefs and actions. Over a period of a few years, this party became the dominant political and social force in Germany, and then in Europe. Although not all Germans became members of the Nazi Party, the consequences of opposition became frighteningly clear, serving to stifle what little voice of dissent may have existed. In fact, there was a total reversal of the social order in that what was blatantly evil became "good," or the norm, and what was previously considered "good" became punishable.

Ellis on Evil

No, we cannot accurately say that some people are essentially evil. Even those who commit many immoral acts would have to do so all the time to be evil people. As Alfred Korzybski wrote in 1933, calling anyone an evil person is to falsely overgeneralize and to completely damn her or him for some evil acts. Invariably, the Hitlers and the Ted Bundys of the world, who steadily commit some of the worst crimes, also do a number of good and kind deeds. And some "bad people," like St. Augustine when young, later achieve sainthood. Humans are fallible and changeable. (Ellis, 2003)

Ellis (1999, 2000) based his model of counseling on the supposition that humans are born with the potential for rational and irrational thinking. Ellis ascribed two categories of predispositions to the human condition: one for self-preservation, happiness, thinking and verbalizing, loving, communion with others, and growth, and a second for self-destruction, avoidance of thought, procrastination, endless repetition of mistakes, superstition, intolerance, perfectionism and self-blame, and avoidance of the actualization of potential. The etiology of these predispositions is founded in learned patterns of thinking.

It would seem that within the second category of predispositions may be found an explanation for evil. According to Ellis's hypothesis, an individual's thinking patterns about oneself and the world are taught by one's immediate social environment. As learning beings in infancy and childhood, with little ability to discriminate between helpful and critical comments, and as a function of egocentrism, children internalize all comments made directly to them, or made about them, into an emerging self-definition. These comments usually include an injunction such as "ought to," "have to," "should," or "must," implying some sort of behavioral imperative, and they conclude with some critical statement about the child's worth should the imperative remain unrealized. For example, an injunction demanding that one should always be the best at what one does becomes "To be second best is to be a loser and to be nothing." This injunction then sets the stage for cheating and other inappropriate actions. Given the lack of room for human error and growth, one who adheres to this notion is under immense pressure not only to do one's best, but to perhaps sabotage the work of others to make sure that one wins.

Glasser on Evil

Glasser (2000) described humans as being motivated by five encoded needs (survival, love and belonging, power or achievement, freedom or independence, and fun). These needs are an aspect of each individual, but are idiosyncratically defined to make up what Glasser labeled as a "quality world" (one's best attempt to fulfill one's needs; designed to close the gap between what one wants and what one perceives that one is receiving or experiencing).

In addition, each individual must assume the responsibility for personally defining each of these needs within one's capability to meet them or to activate one's environment in healthy ways to address each need. By "healthy ways," Glasser stated that one cannot have one's needs met at the expense of others' needs. To exploit or manipulate other individuals is to view others as being at one's beck and call and to expect others to abandon their needs in order to meet one's own needs. In such cases, one becomes exploitive and uncaring of others, sabotaging their needs. For example, *Mein Kampf* contains a justification for the survival of the German race at the expense of those people labeled as *untermenschen,* or subhuman. This rationalization was used to justify the extermination of millions of persons identified as such on the mistaken assumption that the survival of the German nation swayed in the balance.

Another aspect in the emergence of evil entails an individual addressing one need at the expense of other personal needs. In such instances, one is self-sabotaging. An example from the classroom illustrates this point: In search of fun, a child acts up in class to disrupt a "dull" lesson. The teacher responds by sending the child to in-school detention, thereby depriving the child of freedom. In this case, the child's initial behavior, although momentarily successful, was at the expense of other needs, specifically the needs for power, belonging, and freedom, which were denied by the sanction of removal from class and isolation from one's peers.

Feminist Therapy on Evil

More than other models of counseling, feminist therapy examines the sociological influences, as well as the psychological factors, that lead to personal dysfunction (Enns & Cox, 1997). Evil seems to be more a function of day-to-day existence within the current social structure than a specific set of actions. On the basis of observations made about the social history of the treatment of women, Bem (1993) and Hyde (1996) identified gender schema as being the basis for the mistreatment of women. Gender schemas involve models of attitude and behavior that become rigidly applied to one gender or the other. Out of these schemas emerge acceptable modes of behavior between genders. Historically, men and male attributes have been extolled as being the preferred way to be, and women have struggled with being oppressed as the subordinate group (Miller, 1986). The evil within this structure involves a discriminatory devaluing of all things feminine. This process of comparison holds male values, attributes, and so forth as the ideal and finds women's values, attributes, and so forth as lacking. Instead, the two viewpoints should be accepted as different but equal. Gergen (2001) challenged the traditional perspective and advocated in favor of an empowering perspective that respects the differences between the genders. For example, the author objected to several *DSM-IV-TR* categories that may include male cultural stereotypes of women and that overlook the significance of sociological factors in women's lives (Scharf, 2004). In this example, depression is explained as a function of sociological factors and gender role expectations that foster a sense of powerlessness in women. Therefore, depression is more a result of dysfunctional factors in women's lives than a cause of them.

Brooks (1998) extended the value of feminist counseling to male clients. Given the isolation in which most men live, they may be unaware of the political and social impact of culture on them. Issues such as an inability to express emotional pain, an overemphasis on achievement, difficulties in establishing and maintaining relationships, and a dependency on drugs or alcohol as a coping mechanism for stress may have their etiologies in the socially prescribed gender role schemas for men. These schemas constrict their awareness of the self and the interaction of the self with others. In addition, men are as susceptible to media portrayals of the ideal male as are women. These portrayals are intended more for selling a product than for fostering any type of life satisfaction.

Social Constructivism on Evil

As a newer perspective on the etiology of people's issues, this model stresses the defining power of subjective reality. The approach emphasizes the responsibility that each individual has in his or her idiosyncratic creation of the reality of any event in one's life. This view suggests that it is far more useful to the clinician to understand the client's interpretation of the event than to know the specific details of the event itself, because it is the client's view of reality that colors his or her intrapsychic responses, such as affect and cognition, and that determines the client's interpersonal behavior (Vaihinger, 1952). When these storied realities are problem oriented or negative, the potential for the emergence of evil may exist.

This approach pays particular attention to the client's use of language because it is considered to be indicative of the client's view of an event and his or her place in that event. *Characterization* refers to the people in the story, *plot* refers to the actions that occurred in the story, *themes* refer to the meaning of the event to the storyteller and his or her emotional experiences, and the *setting* is where and when the event occurred (Scharf, 2004).

For example, if a parent describes a child's misbehavior (e.g., spilling a pitcher of milk) as *purposefully clumsy and stupid* in comparison with *uncoordinated,* the former perception of the event may have triggered disciplinary action or perhaps help in cleaning up the spill, along with the advice to "be more careful next time." In the second perception—that the child is simply uncoordinated—the parent's interpretation of the event (both in terms of cognition and affect) generated a behavioral response on the part of the parent that was congruent with the parent's self-created impression of the child's actions. It is the story that generates the pain, more so than the actual event (Zimmerman & Dickerson, 2001).

Case Example Revisited

Alden discovered a multiplicity of viewpoints from both offenders and victims that substantiated their situations, actions, and affects. He noted that some victims had empathy for the plights of their offenders, but that the offenders had a lack of empathy for the victims. Being more puzzled by this latter discovery, Alden learned of the multiple justifications used by offenders to support their criminal behavior. He was dismayed to realize that any punitive sanctions for their crimes which did not address and challenge those justifications could not be truly effective, and, sadly, this meant that there was a high probability of more crime.

Conclusion

As human beings and as counselors, we are faced with an undeniable need to make sense of evil and of the roles of victim and aggressor. One must do this through the integration of personal spiritual/religious beliefs and clinical orientations in order to present a congruent image to clients and, in doing so, offer them hope for the same resolution in their personal lives.

Self-Understanding Exercises

1. If evil exists within your ontological perspective, to what extent are we its random victims and to what extent do we bring this evil on ourselves?
2. To what extent are we born flawed and need to be rescued from our base nature? Or are we born "in goodness," requiring only an opportunity for our innate potential for growth to emerge? How does this view direct the course of your career in counseling?
3. If good people can do bad things, how do we distinguish this group from "evil persons"?
4. If one makes the assumption that evil is innate, to what extent is evil impervious to counseling?

Opportunities for Further Growth

1. Survey other members of your religious or spiritual community regarding their understanding and explanation of evil.
2. Explore the concept of evil from cross-cultural perspectives. How might gender, ethnicity, or age affect individuals' definitions of evil?
3. If evil were to be controlled by the enactment of laws, pick one social issue (abuse, alcoholism, etc.) and trace the evolution of laws that define, monitor, and sanction this behavior. What do you see to be the next step toward the eradication of this evil?
4. To what extent do you believe that it is possible to eradicate evil, or must we, in some manner, learn to live with evil, but not become contaminated by its presence in our lives?

9

∎ ∎ ∎

Balancing the Concepts of the Divine and the Penitent

The confession of evil works is the first beginning of good works.

—SAINT AUGUSTINE (354–430 BCE)

CASE EXAMPLE

Ambrose entered the field of school counseling because he wanted to help children who had had experiences similar to those of his own disrupted childhood. He was raised by a single mother, but after the death of his father when he was 8 years old, there were two subsequent marriages, and stepfathers, in the home. Ambrose disclosed that each male figure was so different that he was still reconciling his understanding of masculinity and his future role as a husband and a father.

Ambrose was raised in the Roman Catholic Church, and he relied heavily on his church affiliation and clergy in times of stress and upheaval. Late in adolescence, he considered becoming a priest, but decided that he enjoyed the secular life too much to do so. He remained an active member of a Roman Catholic congregation on campus, but remarked that his priest back home was better.

As Ambrose progressed through his counseling program, he began the course on counseling theory and was intrigued to learn that learned scholars could provide so many different ways to help people. He watched the "Gloria" tapes and was amazed to observe that Ellis, Perls, and Rogers all seemed to be effective in treating Gloria. He also was amazed, and then confused, that such differing clinical styles could each have such a positive impact, and he questioned how he could ever learn to "do counseling right." Even in his role-play simulation exercises, he felt frozen, undecided about which was the best direction to follow. In his own counseling sessions, he discussed his confusion about multiple treatment styles that "all work" and his uncertainty concerning how to be a good counselor. He felt unsure about what to expect of himself within the counseling session and what to expect of his clients. He felt immobilized.

Ambrose sensed that becoming proficient in counseling was more than skill mastery, but he was unsure about how to articulate what was missing. Having learned to play the piano and to play tennis, he had expected to once again feel the awkwardness that is a natural part of learning new

149

skills, but his discomfort exceeded what he had felt previously. He feared that he might be deficient in some core attribute that is necessary to become an effective and caring mental health professional.

■   ■   ■

INTRODUCTION

According to Augustine's statement, confession is the first step in recovery. What does not appear in the quotation is clarification as to why such an act is important; to whom that confession is to be made; how the listener is expected to respond; and, after confession, whether there is a next step on the road to salvation or whether the confession itself is sufficiently redemptive.

Similar questions apply to mental health services. What does the service provider do, what does the client do, and why? What makes this process successful from the perspective of each participant? These questions stemming from the Augustinian proclamation imply a behavioral exchange, while the essence of psychological intervention rests within the qualities of the therapeutic relationship itself. Such qualities form the foundation for the delivery of services and intervention, with the codicil that the efficacy of any intervention, no matter how tried and true, must materialize from the relationship between the clinician and the client.

Therefore, this chapter will focus on the relational expectations of the mental health services provider, in terms both of the self and of the client. The main question to be explored is "Given that the role of the clinician carries more power, and therefore more responsibility for the success of the clinical services, than does the role of the client, how is one to be therapeutically powerful, from where do these role expectations arise, and what recursive expectations apply to the client?"

This chapter will also focus on the qualities of a successful therapeutic relationship. Although existing texts of very high quality, clarity, and utility already provide similar information, what will distinguish this chapter is an exploration of the clinician's subconscious formation of the role of the clinician and the concomitant role of the client. This investigation centers on the clinician as an authority figure and on the possible etiologies of that foundational concept. One possible explanation for the nature of a clinician's role as an authority figure might be based on a possible link between perceptions of God or a Supreme Being and perceptions of the penitent before God and the qualities of the therapeutic relationship between the clinician and the client.

Even as hypothesized, this connection is extremely tentative, awaiting input from clinicians and scholars. However, it may be worthy of conjecture for the clinician to imagine how his or her images of God, Allah, Yahweh, or the Divine may color the subconscious expectations of the self and of the client within counseling. In addition, although one may "play God" as a clinician, one also plays the role of the penitent in one's religious practices. Thus, awareness of, and comfort with, both roles within religious or spiritual practices may be important to better understand the nuances of the therapeutic relationship.

Any scholarly work on religion or spirituality must address, in some manner, the concept of God, the Divine, a Supreme Being, or a Universal Constant. However, as this book is intended for clinicians, not theologians, it is far beyond the scope of this work or this author's knowledge to discuss theologically based concepts of the divine. Nonetheless, it is within the scope of the book to explore whether one's perceptions of God may color one's perceptions of the role of the professional helper. If so, a case could be made that one's image of God as a primary authority figure serves as a blueprint for the self as the authority in the provision of mental health services.

THE RELATIONSHIP BETWEEN THE DIVINE AND THE WORSHIPPER

Armstrong (1993) traced how notions of God evolved over 4000 years to meet the social, religious, and spiritual needs of the times. This chronology is fascinating reading in and of itself for those who are interested in a deeper understanding of this social and religious phenomenon. However, of specific interest to clinicians is the discussion of God during the appearance and advancement of psychology and mental health intervention.

In the 19th century, social thinkers questioned the centrality of God in the universe throughout human existence and began to elevate the rights of the individual over an obligation, deference, or obedience to the Divine. As an outgrowth of the Renaissance and Scientific Revolution, secularists of the 19th and 20th centuries "saw atheism as an irreversible condition of humanity in [the] scientific age" (Armstrong, 1993, p. 377). A vigorous belief in science liberated one from the terrifying God of one's childhood or the vengeful God who threatens one with eternal damnation if his rules are not strictly followed.

Over time, the God of mercy, love, and compassion had been replaced by the God of judgment, retribution, and punishment. This was not a God to be embraced or willingly adored, but a God to be avoided, discounted, dismissed, or eliminated. It is important to remember that the experiences of that time centered more on the practice of organized religion than on individual spiritual paths, so the revolt against God could perhaps better be viewed as a rebellion against the practices of institutional religion. Moreover, given the perception of religion in the 19th and 20th centuries, one could not easily dismiss dogma without dismissing God because the two were so closely intertwined through practice as to be virtually synonymous. Accordingly, a dismissal of dogma encompassed a refutation of God, whether purposefully intended or not. There seemed to be no social venue in which to believe in God outside of institutional religion.

In response to the need to generate distance from formal religion yet maintain a sense of God, Armstrong (1993) suggested that the surfacing of the concept of a "personal God has helped monotheists to value the sacred and inalienable rights of the individual and to cultivate an appreciation of human personality" (p. 209). It is not that individuals must appreciate God; rather, it is that God must love and honor each individual. There was a move away from a collective identity and experience of God to a truly individual experience, a shift from the hierarchy between God and humans to a supposed equality.

This was a vital shift in orientation. Originally, people were to serve God; yet in this script, God exists to meet the needs of the individual. Prayer is not for guidance or forgiveness from the All-Knowing, but rather for personal indulgences or favors. Acceptance of God becomes conditional, based on the granting of prayed-for wishes. Should prayers go unanswered, then God can be dismissed as uncaring and undependable—human traits applied to a transcendent being. In this vein, God must prove his or her "utility" to humans because belief and faith have been replaced with pragmatic outcome and observable results as an indication of existence or validity.

This new version of God encompasses another fundamental transformation. Religion teaches that humans are created in the image of God and that they should aspire to God's ideals and continue to aspire even in the face of failure or tragedy. This marks the appearance of a personal God created in the image of humans—a God who does everything that a person does (loves, judges, punishes, creates, hates, destroys, and so forth). Such attributes are displayed by God not by divine principle, but rather as a response to the prayers of an individual. As a perhaps overly dramatic metaphor, God could be seen as having been reduced to a "vending machine," awaiting the input of a specific amount of spiritual coinage, in the form of prayer or belief, and dispensing fulfilled wishes in response. However, such a perception of God carries a grave liability. Given the projection of individual needs, fears, and desires, the "acts of God" may endorse our prejudices without compelling us to transcend them (Armstrong, 1993, p. 210). For example, the history of human existence is scarred by wars fought in the name of religion and God, with the notion that the God of the winning side is more powerful than the God of the losing side. Praying against social issues such as gay rights, the Equal Rights Amendment, or abortion rights may be seen to maintain bias in the name of piety, but one may wonder where the virtues of kindness, compassion, and neighborly love have gone within this practice.

There are other issues related to one's perception of God. One question might revolve around the issue of the will of God: Does acceptance of God's will mean that one must accept that which is fundamentally unacceptable, either on a societal level, such as genocide, or on a personal level, such as fatal illness? Doing so, in either case, suggests the concept of a divine plan, unknown to humans either collectively or individually, for every life and every event. Doing so also implies some degree of predestination—that the course of one's life is more preordained than one might imagine. In that case, boundary issues surface regarding how much free will one may actually exercise within the confines of one's preset life script. It is interesting how the stars, the runes, numerology, birth signs, tarot cards, and the year of birth have all been consulted to explain one's current life situation. Such practices may be dismissed as being unscientific or superstition. However, such a dismissal does not account for the millions of people who have sought answers through these practices across countless cultures and over the entirety of human history. How many readers of this book access their horoscopes on a daily basis or consult with psychics before making a critical life decision?

A related question is "Who has access to God's will?" Is his will communicated only to members of the clergy through ancient texts, or does each person have direct access to the will of God? If the latter, then under what conditions and through what medium might this communication, if two-way, or transmission, if one-way, occur? This question is vital to understanding the self as a clinician as a prelude to the dynamics in session. Are clinical services about absorbing the client's input and making pronouncements of diagnoses, etiology, or remedy (a transmission), or are clinical services a dialogue on two distinct perceptions of the same concern, with the client's perception based on personal experience and the clinician's perception based on professional knowledge, but with each being only one half of the complete picture, requiring the other, complementary perspective for wholeness?

Is this knowledge the outcome of transcendent experiences that provide certainty as to God's purpose for an individual? If it is based on personal transcendence, then how might clergy know with any degree of certainty what God intends for one individual as opposed to another? Or, in an increasingly individualistic society, can clergy only offer broad ways of being as opposed to individualized guidance? The notion of transcendence can be equated with the experience of clinical catharsis. Both peak experiences involve an awakening of consciousness, an awareness of the self in a larger context, and the heartfelt recognition of a thread of consistent truth in one's existence. These experiences, under the guidance of clergy or the clinician, allow the individual to honor the "divine within" and to create a forum for self-understanding that far surpasses problem solving or atonement. Not only is the experience itself transformative, but the acknowledgment of one's capacity for such experiences and the ability to access the experiences must, in some noncomparative and noncompetitive manner, elevate one's sense of self-potential. These two adjectives—noncomparative and noncompetitive—are vital aspects of an emerging higher way of being, where the locus of control and comparison shifts from multiple external loci of reference to a single internal locus of reference. The challenge for clinicians is to consider to what extent they seek to promote such personal growth that far exceeds simple problem resolution or symptom amelioration. It may be overreaching to claim that clinicians can "do" this experience for their clients, but it may be reasonable to suggest that the types of questions utilized and the interventions chosen will lead more directly, perhaps, to one or the other outcome.

On a very elemental level, this issue confronts clinicians with the basic question of belief in the human potential for transcendence. A similar question exists within the hierarchy of formal religious institutions. By virtue of its triangular shape, Maslow's hierarchy of needs implies that fewer individuals achieve the higher levels than the lower levels. Maslow made the statement, however, that spiritual needs exist on all levels and can be achieved by all individuals. The challenge within this issue centers on the belief system of those who provide care as to the innate potential of the receiver of the care in terms of the capacity for growth and for transcendence. If a caregiver believes that clients or penitents are in some way flawed by their errors or sins, and by committing such acts they have forfeited some right to growth, then the admission of such conduct will be followed by some redemptive behavioral intervention. If, however, the same caregiver, be he or she clinician or clergy, viewed the error or sin as a vital stepping-stone on the road to this individual's transcendent or cathartic experience and an opening toward the "universe of self-redefinition," then the focus of the dialogue is less on "What have you done and how can you do better?" and more on "How are you now and forever changed?"

This topic is of vital interest to clinicians because adhering to the initial set of beliefs (exploration of the presenting problem) dictates that clinical services must dwell on and around the presenting issue, while adhering to the second set of beliefs (growth possibilities) directs attention more toward the outgrowth of that experience. In the former orientation, the client becomes defined by that negative experience and is labeled a "dropout," an "addict," or a "manic-depressive," while in the latter orientation, such labels are irrelevant and speak much more to the individual's past than to his or her future.

Another issue concerning the perception of God may revolve around issues of gender imbalances. A review of deities based in antiquity reveals that all original god figures were representative of the female. On the basis of a lack of understanding of conception and birth, these events were seen as being miraculous and as being physically beyond the ability of men. The very terms *Mother Earth* and *Mother Nature* stem from that primitive awe. Both honorifics venerated the qualities that modern society designates as being "female." However, over the years, and with the ongoing redefinition of social and religious mores, polytheism offered male and female god figures, with each figure representing another human quality.

It took the advent of monotheism to present the figure of God as a "father." However, a subsequent query must be "What kind of father?" This shift is again worthy of reflection, as the qualities ascribed to God became only "male" qualities. It may be of interest to access any dictionary and compare the definitions of the terms *father* and *mother*. Prior to such research, it would be reasonable to expect that both simply refer to the process of parenting. According to Merriam-Webster OnLine, a *father* is "a man who has begotten a child" and a *mother* is "a female parent"—"maternal tenderness or affection." According to the online version of the Oxford English Dictionary, *father* means "to beget a child" and *mother* means "to also look after kindly and protectively." Although both definitions acknowledge the biological aspects of parenting, it is only the definition of the mother that describes the qualities of caring and, on a basic level, assumes a post-birth relationship. There was no equivalent description of a "fatherly" relationship with the child. Although based on a cursory exploration at best, this discrepancy serves to acknowledge the ramifications for gender roles within relationships. Whereas the role of the father is more open to creation, interpretation, or dismissal, the role of the mother is carefully described.

The question may then be raised as to how these role expectations are interpreted by both men and women in their ongoing professional relationships. Do those qualities include judgment, condemnation, and marginalization, versus compassion, mercy, and love? Or is the perception of the Divine one that embodies both what humans have categorized as male and female qualities? Since God is all-seeing and all-knowing, how does one expect God to respond to what is seen and known?

As a clinician, does one expect oneself to be empathic, encouraging, and unwaveringly supportive, or does one expect oneself to be judgmental, punishing, and threatening? Although perhaps a drastic polarity of positions, these qualities must be expressed within the therapeutic relationship. While in no way suggesting equality between the Divine and a mental health clinician, it may be worthwhile to consider what qualities the clinician seeks to embody and the extent to which these qualities are expressed and experienced in session by the client. The qualities listed were intended to be dichotomous in order to prevent a clinician from claiming that he or she can take either stance on the basis of the requirements of the client and the case. It would be difficult to fathom how one might claim both stances and also claim genuineness and authenticity in one's presentation of the self in session. Therefore, it is again worthwhile to consider how one envisions the qualities of the Divine within one's spiritual or religious tradition and how well one mirrors those qualities in session.

Armstrong (1993) also made distinctions between the God of the West, focusing on action (behaviorism), and the gods of the East, focusing on contemplation. One axiom states that "actions speak louder than words," implying that "if one talks the talk, then one must walk the walk." This adage speaks to the importance of genuineness and congruence for an individual, warning of the perils of declaring a virtue or intent and not acting in accordance with that statement. Another interpretation suggests that until one can demonstrate, in an observable manner, some intent, then whatever one thinks of the intent is irrelevant. In such cases, words or thoughts have no meaning or value until put into action. Although action is necessary for client change to occur, one must ponder on what basis that action is taken. Problem solving has come to be equated with action: "the sooner, the better" and the more forceful, the more right-minded. Perhaps this bias toward behavior has become extreme. In one's haste to act, lest one be accused of being weak-willed or indecisive, actions may be taken impulsively and without proper consideration. So one may ponder, "What is the place of contemplation and how does one know when to act?"

The Tao Te Ching suggests that "right action" is founded in "right thinking." One way to consider right thinking is to wonder whether one's conduct in any given situation reflects one's value system. A second consideration, taking the context into consideration, is whether choosing to accept a situation in which one was railed, but was powerless to affect direct change, is a sufficient response. For example, in a marriage, one spouse may be a "morning person" while the other spouse is not. Trying to make the other person become more of a "morning person" is bound not only to fail, but to generate conflict and tension in the marriage. Perhaps accepting the individual as he or she is presents the only viable solution, assuming that one's core value is to maintain a happy, harmonious marriage. In that case, the action that is taken is not about changing the other, but about changing one's own attitude toward acceptance and, in fact, may be noticeable by the lack of previous actions intended to try to change the other.

The idea of contemplation brings to mind the issue of the reading of scripture, holy writings, and so forth. To what end is such literature intended? Debate rages as to whether a literal or figurative interpretation of scripture is correct. Perhaps that debate is too simplistic. Perhaps both styles of reading holy texts are necessary. If one reads a passage in light of its literal meaning, what message is gleaned? If one reads it in light of a figurative or metaphorical meaning, what message is gleaned? If written thousands of years ago, how does each message apply to life in the 21st century? More immediately, how does each message apply to one's understanding of oneself within one's life context?

Although a time must come for action in order for any improvement to be made, that action must be based on and balanced by careful contemplation of the factors mentioned. However, this contemplation is not just to be conducted prior to taking action. Once action is taken it must be evaluated on two levels. First, how well did one do what one set out to do? Second, how closely did the result of one's action approximate its intended effect? Even if the answer to the first question is positive, anything less than satisfaction in the second query indicates a need for further learning. As a clinician, one is confronted by clients in pain who are hoping for immediate relief. Although endless contemplation would result in client frustration with clinical services, hasty action could lead to repeated failures by the client to "fix" what has brought him or her to clinical services, as well as increased despair and frenetic action.

Armstrong (1993) also posed fascinating questions, such as "Does God negate our freedom, as Sartre alleges?" This question may hold more relevance for those in the mental health professions than for other professionals. As presented earlier in the chapter, the notion of free will seems to underlie most psychological theories. If one adheres to the belief that God creates and then micromanages the lives and events of individuals, then the balance of power rests wholly with the Divine, and the human is relegated to being a pawn in a greater cosmic strategy that exists far beyond the knowledge or comprehension of humankind. If, by contrast, one eschews the notion of God as the creator, ignores the issue of how one came to be, and focuses entirely on one's function/purpose and actions in life, then the issue of free will is of vital concern.

What motivates humankind if one is not guided by transcendent virtues? What prompts one individual to evolve from pursuing actions of self-interest to pursuing actions in the service of others and yet another individual to remain fixated on self-interest throughout his or her life? The main query in this puzzle could revolve around issues of inspiration. However, if one believes in free will and creation, then individuals are placed on earth with the potential to act and develop in myriad different ways. The question may then emerge as to how each person navigates and negotiates social relationships when guided by a particular value system.

Although every faith tradition provides a code of values, the process of accountability is less to the congregation or clergy and more to one's concept of the Divine. The amount of risk accepted by an individual may be related to the anticipated reaction from the Divine. Working on the assumption that God hears all and sees all, are risk and failure rewarded for the effort or condemned for the lack of positive results? This continuum of projected responses forms a critical blueprint for the process of counseling.

Counseling assumes that the client takes two risks: (1) to reflect on oneself and (2) to take risks without the promise of success or the lessening of immediate pain. Clients who are reluctant to change may fear judgment, ridicule, and punishment should they not succeed. Perhaps this disinclination has its roots in an apprehensive vision of the Divine as projected onto the clinician.

From an ontological perspective, Sartre also wondered if there might be a "God-shaped hole in the human consciousness" (Armstrong, 1993, p. 378). Without speculating about the cause of such a phenomenon, the presence of this facet of human consciousness implies a metaphysical vacuum that needs to be filled. The history of human existence may support such an assertion. Any reviews of cultures past and present hold in common the identification of god figures that are relevant to the history and culture of each period. Although relegated to history as they are replaced by more modern visions of the Divine, it can be imagined that primitive gods provided a sense of unity, cohesion, and purpose for those ancient civilizations. Moreover, the qualities of these god figures offered a template for what was considered to be heroic or valiant at the time. In that way, the gods served as the exemplification of societal virtues and, as such, provided the core societal values.

If there is indeed a deeper human yearning to experience life beyond the physical senses and physical and material needs, then it is God who is the manifestation of eternity and universal continuity. A belief in the Divine, no matter which name is applied, places the individual into a collective amalgam of humankind, past, present, and future. This sense of the self in relation to others and the universal constants may be the antithesis of the issue of anomie, or existential despair, that is so destructive to the human spirit, because if one believes in nothing beyond oneself, then the demise of the individual is equated with the death of the universe. This burden would seem to be far too great for any individual to bear.

It is of relevance to this discussion that the 2007 conference of the Association for Counselor Education and Supervision held the issues of social justice and social advocacy as its two themes. Both themes imply a contribution to society that is beyond oneself, an implicit call for the moral imperative of service on behalf of others, and the connotation that one may not see the direct results of one's actions, but is called to act nevertheless.

One may reflect on the idea that to be of assistance to others without expectation of reward manifests the human example of God-like caring. Such an ideal may emulate the construct of "social interest," as introduced by Adler, as the epitome of human interaction. This notion also has ramifications for how the counselor approaches the client's presenting issue. Notions of problem solving seem to be anchored within the material, physical world and seem to be entirely client-oriented. However, notions of spiritual growth through immediate problem solving, with such an experience being a motivator for personal insight and development, seem to be consistent with goals that are loftier than just "getting one's house in order."

Armstrong (1993) also introduced the role of wonder, offering the sentiments of Camus: "Does God lessen that wonder as all things spring from and return to God?" Camus suggested that a rejection of God might allow humans to direct their kind emotions toward the betterment of the human condition. Perhaps on an elementary level, the standard answer of "God created . . ." may appear to reduce the notion of wonder. However, much like a spiritual hunger, it may be posited that inquiry and curiosity are also basic human characteristics. One need only spend time with 3- and 4-year-olds to marvel at their thirst for answers to "why" questions.

As proffered by process theology, God can also be seen as the great companion—the fellow sufferer who understands. If one includes such a perception of God, then the core values of God may be seen as acceptance, empathy, and support, but not interference. The call to God is then for strength and guidance but not for favors. This type of appeal is founded in a firm belief in one's own as-yet untapped resources and strengths.

A debate might ensue on the limits of personal power and, should one not succeed to the level to which one aspires, to what extent such shortcomings might be perceived as a lack of effort and to what extent they are a realistic appraisal of the limits of one's capacities. Perhaps part of being a fellow sufferer entails observing individuals who are confronting their own limits without a sense of humiliation or defensiveness. This ability as a mental health services provider would seem to be a great asset in terms of role modeling an acceptance of self. An extension of this growth experience might be that one cannot fully accept another, with his or her particular competencies and inabilities, until one can fully accept and live with oneself.

Another extension of this concept revolves around a transition in relational dynamics from seeking out approval to wanting acceptance. Approval, as a dynamic, places one in the position of allowing another to pass judgment on the self, while acceptance requires a meeting of equals with the polite request that one's judgment of the self be on par with that of the other. This represents a shift in the locus of evaluation from external sources to an internal source. It also manifests a vital transition from deciding on right and wrong from what others say, which may vary on the basis of one's reference group, to a single source of morality—one's own value system.

God also "represents our aspirations, capacities and potential; that which once seemed miraculous" (Armstrong, 1993, p. 385). As such, the figure or image of God represents, on a figurative level, the epitome of potential. Although unattainable, this paragon offers guidance on how to live one's life. On a more human level, those qualities are approximated within cultural heroes (assuming that there are heroic figures of both genders). This intermediary figure provides a more achievable role model for human conduct. Every culture offers heroic figures as more down-to-earth examples of godly virtue, and the recounting of their struggles serve as inspiration for everyday life.

Buber (1970) added that God as a presence affords a moral imperative with the meaning left for individuals to decipher. However, belief in the presence of God provides a sense of accountability beyond that accorded to social institutions, such as family, friends, the legal system, and so forth. Given the all-knowing and all-seeing capacity of God, the relationship with God exemplifies the ultimate I–thou connection: a transparency of the self as mirrored in an openness to the scrutiny of God. Whether on the basis of fear of judgment and condemnation or on the basis of an inspirational model of virtue personified, standing before God, either figuratively or literally, the individual is confronted by his or her own worth and worthiness.

This measure taking is a worthwhile, ongoing human endeavor. Every life challenge or developmental milestone offers an opportunity to consider the extent to which one's life is unfolding in patterns of personal and relational integrity and virtue. The main question being posed might be "How much of the person that I hope I am, am I?" This question, although complicated, indicates a setting aside of time for the process of self-reflection and the critical nature of such introspection. Any acknowledged virtues (that which one feels proud of and wishes to continue) and admitted vices (that which one feels regret or shame for and wishes to change) must be balanced. An overemphasis on virtue may imply false pride and perfection and could preclude further growth. An overemphasis on vice may imply an exaggerated negative self-image that could lead to despair and resignation.

A belief in God as spiritual transcendence illustrates a personal belief in an individual's ongoing evolution of the self through life stages and tasks with a focus on the future and self-betterment, the "not-knowing, not yet" (Armstrong, 1993, p. 389). This belief reflects personal faith in one's potential to move forward in one's life quest without being certain of what one may discover. This devotion to one's own growth, spiritual and otherwise, marks the impetus for conscious choice and ever-expanding awareness. In this instance, transcendence may take on the meaning of evolving beyond that which one was toward that which one hopes to become, all the while being truly uncertain as to what that might be.

This section initiated consideration of one's views of God; the next section will offer a very brief overview of both attachment theory and object relations theory as explanations for the development of a personal "God image."

THEORIES OF SPIRITUAL RELATIONAL DYNAMICS

Attachment theory seeks to explain how a weaker person creates a relationship with a perceived stronger person in order to achieve physical survival and psychological security (Miner, 2007). Attachment theory is based on two fundamental hopes: (a) The self is worthy of care, and (b) others are dependable caregivers who are willing and able to care for the self. According to Ainsworth (1985), attachment theory describes the seeking of a haven of safety from an attachment figure and the surfacing of anxiety when separated from that figure.

God is viewed as being supportive and strong, generating confidence with which to face new life challenges and risk taking, and providing the courage and readiness to face doubt, self-criticism, and the knowledge of one's incompleteness. Batson, Schoenrade, and Ventis (1993) spoke to the need for a strong attachment to God as a foundation for one's spiritual quest. This is a developmental stage during which one comes freely to God. Although the searcher may experience anxiety in this process, the searcher can rest comfortably in the assurance of God's love and support.

Beck (2006) described God as an attachment figure as being the ultimate means of avoiding anxiety about abandonment. Beck hypothesized that the qualities sought in an attachment to God were based on compensatory motives for the parent/caregiver–child relationship.

Miner (2007) considered previous notions of attachment with God to be cognitive projections whereby one ascribes human qualities to God, such as power, protection, and availability. Instead, Miner advocated that attachment to God is based on "genuine personal knowledge" (p. 116) as a function of the presence of the spirit and is expressed as a "built-in yearning for God" (p. 119). Formed in God's image, each individual shares some of God's attributes, such as love, mercy, patience, grace, and justice; however, humans cannot hope to emulate all of God's attributes. The teachings of a loving God and the knowledge of God through recognition of acts of salvation motivate attachment as do models of secure attachment within one's religious or spiritual community.

From the perspective of object relations theory, Rizzuto (1991) posited that the development of the God image in childhood mirrors the child's experiencing of the parents as object representation internalizations of significant individuals and relational dynamics with those individuals. The God object is therefore designed around an individual's needs and is internalized as an "introject"—an amalgamation of a mental model of primary attachment figures (Hall & Gorman, 2003, p. 2). Rizzuto's interest centered on the possibility of the "updating [of] one's God's representation" (p. 57).

In response to Rizzuto's interest, Hall, Brokaw, Edwards, and Pike (1998) asserted that the image changes over time and experience as a reflection of one's relationships with other humans. The issue remains as to how an individual creates or adopts an image of the Divine, a Supreme Being, or God and how that image may evolve over time. If the evolution of one's image of God over the course of anticipated human development is, in fact, more psychologically healthy than the foreclosure of one's vision of God, what differences exist in individuals who undertake such transformative experiences in comparison to those who retain the same image of God throughout life? Many scholars have dedicated their professional lives to this question, but the focus of this chapter is to attempt to link these notions to the roles of the clinician and the client within the therapeutic relationship.

With regard to the therapeutic relationship, it is of interest that Armstrong (1993) wrote about the risks of a journey to the depths of the mind because we cannot know what we will find there. Such a trek must be undertaken under the guidance of an expert who can "monitor the experience, guide the novice past the perilous places, and make sure [that] he is not exceeding his strength" (p. 213). The expert must know how to get there and when one has arrived, rather than confuse the pain for the end. Such cautions hold true for both one's search for God and for the process of delivering clinical services.

IMPLICATIONS FOR THE THERAPEUTIC RELATIONSHIP

Frame (2003) alleged that whether "a client's God is loving, benevolent, merciful, forgiving, involved, and accessible or vengeful, aloof, punishing or impersonal," that perception shapes relationships with other people, especially relationships with those in authority (p. 100). It may be conjectured that such dynamics apply equally to the clinicians' perceptions of those who arrive as clients. It may be worthwhile to consider how such complementary roles emerge within the clinical relationship and to what extent these dynamics are observed and overtly addressed. For example, should both the client and the clinician affiliate with a faith tradition in which the verbal declaration of a misdeed is a required part of the healing process, then both would come to clinical services with expectations—the client expecting to disclose, or perhaps confess, and the clinician ready to advocate such behavior.

What might happen, however, if the clinician's and the client's faith traditions hold differing views of disclosure, where, in the client's case, acknowledgment to the self is sufficient, but in the clinician's case, open declaration is important? In either case, what does each person expect to happen after the disclosure has taken place? Does the client expect to be told or directed how to be different in the future, and if so, how does that expectation correlate with the clinician's expectation for the expansion of client insight?

What is central to this discussion are the core values that prompted an individual to choose to become a mental health professional and his or her values regarding those whose status is that of a client. Values arrive with the clinician-in-training, set in place by social institutions long before clinical training began. It may be suggested that those values predispose the future therapist to a genuine expression of relational dynamics and theory-specific interventions.

Egan (2007) offered the thesis that the goal of clinical services is to explore human meaning, purpose, and values. However, implicit in the depth required for this exploration is the development and maintenance of a therapeutic relationship based on mutual trust, honesty, and forthrightness. Rogers (1980) identified unconditional positive regard, empathy, and genuineness as core relational values and experiences, both as ends in themselves and as the means to the resolution of the client's pain. Patterson (1985) stated that clinical services do not involve a relationship, but it is still the relationship itself (if there were one) that is curative.

If conceptualized as a vehicle for socio-emotional relearning, the therapeutic experience for the client must be facilitated through the clinician's use of the self as a role model of "ways of being." For example, to return to Roger's concept of genuineness, the clinician must be totally aware of his or her personal responses to the client, and through the judicious use of immediacy, the clinician must "own" those responses and share them in a way that may be of help to the client.

From another perspective, the therapeutic relationship can be envisioned as a forum for client relational experimentation with another individual to confirm the parts of the self that have not been accepted or welcomed by significant others to date. For example, if the client was previously judged harshly and criticized by family members for being "too emotional," clinical services may provide an alternative "corrective emotional experience" for the client when such expression is legitimized by the clinician. However, should the clinician inadvertently mirror the judgmental stance of family members, the client receives a second condemnation of that aspect of the self, this time by a "professional."

These examples speak to the most challenging task for the clinician, who may ponder not "What am I doing with a client?" but instead "How is what I am doing being perceived?" Given the relative power imbalance within clinical services and the reluctance of a client to confront a clinician's actions except perhaps through premature termination of services, the clinician must determine how to manifest a personal stance of therapeutic authority that may incorporate aspects of one's notions of divine authority. Again, this idea does not appear in any of the professional literature to date and will require further contemplation and study to be rejected or confirmed.

This section will present four examples of relational values. It is the professional responsibility of every clinician to articulate the values that direct his or her delivery of clinical services and, if in agreement with the thesis of this chapter, to consider the origins of those values. Such values provide the foundation for how one "is" with clients in a core belief that the experiencing of such values by the client will both be of assistance to the client and set the stage for effective client introspection and growth. The following are four examples of relational values:

1. **Respect** is exemplified by doing no harm. It is a nonmanipulative and nonexploitive approach. The clinician is competent and committed. One takes the client's viewpoint seriously even when disagreeing, helps the client place demands on him- or herself, assumes the client's goodwill (that a client wants to work on his or her presenting concern(s) until proven otherwise), enters the world of client reluctance, does not rush to judgment (identifies, explores, reviews, and challenges the consequences of personally chosen values), and keeps the client's agenda in focus.

2. **Empathy** is accepting, confirming, and understanding the human echo (Kohut, 1978, p. 705). There is "psychological air" to allow those in the relationship to breathe more freely (a freedom for one to speak one's truth) (Covey, 1989) and social radar as a way to take active interest in the feelings of others. Rogers (1980) wrote,

> [I]t means entering the private perceptual world of the other and becoming thoroughly at home in it. It involves being sensitive, moment by moment, to the changing felt meanings which flow in this other person, to the fear or rage, or

tenderness or confusion or whatever that he or she is experiencing. It means temporarily living in the other's life, moving about in it delicately without making judgments. (p. 142)

There seems to be three kinds of empathy: (a) understanding the client's point of view, (b) understanding the social context in which each client lives, and (c) understanding the dissonance between the client's point of view and the societal reality. Basic to multicultural approaches to counseling, empathy also involves an acknowledgment of one's "blind spots" in the world in which we operate and, specific to this work, any spiritual values and biases.

3. **Genuineness** is the congruence of belief, affect, and behavior, including values lived apart from the helping role. The clinician expresses immediacy, communicates clearly, listens without distortion, reveals true motivations, is spontaneous rather than rehearsed, and responds immediately to the needs or the state of the client. He or she also models vulnerability, lives in the here and now, practices interdependence, enjoys psychological closeness, and remains committed to others.

4. **Empowerment** is the identification and accessing of client resources, both within the individual and within the client's social context. The clinician acknowledges the inherent imbalance of power in the provision of professional services, exerts his or her influence as an expression of that power, and influences the client without robbing him or her of self-responsibility. There is a tension between the right of the client to live a life of one's own choice and the clinician's obligation to help the client live a better life. The clinician sees the client as having resources that are blocked, rather than lacking strength. The clinician also questions the "cult of victimhood" as a defining individual characteristic and works with the freedom that is present in the client, sharing the helping process with the client to increase the client's investment in the process. The process of change can be a combination of adaptation, acceptance, or amending. The clinician serves as consultant, not a director, and focuses on client learning, rather than on directly helping the client. Client fragility is seen as self-protection.

Buber (1970) wrote on the differences between the authentic I–thou relationship and the incomplete I–it relationship. The I–thou relationship demands a level of psychological contact, from human to human, emphasizing the similarities and downplaying the differences. This orientation looks beyond the presenting issue, through cultural variables, to recognize that another person is dealing with lost dreams, life challenges, and failures. If the situation is approached in this manner, it would be hard to imagine a mental health service provider who has not had experiences similar to almost any presented by a client. In contrast, the I–it relationship allows the clinician to relate to the client as a diagnosis (ADHD, depressive, obsessive, or anxious) or as a problem (an alcoholic, a dropout, or a person with low self-esteem). Such a focus elaborates on the differences between the client and the clinician at the expense of the similarities. In addition, the distance thereby created increases the possibility of clinician judgmentalism and reduces the opportunities for empathic bonding. It may be characteristic of the I–it relationship to state, "I've never been a . . . so I cannot treat one."

Peck (1993) spoke to the preciousness of every human being. He offered that the term *religion* is based on the Latin *religio*, meaning "to connect, to attempt to be in harmony with [the] unseen order of things" (p. 46). Such a definition is not remiss when applied to clinical services if one can interpret "[the] unseen order of things" as referring to the individual's subconscious. Peck also addressed the idea of God in a direct, perpetual, and loving relationship that balances the exalted and fallen sides of the human condition. This compassion may be extended to one's version of one's clinical role and, on a secular level, to one's hoped-for outcome for each client.

Peck spoke to the inherent worthiness of each individual and of unconditional love. This concept of not having to "earn" respect or acceptance is a challenge for anyone who has been taught to value action and outcome. In such circumstances, effort may be applauded; however, victory is rewarded. The world then becomes a dismal place for those whose efforts are never sufficient to garner the "prize" but who dare not abandon the competition altogether. It is this atmosphere that fosters dishonesty, duplicity, cheating, and sabotage as the pressure to win overrides the pressure to be a true winner in life. To be a winner in life transcends the immediate competition for wealth, status, or fame and implies submitting oneself to something greater—a submission of the human will to a higher order of directive or imperative, the notion of harnessing the will to a greater aspiration of the self.

In summary, the reader may ponder whether a personal view of God and God's characteristics is related to one's sense of the self as a helping professional. If this connection is in any way valid, one must also consider how one's view of a penitent may color one's expectations of clients or whether the clients' images of the self in penance dictate or influence the self in clinical services.

EXPECTATIONS OF THE ROLE OF THE CLIENT

If one has been raised within a religious or spiritual tradition, one becomes accustomed to the mores of being a congregant. Contained in these faith-based traditions is a prescribed ritual or process for seeking redemption. It is worthwhile to consider how deeply this experience may influence the expectations that novice clients bring to mental health services.

The decision to seek clinical help is usually based on a life event in which one used poor judgment or in which one has suffered in some way. In the first instance, one realizes that one's course of action may not have prompted the optimal results. In the second instance, one may feel victimized and powerless in the face of the activating event. In the former, the client may be reluctant to overtly acknowledge the mistake; in the latter, the client may be reluctant to explore any contributing role that he or she may have played, if not in the etiology of the distress, at least in the maintenance of this issue. In the first case, the client may come to clinical services fearing judgment and being determined to withhold as much "incriminating information" as possible. In the second case, the client may come to clinical services expecting sympathy and may bridle at any focus on his or her contribution to the presenting issue. Probably, in both cases, there is the expectation that the "knowing clinician" will provide a cure or tell the client what to do (Teyber, 2006, p. 43). "Many clients believe [that] the process of therapy is primarily having the therapist tell them what to do" (p. 28). This one-up, one-down relationship fosters dependency and a sense of client inadequacy as a function of the client's belief in the greater potency of the therapist at the expense of the self. Such an orientation may bear a strong resemblance to the experiences of many penitents in many faith-based traditions.

However, the experience in clinical services is designed to be drastically different, not for the sake of difference, but for the curative powers within a different sort of helper–person-helped relationship. Teyber (2006) stated that the purpose of clinical services is to help the client gain a sense of mastery of and competence in the issue specifically and in life in general. The main expectation for the client is that he or she will become an active participant rather than expecting to be passively cured or told what to do. In addition, the client comes to learn the subjective meaning in the story, the themes, and the conflict, and to appreciate that it is the combination of personal experiences on the client's part and professional knowledge on the part of the clinician that can generate an issue that is more amenable to resolution.

An issue that arises in summarizing this section of Chapter 9 involves the role that the individual assumes when being helped within his or her religious or spiritual community. Do these role expectations "travel with" the client to the therapeutic setting? How might these dynamics affect the therapeutic relationship and the expectations held by the therapist? How might such dynamics dictate the expectations that the client has for the self within mental health services?

Case Example Revisited

Ambrose began to realize that his personal values, as founded in his narratives regarding the process of confession and the presence and role of God in his life, deeply influenced his acceptance of the teachings of his clinical program. His insight was, at first, frightening for him as he sincerely questioned his potential to become the kind of clinician to which he aspired, yet retain his Roman Catholic identity. His faculty advisor suggested that his answer lay not in surrendering either the spiritual/religious or the emerging vocational aspect of his identify, but in balancing or reconciling them. The exercise that she prescribed for him involved an objective comparison of the qualities of God as Ambrose perceived God with those of the best clinicians that Ambrose could observe.

This exercise troubled Ambrose because he claimed that he did not hold an independent vision of God apart from the teachings of his childhood. His advisor reassured him that his situation was common and, over several meetings, helped him to verbalize that child-based vision, gently leading Ambrose to consider how much of that vision was still a good fit for him.

This notion of "reinventing God" remained problematic for Ambrose on a very core spiritual level, but he persisted in the exercise. By contrast, he was more successful in the academic exercise of observing and interviewing clinicians regarding ideal clinical attributes, because he was able to identify several similarities between the qualities of God and those of the "ideal clinician," and this discovery has proven to be comforting to him in his search. As of the completion of this chapter, it is safe to say that Ambrose's vocational identity seems to be more settled for him than his religious perspective.

Conclusion

This chapter has introduced what is hoped to be viewed as an area worthy of personal meditation and professional dialogue: the possible connection between the worshipper–worshipped relationship and the client–clinician relationship. Given the pervasiveness of religious affiliation in society, it can be assumed that most individuals come to embrace an image of God—a Supreme Being of one kind or another. That image dictates the expectations of the role of those who have a relationship with that deity. Within both of those roles—the worshipped and the worshipper—are implicit values that are hypothesized to influence similar dynamics within the therapeutic relationship. Although this idea is truly in its infancy, perhaps input from scholars and clinicians will confirm—or refute—the legitimacy of such an exploration of the reconciliation of one's spiritual/religious identity and one's vocational values and ways of being.

Self-Understanding Exercises

1. List three adjectives that you would apply to your notion of God and three adjectives that you would apply to the "ideal" clinical practitioner. What do the similarities or differences between the two lists illustrate for you?

2. In your opinion, how curative is the therapeutic relationship? Why?

3. How feasible is providing efficacious mental health services without client verbalization of the presenting issue (i.e., without a client "confession")?

Opportunities for Further Learning

1. Discuss with clergy from other faith traditions their versions of God or whatever Supreme Being they acknowledge. How similar are their descriptions to what your chosen faith professes?

2. Read scripture from a faith tradition other that your own and discern the vision of the god figure put forth.

3. Ask practicing clinicians within your mental health discipline to respond to the thesis of this chapter: that there may be a connection between the worshipper–worshipped relationship and the client–clinician relationship. How informative are their responses in your quest to find such a connection?

10

...

Spirituality and Ethics

Men are not made religious by performing certain actions which are externally good, but they must first have righteous principles, and then they will not fail to perform virtuous actions.

—MARTIN LUTHER

CASE EXAMPLE

Jorge was employed as a family counselor on a college campus with a very diverse student body. He recognized that his own cultural background provided him with a way to build strong therapeutic relationships with Hispanic students, and his fluency in Spanish allowed him to counsel comfortably in two languages. However, he also recognized the importance of religion in his own personal and interpersonal relationships within the Hispanic community and was sensitive to its influence on his clients.

Wanting to provide optimal clinical services, Jorge also was concerned about any possible ethical issues pertaining to spirituality when providing counseling on a public university campus, and so he looked to existing codes of professional behavior for guidance and direction. In his search, he found general principles of practice, but no specific guidance in spiritual or religious counseling. He realized that he would need to apply the common ethical precepts to his concerns and utilize his supervisor and his peer consultant to ensure that he was not overlooking any ethical issues as he broached religious and spiritual issues with his clients.

■ ■ ■

INTRODUCTION

Ethical behavior forms the cornerstone of professional practice as a counselor, social worker, psychologist, or family therapist or any other recognized mental health professional. The principles outlined in the various codes of ethical and professional conduct, as developed by their national associations, are intended to ensure the well-being of the client. The clinician has sole responsibility for facilitating the client's well-being, both within and throughout the therapeutic context (Frame, 2003). All graduate training program curricula and all professional licensing exams address ethical concerns, and the helping professional's response to these concerns should epitomize ethical conduct.

For example, the American Counseling Association (ACA) Code of Ethics (2005) states that its contents serve four main purposes:

1. The *Code* enables the association to clarify to current and future members, and to those served by members, the nature of the ethical responsibilities held in common by its members.
2. The *Code* helps support the mission of the association.
3. The *Code* establishes principles that define ethical behavior and best practices of association members.
4. The *Code* serves as an ethical guide designed to assist members in constructing a professional course of action that best serves those utilizing counseling services and best promotes the values of the counseling profession. (Purpose).

ETHICS, SPIRITUALITY, AND CLINICAL SERVICES

More than 15 years ago, Bergin (1991) advised that ". . . there is a spiritual dimension of human experience with which the field of psychology must come to terms more assiduously" (p. 401). Currently, and specific to the theme of this book, "counselors have been urged to take more seriously clients' religious and spiritual issues" (Frame, 2000, p. 72). Given the continued and expanded focus on religious and spiritual issues in counseling, ethical concerns emerge when clinicians utilize spiritual interventions in professional mental health services and, conversely, when clinicians choose to omit these interventions when their inclusion is appropriate (Weld & Eriksen, 2007). "[P]sychotherapists who use a theist, spiritual strategy are faced with a number of potentially difficult ethical questions and challenges" (Richards & Bergin, 2005, p. 143).

Issues such as attention to client welfare, personal limitations, the setting of boundaries, increasing one's knowledge, knowing when to refer a client, and personal awareness are relevant concerns (Faiver & Ingersoll, 2005). In addition, Eck (2002) stated that mental health professionals must "obtain the training necessary to demonstrate competence in understanding the role of spirituality and religion in their clients' lives" (p. 267). "These and related dilemmas may challenge or hinder counselor educators, supervisors, practicing mental health counselors, and school counselors from adequately addressing spirituality as a counseling component" (Steen, Engels, & Thweatt, 2006, p. 106).

In addition to clinical skills, clinicians need to "emphasize the necessity and importance of tolerance, respect and mutual understanding in a world of diversity" (Wolf, 2004, p. 364). From an ontological perspective, Wiggins-Frame (2003) identified four possible views that clinicians may hold regarding religion and spiritual traditions: (a) exclusivist (the clinician's religion has a monopoly on the truth; that is, it is the one true path), (b) "inclusivist" (religion is viewed from the client's perspective), (c) pluralist (all religions hold some truth), or (d) empathic interest (religion is a way in which to learn about people). Wiggins-Frame challenged clinicians to consider which description most accurately portrays their orientation toward religion/spirituality in counseling and the ramifications of that personal choice with respect to the quality of the services that clinicians provide to clients.

Another way to examine religious traditions is to establish the commonalities among belief systems, such as ". . . [the] universal human ethics found across many different religions [which] include ideals such as kindness, love, forgiveness, and treating others as you would want to be treated" (Wolf, 2004, p. 365). Given the rising expectations from clients that their spiritual or religious issues are welcome within mental health services (Sperry, 2007), professionals who wish to respond to those clients' needs have an obligation to ensure that they do so in a manner that exemplifies the highest standards of ethical conduct.

A review of current ethical codes as established by the various professional associations offers similar themes of relevance to the study of spirituality and counseling; however, there are no statutes or guidelines that specifically address spiritual or religious concerns. The ethical codes that were reviewed include those of the American Counseling Association (ACA, 2005), the American Psychological Association (APA, 2002), the American Association for Marriage and Family Therapists (AAMFT, 2001), and the National Association of Social Workers (NASW, 1999).

A review of the relevant scholarly literature found 10 issues that various authors consider to be of importance for clinicians responding to the religious and spiritual concerns of clients:

1. client welfare,
2. respect for diversity,
3. informed consent,
4. competence and training,
5. the person-of-the-counselor issues,
6. imposition of values,
7. dual relationships and boundaries,
8. workplace boundaries,
9. respect for other professionals, and
10. consultation and referral.

In order to explore each of these issues, the relevant language from one ethical code will be cited, followed by references to the relevant sections of other ethical codes. A discussion of the ethical concerns that are specific to spirituality and counseling, as well as recommendations for helping professionals in order to prevent ethical lapses, will follow.

Client Welfare

This issue is listed first in the multiple codes of ethical conduct that were reviewed. The ACA Code of Ethics (2005) states that "the primary responsibility of counselors is to respect the dignity and to promote the welfare of clients" (Section A.1.a); "[to] attend to client worth, dignity, uniqueness and potential"; and "to avoid harming their clients" (Section A.4.a). These principles are mirrored in Section 1.01 of the NASW Code of Ethics (1999) and Section 1.1 of the AAMFT Code of Ethics (2001).

The Preamble to the APA Ethical Principles of Psychologists and Code of Conduct (2002) lists five principles: (a) beneficence and nonmaleficence, (b) fidelity and responsibility, (c) integrity, (d) justice, and (e) respect for people's rights and dignity. The text is as follows:

BENEFICENCE AND NONMALEFICENCE   Psychologists strive to benefit those with whom they work and take care to do no harm. In their professional actions, psychologists seek to safeguard the welfare and rights of those with whom they interact professionally and other affected persons, and the welfare of animal subjects of research. When conflicts occur among psychologists' obligations or concerns, they attempt to resolve these conflicts in a responsible fashion that avoids or minimizes harm. Because psychologists' scientific and professional judgments and actions may affect the lives of others, they are alert to and guard against personal, financial, social, organizational, or political factors that might lead to misuse of their influence. Psychologists strive to be aware of the possible effect of their own physical and mental health on their ability to help those with whom they work.

FIDELITY AND RESPONSIBILITY Psychologists establish relationships of trust with those with whom they work. They are aware of their professional and scientific responsibilities to society and to the specific communities in which they work. Psychologists uphold professional standards of conduct, clarify their professional roles and obligations, accept appropriate responsibility for their behavior, and seek to manage conflicts of interest that could lead to exploitation or harm. Psychologists consult with, refer to, or cooperate with other professionals and institutions to the extent needed to serve the best interests of those with whom they work. They are concerned about the ethical compliance of their colleagues' scientific and professional conduct. Psychologists strive to contribute a portion of their professional time for little or no compensation or personal advantage.

INTEGRITY Psychologists seek to promote accuracy, honesty, and truthfulness in the science, teaching, and practice of psychology. In these activities psychologists do not steal, cheat, or engage in fraud, subterfuge, or intentional misrepresentation of fact. Psychologists strive to keep their promises and to avoid unwise or unclear commitments. In situations in which deception may be ethically justifiable to maximize benefits and minimize harm, psychologists have a serious obligation to consider the need for, the possible consequences of, and their responsibility to correct any resulting mistrust or other harmful effects that arise from the use of such techniques.

JUSTICE Psychologists recognize that fairness and justice entitle all persons to access to and benefit from the contributions of psychology and to equal quality in the processes, procedures, and services being conducted by psychologists. Psychologists exercise reasonable judgment and take precautions to ensure that their potential biases, the boundaries of their competence, and the limitations of their expertise do not lead to or condone unjust practices.

RESPECT FOR PEOPLE'S RIGHTS AND DIGNITY Psychologists respect the dignity and worth of all people, and the rights of individuals to privacy, confidentiality, and self-determination. Psychologists are aware that special safeguards may be necessary to protect the rights and welfare of persons or communities whose vulnerabilities impair autonomous decision making. Psychologists are aware of and respect cultural, individual, and role differences, including those based on age, gender, gender identity, race, ethnicity, culture, national origin, religion, sexual orientation, disability, language, and socioeconomic status and consider these factors when working with members of such groups. Psychologists try to eliminate the effect on their work of biases based on those factors, and they do not knowingly participate in or condone activities of others based upon such prejudices.

DISCUSSION These five principles set forth in the Preamble of the APA Ethical Principles of Psychologists and Code of Conduct (2002) speak clearly of the primary mission of all mental health professionals (Frame, 2003). Given the potential impact of mental health services on client growth or on client decline, professionals who seek to intervene in meaningful ways with clients must do so with the intent and purpose of supporting the betterment of client welfare. Clients who seek clinical services do so in the hope and belief that their concerns, issues, identity, and potential will be confirmed by the helping professional and that committing one's resources to the counseling relationship and process will result in an amelioration of the presenting issue and the probability of a more personally satisfying future. However, as clients come to mental health services in personal pain and are also unaware of the professional obligations of the mental health professional, it is the responsibility of that professional to monitor his or her professional interactions to ensure, as much as possible, that such interactions are for the client's greater good.

Especially with regard to spiritual or religious issues in counseling, mental health professionals are charged with respecting the dignity of clients, fostering positive growth and development, and understanding the cultural background of clients (Frame, 2000). Unlike mental health professionals in the past, who may have viewed religious affiliation as a defense mechanism or an indication of emotional dependence and therefore discounted it in therapy, current clinicians must take seriously clients' religious or spiritual questions, become familiar with a client's spiritual language, and work within a client's belief system to understand how such beliefs act either as stressors or as buffers to stress. In summary, it can be asserted that the demand for the integration of religious issues into mental health services comes from the clients themselves, and those who provide mental health services would be remiss in their professional obligations if they overlooked such concerns.

ETHICAL RECOMMENDATIONS TO ENSURE CLIENT WELFARE   With regard to client welfare, helping professionals are charged with

- creating an environment that is flexible and open to religious and spiritual exploration and questioning (Steen et al., 2006),
- directing purposeful attention to the "subjective phenomenon of personal spirituality" (Steen et al., 2006, p. 110),
- incorporating qualitative appraisal techniques to investigate clients' evaluations of their own spiritual health, spiritual stressors, and spiritual supports, and
- viewing counselor rigidity around spiritual issues as immediate grounds for client referral to another practitioner.

Respect for Diversity

All mental health fields currently espouse language that validates the vitality and importance of cultural factors in the description of individual identity and the relationship of each individual to the greater society. Multiple factors have been identified as being relevant considerations in the way in which each individual defines him- or herself and how each individual may be accepted by society as a whole. Although mental health counselors cannot be expected to know how each factor affects each client in each life context, these professionals are responsible for acknowledging the presence of such factors, the potential importance of their impact on each client, and the need for the process of therapeutic services to attend to these characteristics of client identity. The NASW Code of Ethics (1999) indicates the following:

a. Social workers should understand the concept of culture and its function in human behavior and society, recognizing the strengths that exist in all cultures.

b. Social workers should have knowledge of their clients' cultures and be able to demonstrate competence in the provision of services that are sensitive to clients' cultures and to differences among people and cultural groups.

c. Social workers should be educated about, and seek to understand, the nature of social diversity and oppression with respect to race, ethnicity, national origin, gender, sexual orientation, age, marital status, political beliefs, religion, and mental or physical disability. (Standard 1.05: Cultural Competence and Social Diversity) (Section?)

DISCUSSION The ACA Code of Ethics (2005) directs that "counselors do not condone or engage in discrimination based on age, culture, disability, ethnicity, race, religion/spirituality, gender, gender identity, sexual orientation, marital status/partnership, language preference, socioeconomic status, or any basis prescribed by law. (Standard C.5)

Currently presented as issues of cultural diversity (Steen et al., 2006), religion and spirituality are included in the listing of relevant cultural factors to which mental health professionals are expected to demonstrate sensitivity, openness, and respect. Clinicians are directed not to discriminate on the basis of multiple factors, including religion (Section A.2.a), and to model professional acceptance and achieve a prompt mutual understanding of the effect that client-identified cultural factors may have on client stress or growth.

In addition, mental health professionals are expected to actively work to understand the cultural backgrounds that have an impact on client identity, including values and beliefs, regardless of the clinician's personal views. Even within religious or spiritual denominations, indicators of spiritual wellness vary among groups. Clinicians are expected to respect cultural diversity and not to force a discussion of spirituality on clients, but still, they are expected to be receptive to such a discussion if clients broach the topic in session. This directive is specifically intended to challenge the notion of religion as a defense mechanism or psychological disturbance and to consider such an orientation to be outmoded thinking and a danger to the client's self-esteem.

ETHICAL RECOMMENDATIONS TO ENSURE RESPECT FOR CLIENT RELIGIOUS/SPIRITUAL DIVERSITY With regard to client diversity, helping professionals are charged with

- becoming more aware of their own biases and assumptions about individuals or groups,
- actively attempting to understand and not to discriminate against a client's expression of religious or spiritual preference,
- accepting the differences between one's personal spiritual/religious path and that chosen by the client,
- recognizing that indicators of spiritual wellness vary among religious groups and within denominations,
- knowing that an attempt to be "spiritually neutral" in session may be construed by the client as being "anti-spiritual,"
- learning about the cultural values and assumptions of certain groups, and
- developing culturally appropriate intervention strategies.

Informed Consent

As an indication of respect for a client's self-direction, mental health professionals are ethically obliged to educate clients as to what to expect in the process of receiving mental health services and to discuss with clients the possible outcomes of any intervention, addressing both positive and negative outcomes. Although such predictions may reflect literature-based evidence or the clinician's previous experiences with those interventions, each client does have the right to decline to participate in a specific intervention or treatment. Such discussion and negotiation are powerful avenues toward client empowerment. The exercise of this right by the client is not equivalent to client resistance and does not justify termination or referral on the part of the service provider. A request for consideration of alternative interventions demonstrates the client's equal participation in and responsibility for the success of counseling. With regard to informed consent, the AAMFT Code of Ethics (2001) states the following:

Marriage and family therapists obtain appropriate informed consent to therapy or related procedures as early as feasible in the therapeutic relationship, and use language that is reasonably understandable to clients. The content of informed consent may vary depending upon the client and treatment plan; however, informed consent generally necessitates that the client (a) has the capacity to consent; (b) has been adequately informed of significant information concerning treatment processes and procedures; (c) has been adequately informed of potential risks and benefits of treatments for which generally recognized standards do not yet exist; (d) has freely and without undue influence expressed consent; and (e) has provided consent that is appropriately documented. When persons, due to age or mental status, are legally incapable of giving informed consent, marriage and family therapists obtain informed permission from a legally authorized person, if such substitute consent is legally permissible. (Standard 1.2)

EXPLANATION   Clinicians use clear and understandable language to inform all parties involved about the purposes of the services to be provided, relevant costs, potential risks and benefits, and the limits of confidentiality, as exemplified in Standard 10.01 (a–c) in the APA Ethical Principles of Psychologists and Code of Conduct (2002) and echoed in Standard 1.05 (a–f) in the NASW Code of Ethics (1999). It is the client's right to know what will happen in counseling and to freely choose the extent of his or her participation after having weighed the risks and benefits of the intervention(s). This consent must be a function of capacity (one's ability to make rational decisions), an understanding of the information provided, and free will, especially for clients who may not expect to have these topics broached in counseling. Clients may not realize that they have a right to question how services are provided and a right to decline to participate in interventions without the risk of censure by the mental health services provider.

In addition, if clinicians are affiliated with a faith-based institution, then, at the onset of the provision of clinical services, they must inform the client about the affiliation and the doctrines of that institution. Once provided with that information, clients have a right to refuse intervention or seek a professional whose spiritual path is more congruent with their own, at which point, the clinician is ethically obliged to offer a referral to another practitioner (Frame, 2003).

ETHICAL RECOMMENDATIONS TO ENSURE INFORMED CONSENT BY CLIENTS DISCUSSING RELIGIOUS/SPIRITUAL ISSUES   With regard to informed consent, helping professionals are charged with

- seeking client agreement before broaching spiritual or religious topics in session;
- explaining to the client the potential risks and benefits of specific interventions;

- accessing the professional literature, clinical supervision, or peer input, wherever possible, in order to determine the potential risks and benefits of certain spiritual interventions prior to using that strategy in session; and
- debriefing the experience with the client prior to the end of that session to evaluate the efficacy of that intervention for that specific client.

Competence and Training

INTRODUCTION   The ethical guidelines referenced for this chapter all insist that mental health professionals honor the limits of their levels of professional competence. For those clinicians seeking to address spiritual and religious topics in session, there exists an ethical imperative to obtain adequate training and acquire additional preparation beyond their graduate programs (e.g., by making an effort to gain insight into the major world religions and looking outside of one's professional discipline to the fields of sociology, psychology, and religious studies). In addition, learning and introducing new interventions require ongoing supervision and consultation to hone the clinician's skill at delivering that strategy and to ensure that the intervention has a reasonable chance of achieving the positive client outcome for which it was intended. The ACA Code of Ethics (2005), Section C.2, states the following:

> Counselors practice only in the boundaries of their competence, based on their education, training, supervised experience, state and national professional credentials, and appropriate professional experience. Counselors will demonstrate a commitment to gain knowledge, personal awareness, sensitivity and skills pertinent to working with a diverse population (Section C.2.b). Counselors practice in specialty areas new to them only after appropriate education, training, and supervised experience. While developing skills in new specialty areas, counselors take steps to ensure the competence of their work and to protect others from possible harm.

These responsibilities also appear in the AAMFT Code of Ethics (Standards 3.1 and 3.2), the APA Ethical Principles of Psychologists and Code of Conduct (Standards 2.01 and 2.03), and the NASW Code of Ethics (Standard 4.01, a–c).

DISCUSSION   The idea of competence in spiritual or religious interventions in counseling is reflected in the discussion of spiritual preparedness (Steen et al., 2006). As part of a developmental life-span perspective and as one component of holistic wellness, clinicians need to professionally prioritize developing clinical knowledge and expertise in this area. Given the relative brevity of graduate training programs in terms of their capacity to prepare future clinicians to address all topics using all available interventions, mental health professionals must choose areas of specialization and seek ongoing training, support, and supervision to build competence and expertise in the delivery of efficacious and ethical services in those areas.

Clinicians may also wish to acknowledge the greater risk of introducing as-yet untried interventions in session and should do so only with adequate preparation and multiple fallback strategies should the new intervention prove to be unsuccessful. In addition, with regard to the misuse of spiritual or religious interventions in session, Tan (2003) cautioned clinicians against (a) misusing spiritual resources such as prayer or scripture to avoid facing painful issues in counseling, (b) focusing solely on religious or spiritual goals to the exclusion of client's nonspiritual agenda, and (c) utilizing spiritual interventions in cases that warrant medical intervention.

ETHICAL RECOMMENDATIONS TO ENSURE COUNSELOR COMPETENCE REGARDING RELIGIOUS/ SPIRITUAL ISSUES With regard to counselor competence, helping professionals are charged with

- obtaining training in multicultural counseling, because spirituality/religion is a component of cultural diversity,
- being responsible for increasing their professional knowledge of the psychology and sociology of religion and of spiritual issues in psychotherapy,
- attending professional development workshops on this topic,
- utilizing at least one comprehensive book as a reference on world religions, regardless of personal preference, because understanding and receptivity are more critical than shared beliefs (Frame, 2003),
- acquiring specific information on the spiritual/religious traditions found in their client population,
- seeking supervision or consultation when first working with clients on spiritual issues or when working with a client from an unfamiliar spiritual or religious orientation, and
- seeking supervision or consultation when introducing new spiritual interventions in their clinical work.

The Person-of-the-Counselor Issues

The nature of the mental health care profession requires the clinician to acknowledge personal issues and unresolved emotional biases not out of a need for the clinician to be "perfect" in order to be of help to others, but rather to acknowledge the common human journey shared by the clinician and the client and to ensure that the full attention of the clinician is directed toward the client and not toward personal needs. In addition, the capacity to "own one's own stuff" provides a model for clients on how to accept their own unresolved issues without fearing scorn or rejection from the professional. This notion of a "shared journey" may be seen as the basis of the therapeutic relationship and a reflection of mutual respect and commitment. Furthermore, such an image refocuses the perception of counseling from a vision in which the counselor "has all the answers" to one in which both the client and the counselor confront similar life questions, but each seeks answers specific to and congruent with one's personal life context and values.

The APA Ethical Principles of Psychologists and Code of Conduct reads as follows:

2.06 Personal Problems and Conflicts

(a) Psychologists refrain from initiating an activity when they know or should know that there is a substantial likelihood that their personal problems will prevent them from performing their work-related activities in a competent manner. (b) When psychologists become aware of personal problems that may interfere with their performing work-related duties adequately, they take appropriate measures, such as obtaining professional consultation or assistance, and determine whether they should limit, suspend, or terminate their work-related duties. (See also Standard 10.10, Terminating Therapy.)

DISCUSSION Specific to the interplay of a client's presenting spiritual and religious counseling issues and the counselor's own personal issues around these topics, the Association for Spiritual, Ethical, and Religious Values in Counseling (ASERVIC, 2005) offers the following: Competency 3—The professional counselor engages in self-exploration of religious and spiritual beliefs in order to increase sensitivity, understanding and acceptance of diverse belief systems.

The ACA Code of Ethics (2005) speaks to the professional hazards of countertransference (Sections C.2.g and F.5.b,c) in general, and this concern is addressed more directly for anti- and nonreligious counselors with religious clients and for spiritual or religious mental health providers with anti- or nonreligious clients (Weld & Eriksen, 2007).

In terms of better conceptualizing one's personal stance toward religion and spirituality and the intersection of one's personal and professional views, Sperry (2007, p. 46) diagramed four stances toward personal and professional views on religion:

Personal		
Professional	Low	High
Low	1	2
High	3	4

1 = Disinterested or agnostic personal stance, positive, value-free professional stance.
2 = Personal spiritual journey, but value-free professional stance.
3 = Disinterested or agnostic personal stance, but interested in the client's religious or spiritual issues.
4 = Personal spiritual journey and sensitive to the client's religious or spiritual issues.
Sperry advised that stances 1 and 2 are out of compliance with current ethical thinking and challenged mental health counselors to accurately assess their own positions on this topic.

ETHICAL RECOMMENDATIONS TO ENSURE COUNSELOR ATTENTION TO PERSON-OF-THE-COUNSELOR ISSUES With regard to person-of-the-counselor issues, helping professionals are charged with

- confronting their own belief systems in terms of the contribution of such systems to personal health and functioning,
- seeking personal therapy for personal religious issues that might impede therapeutic efficacy,
- avoiding the placement of personal needs (e.g., proselytizing, presenting one's personal hostility to religion, etc.) over the client's needs,
- refraining from trying to convince the client of the dangers of his or her religion (Frame, 2003),
- assessing their understanding of the client's spiritual or religious worldview (Wolf, 2004), and
- being "involved in their own spiritual journey" (Faiver & Ingersoll, 2005, p. 176).

Imposition of Values

The understanding of the therapeutic process has evolved to the point that the communication of values between the mental health professional and the client is an expected aspect of that process. However, there is an important distinction between the communication of one's personal values and the imposition of those values. By imposition, Richards and Begin (2005) mean ". . . using coercive methods to indoctrinate or influence clients, especially concerning therapy session content that is not relevant to the disorder or problem being treated" (p. 153).

The NASW Code of Ethics (1999) addresses this concern by stating that social workers respect and promote the right of clients to self-determination and assist clients in their efforts to identify and clarify their goals. Social workers may limit clients' right to self-determination when, in the social workers' professional judgment, clients' actions or potential actions pose a serious, foreseeable, and imminent risk to themselves or others. (Standard 1.02)

This professional sentiment is echoed in the AAMFT Code of Ethics (2001), Standard 1.

DISCUSSION Clinicians risk a serious breach of ethical standards if they preach, teach, or try to persuade clients that the clinician's personally held belief system is more valid than the client's. Examples of such ethical violations may include (a) offering literature about the therapist's religious denomination, (b) inviting clients to attend services at the counselor's choice of place of worship, or (c) teaching clients about the counselor's religious beliefs when those beliefs are irrelevant or tangential to the client's presenting issue.

A second example of the values imposition would be for the mental health professional to criticize or condemn the client's choice of lifestyle, including issues such as gender roles, marital fidelity, and sexual orientation. Although the counselor has an obligation to offer professional input regarding the possible consequences of a client's choices, the counselor has no right to make the choice for the client.

A third example of values imposition would entail a covert agenda to change the client toward ways of being that are more in line with the mental health professional's notion of the "right" way to live one's life. Examples of such agendas include conversion therapy for homosexual clients or trying to convince a female client to adhere to a more traditional gender role as a way to resolve her career concerns. Conversely, this issue is equally important to liberal therapists who may try to convince clients to become more accepting of alternative lifestyles or values as a reflection of the counselor's own approach to life. Richards and Bergin (2005) succinctly stated, "Regardless of their personal views, therapists should not attempt to coerce clients into decisions or lifestyles that are contrary to clients' values, wishes, and cultural context" (p. 156).

A fourth example of values imposition is the use of spiritual interventions without the client's explicit consent. Such impositions may include a prayer at the beginning of the session, the use of religious imagery in guided imagery exercises, and the offering of scripture as bibliotherapy. The use of such techniques without the client's overt consent implies that the values associated with such practices are beneficial for the client and that the client agrees with such values. Given the previous discussion of the ethical obligations around the issue of informed consent, such an assumption on the part of the mental health professional would be inappropriate.

Given the ethical concerns discussed in the previous paragraphs, the notion of professional neutrality might provide a false sense of security. Although nondiscussion avoids the issue of values imposition, that omission suggests that such topics are irrelevant in counseling (Steen et al., 2006). It is a basic supposition that a spiritual perspective generates a spiritual reality which ". . . influences the identity, agency and lifestyle of human beings" (Bergin, 1991, p. 398). Therefore, "the real issue is how to use values to therapeutic advantage without abusing the therapist's power and the client's vulnerability" (p. 396).

ETHICAL RECOMMENDATIONS TO ENSURE THE AVOIDANCE OF THE IMPOSITION OF VALUES

With regard to avoiding the imposition of values, helping professionals are charged with

- respecting a client's right to hold beliefs different from the clinician's, even if both are members of the same religious denomination;
- refraining from trying to convert the client even if it is believed to be in the client's best interests;
- remaining accepting of a client's lifestyle choices even if the clinician does not agree or deems those choices to be possibly destructive to the client (however, exploration of the consequences and implications of such choices are clearly within the therapeutic mandate);
- overtly discussing any disagreements with regard to values, with the intent of either resolving the issue or recognizing that the issue is grounds for client referral to another practitioner;
- obtaining the client's explicit permission prior to pursuing religious goals in counseling;
- obtaining the client's consent prior to using a spiritual intervention, but only after explaining the purpose, intent, and procedure for such a strategy;
- seeking agreement on spiritual themes in the client's life as a source of strength, guidance, and coping; and
- pursuing a deeper understanding of how a client's beliefs support his or her identity and ability to respond in positive ways to life's challenges.

Dual Relationships and Boundaries

INTRODUCTION   The sensitivity and vulnerability implicit in the therapeutic relationship on the part of clients demands that the mental health professional be explicit in word and action about the characteristics, dynamics, and limits of the clinical relationship. Accepting an individual, group, or family as a client implies that the therapeutic alliance supersedes any other relationship between the parties involved. It is the responsibility of the mental health professional to maintain the primacy and exclusivity of the clinical relationship, because any blurring of that relationship through other counselor–client contact will seriously imperil the objectivity of the clinician and be detrimental to the quality of the counseling services provided.

The APA Ethical Principles of Psychologists and Code of Conduct (2002) offers the following with regard to dual relationships within a therapeutic setting:

a. A multiple relationship occurs when a psychologist is in a professional role with a person and (1) at the same time is in another role with the same person, (2) at the same time is in a relationship with a person closely associated with or related to the person with whom the psychologist has the professional relationship, or (3) promises to enter into another relationship in the future with the person or a person closely associated with or related to the person [receiving services].

A psychologist refrains from entering into a multiple relationship if the multiple relationships could reasonably be expected to impair the psychologist's objectivity, competence, or effectiveness in performing his or her functions as a psychologist, or otherwise risks exploitation or harm to the person with whom the professional relationship exists. Multiple relationships that would not reasonably be expected to cause impairment or risk exploitation or harm are not unethical.

b. If a psychologist finds that, due to unforeseen factors, a potentially harmful multiple relationship has arisen, the psychologist takes reasonable steps to resolve it with due regard for the best interests of the affected person and maximal compliance with the Ethics Code. (Standard 3.05)

c. When psychologists are required by law, institutional policy, or extraordinary circumstances to serve in more than one role in judicial or administrative proceedings, at the outset they clarify role expectations and the extent of confidentiality and thereafter as changes occur.

Similar guidelines appear in the NASW Code of Ethics (1999, Standard 1.06c) and the AAMFT Code of Ethics (2001, Standard 1.3).

EXPLANATION   Dual relationships make clients vulnerable to exploitation by counselors by provoking competing agendas and needs that may impair the mental health professional's clinical judgment (Frame, 2003). There are two main instances of concern: (a) when the clinician is also in the capacity of a religious leader and (b) when the counselor is a member of the congregation.

If the clinician is also the religious leader, clients may personalize sermons or other teachings that were meant for a general audience. Given the issues of (1) a power imbalance between the clergy member and the congregant/client and (2) a lack of anonymity, clergy/counselors are advised to consider (a) consultation services for clients in order that they may seek counseling elsewhere; (b) referrals among clergy so that one does not see members of one's congregation; (c) counselor discretion about what to divulge about a client/congregant; (d) that clergy not participate in activities such as meditation groups or other congregant experiences where self-disclosure is expected; and (e) policy regarding home visits, emergencies, and social contact (Richards & Bergin, 2005).

Such dual relationships also (a) blur job functions and responsibilities, (b) may make clients feel unsafe disclosing information when the counselor has religious authority over them, and (c) call into question the purity of one's motive for referring clients to one's own practice. There is a similar concern if the counselor is part of the congregation. Social contact with clients, the blurring of professional boundaries with regard to friendship or other nontherapeutic relationships, and the level of client comfort when meeting in a nontherapeutic setting all provide strong arguments against this practice. Furthermore, clients may begin to avoid the religious or spiritual institution for fear of running into the clinician and experiencing the ensuing embarrassment. Such a relationship also risks accidental violation of client privacy and confidentiality. Finally, clients may confuse the counselor's presence at the religious or spiritual institution with the counselor's clinical availability.

ETHICAL RECOMMENDATIONS TO ENSURE THE AVOIDANCE OF DUAL RELATIONSHIPS   With regard to dual relationships, helping professionals are charged with

- avoiding role duality between professional and religious affiliations,
- consulting with a supervisor or colleague if one is considering overlapping the two roles,
- clearly defining the limits and extent of the relationship with the client and explaining the boundaries and possible risks (if warranted), and

- maintaining careful documentation of each aspect of the services provided and ensuring that this pattern of documentation continues throughout the therapeutic relationship.

Workplace Boundaries

INTRODUCTION Another concern deals with possible violations of laws or policies separating church and state (Richards & Bergin, 2005). Richards and Bergin's (2005) discussion of the interpretations of the First Amendment spoke to two vital issues of relevance to mental health professionals: (a) One religion cannot be favored over another and (b) participation in religious activity cannot be compelled. Although such ethical guidelines have not been put into writing as of yet, the ethical codes of all mental health professions demand that professionals adhere to the law. For example, the AAMFT Code of Ethics (2001) asserts the following:

Marriage and family therapists maintain adequate knowledge of and adhere to applicable laws, ethics, and professional standards. (Standard 3.2)

DISCUSSION The fourteenth amendment to the Constitution of the United States, which incorporates the first amendment, is applied to all "state actions" and limits behavior in governmental settings, including public schools. Teachers and other school-based personnel within the public school system cannot "do anything in the work setting that would make it appear that the government or its employees seek to promote, endorse or establish religion" (Richards & Bergin, 2005, p. 160). Although sharing values and exploring beliefs is acceptable and is permitted within state-funded agencies, any activities that might be seen as advocating one specific belief system over another would be unethical and illegal (Frame, 2003). Students may sponsor such activities within a school setting; however, a teacher or administrator cannot initiate such an action (Wolf, 2004). With younger children, the teacher must exercise even greater care because young children cannot separate the actions of one teacher from an endorsement by the school.

In a civic setting, such as a mental health care setting, these topics can be broached by the client and responded to by the counselor, but only when initiated by the client. Clinicians in an agency setting are advised to get formal permission from a supervisor before using spiritual interventions such as praying with a client, reading scripture, and assigning spiritual bibliotherapy as homework. Written permission may also be requested from one's client, thereby granting informed consent for that specific intervention. In addition, care must be taken not to usurp or displace the authority of religious or spiritual leaders. Clinicians are not to conduct religious rituals or give blessings. Conversely, mental health professionals are cautioned against denigrating a client's religious leaders or making negative comments about belief systems.

ETHICAL RECOMMENDATIONS TO ENSURE THE HONORING OF WORKPLACE BOUNDARIES With regard to honoring workplace boundaries, helping professionals are charged with

- adhering to workplace policies honoring the separation of church and state when practicing in civic settings,
- working within a client's value system,
- refraining from using spiritual interventions to impose a specific viewpoint and, when they do use such interventions, using them only with the written permission of the client and the agency, and
- obtaining written permission from the parents of children before using any type of spiritual intervention.

Respect for Other Professionals

INTRODUCTION   Congruent with the previous discussion regarding the limits of competence and the imposition of religious or spiritual values, mental health professionals are cautioned against usurping the role and function of the client's religious leaders. Specifically, professionals are cautioned against (a) advocating that the client revise his or her current belief system or consider other spiritual paths and (b) imposing interventions that are more consistent with the role of an ecclesiastical leader. Such actions show a lack of respect for sources of support in the client's life and obstruct the facilitation of collaborative relationships with those supports to better serve the client.

With regard to these concerns, the NASW Code of Ethics (1999) states the following:

a. Social workers should treat colleagues with respect and should represent accurately and fairly the qualifications, views, and obligations of colleagues.

b. Social workers should avoid unwarranted negative criticism of colleagues in communications with clients or with other professionals. Unwarranted negative criticism may include demeaning comments that refer to a colleague's level of competence or to attributes such as race, ethnicity, national origin, gender, sexual orientation, age, marital status, political beliefs, religion, and mental or physical disability.

c. Social workers should cooperate with colleagues within and outside of the social worker's field of expertise when such cooperation is in the interests of the client. (Standard 2.01)

The APA Ethical Principles of Psychologists and Code of Conduct (2002), Standard 3.09, provides similar guidance, and the ACA Code of Ethics (2005), Standard A.11.d adds the following:

Professional counselors recognize that the quality of their interactions with colleagues can influence the quality of services provided to clients. They work to become knowledgeable about colleagues within and outside the field of counseling. Counselors develop positive working relationships and systems of communication with colleagues to enhance services to clients.

DISCUSSION   A concern when clients come for help with issues related to religious or spiritual issues is that the counselor might challenge the credibility of the client's religious leaders. Although psychology historically sought to discredit the function of religion and religious leaders in individuals' lives and to demean reliance on religion, this perspective is in need of revision on the part of mental health professionals. The inclusion of this topic within this chapter on ethical behavior will hopefully serve as confirmation of the evolution of a positive working collaboration between clergy and mental health professionals.

The most subtle expression of a lack of respect for religious leaders is a failure to consult or cooperate with them. Such an omission may prevent the client from receiving the social support of church members or from accessing church-based programs for financial support or other assistance. In addition, the service missions of many religious institutions may help clients find a purpose or meaning in life at a time when its absence is most keenly felt.

Another concern is that the use of spiritual interventions in session may cause the mental health professional to overstep his or her role and infringe on the role of the religious leader. The most obvious manifestations of this concern involve overt denigration of religious leaders and of the client's affiliation with a specific religious institution and outright rejection of advice given to a client by clergy. Additional professional infringement on the role of religious leaders occurs if the clinician assumes ecclesiastical competence or performs ecclesiastical functions such as hearing confessions, granting pardons, and so forth (Tan, 2003). Such actions not only convey a lack of ethical respect for the duties of clergy, but also show a disrespect for professional boundaries.

In summary, in holding with the initial ethical mandate regarding attention to the welfare of clients, respect for a client's choice of religious or spiritual belief system must be extended to the client's clergy member(s), whether or not the clinician personally shares such an orientation (Richards & Bergin, 2005).

ETHICAL RECOMMENDATIONS TO ENSURE RESPECT FOR RELIGIOUS AUTHORITIES With regard to respect for religious authorities, helping professionals are charged with

- determining the client's affiliation and whether the client may identify specific religious leaders as a source of support and assistance (should be done during the intake process),
- requesting the client's permission to contact any such individuals for a possible consultation and coordination of services if such collaboration seems to be appropriate,
- explaining the parameters of the consultation to the person contacted and stating that permission was given by the client for the contact to be initiated,
- explaining the purpose of any proposed spiritual intervention and stating that its use in no way implies that the mental health professional is assuming the role or function of the religious leader, and
- consulting the religious leader to determine how his or her role and functions may support the therapeutic agenda.

Consultation and Referral

INTRODUCTION The mental health services professional has a primary ethical obligation to be of service to clients; however, the professional must also recognize the limits of his or her professional competence. Clinicians have an obligation to consult with other professionals, both within and outside one's clinical field, and to provide referrals to other professionals in the event that the clinician's services are ineffective or if additional help is warranted or requested. The ACA Code of Ethics (2005) states the following:

> **A.11.b.** (Inability to Assist Clients) If counselors determine an inability to be of professional assistance to clients, they avoid entering or continuing counseling relationships. Counselors are knowledgeable about culturally and clinically appropriate referral resources and suggest these alternatives. If clients decline the suggested referrals, counselors should discontinue the relationship.

In addition, the NASW Code of Ethics (1999) states the following:

> ### 2.05 Consultation
> **a.** Social workers should seek the advice and counsel of colleagues whenever such consultation is in the best interests of clients.

---

b. Social workers should keep themselves informed about colleagues' areas of expertise and competencies. Social workers should seek consultation only from colleagues who have demonstrated knowledge, expertise, and competence related to the subject of the consultation.

c. When consulting with colleagues about clients, social workers should disclose the least amount of information necessary to achieve the purposes of the consultation.

2.06 Referral for Services

a. Social workers should refer clients to other professionals when the other professionals' specialized knowledge or expertise is needed to serve clients fully or when social workers believe that they are not being effective or making reasonable progress with clients and that additional service is required.

b. Social workers who refer clients to other professionals should take appropriate steps to facilitate an orderly transfer of responsibility. Social workers who refer clients to other professionals should disclose, with [the client's] consent, all pertinent information to the new service providers.

c. Social workers are prohibited from giving or receiving payment for a referral when no professional service is provided by the referring social worker.

Both the APA Ethical Principles of Psychologists and Code of Conduct (2002, Standard 4.06) and the AAMFT Codes of Ethics (2001, Standards 1.10 and 1.11) present similar statements about the mental health professional's ethical responsibilities with regard to consultations and referrals.

DISCUSSION Specific to this area of ethical review, the Association for Spiritual, Ethical, and Religious Values in Counseling (ASERVIC, 2005) offers the following prescription: Competency 6—The professional counselor can identify [the] limits of his/her understanding of a client's religious or spiritual expression, and demonstrate appropriate referral skills and generate possible referral sources.

Frame (2003) recommended that clinicians make referrals to clergy for the use of techniques that are congruent with the client's belief system, as was suggested in the "limits of competency" section discussing maintaining ethical respect for the authority of other professionals in the client's life. A second opportunity for such referrals involves religious issues such as conversion from one faith to another, which is clearly beyond the competence or area of expertise of most mental health professionals. A clinician must also consider that, should such an issue be within his or her area of expertise, entering into or continuing a therapeutic relationship may cause a blurring of professional boundaries and thereby be detrimental to the client. A third opportunity to make a referral involves a client's request for the interpretation of scripture or other religious writings, a task that would be more congruent with the professional practice of clergy.

Frame also suggested that clergy be contacted to provide a referral for clients who are seeking specialized knowledge in religious traditions, such as Native American religions. From a slightly different perspective, Wolf (2004) advocated referral to, and consultation with, clergy regarding those clients who may be considering the ministry or a religious vocation as a career choice.

ETHICAL RECOMMENDATIONS FOR PROFESSIONAL CONSULTATIONS AND REFERRALS   With regard to consultations and referrals, helping professionals are charged with

- developing a network of friendly clergy who represent the diversity of the religious/spiritual traditions encountered in one's professional practice,
- building collaborative relationships with clergy who can be trusted to support a client's psychological and spiritual health and to be positive adjuncts to the therapeutic process,
- ascertaining the clergy member's perspectives on mental health services to facilitate an open exchange of information that is or might be relevant to the client's welfare, and
- maintaining contact with referred clients, if possible, in order to ensure that the referral has been successful and, if it has not, investigating what happened in order to remedy any such issues prior to future referrals.

Case Example Revisited

Jorge's first on-the-job encounter with ethical concerns involved the legal guidelines for working at a public, state-funded institution and the restrictions against introducing the topic of religion or spirituality in session. Although his supervisor confirmed that he could pursue this area of inquiry once it had been raised by a client, Jorge recognized his limited ability to discuss religious or spiritual traditions other than his own.

To remedy this situation, Jorge vowed to increase his knowledge of other spiritual traditions. He also made use of the extensive religious support systems on campus by developing a list of supportive clergy to whom he could refer clients. In working with his peers, he identified two professional organizations that he

could explore and several upcoming conferences where he could attend workshops on the themes of gaining knowledge of other faith traditions and the ethical use of religion and spirituality in counseling. He also asked each member of the clergy with whom he spoke to recommend one basic source that he could consult in order to develop a fundamental understanding of, and working vocabulary pertaining to, diverse religious and spiritual traditions.

In Jorge's opinion, increasing his knowledge and developing new skills while relying on established sources of religious or spiritual authority offered an optimum way for him to attend to the needs of his clients and make a commitment to expand his ability to be of help to them.

Conclusion

Given the attention currently being paid to spiritual and religious issues in the provision of mental health services, it is vital that professional enthusiasm not outpace the ethical guidelines for professional practice. Although perhaps not specifically addressing the themes of spirituality and religion, all ethical standards provide applicable guidance and direction. It is the responsibility of each mental health professional to ensure that he or she has knowledge of, and adheres to, these standards. In addition, ongo-

ing discussion of these issues will promote greater understanding and clarity, for ". . . wherever spirituality is concerned, there is bound to be ambiguity" (Faiver & Ingersoll, 2005, p. 181). The final words of this chapter are offered by Richard and Bergin (2005), who stated, "[W]e believe more discussion, debate and research is needed as this approach evolves to ensure that therapists continue to progress in their capacity to use spiritual strategy ethically and effectively" (p. 169).

Self-Understanding Exercises

1. How do you define a *spiritually competent counselor*? How do you measure up to this definition and what is needed for you to grow in this area? (Faiver & Ingersoll, 2005)
2. For which religious or spiritual questions would you refer a client?
3. Identify any potential personal transference issues regarding spirituality that you might have. How would you address these concerns so that recognition of the issue prompts helpful self-disclosure rather than transference?

Opportunities for Further Learning

1. Interview a licensed mental health professional who is also a member of the clergy and discuss how that individual addresses the types of ethical concerns raised in this chapter (Frame, 2003).
2. Review original works by Freud and others on the separation of psychology and religion. Given the cultural context in which those theorists operated, how sensible was that schism? How sensible is it in today's cultural context?
3. Compare the ethical code of your professional association with state licensing laws governing your clinical practice. Where do the two codes of conduct overlap? Where do they diverge?

11

Theory-Based Approaches to Wellness in Counseling and Spirituality

Thinking is the talking of the soul within itself.
—PLATO (428/427 B.C.–348/347 B.C.)

CASE EXAMPLE

Constance earned a professional degree and her Licensed Professional Counselor designation. She was a counselor in a community mental health center that relied on third-party reimbursement as payment for clinical services. Thus, Constance was required to complete a "diagnostic ticket" for each client, specifying the diagnosis for the insurance company.

Although Constance enjoyed the professional puzzle of diagnosis, she was becoming more and more troubled by the lack of corresponding criteria for assessing client growth, apart from the reduction of symptoms. Her review of the *Diagnostic and Statistical Manual of Mental Disorders* provided little guidance, from her standpoint, so she returned to her study of theory to develop an alternative notion of how to describe "successful counseling," not in terms of delivery of services, but in terms of client growth toward wellness.

In her search, she discovered models of wellness that pertained to many topics, but none that applied specifically to client spirituality. She realized that she would have to develop a personal model that integrated spiritual and clinical wellness within her counseling model in order to be able to observe client change both away from dysfunction and toward a sense of "optimal functioning."

INTRODUCTION

The Purpose of Theory in Clinical Service and the Evaluation of Clinical Success

A theory can be defined as "a group of logically organized laws or relationships that consti- tute [an] explanation in a discipline" (Heinen, 1985, p. 414, as cited by Sharf, 2004, p. 1). Theory encompasses

> a set of principles that (a) explains a group of phenomena or facts, (b) can be used to make predictions about future or coexisting phenomena, (c) can be tested by checking the accuracy of those predictions, and (d) helps comprehen- sion of the phenomena [that] it explains and guides action in relevant situations. (Day, 2004, p. 22)

Within the profession of counseling, theories are also referred to as treatment systems, the- ories of change, and treatment approaches (Seligman, 2006, p. 10). Theories, in general, provide information about (a) different stages in an individual's development, including both healthy and abnormal development; (b) techniques to help clients both remediate life obstacles and grow in healthier ways; and (c) barometers of success in counseling and psychotherapy.

Professional counseling and mental health services are based on the notion that an understanding of the client's issue, in a manner distinct from that presented and yet based on a model applicable to the client in each similar context, guides the way in which the coun- selor makes sense of the client's stories of life dissatisfaction (Corey, 2005). Theory also offers a "rationale, conceptual scheme or myth . . . that you and your client agree on what has gone wrong, and what life would look like if the problem were set right" (Day, 2004, p. 11). Furthermore, theory provides a series of goals for insight or self-understanding and for change (acceptance of a life circumstance that has heretofore been fought, or an amendment to a life circumstance that might have interfered with the development of a quality life) that the client and the counselor may negotiate and, based on that compromise, to which thera- peutic effort is directed (Sharf, 2004). Finally, the specification of counseling goals facilitates the identification of benchmarks of client progress and of the counselor's self-evaluation of clinical efficacy (Sharf, 2004). Implicit in this adaptation of theory and direction in counseling is a philosophical challenge to balance the biomedical approach, the biopsychosocial approach, and the actualization approach to treatment.

The biomedical approach seeks to categorize client behavior into a diagnosis that is founded in an etiology of chemical imbalance in brain functioning. On the basis of that foundation, one treatment focus may require the introduction of a particular medication to control that specific brain functioning in order to reduce the observable symptoms. Another approach emphasizes a biopsychosocial understanding of client dysfunction and directs in- tervention toward any of the three contributing factors: biology, ego functioning, or social relationships.

Whichever approach is chosen, the mental health professional is still confronted with a philosophical question: What constitutes therapeutic success? Is success considered to be the alleviation of presenting symptoms, or is it their reduction to a point where there is no longer significant interference in life functioning, or does that goal serve as the initial goal for prompting optimal client development toward a model of wellness? As Hattie, Myers, and Sweeney (2004) stated, "[E]nhancement of functioning is a very different emphasis than simply attempting to restore adequate functioning" (p. 362).

Conceptualizations of Wellness

One challenge in helping clients move toward wellness or functioning is the lack of a concise definition of what this type of growth or level of functioning entails. As an overarching principle, Diener (1984) specified that such a formulation must be based on a subjective evaluation: the measurement of all of the components of one's life. However, more than a decade later, in 1995, Ryff and Keyes noted that "the absence of theory-based formulations of well-being is puzzling" (p. 720). This need for the development of such a formulation reflects the contentions of theorists such as Jung and Maslow that humans have an innate drive to actualize personal potential and excellence (Hattie, Myers, & Sweeney, 2004).

Savolaine and Granello (2002) discussed the paradigm of a "salutogenic (or health-enhancing) focus" (p. 178). However, the naming of the paradigm seems to have come before the application of its concepts. The World Health Organization (1958) claimed that health is "a state of complete physical, mental and social well-being, not merely the absence of disease" (p. 1). This definition was a crucial acknowledgment of two concepts: (a) distinct areas of functioning exist that affect overall functioning and (b) health transcends the mere absence of illness. As Dunn (1961) remarked, more from a psychological orientation than from a medical perspective, wellness involves the inherent drive in individuals to seek their highest potential. Seligman and Csikszentmihalyi (2000) stated that "social and behavioral sciences can articulate a vision of a good life . . . and can show what actions lead to well-being" (p. 10). These authors also asserted that "treatment is not just fixing what is broken; it is nurturing what is best" (p. 9). The notion of "what is best" can be viewed as the foundation for differing notions of psychological wellness.

The models of psychological wellness that follow are presented in chronological order according to their appearance in the professional literature. Opatz (1986) drew up a six-factor model of wellness. The six factors are the intellectual, emotional, physical, social, occupational, and spiritual arenas. The evolution of counseling models that has taken place over the past century focuses on a more comprehensive and holistic approach to clients (Seligman, 2006). More than a decade ago, Wittmer and Sweeney (1992) offered a five-aspect model for optimal functioning consisting of

- spirituality (values, beliefs, ethics, purpose and direction, optimism, and inner peace);
- self-regulation (sense of worth, mastery of one's own life, spontaneity and emotional responsiveness, sense of humor, creativity, awareness of reality, and physical health);
- work (paid employment, volunteer experiences, child rearing, homemaking, and education);
- friendship (positive interpersonal relationships and social supports that provide rewarding activities and interactions); and
- love (intimacy, trust, sharing, and cooperative long-term relationships).

As with the concept of psychological wellness, there is also no concise definition of what constitutes spiritual wellness. The current focus on aspects of spiritual functioning is more elaborate and concise in terms of pathology or dysfunction. The latest *Diagnostic and Statistical Manual of Mental Disorders* (*DSM-IV*, 2000) lists hundreds of diagnoses, yet there is only a single category for a "religious or spiritual problem" (V62.89). The description of that problem is as follows:

> This category can be used when the focus of clinical attention is a religious or spiritual problem. Examples include distressing experiences that involve loss or questioning of faith, problems associated with conversion to a new faith, or questioning of spiritual values that may not necessarily be related to an organized church or religious institution. (p. 741)

Although the preceding description is intended to be inclusive, clients and clinicians are left to ponder the definition of "spiritual health." In fact, the purpose of counseling—to remediate dysfunction and/or to move toward optimal functioning—is being debated; however, that debate is beyond the scope of this book. For the purposes of this chapter, a guiding principle would be that remediation of dysfunction is a necessary step toward being healthy, but remediation is insufficient to promote health without purposeful intervention to strengthen and hone functioning and to support personal initiative and experimentation in how to live a healthier lifestyle within that specific component of one's life.

Given the paucity of diagnostic guidelines for "spiritual dysfunction," this chapter will address three related themes:

1. How does the current professional literature speak to the topic of spiritual wellness?
2. How do or might traditional models of counseling describe optimal functioning?
3. How can models of spiritual wellness and optimal functioning as a reflection of counseling theory be merged to help counselors and clients define *growth* for the purposes of their spiritual journey in counseling?

Pondering Spiritual Wellness

As a prerequisite to the specific study of spiritual wellness, one must be accepting of a professional approach toward wellness or strength-focused counseling or helping, compared with pathology-oriented psychotherapy. Smith (2006) cited one study which confirmed that clients may be more appreciative of a counselor who focuses on personal potential than one who spends a lot of time diagnosing the problem. It was reported that this emphasis resulted in enhanced feelings of confidence, motivation, and personal power on the part of the client. Smith concluded the article by identifying four challenges in understanding spiritual health: (a) the development of a taxonomy of spiritual strength, (b) the lack of a model for developing strengths, (c) the language that details pathology and deficits, and (d) the integration of cultural interpretations of spiritual strength.

James (1902) noted that religion is a unifying force in personality, which is the core beliefs and values that come to epitomize personal identity and uniqueness (Kneezel & Emmons, 2006). More than a century later, Griffith (2004) suggested that people's initial need for spiritual fulfillment has garnered attention from writers in the fields of psychology, theology, and philosophy.

Transcendence meets the human need for purpose, which is the human desire for generativity, service, and spirituality in order to offset the human fears of hopelessness and meaninglessness. This spiritual growth is characterized as an investment of life energy in a cause or principle that is greater than oneself. Leak (1992) stated that spiritual maturity is connected to social interests, "in which life is seen as part of a larger unfolding of divinely inspired events" (Griffith, 2004, p. 172). Kneezel and Emmons (2006) referred to spirituality as "the fount of meaning and a provider of a global interpretation of one's everyday experience . . . as a catalyst for personality development" (p. 266). Within this framework, life is seen as an opportunity not to receive, but to give and to contribute to the sacredness of relationships and of life.

Spiritual wellness has been defined by many writers. Myers (1990) defined spiritual wellness as "a continuous search for meaning and purpose in life; an appreciation for depth of life; the expanse of the universe, and natural forces which operate in it; a personal belief system" (p. 11). Ryan and Deci (2002) spoke about the three components of spiritual wellness: autonomy, relatedness, and competence. *Autonomy* refers to those notions which are personally chosen and valued. *Relatedness* is a feeling of mutual connection with others, a sense of personal belonging, and the identification of a community in which one feels welcome. *Competence* can be described as a sense of efficacy in one's interactions with the social world and the environment. These components are consistent with Benson, Roehlkepartain, and Rude's (2003) notion of spirituality as a search for meaning, purpose, contribution, and connectedness.

A solid spiritual self can provide a consistent theme for one's life and a venue for the ultimate connection with a Supreme Being or God. This motivation behind one's relatedness to the Divine is vital to a picture of overall spiritual wellness. One who feels loved and safe with God will enjoy participating in religion; one who feels criticized or judged by God may participate in religion, but such participation is founded on external pressure or a fear of God.

Briggs, Apple, and Aydlett (2004) identified four constructs of spiritual wellness: (a) *meaning and purpose in life* speaks to those events and relationships that contribute to a sense of personal significance, hope, and a motivation for living; (b) *positive connectedness* is a healthy relatedness with one's self, other people, and the Divine; (c) *transcendence* can be described as a move away from a sense of responsibility to one's own ego needs toward a focus on others and the world in general; and (d) *inner resources* include one's capacities and values as a consistent source of empowerment and guidance. Note that these values are a result of a consideration of, and negotiation with, external value systems.

Purdy and Dupey (2005) included six elements in their Holistic Flow Model of Spiritual Wellness:

a. **A belief in an organizing force in the universe** creates a dynamic connection and an ability to commune with nature.

b. **A notion of connectedness** generates an appreciation of the world beyond one's own self. Oneness with others, nature, ideals, and so forth provide a sense of healthy interdependence.

c. **Faith** refers to a belief that one's view of the world is indeed reality. The authors offer as an example the tenet that hard work will generate positive outcomes, even if the goal that has been identified is not yet met. "Faith provides the motivation to act with purpose" (p. 101).

d. **Movement toward compassion** speaks to a tendency to act unselfishly in order to help others and to create a more positive world. This movement is also evident in an individual's capacity to offer and receive forgiveness.

e. **The ability to find meaning in life** is tied to the notion of free will as espoused in logotherapy, but balanced by an individual's responsibility to make sense of meaning in life and to make peace with that meaning.

f. *The ability to find meaning in death* offers a balanced perspective on life. Although identified as an existential issue, the practical resolution of this challenge directs one's life energy and purpose in order to make one's life of meaning, value, and worth. In addition, Purdy and Dupey (2005) emphasized that "spirituality is innate and ever present; perpetuates the drive for transcendence; and, when in a healthy state, is adaptable and embraces change. It is open-ended and ever unfolding" (p. 98).

Most recently, as an overarching view, Briggs and Shoffner (2006) identified spiritual wellness as being the integrational force for other aspects of human functioning and as being central to wellness in all areas.

Summary

There are two related points of view: wellness as espoused in counseling theories and spiritual wellness. However, there is no proposed overlap between the two views. Such an overlap is a necessary step toward incorporating ideas of spiritual wellness into a clinician's view of wellness as espoused by his or her integration of counseling theories. Although it is beyond the scope of this chapter to address all possible integrations of counseling theories with each other, the next section will provide an overview of possible models of wellness from the perspective of traditional counseling theories and then propose a model of spiritual health tentatively intended to fit within that conceptual framework. Included will be psychodynamic theories, humanistic/existential theories, cognitive theories, and behavioral theories.

INTRODUCTION

Integrating Clinical Orientations and Spiritual Wellness

To reiterate, Seligman and Csikszentmihalyi (2000) stated that "social and behavioral sciences can articulate a vision of a good life . . . and can show what actions lead to well-being" (p. 10) and that "treatment is not just fixing what is broken; it is nurturing what is best" (p. 9). The challenge is to offer one application of this vision to samples of traditional models of counseling or psychotherapy by itemizing barometers of wellness within the framework of each theory and then hypothesizing how spiritual wellness might be integrated within that theoretical framework. The theories to be addressed were selected at random, and due to space limitations, no more than two theories from each major perspective were included. Readers are asked to view the material as examples of this orientation, which are then applicable to theories of their own choosing. This section will illustrate how spiritual wellness can be infused into current approaches to counseling or psychotherapy.

Integrating Spiritual Growth Into a Psychodynamic Clinical Orientation

This section will review the current professional literature on psychodynamic theory in order to hypothesize barometers of psychodynamic wellness. Divided into psychoanalytic and Jungian models, each possible measure of client wellness will be presented together with a brief explanation.

CONCEPTUALIZING PSYCHOANALYTIC WELLNESS   These barometers represent an attempt to outline aspects of wellness from a psychoanalytic perspective:

- *Making the unconscious conscious* **(Novie, 2003; Sharf, 2004)**   results in an awareness of the mythology of one's childhood and relationships with adult figures as seen through the eyes of the rational adult compared with the emotionally focused child.
- *"Strengthen[ing the] ego so [that] behavior [is] based more on reality and less on instinctual cravings or irrational guilt"* **(Corey, 2005, p. 65)**   requires the use of ego processes to control sexual and aggressive drives (Freud, 1963; Seligman, 2006) and is a pro-active stance that channels life energy into other-focused endeavors.
- *Re-analyzing and reconstructing childhood experiences* **(Sharf, 2004)**   produces a resolution of childhood trauma and a reinterpretation of one's childhood experiences in order to provide closure and relief from ongoing worry about an event that occurred in the past.
- *Probing into the past to develop a level of self-understanding*   results in an acceptance of the reality of one's past, not as permission to blame either the self or others, but as a foundational experience that has unconsciously dictated one's identity, but can now be refined, edited, or dismissed as a personal vision of ego identity.
- *Relating to the self and others more meaningfully* **(Novie, 2003),** *understanding ego defenses, and adapting in positive ways to the external world* **(Sharf, 2004)**   involves a recognition that one utilizes defense mechanisms to shield oneself from the truth about who one truly is and to honor the pragmatism of those defenses, especially at the time in life in which they were created; however, one must also confront the personal dishonesty allowed by their use. This insight is to lead to self-monitoring in social situations in order to maintain one's stance of honesty and openness, and, in those instances when the ego defense mechanism reappears, to question what unresolved childhood issue is being triggered that caused the defense mechanism to reemerge.
- *Coping more effectively with the demands of society* **(Seligman, 2006)**   produces a recognition that social living carries norms and values that are perhaps more characteristic of the group than of the individual and that one must intentionally decide how to balance one's values and those of the social group in a way that meets the needs of the individual for both affiliation and a separate identity.
- *Replacing the idealized views of parents* **(Sharf, 2004)**   involves transcending the childish view of one's parents as all-loving or all-cruel and replacing it with a more realistic view of the parents as adults, with strengths and limitations, who also function out of the joys and sorrows of their personal and marital pasts.
- *Reducing the perfectionism, rigidity, and punitiveness of the superego* **(Seligman, 2006, p. 57)**   argues for a redefinition of the purpose of the conscience from one of critical judgment imbued with terrible consequences and harsh self-denigration to a set of ideals with the recognition of times of success, struggle, and disappointment. However, even in times of struggle and disappointment, the individual faces personal challenges rather than deflecting those concerns by use of ego defense mechanisms.

CONCEPTUALIZING JUNGIAN WELLNESS   This section will review the current professional literature on Jungian theory in order to hypothesize barometers of "Jungian wellness." Each possible measure of client wellness will be presented, together with a brief explanation:

- ***Increasing individuation* (Schwartz, 2003; Seligman, 2006).** Sharf (2004) defined individuation as "a conscious realization of psychological reality that is unique to one-self" (p. 93). This growth fosters awareness that one's perception of any life event re-veals more about the individual's personal values and beliefs than about the event itself. Given that premise, the understanding of the self in the context of that event must cen-ter on the individual rather than the details, participants, and unfolding of the event.
- ***Moving toward personality unification* (Schwartz, 2003).** Given the theoretical precepts of masks, shadows, and so forth, an individual's exploration of the self must include all aspects of the self, not just those which may be socially conventional or pleasing to the self and others.
- ***Honoring both strengths and limitations* (Seligman, 2006).** This is an aspect of growth toward a sense of fullness, or acknowledgment of all parts of oneself, both as a statement of one's growth as an individual and as a declaration of one's commit-ment to further growth.
- ***Accepting and attaching meaning to repressed memories* (Seligman, 2006).** Part of growth may involve revisiting unresolved issues that occurred at a time in one's life where one did not have the understanding to make appropriate sense of that event or the emotional resources to confront the ramifications of the event openly. The consequences of that event have been carried as "emotional bag-gage," influencing ongoing life choices; however, that influence has yet to be overtly acknowledged.
- ***Growing in creativity and energy* (Sharf, 2004).** The acceptance of previously repressed issues will release the energy that has been used to hide those issues and will provide a sense of personal relief and the lessening of one's personal burdens. The freeing process generates a flow of personal energy that can be redirected in more personally fulfilling ways than hiding old secrets.
- ***Expanding spiritual feelings* (Seligman, 2006).** The release of the damaging parts of one's past and the understanding of one's collective unconscious provides an opportunity to attend to one's spiritual connections, both with others and with a Supreme Being.
- ***Coping with pain and suffering* (Seligman, 2006).** Finding a balance between joy and sorrow transforms one perception of one's own life story from misery laden to a more evenhanded version that accepts both struggle and success as normative life experiences and celebrates both as reflections of one's ongoing life journey.

SUMMARY OF THE INTEGRATION OF PSYCHODYNAMIC COUNSELING MODELS OF WELLNESS AND SPIRITUAL WELLNESS   The following list presents six common themes among the pre-viously discussed concepts of spiritual wellness and psychodynamic wellness:

- ***Exploring the unconscious motivation between religious or spiritual affilia-tion and between oneself and God or a Supreme Being.*** Both models stress the exploration of ways of relating to others in order to determine whether current rela-tional patterns are based on a response to "childish" needs or on mature interdepend-ence. Endemic to troubling relationships is the hypothesis that the individual's way of functioning is more a replication of childhood fears and patterns than adult functioning.

- *Exercising a drive for personal development to augment the Freudian expression of aggression and sexuality or the resolution of issues of inferiority.*   The addition of a drive or instinct for spiritual growth expands the motivation for a person's actions beyond self-care and toward an attempt to commune with others and contribute to the greater society.
- *Building a solid versus pseudo-spiritual self.*   Both epistemologies speak to the need to discern which identity is true to one's self and which is an accommodation of the pressures inflicted by society. The distinction encompasses whether one performs a behavior based on fear or on a desire to conform (reflecting an external evaluation of the self), in comparison with the honesty of what the individual contributes to, and receives from, such participation (reflecting an internal evaluation of the self).
- *Creating a healthier relationship with one's self.*   In both approaches to understanding oneself within the context of one's life, personal honesty is a common objective. This honesty reflects an open admission, at least to oneself, of the use of defense mechanisms to protect oneself from personal pain and a willingness to confront the defenses on the way to directly exploring and resolving the hidden pain. Given that one's "spiritual/religious self" and "secular self" are purported to be initially formed during childhood while one is pressured by parents, religious leaders, and peers to adhere to a certain standard, the emergence of these defense mechanisms as a way to cope with the unwanted or feared aspects of the self would be an expected coping strategy.
- *Balancing the superego and the punitive aspect of religious beliefs.*   The childhood fear of the consequences of nonconformity must be reexamined for current relevance, and the true expression of one's values must be reexamined for the development of a conscious based on individual principles and aspirations rather than on the imagined scrutiny of peers or society.
- *Committing to a cause greater than oneself (social interest).*   Both psychoanalytic wellness and spiritual health describe the need for generativity and the need to contribute to a goal that is greater than just the satisfaction of personal needs. This desire to reach beyond oneself in order to establish a community based, not on the satisfaction of personal needs, but on a perceived contribution to that community is indicative of an individual who recognizes his or her personal strengths and, more importantly, recognizes the value of sharing those gifts for the betterment of all rather than hoarding those gifts for personal use only.

Integrating Spiritual Growth Into a Humanistic/Existential Clinical Orientation

This section will review the current professional literature on humanistic/existential theory in order to hypothesize barometers of humanistic/existential wellness. Separated into existential and person-centered approaches, each possible measure of client wellness will be presented with a brief explanation.

CONCEPTUALIZING EXISTENTIAL WELLNESS   This following list focuses on those possible barometers of wellness from an existential viewpoint:

- *Acknowledging existential concerns.*   This task speaks to a need to accept the fact that living provokes normative anxieties around core life issues such as meaning, freedom, responsibility, and death. In addition, wellness is equivalent to a personal willingness to face these issues openly and honestly rather than project their burden onto others or deny their existence.

- *Building meaning* **(Corey, 2005).** This task speaks to a need for each individual to signify a personal relevance to existence. This meaning need not be heroic or epic, for meaning may arise from common worldly endeavors (Frank, 2003); however, such a meaning provides a core value for each individual.
- *Embracing freedom* **(Corey, 2005; Kelly, 1995).** This license to define oneself is a basic existential right. On the basis of the individual's desired identity, freedom must be exercised in order for one to live a truly authentic life that is congruent with that identity.
- *Assuming responsibility* **(Corey, 2005; Kelly, 1995).** With freedom comes the responsibility that one must assume for all life decisions and for all of the consequences of one's choices.
- *Honing personal authenticity* **(Corey, 2005; Kelly, 1995).** Frankl (1965, as cited by Sharf, 2004, p. 172) saw authenticity as "achiev[ing the] highest possible activation" as an individual. Within this refinement of personal identity and values, one must identify barriers to authenticity (Seligman, 2006), recognize instances of self-deception (Sharf, 2004), and evaluate the reality of one's lived experiences in comparison to simply adhering to cultural expectations (Sharf, 2004).
- *Facing suffering, dread, anxiety, and death* **(Frank, 2003; Kelly, 1995).** The inevitability of suffering is an aspect of one's inability to predict the outcomes of one's choices, coupled with the lack of any guarantee that one's life will turn out in a specific way. Given that uncertainty, one may be tempted to put off any decision making until some unspecified later date. However, given the time constraints of mortal existence, time lost cannot be recaptured; thus, a decision deferred is a decision not made, which still does not make time stand still. Therefore, the individual must be prepared to choose, utilizing one's values and assets as guides, confident in one's ability to adapt and cope but not wholly certain of a positive outcome.
- *Making choices to reach personal potential* **(Corey, 2005).** An individual is responsible for defining an "aspirational self"—an identity and way of being that one would envision as the epitome of one's existence. This identity is less about a peak experience and more about an optimum way of living.
- *"Recognize[ing] and challeng[ing] narrow and compulsive trends [that are] blocking freedom"* **(Corey, 2005, p. 145).** As part of one's identity and aspirations toward ongoing growth, one must also confront one's tendency to sabotage oneself, including one's ability to deceive oneself (Sharf, 2004).
- *Living a life that reflects one's values and priorities* **(Seligman, 2006).** This objective is based on the assumption that the individual can freely own personal values and is prepared to live according to them regardless of pressure from others.
- *Building a "life with interest, imagination, creativity, hope and joy rather than dread, boredom, hate and bigotry"* **(Sharf, 2004, p. 172).** These two sets of characteristics provide a barometer by which one may evaluate one's experiences in day-to-day living with the knowledge that voluntary progress toward the first set within everyday living will bring one closer to one's version of an individually real or authentic life.

CONCEPTUALIZING PERSON-CENTERED WELLNESS The following list focuses on those possible barometers of wellness from a person-centered viewpoint:

- *Celebrating independence and the integration of the self* **(Corey, 2005; Hazler, 2003).** Seligman (2006) advised clients to overcome the "remoteness, rigidity and limited awareness of [their] inner selves" and move toward congruence of all aspects of one's personality (p. 175). Clients recognize that they get behind masks in the process of socialization, but become flexible and creative in thought and action when they are freed from stereotypes and imposed conditions of worth (Hazler, 2003).

- *Practicing self-honesty* **(Seligman, 2006).** This task is characterized by an openness to experience, moving away from phoniness or superficiality in order "to be that self which one truly is" (Kierkegaard, 1941, as cited by Sharf, 2004, p. 209).

- *Trusting the self* **(Seligman, 2006).** This task is characterized by confidence in the expression of feelings and a trust that one can take action to overcome feelings of helplessness, powerlessness, and the inability to make decisions about the present and the future (Hazler, 2003).

- *Relying on an internal source of evaluation* **(Sharf, 2004).** One is self-directed rather than focused on meeting the goals of others, either for the self or for those others, and one honors one's subjective experience of an event or an individual.

- *Willing to continue to grow* **(Hazler, 2003).** This is a lifelong commitment to oneself to continue to question the emergence of one's potential in any given situation rather than settle for what others may accept or for what others may do.

- *Perceiving one's own positive nature* One "accept[s] both strengths and weaknesses as legitimate and evolving parts of [one's] positive nature" (Hazler, 2003, p. 167). Strengths provide one with a foundation on which to rely; weaknesses are areas for future or further growth should such growth prove to be congruent with one's overall picture of oneself. Otherwise, one must accept these weaknesses as part of oneself, not as a statement of inferiority, but as a simple condition of the human experience that one cannot be proficient and able in all things to equal extents.

- *Becoming accurate in self-perception and communication with others* **(Sharf, 2004).** This emergence involves the self in the relationship. The questions implicit in this stage of wellness include "How am I seen or perceived by others?" "How do I want to be perceived?" "How do I account for any difference?" "How real or genuine am I with others?" and "How do I account for my lack of genuineness in specific relationships or situations?"

- *Living and experiencing the present* **(Seligman, 2006).** This is the goal of living one's current experiences in the "now" (the present) rather than through past events or trying to control the future. One's experience of the self in the present is the truest evaluation of the correctness of this experience for that individual.

- *Expressing emotions and thoughts—even those seen as being painful or unacceptable to others* **(Corey, 2006).** This aspect of wellness involves being open to one's immediate experiences in a situation in terms of feeling, thinking, and communicating those reactions in a manner in which the individual completely owns the feelings or thoughts and accepts responsibility for acting on those reactions.

SUMMARY OF THE INTEGRATION OF HUMANISTIC/EXISTENTIAL COUNSELING MODELS OF WELLNESS AND SPIRITUAL WELLNESS This section will present those areas in common between the previously discussed concepts of spiritual wellness and humanistic/experiential wellness. There are eight common themes between the two definitions of personal wellness:

- ***Developing a personal meaning of life and death.***   Both knowledge systems speak to the need for a personally created and relevant resolution of the core issue of human existence: "Why am I here?" It is the resolution of this question in positive ways that generates values consistent with the individual's answer to that question with the beliefs about how to live one's life that flow from it. Kelly (1995) spoke to the notion of "theist existentialism" as a way to infuse the possibility of a Supreme Being into the existential framework or at least to question the need to exclude either belief because of one's holding the opposing belief.

- ***Developing a purpose in life as a function of exercising one's personal assets.***   This focus on strengths is a foundation on which to grow and an opportunity to develop coping strategies. It is a perspective that is in opposition to the "human deficiency" model, and it acknowledges the tendency of individuals toward actualization in unique and individual ways.

- ***Exhibiting sensitivity to relational awareness.***   This awareness of the self in the context of varying relationships draws attention to individual patterns within the diversity of one's relationships and questions instances of inconsistency or incongruence. In addition, attention is directed toward defining one's ideal self in the relationship. Also, one begins to focus on relationships based on mutual respect, healthy interdependence, and support for one's individuality.

- ***Living a holistic experience of life.***   Rather than negate aspects of one's being, both spirituality and these theoretical models stress fully experiencing the events of one's life. Affect, cognition, behavior, and physical sensation combine for a "lived existence," rather than relying on only one meaning-making process. In addition, paying close attention to all four barometers of experience allows for the identification of those instances where one meaning-making process may be at odds with another or may be overlooked completely. Identification of the self within these specific events provides distinct areas for further self-understanding, acceptance, and growth.

- ***Developing a healthy relationship with the self.***   Although notions of "the ideal" are present in both theoretical models and spiritual traditions, this concept is more about aspiration than achievement. It is the attempts to grow and better oneself that confront each person with strengths to be rejoiced and limitations to be accepted. Although one may not succeed to the extent desired, the failure is far less a character flaw than not trying at all.

- ***Practicing healthy interdependence.***   True knowledge of the self is a vehicle toward acceptance of others on a deeper basis than one's role in society. The transition from the I–it relationship to the connection of the I–thou relationship is based on an understanding of personal needs, a respect for the needs of the other, a willingness to legitimize the experiences and needs of the other without relinquishing one's own needs, and a commitment to balancing the health of the self and the health of the relationship.

- ***Encouraging the practice of compassion through empathy.***   Both traditions advocate a connectedness with others that transcends mere formality. Compassion is not to be confused with pity, because compassion is "feeling with" another, while pitying involves "feeling for" that other person. The willingness and ability to truly experience life through the eyes of another as a way to legitimize and respect similarities and differences, rather than to judge, condemn, or exploit weaknesses, is the basis for true connection and mutual respect.

- **Demonstrating honesty and openness to give and receive forgiveness.** The process of letting go of past wrongs, either those committed by oneself or those committed by another, is a vehicle toward freedom from guilt, remorse, and anxiety. Once one can admit that one may have caused harm to another no matter how kind one's intent, one can begin to separate intent and outcome by others. Although a positive intent does not excuse harm to another, the recognition of such an intent may diminish the animosity felt by the injured party. It is in this spirit that an apology sincerely offered can be gratefully accepted. Both spiritual/religious traditions and these models of counseling speak to the need to resolve past hurts, to atone where possible, and to learn and grow from both experiences.

Integrating Spiritual Growth Into a Cognitive Orientation

Kelly (1995) spoke to the commonalities among cognitively focused counseling approaches by identifying six continua of distorted thinking:

a. **Undercontrol versus overcontrol.** Individuals in the first group believe that one is responsible for nothing and is a victim of everything, while those in the second group believe that one is responsible for every aspect of one's life and relationships.

b. **Attention focused on the past versus attention focused on the future.** Individuals in the first group spend countless hours reliving past events as though the solution to present complaints is somehow hidden there, while those in the second group dedicate much energy to imagining an ideal future.

c. **Avoidance or denial of positives versus acknowledgments of personal strengths.** Individuals in the first group tend to negate personal strengths or potential and tend to either avoid contemplation of such possibilities or counter suggestions for change with the characteristic "Yes, but . . ." while those in the second group accept personal limitation as a natural aspect of life, can balance that recognition with acceptance of personal strength and use the latter as vehicles toward ongoing personal growth.

d. **Defeatism versus perfectionism.** Individuals see all life events as either wholly disappointing or wholly ideal. Given that very few situations are so clearly one extreme or the other, these individuals' emotional responses swing from despair to euphoria, with the majority of the affective responses revolving around expressions of despair and frustration.

e. **External focus versus internal focus.** Individuals attempt to decipher and interpret the world around them without confirmation or feedback from others, or else they ruminate continually on their personal failings.

f. **Meaninglessness versus rigidity of belief.** Individuals who believe in meaninglessness, as well as those who are rigid in their beliefs, tend to dismiss all life events and the significance of those events as trivial or ill fitting to a preconceived belief about the world. The sum of all of these belief systems, most of which tend to function without the awareness of most individuals, are affective responses that are characterized as miserable, defeated, hopeless, and despairing.

This section will review the current professional literature on cognitive theory in order to hypothesize barometers of cognitive wellness. Categorized into Rational Emotive

Behavior Therapy (REBT) and Reality Therapy, each possible measure of client wellness will be presented with a brief explanation.

CONCEPTUALIZING REBT WELLNESS   The following list focuses on those possible barometers of wellness from the viewpoint of Rational-Emotive Behavior Therapy.

- ***Separating behavior and the self* (Corey, 2005).**   An individual understands that one can perform or act poorly or disappointingly without being "a bad person."
- ***Accepting the self in spite of imperfections* (Corey, 2005).**   Self-acceptance is not to be confused with self-approval. Self-acceptance recognizes that one will fail, disappoint, and frustrate, but that such experiences are a natural part of life and relationships and can be balanced with experiences of success, trust, and confirmation. In contrast, one's need for self-approval motivates one to live more rationally and purposefully.
- ***Moving toward unconditional self-acceptance* (Ellis, 2001).**   Previous belief scripting interferes with an individual's ability to accept oneself regardless of the behavioral consequences or the emotional upset, because previous scripting tends to place unachievable standards as conditions of worth on individuals, but does not support any effort or attempt toward meeting those standards, demanding total and immediate success.
- ***Reducing emotional distress* (Vernon, 2003).**   "[A] rational philosophy of life . . . will reduce emotional distress and self-defeating behaviors and [result in an] ability to be happier and live more meaningfully" (p. 241).
- ***Becoming less "disturbable"* (Seligman, 2006).**   By practicing logical and flexible thinking, tempered by principles of self-acceptance, one will tend to attribute reasonable amounts of distress to life's failures and "catastrophize" less and less, leading to fewer episodes of overwhelming and enduring emotional disturbance.
- ***Decreasing self-defeating behaviors* (Sharf, 2004).**   One needs to better assess the impact of one's behavior in light of the intended impact and to integrate feedback from others in a way that modifies one's behavior in favor of those behaviors which are more efficient and effective in terms of achieving one's purpose.
- ***Thinking more clearly and rationally* (Sharf, 2004).**   Given any situation from which emotional disturbance arises, the question to be considered is "As I processed this event, what did I tell myself about my part in it, its importance, and so forth that generated such feelings of misery and despair?"
- ***Dealing effectively with negative feelings such as sorrow, regret, frustration, and annoyance, and handling depression, anxiety, and worthlessness* (Seligman, 2006).**   Such feelings are the natural result of life events or plans gone awry or unfulfilled. The concerns are the intensity of the emotion (How appropriate is it, given the actual event?), its duration (Does one "hang onto it" long after it has passed?), and its lesson for the future (What can one learn about one's contribution to the failure or the disappointment in order to act more effectively in similar situations in the future?).

CONCEPTUALIZING REALITY THERAPY WELLNESS   The following list focuses on those possible barometers of wellness from the viewpoint of Reality Therapy.

- ***Defining one's "quality world"* (Wubbolding, 2003).**   Each individual must assume the responsibility for, and ownership of, a definition of his or her optimal life.

- *Getting connected with people in a quality world* **(Corey, 2005).** Each individual fills the need for love and belonging with people who respect one's personal use of these constructs and are willing to participate in relationships based on mutual fulfillment.

- *Hoping for a more personally-fulfilling future* **(Corey, 2005).** One must remain optimistic that even if a specific need is currently unmet that if one becomes more analytical in understanding one's specific needs in this area and critically evaluates the inclusion or exclusion of other needs within this life sphere, one can make better decisions about how to continue to legitimize that need but work differently toward getting the need met.

- *Practicing appropriate self-sufficiency* **(Sharf, 2004).** This notion of wellness reflects one's ability to process life events utilizing this approach in a way that is evaluative, but nonjudgmental, and that leads to better self-understanding and better future choices.

- *Evaluating current needs fulfillment* **(Sharf, 2004).** Each person is responsible for determining how completely his/her quality world is evolving. However, one cannot create one's own quality world at the expense of another person's. The admission by another person that he or she cannot meet a specific need in the moment does not negate the importance of the need, but merely redirects the individual toward a more responsive resource.

- *Assessing how realistic needs are* **(Seligman, 2006).** Although one may have a specific dream for parts of one's life, the guiding question is "How achievable is this dream?" If the dream is not truly achievable regardless of personal effort and support, then failure and disappointment are likely.

SUMMARY OF THE INTEGRATION OF COGNITIVE COUNSELING MODELS OF WELLNESS AND SPIRITUAL WELLNESS This section will present commonalities between the previously discussed concepts of spiritual wellness and cognitive wellness. A review of the two schemata offers five common barometers of well-being:

- *Building a personally cogent belief system distinct from knowing.* An important distinction between knowing and believing is the irrefutability of fact compared with the subjective validity of belief. The main issue in both approaches to the world is whether or not one's knowledge and beliefs generate a sense of harmony or emotional distress. Such a comparison is equally apt for spiritual beliefs and nonspiritual beliefs and knowledge. In addition, although knowledge may be fairly fixed, beliefs can evolve over time with greater self-awareness and identification of personal needs.

- *Focusing on personal assets in contrast to personal limitations.* Both cognitive and spiritual notions of wellness emphasize competence over ineptitude. One interesting dynamic is whether an individual creates a foundation of identity based on strengths and capabilities or on weaknesses and limitations. Although acknowledging both assets and limitations is part of accepting the human condition, those aspects of the self which one chooses to emphasize indicate a core belief in one's potential to deal with life's struggles and challenges or a resignation that one cannot do so.

- *Evaluating need fulfillment on an ongoing basis.* Given the evolving nature of self-understanding, one has the right and the responsibility to continually assess how well one's particular lifestyle, including the choice of religious or spiritual affiliation, meets one's personal needs. Although the affiliation may not change, one's needs enter into a constant state of flux as one becomes more aware of the self within differing life contexts. This is not to suggest that one must outgrow one's spiritual or religious affiliation, simply that one may revise which needs can be met within that context and which needs, perhaps previously assigned to that context, must now be met elsewhere in one's life.

- ***Assuming the responsibility for defining one's spiritual "quality world".*** Assuming the responsibility for defining one's quality spiritual world, much like defining one's quality world in other aspects of one's life, is a great challenge. Regardless of affiliation, questions such as "What do I need from my choice of religious or spiritual tradition?" and "What do I believe about a Supreme Being?" provide a blueprint against which to measure what each religion or spiritual tradition has to offer. Although no single religion or spiritual tradition will meet all of one's needs, it can be hypothesized that the tradition that offers the most congruence between what is asked for and what is provided will prove to be the most supportive for that particular person.

Integrating Spiritual Growth Into a Behavioral Orientation

This section will review the current professional literature on behavioral theory in order to hypothesize barometers of behavioral wellness. Each possible measure of client wellness will be presented with a brief explanation.

CONCEPTUALIZING BEHAVIORAL WELLNESS   The following list focuses on those possible barometers of wellness from the viewpoint of Behavior Therapy.

- ***Specifying ill-serving behaviors in light of client goals*** **(Kalodner, 2003).**   Although the intent of an action may be noble, its impact on others can best be assessed by their reactions to the behavior. Given a specific client goal in an important life context, behaviors that seem either counterproductive or neutral must be identified for remediation.
- ***Exploring the rigidity of the behavioral repertoire*** **(Kalodner, 2003).**   Personal comfort and making changes do not go well together. Behavioral change implies awkwardness, self-monitoring, and some disappointment before the new behaviors totally replace the previous ineffective behaviors. Clinging to obsolete behaviors, meaning that certain actions do not provoke the desired response, merely extends the duration of the presenting complaint.
- ***Setting personal goals in order to create a life direction*** **(Corey, 2005 Sharf, 2004).**   On the basis of one's notions of wellness and happiness, one must choose outcomes specific to one's belief system. These goals must be guided by what the individual can accomplish and must revolve around personal change within one's life contexts and relationships.
- ***Focusing on learning, practicing, and evaluating*** **(Corey, 2005).**   The objective of this process is to refine new behavioral repertoires that must be evaluated, not on the skill of the performance, but in light of the desired environmental response.
- ***Describing positive changes*** **(Corey, 2005).**   Individuals must revise their goal-setting process to specify what they would like to see happen, as opposed to what they would like to avoid.

- *Assuming personal power in order to change life circumstances* **(Corey, 2005).** By revising one's perspective—moving away from weaknesses and incompetencies and toward strengths and assets (Kalodner, 2003), the individual is recognizing his or her personal assets and resources for use in achieving a desired outcome.

- *Weighing the costs and benefits of goals* **(Sharf, 2004).** Given the absence of the "perfect solution," an individual must carefully assess what he or she will gain by making a specific change and what will be sacrificed or lost within that process. Doing so allows a person to consciously make a life change, ready to rejoice in what is gained and to mourn what must be abandoned for the sake of that change.

- *Discovering the relationships among problems* **(Kalodner, 2003).** This idea emphasizes that an episode of concern is merely an example of an ongoing pattern of relational behavior. Rather than concentrate on understanding the specific activating event, it is suggested that one explore common personal behavioral themes and patterns within all relational contexts in order to provide an overarching theme to address the multiple contexts in which to practice new ways of being.

CONCEPTUALIZING SPIRITUAL WELLNESS FROM A BEHAVIORAL ORIENTATION The following list presents two commonalities between the previously discussed concepts of spiritual wellness and behavioral wellness:

- *Assessing the efficacy of one's goals.* On one level of functioning, concern can be directed toward how well an individual performs a certain behavior and the reinforcement that one receives from one's social environment. Although competence is crucial to potential success, a deeper issue concerns how well that action, within a given social context, resulted in the desired outcome. On this second level of functioning, the intentionality of the action, regardless of the skill of its enactment, becomes the barometer of success or failure. From a spiritual perspective, the question is not only how well an individual performs a specific ritual, but also how clearly that individual has defined what he or she hopes to gain from that action and, by means of an internal locus of evaluation, how completely that need was met.

- *Evaluating personal competence in one's interactions with others and one's environment.* Behaviors in everyday life or in ritual and practice in religious and spiritual traditions are intended to foster a specific response from the external world and to meet a particular idiosyncratic need. Should that response not be generated or that personal need not fulfilled, there are two questions that must be asked: "How feasible is it to have this 'need' met within this context?" and "How might I adapt, change, or improve my actions to achieve a more favorable response?"

Case Example Revisited

Constance found her dilemma to be a common struggle within her group of professional peers. She determined that her notions of clinical wellness needed to include notions of spiritual wellness and that counseling might be more effective if she could offer this perspective to her clients. She stated that a conjoint demarcation of counseling goals, including spiritual goals, might facilitate more client initiative and energy in counseling by fostering a sense of shared direction and responsibility for therapeutic progress.

However, she recognized that her first task was to formalize her personal conceptualization of these constructs of wellness within her own epistemology. She utilized tapes of her counseling sessions to help her identify common themes, theories, and assumptions in her clinical work and found that she adhered to an Adlerian model of developing client insight and a cognitive–behavioral model of change. Constance then requested peer supervision in order to confirm the accuracy and validity of her own findings. Her analysis was corroborated.

This information allowed her to focus her research on notions of wellness from each theoretical orientation and to begin to formulate a notion of spiritual wellness. Although her notion was still evolving, she was able to develop six concrete views of client functioning with regard to insight and change, as well as an experimental utilization of Purdy and Dupey's (2005) Holistic Flow Model of Spiritual Wellness. When she first introduced these notions into counseling, she found validation through client statements such as "I always wondered what counselors thought as they sat there nodding," "Wow, that seems so clear to me now. I can see how confused I was making myself," and "What a valuable way for me to think about my spirituality as part of my growth process through my divorce." This feedback was legitimizing for Constance. However, she worked to develop negotiating skills with clients around these goals, both to ensure client ownership and to ensure relevance to, and priority in, the client's life.

Conclusion

This chapter has endeavored to honor Plato's quote advocating the "quiet exchange" of the integration of ideas within a personally relevant clinical framework by offering conceptualizations of a wellness orientation to clients, concepts of spiritual wellness, and the integration of these two topics. For the purposes of this discussion, the "thinking" process to which the citation refers speaks to the counselor's conceptualization, infusion, and refinement of his or her own blending of these notions.

As helping professionals, our task is less to provide answers for clients and more to challenge clients to answer the same questions that guide our own life journey—in this case, "How do I move my thinking from reflecting on my problem to imagining my future?" and "How can I utilize my spiritual/religious beliefs and traditions to complete a full picture of my notion of optimal human functioning?"

Self-Understanding Exercises

1. Compare your definition of *wellness* with that of colleagues or other students. In what ways are your definitions similar and in what ways are they distinct?
2. How well are you living up to your standards of "personal wellness" in the different areas of your life? How do your relative strengths and areas of challenge affect your efficacy as a counselor?
3. How does your spiritual/religious faith define *wellness*? How well does that description fit your concept of wellness?

Opportunities for Further Learning

1. When you have identified those theorists whose work informs and directs your clinical approach, read original source material regarding their notions of actualization.

2. Speak with mental health professionals (clinical social worker, psychologist, family counselor, etc.) who have sought training that differs from your own, and ask each professional how he or she defines *client wellness*. How does each respondent see his or her training as leading to that definition?

3. Seek out clergy from differing faiths, and explore with each one his or her definition of the *fully functioning individual*. How similar or distinct are their descriptions?

12

••••

Spirituality and Marginalized Groups

Faith is like love: it cannot be forced. As trying to force love begets hatred,
so trying to compel religious belief leads to unbelief.

—ARTHUR SCHOPENHAUER (1788–1860)

CASE EXAMPLE

As a pastoral counselor, Andrea was conducting a group for women who are "coming out of the closet" and announcing their lesbian sexual orientations. As part of the exploration of coping strategies, several of the women tearfully stated that they no longer felt welcome in their respective churches and felt bereft of spiritual comfort and direction at a time in their lives when they felt most vulnerable. They reported feeling stigmatized by clergy to whom they could previously turn for support and could not understand how the church, which had previously seemed to be a sanctuary for them, could now seem so cold and judgmental. In response, Andrea wanted to affirm their affective experiences but not condemn the church that employed her. She felt pulled between defending the life experiences of her group members and her personal belief in the welcoming power of the church.

••••

INTRODUCTION

The notion of universal religious or spiritual belief confirms that all are made in God's image and all are deserving of his blessing. "Persons need not claim a specific religious affiliation to have a significant spiritual dimension to their lives" (Turner, Center, & Kiser, 2004, p. 419). However, this idea is utopian, and the reality is that different groups experience different levels of acceptance within mainstream religious communities. The study of the experiences of specific subpopulations within faith-based institutions honors their diversity and the challenges facing spiritual or religious traditions or institutions in trying to be "all things to all people." More specifically, such study explores the challenges faced by specific traditions or institutions and how well they respond to those challenges. For the purposes of this chapter,

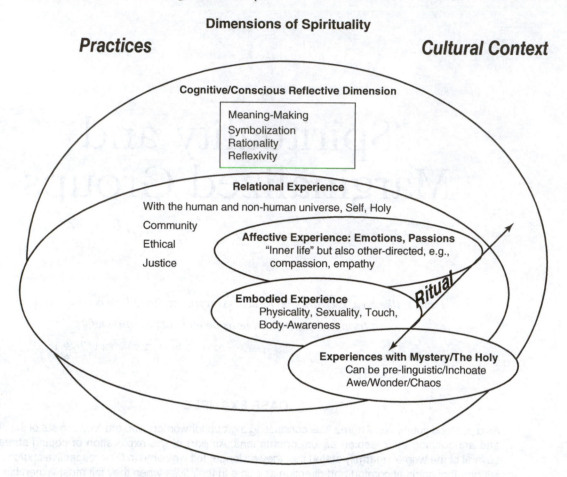

Dimensions of Spirituality

Practices

Cultural Context

Cognitive/Conscious Reflective Dimension

Meaning-Making
Symbolization
Rationality
Reflexivity

Relational Experience

With the human and non-human universe, Self, Holy

Community

Ethical

Justice

Affective Experience: Emotions, Passions
"Inner life" but also other-directed, e.g.,
compassion, empathy

Ritual

Embodied Experience
Physicality, Sexuality, Touch,
Body-Awareness

Experiences with Mystery/The Holy
Can be pre-linguistic/Inchoate
Awe/Wonder/Chaos

the experiences of four specific groups will be presented: (a) women; (b) lesbian, gay, and bisexual (LGB) persons; (c) children; and (d) adolescents.

As a way to conceptualize the dimensions of spiritual interrelatedness, Mercer (2006) offered the above visualization of dimensions of spirituality:

This visualization offers a perspective on the ever-expanding process of spiritual experience. However, each individual receives differing messages about his or her relationship with the greater society, of which religion is one of many institutions. While any religious or spiritual practice may claim to be open to all and to be responsive to the needs of all, in actuality, this hope may be rarely achieved. The gap between the intent and the experience may be unintentional on the part of the religious leaders; however, helping professionals need to understand the unique lived experiences of each person within this vital aspect of his or her life.

THE RELIGION AND SPIRITUALITY OF WOMEN

The exploration of the experiences of women with respect to spirituality has undergone, and continues to undergo, a transition (Howell, 2001), with women's satisfaction with traditional faith practices diverging widely both within those practices and between different faiths. Heath (2006) asserted that

[R]eligion has a positive effect on mental health primarily because religion provides a sense of meaning as well as hope and optimism. Religion is thought to set
up positive social norms that elicit approval, nurturance and acceptance from
others while providing a social network. (p. 157)

However, empirical study has yet to substantiate this hypothesis. This gap between
theory and observation is due partly to the initial thrust of research that questioned only behavioral indicators of religious affiliation or practice (such as church attendance) and blurred
the conceptual frameworks of religion and spirituality. The problem was that the reliance on
behavioral indicators did not encompass the lived experiences of women within their faiths.
What remain to be studied are the experiences of women within traditional and nontradi-
tional spiritual practices in terms of the perceived benefits, the contribution to personal identity, and the sense of spiritual community and feelings of disappointment.

Frame (2003) spoke to the diversity of women's spirituality and its expression. It has
been suggested that many women feel supported, secure, and affirmed through an affiliation
with mainstream religion and are less interested in questions regarding issues of gender and
feminism that have been raised by those within and outside of those institutions. In fact, Frame
cautioned professional counselors to be aware that there is a population of women who decry
feminist challenges to mainstream religion. There is a great diversity of thought and opinion
with regard to women's views of their spiritual and religious needs and experiences.

From a historical perspective, Lauver (2000) spoke to the core foundation of Western
religions in which the spirit, the mind, and the intellect were elevated over the biological aspects of life. In comparison to the ancient female-focused religions, this transition represented a purposeful male-dominated shift in perspective, relegating all things female to a
lower status and elevating all things masculine to the upper echelons of the hierarchy.
Lauver explained that such a prejudicial foundation was based solely on bodily functions
such as childbirth, breastfeeding, and menses. By their very physical nature, women were
assigned a lower status within the religious hierarchy. Ruether (1995) suggested that traditional religions should reconsider their biases against women's bodily functions, which have
been used as tools of discrimination, and instead view them as life-affirming. Mind, body,
and spirit are seen as interrelated aspects of the self, with growth (or stagnation) in one area
being transferable to functioning in other areas.

According to Townes (1995), this emergence of hope in the midst of inhumanity has its
basis in the challenge to dominant norms and the rise of new visions for humanness. This
spirituality is founded in a "protest against the dominant religious status quo, seeking justice
in the midst of evil, peace in the midst of violence, and freedom in the midst of oppression"
(Heath, 2006, p. 161).

Townes (1995, p. 52) spoke to the uncovering of a "powerful spiritual awakening" that
was centered on wholeness and on attention paid to the previously neglected aspects of the
personal unconscious. The thrust of this exploration was on the process of self re-focusing,
in order that one might live in the present. The study included those women who had
moved away from the faith traditions of their childhood. Few of the women mentioned the
benefits of belief in a Higher Power; most spoke of a search for "personal essence and the
clarification of what was important to them" (p. 54). The women related how their childhoods were dominated spiritually by the attempt to obtain from structured religions a sense
of community, a sense of the self, and direction on how to relate to the everyday world.
However, later in life, these women expanded their search for direction beyond the traditional

religious institutions. They shared a midlife experience of withdrawal from external spiritual stimuli and mourning, and a purposeful search for renewed spiritual awareness.

A review of the literature that focused on developmental models of women's spirituality offered a framework—the five-phase model of spiritual development of St. John (2000)—Christ (1995), and Harris (1989), which is summarized as follows:

	Stage I (Doormat Me)	Stage II (Grand Me)	Stage III (Why Me?)	Stage IV (Who Am I?)	Stage V (Real Me)
Views of the Self	Apologizer, unworthy, pleaser, fearful	Competitive, impressive, superior	Uncomfortable being alone with oneself, despondent, feels victimized	Aware of feelings, growing sense of inner worth, desire to direct one's own life, rejects authority figures, rejects traditional ways of doing things, takes responsibility for the self	In touch with one's roots, conscious of the self, accepts the self as human, harmonizes inner and outer life, balances autonomy & interdependence
Views of Others	Power belongs to others, criticism from others must be true, nurtures others to be needed & accepted	Controls/ dominates others, oppresses others for personal gain	Feels trapped, feels detached from others, feels better toward others	Acknowledges one's feelings to oneself, casts off bitter friends, demands honesty, feels anxiety when relating to others	Open to diverse ideas, relationships are based on mutual trust and caring, senses the interconnectedness of all things
Views of Women	Lacks a sense of kinship with women	Lacks a sense of kinship with women	Lacks a sense of kinship with women, continues to stereotype others	Notices other strong women, sees sisterhood as a tie that links all women	Deep kinship with women
Views of God	God is the father, you are the child; God is on my side, not yours; God is a judge; God rewards and punishes	God is the father, you are the child; God is on my side, not yours; God is a judge; God rewards and punishes	Blames God, angry with God, feelings of betrayal, fears God	Open to seeing God in new ways, God is a healer, God is the beloved	Close personal relationship with God, the wisdom within; God is in everyone

Note. St. John, 2000.

Frame (2003) offered a seven-step process for women who develop and own a specific model of spirituality. This process is based on the work of Harris (1989). The seven steps are

1. becoming in tune with one's present identity,
2. resolving one's personal spirituality,
3. creating an integrated model of personal spirituality,
4. listening to an inner presence,
5. engaging in practices that foster that inner spiritual voice,
6. serving as a guide or mentor, and
7. engaging in a transformation toward a cosmic connection and personal responsibility for that transformation.

In summary, although this chapter has focused primarily on dissatisfaction with traditional religious institutions and those institutions' responses to the needs of women congregants, it must be remembered that many women feel welcomed and supported by those very same houses of worship.

THE RELIGION AND SPIRITUALITY OF LESBIAN, GAY, AND BISEXUAL PERSONS

In recent history, society in general and religious institutions in particular have been challenged to accept the population of lesbian, gay, and bisexual persons. In 1973, homosexuality was deleted from the list of mental disorders contained in the *DSM-IV-TR*, which is the current edition. A more recent American Psychological Association statement asserts that "homosexuality is not an illness, [a] mental disorder or [an] emotional problem" (APA, 1999). However, many Christian denominations and others cling to the more established beliefs.

Lynch (1996) described the mainstream religions of Christianity, Judaism, and Islam as being at best negative and at worst destructive toward homosexual and bisexual persons. The Holy see, the central governing body of the Catholic Church (also known as "the Vatican"), claimed that homosexuals are "objectively disordered and inclined toward evil" (Buchanan, Dzelme, Harris, & Hecker, 2001, p. 435). Recent research reported that such statements were at odds with opinions held by the general population. The idea that one cannot be openly gay and either Catholic or Pentecostal speaks to the conflict around the issues of sexuality and spiritual identity (Ritter & Terndrup, 2002).

The views of differing denominations range from the punishing policy of Fundamentalist Christianity to the full acceptance offered by Quakers or Unitarian Universalists (Davidson, 2000). Other churches offer a perspective that encompasses both ends of the spectrum by advocating that one should "love the sinner" (the specific person), but "hate the sin" (the sexual act between two same-gender persons). Within the Church of Jesus Christ of Latter Day Saints, or the Mormons, homosexuality is considered to be perverted and carries the possible punishment of excommunication (Frame, 2003). On the basis of these perspectives, mainstream religion has not been supportive of LGB persons and has excluded them from ordination to the clergy and from institutionally supported rites of passage, such as marriage.

Rodriquez and Ouellette (2002) also found that LGB persons participate in organized religion less than their heterosexual peers and that participation itself may be detrimental to their mental health. The rationale for this claim is that negative messages about one's sexual orientation are communicated through religious teachings, the prohibition against gay clergy, and the institutionally imposed sanctions against openly gay members (Lease, Horne,

& Noffsinger-Frazier, 2005). The conflict between one's sexual orientation and one's religious identity can cause severe dissonance because full acceptance of one aspect of the self implies full rejection of another.

The belief in a Higher Power or Supreme Being is a central characteristic of more than two thirds of the American population (Miller & Thoresen, 2003). In addition, considering that the U.S. gay population has been estimated to be approximately 50 million persons, it is inevitable that issues of sexuality and spirituality will occur in the context of professional helping relationships (Buchanan et al., 2001). Furthermore, it can be assumed that most individuals are raised in a spiritual or religious environment, which influences one's values and beliefs about the world in general and sexuality in particular (Lottes & Kuriloff, 1994). The link between this belief system and physical and mental health is expanding. However, the linkage is less clear for LGB persons.

Given that the majority of the mainstream religions (Protestantism, Catholicism, Judaism, and Islam) prohibit homosexuality, individuals are confronted with a self-definition and values that are at odds with one another. Many persons report abandoning or being abandoned by their faith traditions during their struggles with their development of a sexual identity (Wagner et al., 1994). Schuck and Liddle (2001) found increased shame, suicidal ideation, depression, and difficulty accepting an LGB identity among those who reported a conflict between their sexual identity and spiritual identity formation processes and support systems. The negative portrayal of homosexuality within religious communities fosters elevated cognitive dissonance as LGB persons try to reconcile the two facets of their identities. From the perspective of major western religions, homosexuality is viewed as immoral and sinful (Barrett & Barzan, 1996). Even if homosexuality is not condemned by a religious institution, it tends to be tolerated rather than celebrated. This kind of atmosphere leaves LGB persons feeling unacknowledged, ashamed, or dishonored.

Traditional Christianity cites two main reasons for viewing homosexuality as immoral:

1. If one believes that the sole purpose of sexual expression is procreation, then homosexuality can be seen as an assault on the family as a basic societal unit.
2. It has been claimed that homosexuality is contrary to God's will, as evidenced in Leviticus 18:22 and Romans 1:27.

Also, the issues of sexual orientation and spirituality seem to be trapped in an emerging conflict between orthodox and progressive worldviews (Van Soest, 1996). Some people of faith and conservatives adhere to a belief in an external transcendent authority that affirms the traditional mainstream tenets of religious traditions (Hodge, 2005). Such beliefs are derived from a sovereign God as revealed in the Bible. Since values are transcendent, believers cannot pick and choose which values to honor and which to overlook on the basis of the prevailing cultural mores. Hodge claimed that those who hold an orthodox worldview believe in the worth and dignity of all people because they are reflections of the image of God.

Some faith traditions advocate abstinence through a relationship with God as a way to curtail same-gender sexual practices. Just as clergy remain abstinent as a way to demonstrate their fidelity to God, it is argued that devout homosexuals should do the same. Engaging in same-gender sexual activities is considered an abandonment of God's law. This transgression then places one in the position of being an unrepentant sinner who is at odds with God's law and with those who willingly follow that creed, making one susceptible to punishment meted out by God.

Hodge (2005) warned that different worldviews, coupled with a systemic power imbalance, promote bias against subordinate worldviews. From that perspective, the issue is less about right and wrong and more about who controls the prevailing social narratives. Hodge (2005) insisted that "every [worldview] refracts reality," but every worldview expands the notion of possibility (p. 215). As an example, many nature-focused religions see homosexuals as spiritual beings. Wilson (1996) spoke to the historical view held by Native Americans who considered gay individuals as holding great spiritual power.

The simplistic solution offered by many religious institutions is for individuals to abstain from homosexual or lesbian behavior (Brooke, 1993). Malloy (1981) holds to a stricter principle, claiming that to live according to God's will demands that all homosexuality be forsaken. The compromise, if such a thing is possible, is for LGB persons to either reject religion or remain closeted in order to participate in religion. Neither alternative seems to be supportive of human rights, individual needs and dignity, and professional ethical codes that support diversity.

In addition, LGB persons must face the effects of AIDS and condemnation from religious institutions (Davidson, 2000). LGB persons may be confronted with the perception that AIDS is a punishment for homosexual and bisexual activities. Those who contract AIDS receive little sympathy or support from traditional religious organizations. Contracting the disease, even if through contaminated blood products, may be interpreted as a punishment from God for one's immorality. Support for the afflicted places all persons in jeopardy of receiving God's wrath; thus, the ill are banished from their religious homes. This dismissal of the AIDS sufferer and his or her partner confronts both persons with the task of either renouncing their homosexuality in order to be welcomed back into the church or seeking alternative spiritual paths to reconcile both the illness and the lack of spiritual support.

These messages also may increase internalized homonegativity (Lease, Horne, & Noffsinger-Frazier, 2005). Since the majority of the mainstream religious doctrines see homosexuality as sinful and same-gender attraction as immoral, LGB persons who are exposed to these messages may develop negative attitudes toward their own sexual orientation and toward homosexuality in general. Such self-condemnation is considered to be predictive of increased levels of shame and mental distress (Allen & Oleson, 1999). In turn, the repetition and pervasiveness of these messages may diminish the individual's sense of spiritual belonging (Beckstead, 2001; Thoresen, Oman, & Harris, 2005). Therefore, LGB persons are charged with reformulating notions of spiritual practices and traditions that will enhance both aspects of their identities.

A recent study sheds some important light on this dilemma (Lease, Horne, & Noffsinger-Frazier, 2005). Researchers who conducted the study surveyed members of Dignity, Lutherans concerned, and Integrity churches—institutions that seek to affirm an LGB sexual orientation among their congregants—in order to determine whether positive affirmations might counterbalance the known research regarding negative messages. The results showed less internalized homonegativity and higher spiritual scores among members. One of the implications of these results is that they confirm the deleterious effects of the negative messages and the need to counter the negative societal messages that have been experienced by many LGB persons. Overt behaviors and attitudes that convey acceptance are important moderating variables in offsetting the negative messages from mainstream religious denominations. The results of this study are promising in terms of identifying potentially curative spiritual experiences within organized religion.

In summary, LGB persons experience being unwelcome within mainstream religious communities. Their options are less than ideal. How reasonable is it to mask one's sexual orientation in order to be accepted by a religious group that may deliberately or inadvertently condemn that which one hides? How acceptable is it to distance oneself from one's spiritual or religious history for fear of being identified as an LGB person? How welcome does one feel in a nonmainstream community in which the cohesive factor may be one's sexual orientation and common spiritual beliefs may be secondary? For helping professionals, clinical intervention and support are sufficiently challenging when the client's choices are viable. Given the current situation, empathy for the spiritual plight of LGB persons must serve as the basis for grieving what may have to be sacrificed and for rejoicing in what must be discovered in order to integrate and live out one's spiritual and sexual orientations.

THE RELIGION AND SPIRITUALITY OF CHILDREN

Spiritual questions, although not necessarily asked as such, are a common characteristic of childhood (Frame, 2003; Mercer, 2006). It has been previously hypothesized that children are incapable of understanding religious and spiritual themes (Koepfer, 2000). However, although children may lack the sophisticated language to express their spiritual experiences, they are intimately aware of the spiritual experience itself (Koepfer, 2000). Hart (2006) advised that those who care for and/or work with children consider that "children's spirituality may exist apart from adult rational and linguistic conceptions and from knowledge about a religion" (p. 163). Instead, children are seen as relying on intuitive ways of knowing, where they are unencumbered by logic or a formalized belief system and are immediately able to access spiritual experiences.

Fowler (1996) described children as "pre-potentiated for faith" (pp. 25–26). This assertion claims that faith development in children will occur naturally through personal development and within the social environment in which each child is raised. Young children develop a sense of being valued and cared for that is based on their interpretations of the words and actions of adults in their lives. This interpretation is transferred to the child's emerging notions about God. If the experience is positive, it creates the foundation for self-esteem, empathy, and the idea that "heaven" or "a perfect place" is a place where those who reside there are trustworthy, loving, and caring, and offer unconditional acceptance. A less positive experience may cause a child to see him- or herself as unworthy and shameful, and God as cruel, judgmental, and fearsome. Young children also learn that rituals can be comforting, which creates a sense of predictability and meaning, an experience that Fowler claimed was the foundation for receptivity to later openness to religious practice and rituals.

"Children's spirituality is based in experience," claimed Mercer (2006, p. 504). For children, spirituality is a phenomenon that is reflected in lived experience rather than verbal expression. Within this experience exists a heightened awareness of a sense of being in touch with something larger and grander than oneself. The experience itself is at the same time both humbling and elevating. *Humbling* conveys a sense of proportion and a relationship with an essence that is vast and cosmic; *elevating* conveys a sense of certainty of place and of the potential to be and become a vital aspect of this larger essence. Children also refer to their awareness with words that speak of wonder, awe, mystery, and a presence that cannot be adequately expressed through rational language. Finally, for children, these experiences confirm their relationship with this essence and with a vast presence that may appear to be impersonal, but is instead truly welcoming and inclusive. However, Mercer warned of a "shadow side" to children's spirituality, which is characterized by chaos, fear, evil, and suffering, and is expressed as monsters that threaten the existence, security, and inner peace of the child (p. 505). Children learn that "the Evil God" is to be feared or placated. Such children have transferred the real-life experiences of poverty, relational neglect or cruelty, violence, or illness to a personal spiritual world that offers little or no comfort in times of great need.

Children bring to their experiencing of religion and spirituality the same inquisitiveness that they have toward other exploration. Questions such as "Who made God?" "What does God look like?" and "Where does God live?" fascinate children. Cloyd (1997, p. 17) received the following answers from 5-year-olds regarding God:

"God is good to us and always by our side."

"God is very special. He is all around you even though you do not know it. God protects you and heals you, too, when you are sick."

Coles (1990) conducted a cross-cultural study of children's concepts of God and came to the conclusion that all children hold a deep sense of God and spirituality. A later study by Nye and Hay (1996) identified four common spiritual themes among children:

1. *Awareness.* This theme refers to concentrating or focusing on the here and now. Children display this ability when they lose themselves in play or attend to some external stimulus.
2. *Valuing.* This theme describes what matters within an experience. Children's experiences of delight and despair mirror their views on good and evil in the everyday occurrences in their lives.
3. *Mystery.* This theme speaks to the wonder and awe that children feel when they experience the world and its complexity. They manifest these views in their use of imagination.
4. *Meaningfulness.* This theme encompasses children's search for purpose in every event and circumstance. Given the relative fragility of their egos and of their sense of identity, each new experience offers clues or insights into an emerging sense of individuality and connectedness with others and the world.

Hart (2006) suggested that children's spiritual experiences and capacities are organized around four themes:

1. *Wonder.* This theme refers to the feelings of awe, reverence, insight, joy, and love that come from the capacity to see the world with the fresh eyes of a child. Uncluttered by adult tasks, cynicism, or automatic assumptions, children can experience the spiritual nourishment that emerges from moments of transcendence. An 11-year-old described the experience as "I was on my swing set by myself and all of a sudden it all opened up to me. I don't know how to say it, but I was frozen right there and felt like everything was perfect and connected" (Nelson & Hart, 2003). This wonder may also involve the awareness of a sacred other. Lost in a timeless moment with the absorption characteristic of children, they have an immediate sense of the "other" and all things, but in a manner in which all things are connected and somehow equal. Nelson and Hart's (2003) survey reported that 12% of their sample reported such an event prior to the age of 6, 27% between the ages of 6 and 12, and 46% between the ages of 12 and 18.
2. *Wondering.* The process of wondering involves children pondering the *big* questions about life and meaning, knowing, justice, death, and reality, seemingly from no specific event nor within any specific context. These questions demonstrate that children

do not take the same life circumstances for granted as do adults. For example, Nelson and Hart (2003) related the story of an 8-year-old watching television with her mother. At a particular point in the show, the mother laughed when the girl was scared by what she had seen. The girl stated, "You know, Mommy, I don't know yet what is real and what's not real." A 6-year-old boy was asked what he thought about during his day. His immediate answer was that he thought about how to get his younger brother to leave him alone, followed by "What are heaven and hell? And what about the devil? Is he real?" Hart (2006) opined that the endless questioning of children reflects a search for "priorities in one's life and serves as a kind of trailhead in the search for meaning" (p. 170).

3. **Relational spirituality.** Hart (2003) offered that a child's relative lack of ego identity allows him or her to be more empathic and openhearted toward others. One 11-year-old related that his decision not to take another child's toy was *not* based on the knowledge that doing so would be wrong, but rather that he refrained because of the distress that the other child would experience. Of the children surveyed by Nelson and Hart (2003), 79% reported such incidents from their childhood. Hart (2006) concluded by stating the following:

> [W]hat we can begin to understand is that children already have a spiritual life; they have access to wisdom and wonder, struggle with questions of meaning and morality, have a deep sense of compassion . . . can we be as willing to let what we learn from children change our theology and theory as we are willing to change children by the imposition of our theology and theory on them? (p. 175)

4. **Wisdom.** Wisdom is both a striving and a tool to reach beyond. Ralph Waldo Emerson defined wisdom as "a blend of the perception of what is true with the moral sentiment of what is right" (Sealts, 1992, p. 257). An 8-year-old related that she realized that in church she prayed for love and wisdom, not as part of a sermon, but as a thought that "came to her" and seemed so right that she was unshakeable in her conviction (Nelson & Hart, 2003). This example is illustrative of the insight necessary to transform information into wisdom and of the additional step that is necessary for this new wisdom to become a guiding life principle. Once again, the survey by Nelson and Hart (2003) confirmed the prevalence of this experience in children: When asked "Have you ever found yourself knowing and/or saying something that seemed to come through you, rather than from you, expressing a wisdom [that] you don't feel you usually have?" 80% answered "yes" and reported incidents from their childhoods.

Mercer (2006) described four dimensions of children's spirituality:

1. **Mysticism.** In terms of the mysticism of spirituality, Jung claimed that the lives of children approach the holy because children are uncontaminated by society and in closer touch with the collective unconscious of spiritual experience. Seen as a huge dream, children report feelings of closeness to God.

2. **Activism.** For some children, their spiritual beliefs lead to demonstrable action. Children will translate a belief in a social cause, such the plight of children in underdeveloped nations, into fund-raising campaigns, letter writing, and so forth. For other children, this sense of activism is expressed by total immersion in a game, a sport, or a musical activity in which they report a sense of transcendence while participating in that activity.

3. **Sagacity.** The notion of a "child–sage," of knowing beyond one's years, is expressed by the immediacy and depth of empathic encounters that cannot be explained through cognitive development or shared experience.

4. **Holy foolishness.** Mercer uses this title as one of reverence for the honesty and straightforwardness of children's expressions of faith, belief, and spiritual attention. The child who claims, perhaps to the laughter of adults, that she got her "cute dimples" from God is speaking the truth as she knows it because, to her, dimples (and all other things) originate from the creator of all things.

On the basis of the efforts of Fowler (1981) and other researchers, the connection between cognitive growth and children's concepts of the Divine has been well studied. Preschool children view God as a special individual (usually a man). Children raised in religious homes tend to see God as someone to be admired, served, and respected—a projection of how they might like to be seen. School-aged children see God as a human who possesses special powers or talents. Children in this age group see God as a creator, a protector, and a judge, similar in many ways to how they view their parents.

Frame (2003) reported on Heller's (1986) gender-based distinctions among perceptions of God. Although both boys and girls saw God as a great father, boys endowed God with rationality and participation in life events. For boys, God was definitely male; in fact, the possibility of a feminine God was reported to generate great anxiety among boys. Girls tended to see God more as an observer than as a participant in life and imbued God with more androgynous characteristics.

Counseling may serve as the spiritual role modeling of openness and receptivity to one's self-definition or one's adherence to prescribed religious/spiritual norms (Lonborg & Bowen, 2004). Such intervention must have its basis in a solid understanding of one's own spiritual preferences and an ethical commitment to honor professional boundaries around the imposition of personal values on clients. Spiritual counseling, as practiced, seems more directed with a specific faith tradition. Counseling on the issues of spirituality, in comparison with spiritual counseling, is embedded in notions of multicultural competency, perhaps more as an ideal to be achieved than as a common practice (Richards, Keller, & Smith, 2004). Counseling on issues of spirituality spans faith traditions, seeking common questions and respecting the diversity of faith-based answers.

Any interaction regarding children's spirituality is a poignant reminder that spiritual thoughts and feelings are as much a part of the growth process for young children as is their physical, mental, or emotional development. However, in a secular society where progress is measured in scientific rather than spiritual terms, researchers often ignore this aspect of a child's existence.

"Spirituality has traditionally been framed in terms of religion, and so the issue of church and state comes up," observed Don Ratcliff, professor of education at Biola University in La Mirada, California, and the author of several books on children's spiritual development. He also stated, "In the research area, a lot of secular universities shy away from it because they think the topic is getting too close to religion. There's concern about objectivity."

Ratcliff's research and his experiences as a parent led him to believe that, at a young age, many children begin to actively search for spiritual understanding. He recalled that, at age 5, his own son became deeply reflective while watching a campfire during a family trip. Gazing into the flames, the child observed that "the fire is like Jesus on the cross, and the stones are like people standing around looking up at the cross." To Ratcliff, the story was a reminder that even very young children have the ability to think abstractly. However, many experts in early childhood development believe just the opposite: Young children's early expressions of faith can be rooted only in the concrete experiences of seeing, hearing, and touching.

"If you ask a preschooler, 'What is God?' you get an answer that God is a person," stated Helen Cohen, director of the Frances Jacobson Early Childhood Center at Temple Israel in Boston. "I remember a child telling me she didn't believe in God. I said, 'Why do you say that?' She said, 'I can't see God or hear God, so I know there is no God.'" Other children seem to be more openly engaged by the concept of a Higher Power, said David Elkind, PhD, professor of child study at Tufts University. He recalled a conversation with a 4-year-old who spoke with authority when asked to describe the difference between God and Jesus. "The difference, according to this child," Elkind recalled with a chuckle, "is that God doesn't have birthdays and Jesus does."

Elkind (1984) identified three stages of faith development:

1. ***The global stage.*** Until age 6 or 7, most children lack an understanding of abstract belief and therefore can't conceptualize the differences among religious faiths. They can appreciate religious symbols and rituals, but don't necessarily connect them to the notion of an invisible God.

2. ***The concrete stage.*** Children ages 7 to 12 are still very grounded in the physical world and are beginning to develop a greater sense of spiritual identity based on personal experiences and religious practices (e.g., "I go to church [synagogue, mosque], and this is connected to who I am and who my family is."). Elkind said that rituals, whether lighting candles in church or opening the ark that holds the Torah in a synagogue, are very effective in helping children of this age understand religious themes.

3. ***The personal connection stage.*** In pre-adolescence, a feeling of personal closeness to God often emerges; it is the budding of what feels like an actual relationship. For some young teens, Elkind said, "God becomes a confidante, because you don't want to share your thoughts with anyone else who will tell your secrets."

Children's thoughts and feelings about God or other spiritual concepts appear to be a natural part of human development, a search for some force in the universe that represents eternity and the absence of change. Even children who are not raised in a religious home are likely to ask spiritual questions.

The presence of children introduces a number of spiritual issues within the family environment. Some of these issues emerge in the context of developmental life transitions. The birth of a child, in all spiritual traditions, carries spiritual beliefs, expectations, and practices. Sometimes the gender of the child dictates specific roles and practices. Some families limit children's contact with those of other faiths and practices, dichotomizing the world into "believers like us" and "nonbelievers." This division is more keenly felt and expressed when adherence to a faith prohibits children's participation in celebrations experienced by the majority. For example, Jehovah's Witness children cannot participate in Christmas celebrations and parties because such events are contrary to that religion's belief system. Specific attire or diets may also generate a sense of social isolation and peer group exclusion. For example, Jewish children whose families follow the laws of kashrut (i.e., they "keep kosher"), are prohibited from eating many common foods (such as cheeseburgers). From a child-rearing perspective, spiritual belief systems about the innate nature of children will direct how parents respond to and rear their offspring. Some parents who view children as having been born into a spiritually gifted state may allow them much more freedom for exploration and expression than parents who believe that children are born into a state of innate wickedness that can be eradicated only through strict discipline.

Previous empirical studies have confirmed a positive connection between spiritual practices and healthful behaviors among children. Mercer (2006) cited six studies that supported the connection between religion/spirituality and resilience and adaptation to illness. In addition, studies indicate that there are fewer incidences of smoking, high-risk behavior, depression, and so forth and a more positive relationship with such healthful behaviors as exercise, a sound diet, and good sleeping habits.

In summary, it is apparent that children are as spiritual as anyone at any age. Perhaps it is necessary for those who care for children and about children to recognize their own level of openness toward spiritual experiences and to recall a time in their youth when language did not hamper the experiencing of wonder, mystery, and awe, and they were content to experience, rather than try vainly to describe.

THE RELIGION AND SPIRITUALITY OF ADOLESCENTS

Adolescence has been considered a life stage of "experimentation and searching, a time when children work to establish autonomy and form their own identities" (Frank & Kendall, 2001, p. 133). A 1992 Gallup poll discovered that 95% of American teens stated that they believed in God, 93% claimed to have a religious affiliation, and 80% categorized religion as being important in their lives. Adolescents tend to develop more abstract notions of God (Cloyd, 1997), seeing God not as a person, but as a spirit. For the vast majority of Americans, spirituality is a central aspect of their identity (MacDonald, 2004); thus, given the effects of family values on adolescent values, spirituality may also be a central consideration for adolescents. In addition, in most cultures, spirituality is inextricably linked to one's worldview on a daily basis (Sue & Sue, 2003).

Just as religion has been shown to be a predictive factor of well-being across the entire life span, Frank and Kendal cited three specific studies which indicated that there is a positive relationship between religion and well-being among adolescents. The studies found that (a) religion is a negative predictor of suicidal ideation and attempt (Donahue & Benson, 1995); (b) religion is a positive predictor of adjustment in school and academic performance (Hyde, 1990); and (c) among African American teens, religion is a positive predictor of a decrease in self-perceived stigmatization (Brega & Coleman, 1999). It has also been suggested that adolescents who consider religious affiliation to be part of their support systems may be more able to resist their peers' injunctions to participate in risky behaviors such as smoking, alcohol or substance abuse, or premarital sexual behavior.

Wong, Rew, & Slaikeu (2006) reported on the inconsistent findings linking religion/spirituality and adolescents' mental health. Based on their extensive review, 18 of 20 recent studies (90%) found positive findings. Studies that utilized institutional descriptions and existential modifiers were the most highly significant for predicting adolescent mental health. This finding is indicative of the need for belonging and structure during the tumult of adolescence. The need for association is stronger for boys and older adolescents than it is for girls and younger adolescents.

Within Western society, often religious institutions and the family have served as sources of morals and values for children. However, participation in religious life as adolescents has been found to be largely dictated by parents (Frank & Kendall, 2001). In addition, although adolescents may give voice to religious morality and the ill-advised nature of high-risk behaviors, such attitudes have not been found to translate into relevant behavior patterns. So the question may arise as to how one can understand the religious development of teenagers apart from that of adults.

Fowler (1981) suggested that the roots of adolescent attitudes toward spirituality are a function of the family and the community. However, there is a danger that, should family members or religious leaders not behave in accordance with sermons and preachings, such a lapse will be seen by the typically idealistic and critical adolescent as being hypocritical and thus condemned to irrelevance.

Added to the importance of family is the notion of "mattering"—a sense of belonging in relationship to others or a feeling that one is important to others (Rayle & Myers, 2004, p. 81), which is a predictor of wellness in adolescence. Mattering was found to be a stronger predictor of spiritual wellness than acculturation, leading to lower levels of depression (citing Taylor & Turner, 2001, bereavement leads to lower levels of mattering). Self-direction, schoolwork, and friendship were not related to perceptions of belonging to the majority culture or ethnic group. What was found to be significant was the adolescent's perceived levels of mattering to others. Given such an identified need, the question then becomes where does the adolescent seek that sense of "mattering" and how well does his or her environment meet that need?

Adolescence is also a time when many teens begin to question their religious and spiritual beliefs and affiliations (Atwater, 1988). Frame (2003) cautioned that this challenge may be more severe for families in which there is a very strong spiritual or religious affiliation. This challenge may emerge if such religious beliefs dictate peer contact, condemnation of sexual experimentation, dress, and so forth, which place the family and peer values systems in conflict. How others, especially parents and religious authorities, respond to this normative searching will determine how strongly the adolescent will heed their input. If the search is considered to be a welcome aspect of developing a strong, autonomous spiritual identity, then the religion of origin remains a viable choice. If the search is condemned as being disrespectful or unfaithful, then the adolescent will hear that he or she has been banished from the religion of origin and will not consider that affiliation to be a viable choice.

Furthermore, adolescents reported increased guilt and anxiety for violating parental codes of conduct that have a spiritual or religious basis. Markstrom (1999) described the resolution of this crisis in identity as being part of what Erik Erikson called the development of the ego. Once fidelity has been established, then the young adult will become personally committed to many societal institutions, including a place of worship. For adolescents from troubled homes, a strong connection to God or a religious institution can provide a sense of support and attachment that is not present in the home. These sources may, in some way, be a substitute for the influence of home by offering values and beliefs that strengthen the adolescent in resisting the lure of peer pressure or gang affiliation.

Wallace and Williams (1997) proposed a model of the influence of socialization to explain how religion affects the health and development of adolescents. The family serves as the original socializing force for the young child. Later, religion, school, and peers exert an influence. All these influences are moderated by the environment into which parents place their children. This process of secondary socialization includes social control, values, identity, and social support. From the adolescent's integration of these messages emerge status, attitudes, beliefs, and behaviors.

It could be asserted that this spiritual drive is what makes adolescents susceptible to recruitment into cults (Lee, 2004). Of particular concern are those religious sects which are described as "spurious or unorthodox" (p. 367). These groups are characterized by psychological and social pressures to distort perceptions, attitudes, and beliefs. Individuals who are attracted to such groups often ask questions such as "Who am I?" "Does God care about me existing?" and "How can I cope with the chaos of life?" (Gesy, 1993).

Such descriptions fit many adolescents as a function of the development of their cultural identity. Erikson (1994) noted this developmental task and asserted that a connection exists between identity and spirituality. Although a previous study found a correlation among adolescent faith maturity, parental influence, peer influence, and congregational influence, parental influence was found to have the most lasting impact on faith development and maturity among adolescents (Martin, White, & Perlman, 2003). However, this transmission of values is a function of the general respect between adolescents and adults. Not only must those elders be viewed as wise, but the adolescent must feel that he or she matters to the elders in question. In the absence of such relationships, substitute groups or religions become more attractive. Lee (2004) spoke to five needs that are met by cult membership: (a) the need to conform, (b) the need not to conform, (c) the need to be led, (d) the need to be devoted to a cause, and (e) the need for parental replacement.

Given the previous studies that link religious affiliation and positive mental health, counselors need to be aware of the importance of religion/spirituality in the coping repertoire and the sense of identity of adolescents. If helping professionals overlook the introduction of this topic when getting to know the adolescent's worldview, they risk the communication of a covert message that these topics are not appropriate for discussion in counseling or in therapy. In addition, a second covert message may be the questioning of the legitimacy of those coping strategies, leaving the adolescent with a greater vulnerability and receptivity to negative peer pressure. According to MacDonald (2004), "the biggest restriction of school counselor–student collaboration is the counselor's belief that a restriction exists" (p. 294).

Frank and Kendall (2001) reached the following conclusions:

> [F]uture research should focus on the meaning and significance of religion, spirituality and culture within the adolescent population as well as investigating where religion fits in the coping processes for these children. Only then will we be able to move toward a more comprehensive conceptualization of the development, prevention, and treatment of serious risk behavior in our youths. (p. 145)

Case Example Revisited

Andrea was initially tempted to dispute her group members' experiences within their faith communities. Personally, she had always experienced warmth and validation from her church community, and hearing these women's stories troubled her. She wondered if perhaps the women might somehow have provoked this ostracism.

During a conversation with her peers, Andrea related her concerns and was referred to an LGB support service. She was concerned that she would be discovered accessing this resource. However, she learned from the support service that, sadly, the women's experiences within their faith communities were all too common. More knowledgeable now, Andrea began to explore issues of faith and sexual orientation to broaden her understanding and to provide more empathic clinical services.

Conclusion

The notions of meaning and motivation seem to be endemic to the search for life purpose and understanding (Turner et al., 2004). However, given the multicultural orientation toward understanding each individual's sense of the world, it must be acknowledged that members of differing groups have different experiences of the same event or affiliation. In the case of reli-gious and spiritual development, this chapter has briefly outlined the differing experiences of women; lesbian, gay, and bisexual persons; children; and adolescents, in order to assist counselors in better recognizing and supporting the needs of and the spiritual challenges facing members of each group.

Self-Understanding Exercises

1. Can you recall a spiritually moving moment from your childhood? Try to relive that epiphany and determine how adequately words describe that event.
2. Consider the extent to which your own sexual orientation is confirmed or rejected by your choice of religious or spiritual affilia-tion. How does that institution explain this acceptance or rejection?
3. Trace your religious/spiritual tradition's historical roots. How have gender roles changed over time? How were gender roles explained in the past? How are they explained now?

Opportunities for Further Learning

1. Identify a local religious education program, and examine the curriculum of that program with regard to either women; lesbian, gay, and bisexual persons; children; or adolescents. What covert and overt messages are sent to and about members of that specific group?
2. Ask a member of the clergy or a spiritual authority about his or her institution's official position on homosexuality. How is that position justified, and what message does that institution wish to send to lesbian, gay, and bisexual persons in society?
3. Interview a lesbian, gay, or bisexual person and ask for his or her firsthand experiences with traditional religion. Ask questions such as these:
   a. What messages does your church [synagogue, mosque, or other religious institution] give you?
   b. How do you make sense of these messages in light of your sexual identity?
   c. If there is a discrepancy, how have you reconciled the two messages?

13

■ ■ ■

Spiritual Strategies for Individual Counseling

CASE EXAMPLE

Teena approached her clinical training eager to learn how to better assist her intended client population of college students. As part of her training, it was recommended that she participate in her own counseling, as a client, in order to discover what being in therapy felt like from the client's perspective. Not only was she eager to participate, but she also confided to her counselor that she had some issues to work through, and she decided that she could attend to both tasks at the same time.

In her journal for class, where she related her experiences as a client, she remarked that her counselor had assigned her tasks that were different from her experiences in high school when she had sought counseling from a member of her clergy to deal with the death of her grandmother. She reported that both experiences were helpful; however, she wondered if there was some line or boundary that separated the counseling provided by a member of the clergy and that provided by a mental health professional.

■ ■ ■

INTRODUCTION

This chapter reflects a growing acknowledgment that client religiosity and/or spirituality is considered to be a significant factor in treatment planning and implementation (American Psychological Association, 2002). In this chapter, intervention strategies are presented that will increase a clinician's range of options for responding to his or her clients' spiritual issues or, more broadly, life issues in which there is a spiritual component.

Nash (1997) described spirituality as "an abiding belief that positive change is achievable [and] . . . encourages a loving acceptance of life, [the] self and others" (p. 2). From this perspective, which seems to be consistent with the overall goals of counseling or psychotherapy, the helping professional is asked to be knowledgeable and skilled in a range of spiritual interventions in order to assist the client on his or her spiritual journey (Frame, 2003).

Pargament, Murray-Swank, and Tarakeshwar (2005) stated that members of many populations have expressed a reliance on various spiritual and religious practices in order to help them in times of stress. Those groups include elderly women facing medical problems, some Americans polled after the 9/11 attacks, combat veterans, hospital patients, parents of children with disabilities, widows, and physically abused spouses. In addition, among the seriously mentally ill, expressions of spirituality have been linked to fewer frustrations, less depression and hostility, and fewer hospitalizations. Furthermore, these authors cited three salient studies which confirmed that clients would welcome an integration of spiritual concerns and healing into their counseling if the helping professional would only offer such an invitation.

An important aspect of this chapter is "informed decision making." This phrase encompasses the gamut of ethical, theoretical, technical, and evaluative questions that clinicians are directed to consider before utilizing any therapeutic technique with any client (Frame, 2003). With regard the consideration of spiritual or religious interventions, such questions may include, but are not limited to, the following:

1. How open is the spiritual stance that I will be modeling for my clients?
2. Which themes and practices of spiritual traditions resonate with me? Which do not?
3. How able am I to express my benevolent connectedness with each client?
4. How do I understand the presence or absence of transcendence in my own spiritual practices?
5. How do my spiritual beliefs contribute to my sense of meaning and purpose? (Briggs & Kelly, 2005)

Within the process of assessment, Briggs and Kelly (2005) offered eight descriptions of clients that may guide counselors in determining the client's level of religiosity or spirituality:

1. *Religiously committed clients* see the world and their issues through their religious convictions. For example, a client who chooses a fundamentalist orientation may utilize religious text as a literal guide for living.
2. *Religiously loyal clients* integrate religious norms into culture in order to create guiding principles. For example, a Jewish client may adhere to culture, as influenced by religion, but not be as invested in the religious practices themselves.
3. *Spiritually committed clients* are oriented toward spiritual themes, but not organized religion. Such clients may choose to live their lives on the basis of meaningful principles, openness to others, and universal kindness, but not belong to a formal community of worshippers.
4. *Religiously and spiritually committed clients* present without an orientation toward any specific religion or spiritual tradition, but may come to welcome the opportunity to integrate such practices. For example, a client presenting with grief issues may be open to considering spiritual or religious practices as part of a mourning ritual.
5. *Superficially religious clients* claim a religious affiliation, but their prime motive for such a connection may be social rather than spiritual. For example, a client may acknowledge that he or she attends church only for weddings, baptisms, and so forth, and not for regular services.
6. *Religiously tolerant and indifferent clients* can accept the need for others to hold such belief systems, but dismiss the relevance of such beliefs to their own lives. For example, a client may see a book of Taoist sayings on the counselor's bookshelf and see its potential value for other clients, but not for him- or herself.
7. *Nonreligious clients* reject the value of religion overtly. They may refer to a belief in the hereafter merely as an excuse to tolerate life circumstances.
8. *Religiously hostile clients* are not accepting of those who see any merit in adherence to such belief systems. For example, a client who refuses to believe in God due to insufficient scientific proof would not accept anyone else's decision to believe in God.

The spiritual strategies presented in this chapter are thoroughly discussed so that the clinician may select an intervention that is congruent with his or her overall treatment approach and with the specific needs of the client. In addition, the discussion includes any available evidence on the efficacy of the intervention, for which clients such evidence is appropriate, and to which issues it is applicable. The interventions addressed include prayer and meditation, the use of ritual, spiritual journaling, bibliotherapy, forgiveness and repentance, 12-step programs, surrender, and consultation and referral. These were the interventions that appeared most frequently within the professional literature. This is intended, not to limit the choice of interventions, but rather to substantiate the efficacy of the chosen intervention.

GUIDELINES FOR USING SPIRITUAL INTERVENTIONS

Prayer

Prayer is reported to be a widespread practice in the United States. Fenwick (2004) reported on three surveys appearing in popular magazines: (a) a 1992 *Newsweek* poll indicating that nine out of 10 Americans prayed at least once each week; (b) a 1994 *LIFE* magazine survey that found similar results for those who believed that God answers one's prayers; and (c) a report in *TIME* magazine stating that 82% of those surveyed believe that prayer heals. Frame (2003) cited a 1993 Gallup poll which reported that "90% of Americans pray, 97% believe that prayer is heard, and 86% believe that prayer makes them a better person" (p. 185).

In addition, Frame (2003) referenced several studies which asserted that women pray more than men and in a more meditative manner, African Americans pray more often than European Americans and report greater satisfaction, and older persons pray more frequently than do younger people. Such opinions are echoed by Koenig, McCullough, and Larson (2001), who reviewed 1,200 studies on the effects of prayer and discovered that the majority of the studies confirmed that prayer encourages better physical health and clinical functioning.

Prayer has no specific religious connotation, although the practice is usually tied to specific rituals and is anchored in a religious orientation. Frame (2003) defined prayer as "thoughts, attitudes, and actions designed to express or experience connection to the sacred" (p. 184). More broadly, prayer can be conceptualized as "a formula of words, sighs, gestures, and even silence that contains some form of entreaty for us or for others" (La Tore, 2004, p. 37).

Such practices provide four coping mechanisms: (a) seeking God's help with difficulties, (b) deferring stressful circumstances, (c) seeking calm, and (d) seeking acceptance (Bade & Cook, 1997). Ameling (2000) stated that prayer is "a simple act of turning our mind and heart to the sacred" (p. 42). Harris, Schoneman, and Carrera (2005) named 10 functions of prayer: "(a) expression of need, (b) affirming faith, (c) self-suggestion, (d) regression, (e) cognitive reframing, (f) relaxation, (g) expression of habit, (h) reduction of anxiety through confession, (i) reconciliation of frustration, and (j) desensitization" (p. 405). From this perspective, the use of prayer in counseling does not indicate the imposition of religious values, but rather denotes the reaching outside of oneself for guidance and support in times of need. The aim or direction of this "reaching" would reflect the individual client's spiritual values system.

The use of prayer in counseling may occur in several ways. The counselor may pray for or with the client, or the client might utilize prayer under the guidance of the counselor (Faiver, Ingersoll, O'Brien, & McNally, 2001; La Torre, 2004; Sperry, 2001). The practice of praying for the client reflects the counselor's use of prayer in his or her own life and also reflects a deep concern for the client and a request for protection or guidance for the client. The practice of praying with the client entails the client offering a prayer in session, which may then be given additional strength or legitimization by the counselor's participation. The third option allows the client to utilize a personally relevant prayer, but it also respects the professional and personal boundaries of the counselor who would serve as a facilitator and observer rather than an active participant (La Torre, 2004).

Within those practices are five different types of prayer that may help counselors direct their clients: (a) contemplative/meditative prayer (being open to experiencing God or a Supreme Being), (b) ritual prayer (the recitation of a memorized or written prayer), (c) petitionary prayer (a request on behalf of oneself or others), (d) colloquial prayer (an informal conversation with God), and (e) intercessory prayer (praying for others) (Bashall & O'Connor, 2005).

Fenwick (2004) offered a historical review of studies of the power of prayer, including the following: In an 1872 study, Sir Francis Galton argued that those who pray should live longer, and he indeed found that priests lived longer than doctors, who, in turn, outlived lawyers. However, his findings were confounded by the discovery that the more eminent a member of the clergy, the *shorter* one's life span. Fenwick also cited a study conducted in India regarding the impact of prayer on the gender of children: Although prayers are frequently offered in favor of a male child, the birthrate in India mirrors that of any Western country, in that there was no significant preponderance of births of male vs. female babies than would occur randomly.

More recently, Byrd (1988) found reduced hospital stays, reduced complications, and reduced drug use among coronary care patients who prayed. Koenig, McCullough, and Larson (2000) reported that regular church participation among those older than age 65 seemed to portend lower levels of cancer and heart disease. Roberts, Ahmed, and Hall (2000) conducted a review of previous studies on the efficacy of prayer and concluded that the results were too inconsistent to support a hypothesis either in support of or against the efficacy of prayer.

Concurrently, Astin, Harkness, and Ernst (2000) conducted a meta-analysis of 23 clinical trials to date and could only acknowledge that the heterogeneity of the samples precluded any generalization of the results. However, since 57% of the studies reported positive outcomes, these authors indicated that the issue was worthy of further investigation.

A subsequent study by Aviles et al. (2000) found that prayer had no significant impact on the medical outcomes for 799 coronary care patients, but suggested that the results offered positive support for the effects of prayer. Although the data did not prove to be statistically significant, the analysis did reveal what was described by the authors as meaningful differences. Cha, Wirth, and Lobo (2001) compared the results of intercessory prayer on behalf of groups of *in vitro* fertilization and embryo transfer patients in South Korea with the results achieved by a control group and found that the prayed-for group had significantly higher success with implantation ($p = .0005$) and pregnancy rates ($p = .0013$) than did the non-prayed-for group. In conclusion, Fenwick (2004) advised that future studies need to formalize and quantify the methods of prayer so that the mental intent to heal can be standardized. He also suggested that the positive and negative results gained to date offer tentative evidence that prayer can indeed work.

Cohen et al. (2000) challenged the "utility of prayer" as a method for controlling events or as an intervention that can be supported as a function of the number of petitions granted.

In contrast, these authors posited that "theists engage in prayer because that is where they encounter God" (p. 42). Rather than view God as a means to human ends, knowing God through prayer becomes the end in itself. Rather than viewing prayer as a way to get God to give humans their way, prayer is to be seen as evidence of a "living relationship between humans and the God who exceeds our understanding and stands above our desires" (p. 43).

According to the beliefs of Christians, Jews, and Muslims, although God is concerned with human welfare and suffering, God responds to prayer on the basis of God's wisdom rather than the desires of those who pray. Cohen et al. (2000) further asserted that, in prayer, one must bow before the superior knowledge and foresight of God, which is beyond the grasp of humans. Although spirituality is integral to how people handle life's challenges and provides meaning, strength, and hope in the face of life's adversities, one should not consider prayer to be a means to control or test God, because such a demand reverses the basic tenet of faith in a Supreme Being.

Townsend, Kladder, Ayele, and Mulligan (2002) identified five randomized control studies of the impact of prayer that could be categorized as rigorously designed. They found the following results:

1. Intercessory prayer was found to decrease mortality in children with leukemia.
2. A group of cardiac care patients who received intercessory prayer required fewer antibiotics, fewer diuretics, and less ventilator support.
3. A group of 1,000 cardiac care patients from the previous study was followed over 12 months, and it was found that those receiving intercessory prayer achieved 10% better outcomes than the control group.
4. No differences in outcomes were found between the prayed-for group and the control group for clients who presented with alcohol abuse issues at a university counseling center.
5. In a study of the reduction of anxiety or depression among Muslim Malays, researchers found that the integration of Muslim-based interventions (advice or encouragement based on the Koran and Hadith) and secular interventions was more successful than secular interventions alone.

However, the helping professional must be cautious in the use of prayer in secular settings. Care must be taken to remain within one's scope of clinical competence and not to blur one's role with that of a spiritual director. A helping professional using prayer also may experience transference as a result of the client's previous experiences with clergy. In addition, the helping professional must be very clear about his or her own spiritual values and prayer practices and not contaminate the counseling session with a personal agenda. Finally, the helping professional must determine whether the client may be using prayer as an avoidance technique, wishing his or her problems away rather than attending to these challenges (Basham & O'Connor, 2005).

Meditation

Meditation is an established practice in both Western and Eastern religions, including Christianity. However, there are clear differences in the way in which each group approaches the practice. In Eastern meditation, the objective is to experience a mind free from ideas and intrusive thoughts. For example, in Taoist practice, meditation is intended to rid one of social artifice and return one to the tenets of "the Way," or Tao, as a vehicle toward personal growth. In comparison, Western meditation emphasizes focusing on one specific idea. Either way, the goal underlying meditation is to bring the power of contemplation to bear on an issue, with the assumption that this practice will resolve it.

Schopen and Freeman (1992) and Miller (2003) stated several benefits of meditative practices, including (a) relaxation; (b) stress reduction; (c) the alleviation of disquieting emotions; (d) changes in one's mental, physical, and emotional states; and (e) a more accurate view of the reality of the situation. Frame (2003) cited research by Martin and Carlson (1988) which found that meditation had a positive effect on stress, anxiety, PTSD, and depression, as well as research by O'Connell and Alexander (1994) which indicated that meditation had a positive impact on the prevention and treatment of addictive behaviors.

The use of meditation, visualization, or focusing may require some direction on the part of the counselor because these practices may not be familiar to clients. The first step involves creating a comfortable physical environment. Next, the client chooses a word, phrase, or object on which to focus; this should be connected to the client's spiritual belief system. The client is then directed to close his or her eyes, to relax, and to repeat the word or phrase, or think about the chosen object, while exhaling. Intrusive thoughts are allowed to pass through one's awareness and to be released; all the while, the person is focusing on breathing and on the chosen object.

This practice can be expanded to include visualization should the counselor direct the client toward specific scenes or events that evoke personal issues or concerns. Sometimes the focus can be on selected spiritual or sacred writings. Such an experience may help the client see "outside of oneself" and may offer a differing perspective on some troubling issue. Focusing involves paying close attention to a puzzle or issue in the client's life in order to allow "new, explicit meaning to emerge" (Frame, 2003, p. 188).

After creating an inventory of concerns, the client is directed to get a "felt sense" of the issue by tuning into emotions, sensations, images, and body movements. Next, the client is directed to put into words the "felt sense" in order to invite the counselor into the experience. By uniting the "felt sense" with the client's cognitive sense of the issue, the client may gain a more complete view of him- or herself within the context of the issue, with the hope that the path toward resolution also becomes clearer.

CASE EXAMPLE

Sophie, a 20-year-old college student, presented with difficulties coping with her grandmother's illness. "Grams" had raised Sophie from infancy, with her only wish being to see her graduate from college. Given the terminal nature of her illness, there was a chance that Sophie's grandmother would not live to see her granddaughter graduate. Sophie was angry that her prayers to God to spare her grandmother had gone unanswered and, in fact, that the illness had progressed. She wondered aloud why God had forsaken her and she began to despair. Her mounting depression over her grandmother's condition and her feelings of disconnection from God were affecting her academic performance; she was in danger of not graduating.

The counselor decided to try to help Sophie separate her sadness at the imminent passing of Grams and to ponder, through peaceful meditation, what Grams sought for herself. Sophie immediately responded with "Grams is praying for an end to the pain and to be with

Grampa again." As she made this statement, she could see that God was indeed responding, not to Sophie, but to the one who had the greater need: her grandmother. At that moment of contemplation, her anger dissipated. She then offered a prayer of thanks to God for heeding her grandmother's wishes, and she felt secure in the knowledge that, whether she was physically present or not, her grandmother would indeed attend her graduation and watch over her.

The Use of Ritual

One aspect of all cultures is the use of ritual to mark salient life events, such as birth, death, marriage, and numerous occasions in between. A ritual can be defined as follows:

> A conventionalized joint activity given to ceremony, involving two or more persons endowed with special emotion and often with sacred meaning, focused around a clearly defined set of social objects, and when performed, confers on its participants a special sense of the sacred and the out-of-the-ordinary. (Denzin, 1974, p. 272)

A ritual that is designed together with the client and is congruent with the client's clinical goals and religious practices uses time, space, symbolism, and access to a multisensory experience to emphasize a life transition or event (Faiver, Ingersoll, O'Brien, & McNally, 2001). By its very planning and execution, a ritual signals an important change that is worthy of one's time and energy to observe. A ritual makes concrete an experience that is often ephemeral in nature.

A ritual can be categorized as liberating, transformative, or celebratory (Basham & O'Connor, 2005). A liberating ritual involves a release from a toxic event, person, or place. For example, leaving a hated job may be ritualized by the destruction of one's parking decal, acknowledging that one no longer has a place in the parking lot, and, even if a return were contemplated, one would not be allowed because there is no longer an assigned spot. This ritual may also celebrate a transition from one job or occupation to another because one severs all ties from one place to anticipate a new success. Transformative rituals integrate change and celebration. For example, the Jewish practice of Bar or Bat Mitzvah acknowledges a change in status from child to adult and rejoices in both states. All spiritual and religious traditions specify rites for welcoming new children, the onset of puberty, marriage, and death. These can be considered rite-of-passage events in which new roles, responsibilities, and powers are bestowed upon the person. Celebratory rituals abound in our society. A cursory journey through the e-cards listed on Hallmark Cards' Web site indicate a wide variety of occasions that are worthy of note. These celebrations are usually annual events that are joyously anticipated. Religious holidays, birthdays, anniversaries, and so forth are listed.

An individually created ritual seems to carry additional power in comparison to those which are already socially sanctioned. Integrating the client's world and spiritual views into a specific event at a specific time and place of importance to the client increases the power and the impact of the ritual. The connection between the details of the ritual and meaningfulness for the client directs the creation and execution of the ritual. Within the event, the counselor may simply be an observer, or he or she may be excluded by the client as a demonstration of the client's readiness to move on. In other situations, family members, friends, and so forth may be asked to join in.

CASE EXAMPLE

Terry came to counseling unable to release his feelings of depression over the loss of his partner in an airplane crash. Although they had not yet "come out" as a gay couple to their families and friends, Terry felt a deep emotional commitment to Frank, whom he saw as a life partner. Terry's clergy member assured him that his friend was now "with God," but Terry was unmoved by such assurances. He knew that Frank had long ago abandoned the church of his youth as a result of an exploration of his sexual orientation, and he had despaired that distancing from his church. Indeed, Frank's homosexuality may have made Frank unwelcome in that house of God. Terry needed some way to be sure that Frank was in heaven, and then he could stop worrying about him.

Terry's counselor focused on helping him to select a ritual from an alternative religion to mourn the loss of Frank. Terry chose a meaningful ritual that involved the burning of memories of the departed and the observance of the flames and ashes reaching skyward. In order to plan the ceremony, Terry gathered members of Frank's family and those of his friends, coworkers, and acquaintances who wanted to bid farewell to Frank. Each attendee was to bring a memento of Frank to add to the funeral pyre, and each was invited to offer some words about his or her loss and hopes for Frank in the hereafter. Terry was also to create a personal time and space early in his day in order to honor his memory of Frank and his grief at Frank's passing and for what might have been in their relationship.

Keeping a Spiritual Journal

Journaling is an activity specifically applicable to the client who finds a release in written expression. This activity allows a client to express his or her thoughts and feelings immediately, rather than "storing up" these insights for the next meeting with the counselor. The client need not concern him- or herself with grammar, punctuation, or even a logical train of thought. Instead of form and protocol, it is the spontaneous substance that gives the exercise its value. Drawings, poetry, ideas, phrases, and so forth are all valid and valuable means for communicating the processing of one's thoughts and feelings. Over time, journaling creates a history of the client's exploration and growth through the presenting issue. The finished work provides the client with a compilation of his or her insights into the presenting issue. Frame (2003) included a definition by Cargas and Radley (1981), who described a journal as

> [a] book in which you keep a personal record of events in your life, of your different relationships, of your responses to things, of your feelings about things—of your search to find out who you are, what the meaning of your life may be. It is a book in which you carry out the greatest of life's adventures—the discovery of yourself. (p. 8)

The process of journaling is also a self-focused exercise. Frame (2003) suggested that journaling provides clients ". . . with a tool for self-discovery, an aid to concentration, a safety valve for their emotions, and a mirror for the spirit" (p. 190). If a client finds that his or her journal content is mostly about others, the client may be confronted with evaluating priorities (i.e., are the opinions of others seen as being more valuable than one's own?). In such cases, a client begins to better understand the frustration inherent in his or her desire to become more self-directing if the primary issue of concern is the opinion of others.

Basham and O'Connor (2005) asserted that "clients gain [a] greater trust in themselves and find personal inspiration" through the process of journaling (p. 153). Journaling also offers the counselor the opportunity to introduce what is known in narrative therapy as "externalizing conversation." Being able to view one's story from a distance, as occurs when it appears on paper, allows the client and the counselor to develop a series of questions about what is said, and what is left unsaid, that may prompt greater client insight and new viewpoints on the client's spiritual practices. Identifying outdated personal beliefs may provide sufficient "thinking room" in which the client may thoughtfully design a personal spiritual belief system that is free from the encumbrances of previous learning.

A portion of this journaling may involve attending to one's dreams. Both James (1958) and Jung (1964) saw dreams as being connected to spiritual life. Sperry (2001) described dreams as "the royal road to the unconscious" and "God's language" (p. 141). Crook-Lyon and Wimmer (2003) cited two recent studies which found that dream content, when brought to counseling sessions, enhanced the session's quality and insight, as well as the working alliance between client and counselor. When the client and the counselor co-author a spiritual interpretation of dreams, three common issues arise: (a) there are conflicts or questions about religion, (b) the client's faith may be strengthened, and (c) the client may embark on a spiritual search. While working through the process of dream interpretation, the client may come to see dreams as a "message for guidance for life or preparation for the future" (p. 42). Crook-Lyon and Wimmer cautioned helping professionals who wish to integrate dream work into their clinical skills repertoire to

- find a model of dream interpretation that is congruent with one's theoretical beliefs and values (see Bulkeley, 2000, or Davis & Hill, 2004),
- indicate a willingness to the client to incorporate dreams and spirituality into counseling,
- demonstrate an awareness and sensitivity to clients' spiritual beliefs about dreams and dream content, and
- recognize that dream exploration may not be a "good fit" for all clients (e.g., those with thought disorders or those who cannot discriminate between fantasy and reality will likely not benefit from the practice).

It may be of therapeutic value to monitor the evolution of dreams over the period of counseling to determine how certain interpretations affect future dream messages. The process of journaling may help clients record their dream impressions as soon as possible, when the dreams are still fresh in their minds. This compilation of dream development may reflect and guide the work of counseling and will offer the client a record of the changes that occur over time.

CASE EXAMPLE

Malcolm, a college freshman, presented for counseling on the issue of possibly dropping out of the university. Stating that there was "no one there like him" and that "it is impossible to make friends," Malcolm was sure that college was "not right" for him. From a religious perspective, Malcolm was certain that God had abandoned him in his quest to become the first member of his family to earn a college degree. He complained that if God had wanted him to succeed, He would not have had him work so hard and that a sign from God would prove to him that he was indeed meant to pursue a college education.

From the counselor's perspective, Malcolm's struggle was twofold: (a) he was questioning his faith and (b) he had a predilection to notice and hold onto only the difficulties, and not the pleasant aspects, of college life. Malcolm was directed to sit quietly for one hour each day, for the next week, in order to attempt to balance the challenges and rewards of college life. He was to address this task at different times of the day—after class, before going to the gym, during lunch, and so forth.

Malcolm was also directed to define for himself what a "sign from God" would look like and to contact the pastor at his home church in order to get some help in processing this experience. It was thought that the signs were all around him; however, because he was unsure of what to look for, perhaps those confirmations of God's desires were being overlooked or ignored. Malcolm and his pastor decided that evidence of God's support for Malcolm would be what Malcolm called "moments of serenity"—those times when he felt no rush to be anywhere or to be doing anything, just moments when he was able to sit in contemplation. Because these signs were now specified, Malcolm was asked to attend carefully to either their presence or their absence.

Over the course of the first week and over subsequent weeks, Malcolm realized that the signs he sought were all around him, and the one who had done the forsaking was him, not God. With this reassurance of divine support, Malcolm felt more dedicated to his studies and to the "rightness" of his fit at the university.

Bibliotherapy

With regard to the practice of integrating spirituality into counseling, bibliotherapy serves a function similar to that found in secular counseling (Basham & O'Connor, 2005). The purpose of this intervention is to offer the client out-of-session reading, videos, and so forth that might serve to broaden his or her perspective on the presenting issue (Frame, 2003). For clients affiliated with a specific religion, those readings may include sacred texts, novels or biographies about others who have faced similar challenges, or books pertaining to the client's presenting issues. A helping professional may wish to consult with a member of the clergy to determine an appropriate reading list for a specific client. Although the literary works need not be specific to the client's religion, those works must be at least compatible with, and never openly critical of, his or her beliefs. There is a danger in recommending only religious texts, because those works may not provide a broad enough perspective to offer the client alternative viewpoints.

Taylor (2004) suggested that bibliotherapy is helpful for those who can transcend their own lives to find meaning in the lives described in the written word. Because the reader is listening to the characters in the story rather than talking with them, reading allows one the opportunity to attend to the characters' struggles and victories in special ways. "We are witnesses to their lives. . . ." (p. 40). Through our observations of the thoughts, decisions, and actions of the characters, "we find ourselves enlarged in ways that we could not have managed on our own" (p. 40). In summary, Taylor advocated bibliotherapy by saying that "a good book, like a good prayer, is one that takes us to the center of ourselves and then leads us back into the world again, with our spirits refreshed and our hearts enlarged" (p. 41).

Sperry (2001) echoed this message, but with the inclusion of an evaluative component. Should a client's choice of books, movies, and so forth serve to maintain the client's defensiveness or rigidity, perhaps alternative books and movies should be offered, to expand the client's perspective, to correct misinformation, to promote a greater perceived relevance of the material to the client's life and situation, and to enhance client investment in the exercise.

The process of bibliotherapy includes the following steps:

1. The client selects a book, myth, or story from a list of resources that is germane to the presenting issue.
2. The client reads the text (or has the book read to him or her if the client is too young to read).
3. The client is then asked to retell the story with a specific focus on the characters and actions.
4. The client shares his or her perceptions and thoughts about the characters and their actions.
5. The client is asked to ponder alternative actions and outcomes that might have been included in the story.
6. The client is directed to personalize the story and determine how it is related to his or her own circumstances.
7. The client is directed to consider ways in which to incorporate the characters' options as responses to his or her own problems.

Pardeck and Pardeck (1993) reported that clients who utilized bibliotherapy mentioned that they experienced a freeing release of suppressed emotions during the unfolding of the story. There was often a resultant growth in insight and in the ways in which the clients could handle similar dilemmas in their lives more effectively.

Frame (2003) offered guidelines for the selection of appropriate materials, cautioning that sources which offer simplistic solutions to complex problems may discourage clients. Likewise, works that portray characters with multiple issues may overwhelm clients who are attempting to discern which issues are related to their own personal struggles. An annotated list of sources that includes the premise, the purpose, the theme, and the possible limitations of each reference may be of help.

Similar care needs be taken in using sacred writings. Although such works have been long advocated by Christian counselors, Frame could offer no evidence of their psychological benefit. However, because the practice is becoming more widespread, some guidelines may be helpful:

1. Be sure that the choice of scripture is within the client's spiritual belief system.
2. Take care to ensure that one is not being viewed as a religious expert.
3. Determine whether the stories used are to be seen as literal, metaphorical, or narrative.
4. Be prepared to refer clients to spiritual leaders if their questions or needs exceed one's competence as a counselor.

CASE EXAMPLE

Teresa presented for counseling on the issue of her growing estrangement from her family of origin. She was raised in a very strict Baptist home, where many members of her immediate family served as church elders and deacons. Teresa left home at an early age to join the military. She later retired and then started advanced training at a technical school. Her estrangement from her family, which began when she left home against her parents' wishes, was reported to be a constant struggle, and her visits home were marked by continual conflict over her refusal to be "saved" and to rejoin her church. Teresa felt uneasy when participating in these arguments because she had never explored other spiritual traditions; she had merely rejected the church of her youth.

Teresa's counselor offered a series of short readings on other denominations of Christianity, as well as on Buddhism and Taoism, because Teresa had mentioned that she had been stationed overseas and had "heard those words" but did not know much about either practice. The theme of the readings was the acceptance of differences.

Teresa was directed to read each text to determine what, if anything, she might gain from each reading. After reading each text, Teresa said that she felt more in tune with the Buddhist reading on the process of acceptance. She agreed with the Buddhist commentary on acceptance and found what she read to be of help. She acknowledged that her family would not be supportive of her selection of any spiritual path other than the Baptist church. However, she said that she felt more centered through her learning about the Buddhist philosophy and its practice of acceptance. Indeed, she felt that she would be able to "hold her own" in family conflicts without needing to preach in return.

Forgiveness and Repentance

Faiver, Ingersoll, O'Brien, and McNally (2001) identified forgiveness and repentance as "the most widely noted spiritual interventions in the current literature" (p. 122). The process of forgiving may address current or past wrongs, including those from long ago in a client's personal history, but to which the client has clung. Christian clients tend to see forgiveness as a biblical mandate, referring to Matthew 18:22, in which Jesus answers the question of how often one should forgive with the response "seventy times seven," implying that the answer is beyond ordinary specification. In addition, both Islam and Judaism honor a God who models forgiveness, albeit in different ways. In Judaism, only the injured can provide forgiveness, because it is the province, not of God, but rather the victim of the wrongdoing, to forgive. From the view of Islam, offenses are more a function of ignorance than evil, and forgiveness on the part of the victim is evidence of that person's compassion. Given these brief examples, it is vital that counselors fully understand the roles of the offender and the victim from within the framework of the client's spiritual belief system.

The counselor must also consider that the time frame for complete forgiveness will vary according to the client. It has been suggested that the process of forgiveness mirrors the process of grieving. In this case, the loss is the trust in the relationship that was damaged or destroyed by whatever action occurred. If forgiveness does indeed mirror grieving, the client must endure the grieving stages of denial, bargaining, anger, and sadness in two contexts—the injury itself, plus the loss of trust in the relationship—before finally reaching the final stage of acceptance. To this list, Richards and Bergin (1997) added justice and restitution, and the prevention of other offenses. They cautioned counselors that the healing process might be lengthy and urged both the counselor and the client to be patient and to endure through that healing. Freedman (1998) identified four possibilities when a client decides whether or not to forgive someone who has caused pain. The client may (a) forgive and reconcile, (b) forgive and not reconcile, (c) not forgive and interact, and (d) neither forgive nor reconcile.

The initial step in repentance must be confession—an open acknowledgment of one's transgression. Klenck (2004) traced the root of *confession* to the Latin word *confessare*—to speak aloud or to utter. The Oxford University Dictionary expands on this definition, stating that *confession* means "to declare or disclose something which one has kept or allowed to remain secret as being prejudicial or inconvenient to oneself; to acknowledge, own or admit; to make one's self known, to disclose one's identity." This definition mirrors that of Jung, who suggested that such actions live in the shadows of our psyches and represent our cast-off elements of the self. The purpose of a confession is forgiveness and reunion.

Acknowledgment forces a confrontation between these shadow elements of the self and the ego. However, this acknowledgment of the self "necessitates a death/rebirth cycle in the psyche that leads to a more integrated psychic structure" (Klenck, 2004, p. 143). This is the process of seeing through one's often-told story and fully exploring its ramifications for the self in context and the self in the world. This effort allows the voice of the self to be heard over the voice of the defense mechanisms. Klenck (2004) saw the process as being inherently freeing, ridding the individual of misrepresentations of the self and presenting an opportunity for the redefinition thereof. Moreover, anecdotal evidence from clinical practice confirms the emotional release of confession on self-forgiveness—the realization that one may be carrying the burden of wrongs that are not deserved and that there must be movement toward those to whom restitution is owed.

Sperry (2001) suggested that the heart of spirituality focuses on interconnectedness, unity, and equality, which are the antithesis of conflict that emphasizes the aggressor and the victim. The use of spiritual intervention in order to interrupt reactive cycles by asking "What does your anger say about you?" or "What is God's will for you in this interaction?" may prompt personal reflection rather than condemnation of the other individual. Sperry also advocated an exploration of the themes of acceptance, forgiveness, caring, and thanksgiving through family-of-origin work in order to provide a perspective on one's present-day functioning.

Success in being able to forgive is also a reflection of one's previous experiences with resolving developmental tasks (Frame, 2003). For example, Frame cited a 1998 study which found that those who had resolved the initial task in Erik Erikson's model of trust versus mistrust in a more positive direction showed a greater ability to forgive later in life. In addition, it has been posited that a client with weaker ego strength may have more difficulty forgiving because he or she may view the harmful action as a reflection of some personal failing rather than ascribing the responsibility to the person who behaved badly. Counselors are also advised to consider the power differential in the relationship between the transgressor and the victim, as well as the power expressed when one *demands* forgiveness as opposed to when one must only *hope* for forgiveness.

CASE EXAMPLE

Christopher presented for counseling around issues with male authority figures. He had previously been in counseling for similar conflicts and had traced the etiology of these issues to a fractured relationship with his father, who had left him and his mother when he was 5 years old and had recently reappeared in order to attempt to reconnect with Christopher. His father told Christopher that he had been too young and "mixed-up" to be a good parent earlier in life, but that he had "turned his life around by finding God" and he wanted Christopher's forgiveness and to be reconciled with him.

Christopher's pastor advised him to "forgive and forget," and to take his father's humility as sufficient atonement for the earlier abandonment. Christopher tried to do so, but he found that his residual anger had resurfaced, and he exploded at his father. He wondered what was wrong with him that he could not take his father at this word, forgive him, and move on. In addition, he related numerous examples from his early church experiences which indicated that the ability to forgive was indicative of a higher functioning person. He decried his inability to forgive his father.

Christopher's initial efforts focused on the four types of forgiveness, and he was empowered to choose among them. Although others may have held differing ideas about what might be "best for him," only he knew the pain that he had suffered and the extent to which he welcomed his father back into his life. Christopher decided that it was his "Christian duty" to forgive his father, but it was his "human duty" to protect himself against any possible further abuse from his father.

In a session hosted by the counselor, Christopher accepted his father's request that he be forgiven. He politely listened to his father's explanation and life story, and interjected conflicting pieces of information or perceptions that he had carried with him since his childhood. He actually empathized with his father's plight and acknowledged that, in his stead, he might have considered a similar course of action. The counselor acknowledged Christopher's empathy for his father, and then the session shifted to Christopher's personal needs and losses. Christopher was equally clear about how his life had been because he had grown up without a father. He stated that there was no way for his father to atone or compensate for his past actions and that his father needed to consider how he wanted to reconnect with him. In a telling moment, Christopher requested permission to call his father by his given name, as a symbol of their possible new relationship. To his surprise, his father refused, saying that he believed that Christopher's request was disrespectful to his status as Christopher's father. The session deteriorated quickly as Christopher retorted that his father abrogated that respect when he left his family many years ago. At that moment, his father stormed out of the room.

In processing these events, Christopher saw that he had no need to acquiesce to his father's demands. He also sadly acknowledged that he was correct to be wary of his father and that he had seen his father's "true colors." Although the relationship was not reestablished, the situation was clarified. While mourning the failure to reconnect on more mutual terms, Christopher credited himself for making the attempt and for forgiving his father both for the past and for his latest departure. With those realizations came a sense of resolution.

12-Step Programs

The most popular expression of self-help programs has been the so-called 12-step programs. Frame (2003) provided data from 1990 which indicated that there were more than eighty 12-step programs and 125,000 members; data from 1993 indicated that, annually, more than 3.5 million individuals participated in some type of 12-step program.

Designed to deal with the issues of addiction (alcohol, narcotics, gambling, codependence, overeating, etc.), these groups focus far less on the individual's etiology and more on day-to-day coping and recovery. The meetings begin with the Serenity Prayer ("God grant me the serenity to accept the things I cannot change, the courage to change the things I can, and the wisdom to know the difference") and progress through personal sharing by those in attendance of triumphs and lapses. Members usually work with a sponsor on whom they rely for support between meetings, and over time, members are expected to provide that service to others in the group.

These programs share several spiritual principles. The first is a belief in a Higher Power, purposefully left undefined in order to encompass all manifestations of this belief spectrum. The second principle is that members are expected to pray or meditate in order to foster a personal relationship with this Higher Power. The third principle is the expectation that adherents will acknowledge the possibility of, and perhaps the need for, a miracle to occur in order for one to be cured of one's addiction. The fourth principle is that daily spiritual renewal must be practiced to show one's ongoing commitment to these principles and as an observable commitment to one's desire to be cured. The last principle is that conflict with others, either within or outside of the group, is seen as evidence of a lack of serenity—serenity that is to be created through one's relationship with the Higher Power.

Although Alcoholics Anonymous (AA) has a formal policy of not participating in research studies, analysis of their data supported the contention that AA programs seem to be successful. For example, Carroll (1993) reported that adherence to step 11 of the 12-step program ("Sought through prayer and meditation to improve our conscious contact with God as we understand him, praying only for knowledge of His will for us and the power to carry that out") was related to attendance at meetings, the length of time that one has abstained from alcohol, and the sense of a greater purpose in life.

Sterling et al. (2006) hypothesized that differing levels of spirituality upon admission to an alcohol treatment program might have an effect on one's success in the program. They could not confirm their hypothesis, however, suggesting that other factors seemed to have a more significant impact on program efficacy. Nash (1997) bemoaned the dilution of spirituality by such programs through the removal of its transcendent dimensions and by the omission of this variable in the healing process.

These programs also have been criticized. The notion of "surrender" may foster learned helplessness, low self-esteem, and a dependency on the group in place of the addiction. There is also concern about the psychological damage that may be caused by the public listing of one's character flaws by individuals who already doubt their personal value and who are extremely sensitive to the opinions of others. Further concerns have been raised about the qualifications of the group leaders: Although former addicts of any type may offer valuable disclosure and validation of the struggle for recovery, questions are raised about their competence to lead such a group, whether their own unresolved issues may contaminate the group, and whether they can actually assist group members in growing further or differently than they have themselves. The final concern centers on the practice of overlooking the causes of the addictive behavior. Because of this practice, one may never address these intrapsychic conflicts, which are sure to resurface in times of stress. If this assertion is valid, then one must wonder whether the addiction to the substance is replaced by an addiction to the group, replicating, rather than truly curing, the initial problem.

CASE EXAMPLE

Maureen came to counseling as part of the sentence imposed by the court for stealing funds from her place of employment. In addition, Maureen tearfully related that she had been "helping herself" to money from her family and from her church. She reported that she had a serious gambling problem and that the money had been stolen to cover past losses and to support what she derided as a futile attempt to win it all back in one huge jackpot. She promised that with her winnings, she would reimburse everyone from whom she had stolen and contribute the rest to the church in the hopes of regaining God's good graces. She believed that her main problem was that she had not yet hit that jackpot.

To her counselor, it seemed that Maureen was stuck in a "wrong solution cycle." The gambling, which was truly her main issue, seemed to be her sole salvation. She said that she was in charge of her gambling; however, a short personal history revealed that she had a compulsion that she could not control. In addition, Maureen felt very alone because she was ashamed of stealing from her place of employment, her family, and her church, and she did not trust herself around others.

On the basis of feelings of aloneness and a desire to help Maureen gain perspective on her addiction, it was suggested that she attend a meeting of Gambler's Anonymous. Although she was skeptical of her need to do so, Maureen understood the court-mandated aspect of her participation in counseling and went, as she put it, to "humor the counselor." At the next session, she reported that she had attended the meeting and had felt welcomed and accepted by the other attendees. She realized that she was not alone in her struggle and that others were fighting the same addiction.

When asked about the more meaningful aspects of her experience, Maureen reported that the opportunity to reconnect with God was a healing experience for her. She had felt as though she had permanently lost that connection and had realized that her hope of "buying it back" had been naïve, when all she needed to do was acknowledge her need for God's help in combating her addiction.

Surrender

This category of intervention is for those clients—and perhaps helping professionals—who try too hard and assume too many of life's burdens. Although society advocates taking responsibility and becoming empowered, little attention is paid to "giving over," as opposed to "giving up." The process of "surrendering" involves both movement away from controlling the world and others in order to create a world that is responsive to one's needs and movement toward acceptance of the direction that one's life may take (Frame, 2003).

Sometimes, in difficult situations, a client must come to accept his or her lack of power in order to influence the situation, and the client must acknowledge that a more fruitful direction for that personal power is toward self-care. With a situation such as a terminal illness, the death of a loved one, an accident, or a natural disaster, a client strains to understand how he or she, and not others, came to suffer. However, a shift toward surrender may foster an experiential openness to transcendence and an arrival at a state of serenity. This process must be congruent with the client's notion of "spiritual surrender" so that the client will not think that the counselor is advocating that the client give up.

Cole (2005) provided a comprehensive review of the literature on the use of religious coping skills and cancer. Strong beliefs are linked to decreased levels of pain, anxiety, hostility, and social isolation, as well as increased life satisfaction (as reported by Jenkins and Pargament, 1995; Pargament, 1997). For individuals suffering with advanced cancer, Cole cited Yates et al. (1981) as reporting increased happiness and positive affect, and less severe and less frequent pain. Later studies linked deference to God as being associated with enhanced quality of life, less depression, and less despair (McClain, Rosenfeld, & Breitbart, 2003; Nairn & Merluzzi, 2003; Nelson, Rosenfeld, Breitbart, & Galietta, 2002). Cole (2005) found similar results in terms of stabilizing depression and reducing the severity of pain. In summary, "[increased] use of surrendering control and positive spiritual/religious coping were associated with better emotional and physical well-being" (p. 224).

Cole and Pargament (1999) directed counselors to ask clients whom they believe are in tune with the process of spiritual surrender, "What would it be like for you to surrender to God?" (p. 192). Clients may also be directed to designate which parts of their presenting issue are within their control and which are beyond their control. When their answers are reviewed, clients may recognize that they are expending emotional energy on issues that are beyond their control, diverting energy from the parts of the issue over which they actually do have some control. This process of "letting go" may also be assisted by the use of guided imagery or ritual. The client would visualize surrendering the applicable parts of the issue, which would provide a more concrete deliverance of symbols of the specific aspects to be given up.

CASE EXAMPLE

Suzanne, a 35-year-old attorney, was referred to counseling because of her obsession with the execution of a client whom she had defended, but whose case she had lost. Suzanne was bewildered by the amount of responsibility that she felt over his death, and she was considering giving up her career. She had reviewed the evidence and her handling of the case, but felt that there was more she should have done. She repeated over and over again, "I cost that man his life."

Suzanne also wanted reassurance that she was not lacking in some way, either as a human being or as an attorney, because of the outcome of the case. From a cognitive perspective, her beliefs about the case and her need to be infallible were apparent, as was her recognition that surely she could not reasonably expect to win every case. From a spiritual perspective, Suzanne was confronted with the idea that she could do her best and still not succeed. She was introduced to the notion that her path in life and that of her client had intersected, as did the client's path and that of his victims. Suzanne began to recognize both the boundary that she needed to protect herself from becoming emotionally involved in her cases and the necessity of weighing the challenges created through her choice of clients.

Throughout this process, Suzanne was confronted with her own notion that acceptance by God was a function of perfection, and she began to grapple with the idea that perhaps God loves humans regardless of their fallibility. She considered the issue of whether it is our fallibility that makes us human and motivates us to continue to strive to grow. She later came to the conclusion that the first step in this process is accepting ourselves as we are now, not as we should be.

Consultation and Referral

Frame (2003) acknowledged that, for all of a counselor's skills and intentions, situations do arise around spiritual issues where referral would appear to be the most professionally appropriate course of action. Counselors are urged to develop references among diverse clergy whose main qualification should be openness to client pain rather than a judgmental attitude about clients failing to follow religious teachings. It would also be helpful if these members of the clergy demonstrated some basic communication skills and had formal training in counseling. Creating a network through contacts with other counselors, congregants, and local councils of churches may prove to be mutually beneficial to clergy and counselors because both are dedicated to working in support of their clients' spiritual, emotional, and psychological growth and health.

CASE EXAMPLE

Sanjay presented for counseling to seek guidance about how to accept his parents' insistence on directing his life. He venerated his parents and had been raised to believe that one's parents always knew best and that to question or disobey them was evidence that one was an ungrateful child. Being in conflict with one's parents or acting in opposition to their wishes brought dishonor not only on the individual, but on the entire family unit.

Sanjay reported that he was now in such a state of dishonor because he had chosen a wife of whom his family disapproved. Sanjay recognized that his culture, his Hindu religion, and his present conflict were interconnected, but could not seem to separate each aspect of his life for consideration. After two sessions, it became clear to the counselor that a Hindu cleric would more easily and completely understand Sanjay's struggle, so a referral was made to the appropriate local cleric.

CONTRAINDICATIONS FOR CHOOSING SPIRITUAL INTERVENTIONS

Regardless of the counselor's receptivity toward including spiritual counseling in the delivery of clinical or psycho-educational services, there are instances in which such intervention may not be appropriate. Sperry (2001) categorized the contraindications for using spiritual interventions as "absolute" and "relative." Absolute contraindications include those instances where such intervention is not warranted and may be harmful. Relative concerns include instances in which the use of such interventions may be risky, ineffective, or inadvisable. The following are *absolute* contraindications:

- clients who are unwilling to participate in such interventions,
- clients who are delusional,
- clients who see no relevance between spirituality and the presenting issue,
- clients who are below the age of consent,
- clients who present in a state of crisis, and
- settings that do not support such an approach (e.g., schools or publicly funded agencies).

The following are *relative* contraindications:

- "clients who are young children and adolescents,
- clients who are severely psychologically disturbed,
- clients who present as antireligious or non-religious,
- clients who present with a significant level of spiritual immaturity,
- counselors who are insensitive to multicultural or spiritual diversity,

- clients who perceive God as distant and punishing, and
- clients who present with [a] deferring or passive religious problem-solving style" (p. 121).

As with all counseling approaches, the use of these interventions must be dictated by the client's needs and receptivity, as well as the counselor's competence in the presentation of the self and his or her skill in using a particular technique.

Case Example Revisited

Teena explored whether there was some overlap that might allow her to integrate the interventions provided by clergy members and those she had just experienced as a counselor-in-training. In her discussions with peers, she received mixed and inconsistent messages about the presence of such overlap and the need to keep both sets of experiences and interventions completely separate. However, in further discussions with faculty members, she began to appreciate the historical rift between the clergy and counselors and the current growing connection between both. Teena felt that her hopes for further reconciliation between the two aspects of her life that provided such meaning and growth were confirmed; she became more dedicated to learning how and when to introduce and practice spiritual interventions in her counseling.

Conclusion

The professional literature repeatedly confirms the potential for clients to be receptive toward the integration of spiritual work in counseling. It appears that the willingness of the counselor to broach the topic may be the determining factor in whether an exploration of spiritual strengths and limitations is part of the therapeutic process. Therefore, the challenge for helping professionals is to expand their current way of helping in order to incorporate what clients seem to want but have yet to request in session. As helping professionals contemplate the integration of spiritual techniques into their therapeutic repertoire, Faiver, Ingersoll, O'Brien, and McNally (2001) admonished them to (a) be aware of their own personal spiritual journey, beliefs, and worldviews; (b) understand the spiritual/religious beliefs and worldviews of the client; (c) ensure the development of their professional competence and ethical adherence as they begin to utilize spiritual interventions; and (d) experience the intervention rather than impose the technique. Helping professionals must also be prepared to join each client on his or her unique spiritual journey.

Self-Understanding Exercises

1. Which of the strategies mentioned in this chapter would you consider using with a client who seemed to be open to such interventions? Which strategies would you not consider using? What are the reasons for your decision?

2. How might you reconcile the practice of "surrendering" with client empowerment?
3. What is your understanding of forgiveness as an integral process of interpersonal healing?

Opportunities for Further Learning

1. Attend an open meeting of your local Alcoholics Anonymous. (In general, only members and prospective members may attend meetings of AA; however, meetings specified as being "open" welcome students, professionals, and nonmembers.) Note your observations, thoughts, and feelings. What about the experience works for you? What aspects fail to resonate with you?

2. Review prayer books from a variety of practices with regard to issues such as grief or loss. How similar or different is each tradition or practice? To what extent does a universal human experience emerge?

3. Explore one of the following Web sites: (a) Explore *faith*, http://www.explorefaith.org; (b) Division 36 of the American Psychological Association, Psychology of Religion, http://www.apa.org/divisions/div36/homepage2.html; (c) Psychotherapy and Spirituality Institute, http://www.mindspirit.org. What might you gain with regard to your personal or professional development?

14

. . .

Spiritual Strategies for Couples and Family Counseling

A happy family is but an earlier heaven.

—Sir John Bowring (1792–1872)

CASE EXAMPLE

Tamara was in training to become a couples and family counselor. She was fascinated by the characteristics of healthy and dysfunctional marriages and families, and could not help but apply her newly acquired knowledge to her own 5-year-long marriage and interactions with her husband and 2-year-old son. Although she appreciated the knowledge that she had gained, she was puzzled by the lack of discussion regarding religion in marriage in her graduate courses.

Tamara and her husband attended six sessions of premarital counseling through their church and found the experience to be both confirming and enlightening. In addition, they both saw themselves as committed church members and participants within that community.

Tamara was now wondering whether this participation was indeed strengthening their marriage and family if such dynamics were not presented in her clinical or academic classes. She also felt very reluctant to broach the topic with her faculty advisor for fear of jeopardizing her status in the program.

■ ■ ■

INTRODUCTION

This chapter offers the clinician a rationale for addressing spiritual and religious concerns within the context of couples and family counseling. After confirming the value of including religious and spiritual issues in couples and family counseling, a brief perspective on family systems is provided in order to create an epistemological framework for the following section.

239

Next, the chapter provides samples of theoretically congruent interventions to offer to clients. Finally, the chapter identifies current and future trends within the integration of religious and spiritual issues in couples and family counseling.

THE RATIONALE FOR ADDRESSING SPIRITUAL AND RELIGIOUS CONCERNS

Hodges (2005) discerned that ". . . [the] last two decades have witnessed a growing interest in spirituality and religion in marriage and family forums" (p. 341). As added evidence of this growing interest, Weaver, Samford, Morgan, Larson, Koenig, and Flannelly (2002) conducted a review of family counseling journals for the period from 1995 to 1999. The authors found that a greater percentage of professional articles on topics related to religion and spirituality had been published in the family counseling journals than in the professional literature on psychology, gerontology, or mental health nursing. Not only are current practitioners and scholars beginning to write about this topic, but, Carlson, Kirkpatrick, Heckler, and Killmer (2002) discovered that 72% of the family therapists polled indicated that spirituality was relevant to clinical work and 54% wanted more preparation in religious/spiritual assessment and intervention. These authors also cited a 1999 study of graduate students in marriage and family therapy programs. The study found that 86% believed that attention to spirituality was vital in order to be of help to couples and families and 67% wanted to learn more about assessment and intervention in the areas of religion and spirituality. This request for specific training was not the first such indication of interest. Carlson (1996) found that 96% of the AAMFT clinical members surveyed agreed that there is a relationship between spirituality and mental health. These findings all imply a growing interest and need for systemic or relational mental health professionals to consider the value of introducing and then perhaps addressing couples' and families' religious and spiritual beliefs and practices.

Hoogestraat and Trammel (2003) referenced a 1996 Gallup poll in which 80% of Americans spoke to the importance of religion within their families of origin and of their adherence to the theological tenets of their chosen faiths in the conduct of their daily lives. Not only is religion important to the family, but the family is crucial to the maintenance and health of religion. Griffith and Rotter (1999) proclaimed that "the family unit is the center of most religious systems" (p. 161). The family is the embodiment of religious or spiritual teachings and practices. Although the mosque, synagogue, or church offers community, it is the family unit that, through observance and practice, translates the teachings into day-to-day endorsement of the family members' faith through their behaviors and interactions. The fact that so many Americans claimed that religion was a vital part of their family system indicates to mental health professionals that they must also attend to this dynamic. Even the respectful omission of questions regarding religion and spirituality within the family system may be interpreted by family members as a covert message not to introduce such topics in session.

However, such reluctance on the part of family therapists may be diminishing. Odell (2003) detailed an increasingly mainstream approach to the inclusion of religious and spiritual issues in marriage and family services. The purpose of these religious and spiritual beliefs is too central to the definition of each family member and of the family unit as a whole to be overlooked. Echoing Frame (2000), Odell (2003) stated that religion and spirituality together define the "worldview [that] is the source of people's foundational beliefs, and it tells people who they are, who or what they worship and serve, what they are to do in life and why" (p. 26). Moreover, clinicians may be wise to consider religion and spiritual beliefs as aspects of structural determinism.

Briefly, structural determinism refers to those values which are central to the identity of the family and each individual. Although largely unspoken, and perhaps not even verbalized within the family itself, these beliefs dictate those aspects of the self, the relationship, and family functioning which cannot be challenged or changed without deeply threatening the fabric of an individual's ego strength and that of the family unit. Although these beliefs define and distinguish each family, they also influence areas of possible change and arenas in which change must take place within the existing family framework. For example, a clinician who advises a family to increase its weekend outings in order to foster family cohesion must consider that regular church, mosque, or synagogue attendance occurs in that same time span. Asking the family to surrender faith-based activities in order to build family cohesion may be seen as being less than respectful. Similarly, clinicians working with aging populations around the issues of death and dying must be sensitive to the religious leanings of the clients. One of the reasons that these clients have chosen and adhered to those particular belief systems may be a function of the peace and optimism that those beliefs offer around post-life issues. The clinician who ignores or overlooks such basic family blueprints does so at the expense of his or her credibility as an empathic helper.

Hoogestraat and Trammel (2003) directed clinicians to consider even more basic questions to which families seek answers within religion. Such questions include concerns about the qualities of a "good" life; issues of morality; concerns about marital, gender, and childhood roles; and the effect of religious or spiritual affiliation on one's sense of family and personal identity. The authors asserted that "religion and spirituality are deeply rooted constructs within many cultures" (p. 413). Hodges (2005b) suggested that family values are shaped by spiritual and religious beliefs. One example of a basic question addressed by every religion or spiritual tradition, in addition to every psychological theory, is whether people are inherently good or evil. Although this is perhaps more of a philosophical issue than a practical one, the answers provided by religions are manifested in such areas of family functioning as child discipline, gender roles, relationships among generations, and the acceptance of others outside of one's own faith. Such a perspective adds credence to Hodges' (2005) assertion that these belief systems "animate every aspect of life" (p. 342) and inform many, if not all, dimensions of family functioning.

This observation is intended merely to caution clinicians to be aware that offering differing views to the family in opposition to the expression of faith-based directives places the family in a tenuous position. It may appear as though the clinician is demanding that the family sacrifice its religious or spiritual connection in order to resolve its presenting issue or else cling to its spiritual connection at the expense of family functioning. Such dichotomous thinking may have detrimental effects, regardless of the decision that the family makes. The family may be more likely to abandon counseling rather than lose their membership in their religious community. In such cases, which may be more prevalent than one might think, it is the clinician's ethical and professional responsibility to acknowledge the predicament into which the family has been put, overtly discuss what may seem to be polarized approaches to resolving the family issue, and seek to build a common understanding and linkages between the religious and spiritual responses and the clinical intents. In such a manner, although change is necessary in order to move forward, such change occurs while honoring the core beliefs of the family members and respecting the importance of their religious or spiritual creeds.

Griffith and Rotter (1999) advocated recognition of the legitimacy of spirituality and religion within family systems as aspects of cultural diversity, a sentiment echoed by Frame (2000) and Wolf and Stevens (2001). Although family character and mores may be defined by other identified cultural factors, such as ethnicity or socioeconomic status, it may be safe to say that no one single cultural factor defines any one family, but instead it may be the interaction among the factors that generate the family's unique distinguishing characteristics. That said, only the family members themselves can identify the relevant cultural factors, and, of equal value, only each family member can share the way in which he or she sees that variable as a defining force in personal and family identity. The task again falls to the mental health professional to initiate the exploration of these factors and their individual and collective contributions.

Aponte (2003) proffered the spiritual underpinnings of clients' emotional and psychological problems. Given the centrality of religious or spiritual belief, it would seem to be difficult, if not impossible, to separate the workings of the spirit from those of the psyche. In most cases, it may be feasible to consider that it is an incongruence between these two powerful influences that brings clients and families to seek professional help and that spiritual and emotional healing takes place within a context of love and forgiveness in the family.

From the perspectives of present and future consumers of mental health services, Bart (1998) discerned that 81% of the general public either wanted or expected an integration of religious and spiritual issues and themes in family counseling. Griffith and Rotter (1999) cited a 1992 Gallup poll which stated that two thirds of respondents would seek a counselor with religious and spiritual values and that 81% preferred to have their own religious and spiritual values integrated into the counseling process.

There seems to be an ever-growing demand that clinicians actively and purposefully acknowledge the importance of religious and spiritual beliefs and practices in clients' lives and that these professionals should intentionally bring these issues into the clinical setting. It is also vitally important for clinicians to grasp that these survey respondents were not seeking "religious counseling." They are not asking clinicians to be experts on their chosen faiths or to be able to guide them within those faiths. What they are seeking is approaches to counseling or other mental health services that acknowledge and legitimize the importance of religion and spirituality as identifying variables in one's psychological and relational structure. Moreover, it may be hypothesized that a client's openness to exploring religion and spirituality in couples and family counseling could signify a vague sense that these themes may be part of either the presenting issue, the future solution, or both, and that the client needs the input of the mental health clinician to determine the roles and contributions of each facet. It would appear that clients are more ready for this exploration than are the professionals who claim a readiness to be of service.

However, there are equally compelling reasons to address religion and spirituality in one's clinical work with couples and families that extend beyond a client's desire. Anderson and Worthen (1997) stated that human experience comprises three dimensions: (a) time (the sequence of events), (b) space (the structure of a relationship), and (c) story (the language that gives meaning to the dimensions of time and space). Those interlocking components of human experience are colored by the threads of religion and spirituality. Other sections of this book affirm that spirituality is an innate human characteristic, expressed more commonly through formal religion, but also through a diversity of spiritual practices. Given the prevalence and popularity of spirituality, even those who disdain any religious affiliation or practice must purposefully fill that life void through other means. The same claim could be made for psychology as a way to make sense of oneself in one's life, relationships, and transcendent relationship.

THE ROLE OF RELIGION/SPIRITUALITY IN FAMILY FUNCTIONING

A review of the current professional literature exploring the interface of families and religion/spirituality found eight potential outcomes that are a direct result of "intrinsic religious practices." Griffith and Rotter (1999) described "intrinsic religion" as being related to all of life and as unprejudiced, tolerant, mature, integrative, unifying, and endowing meaning. Religious or spiritual practices that are characterized by these ideals can be forecast to provide the following items:

1. Social support as an extended family (Abbot, Berry, & Meredith, 1990; Griffith & Rotter, 1999; Hoogestraat & Trammel, 2003; Sperry, 2001): The religious or spiritual community may serve the family system in times of upheaval or transition, or through the celebration of normative life transitions. Given the increased social mobility of the 21st century, a connection to such a community in a new living environment can foster the social networking and connections sought by recently arrived families.

2. Source of answers to questions about meaning (Abbot, Berry, & Meredith, 1990; Hoogestraat & Trammel, 2003): Spirituality and religion offer faith-specific answers to questions about meaning, purpose, and post-life expectations, in addition to guidance for day-to-day living.

3. Family activities (Abbot, Berry, & Meredith, 1990): These institutions engage family members of all ages in activities such as children's worship, teen groups, adult study groups, and regular services. By satisfying religious or spiritual needs on all levels and for all ages, not only is the present generation of a family welcomed, but so, too, are future generations.

4. Social and welfare services (Griffith & Rotter, 1999): Participation at a church, mosque, synagogue, or other place where people gather to worship fosters social connections. For those seeking a religious or spiritual path or those new to the community, these services provide a warm welcome and the hope that one's family may be accepted. Many religious and spiritual communities nurture congregants who are in pain or are suffering. Both clergy and caring groups within the community respond to those who are experiencing health issues, job loss, the death of a loved one, and so forth.

5. Connection to a Higher Power (Hoogestraat & Trammel, 2003): Each spiritual organization offers to its members a belief in their "specialness" in terms of a comforting relationship with a Higher Power. Gallup (1996) reported the widespread use of prayer (90% of the respondents claimed to pray weekly, and 75% of the respondents said that they prayed daily), which implies a personal belief in, and a connection to, God or a Higher Power.

6. Increased family intimacy (Sperry, 2001): The closeness fostered within a couple or a family through a common commitment to a religious or spiritual ideal reflects a statement of shared values. Since values direct behavior and interaction, the unity of direction with regard to the more complex life questions must express itself in greater day-to-day family harmony.

7. Increased family cohesion through ritual and tradition (Sperry, 2001): The place of ritual and tradition provides a reason for families to gather, celebrate, and strengthen their sense of family identity. Although secular celebrations such as birthdays, anniversaries, graduations, and so forth mark the passage of time in a family's life, the commemoration or celebration of religious or spiritual events adds a sense of timelessness. In addition, the observance of such rituals allows the family unit to connect with the larger

"religious family." Such practices, year after year and generation after generation, also uphold family stability and cohesiveness (Griffith & Rotter, 1999).

8. Framework of morality (Griffith & Rotter, 1999): Every faith offers guidelines for living a "good and just life." For those seeking direction, bolstered by a community of like-minded believers, the morality offered by a religious society may offer a welcome clarity in what may seem to be a confusing debate among the Far Right, the new Left, and moral relativity.

In summary, Sperry (2001) cited Brigman's (1984) survey of family-life professionals, who indicated that they found that spiritual and religious practices were helpful to families in terms of fostering love, faith, hope, forgiveness, grace, reconciliation, a relationship with God, and the divine worth of people. It could be imagined that these outcomes illustrate the true potential of spiritual and religious practices for couples and for families; however, it is also important for the mental health professional to be able to distinguish between the intrinsic religious or spiritual practices that hold the potential for such accomplishments and those which are deemed to be extrinsic and may prove to be harmful to the individual and the family.

Griffith and Rotter (1999) explained extrinsic religion as religious expression that is compartmentalized, prejudiced, exclusionary, immature, utilitarian (used to gain comfort and status), and self-serving. In short, such practices would include those that serve either one individual or the institution itself at the expense of the congregants. Those faiths which profess a rigid doctrine that is insensitive to human need appear to be more invested in conformity and obedience than in the spiritual growth of their members (Griffith & Rotter, 1999). The practice of questioning is a vehicle toward learning, personal understanding, and maturity; a faith that does not tolerate or that condemns a spirit of inquiry cannot be supportive of the spiritual growth of its members.

Another concern, especially for mental health professionals who work with couples and families, is those dogmas which speak negatively about sexuality, divorce, and remarriage. This issue is not about those matters per se; rather, it is about those religious groups which may punish or expel members who demonstrate age-appropriate sexual behavior or who, for some reason, end a marriage. Although these transitions may be uncomfortable for those around the individual, these are times in which the person is in need of additional support and caring, and is often depending on his or her religious community for those kindnesses. When the person is rebuffed because of his or her actions, there may be a tendency for the individual to feel lost, bereft of support, and perhaps disgraced in the eyes of God. This type of judgmental practice leads to feelings of guilt, confusion, and low self-esteem on the part of the "fallen" member. In addition, an overemphasis on sin, on the basis of negative assumptions about human nature and the human condition, may keep affiliates constantly in a state of anxiety regarding their own value and worthiness. Such chronic anxiety is hazardous to psychological well-being and relational health.

Sperry (2001) cautioned about those faiths which promote traditional patriarchal gender roles. There is a subtle tension between a respect for a faith institution's right to proclaim its beliefs and the right of that faith to use that dogma to oppress family members. One of the beliefs of family-focused mental health professionals is that the family unit, as a whole, can be no healthier or happier than each of its members. The imposition of gender roles that are designed to elevate one person and suppress another is not a path toward fostering the health or happiness of the family unit.

Finally, Hoogestraat and Trammel (2003) introduced the issue of spiritual or religious abuse. Sadly, there are more and more reports of abuse by religious leaders. In such cases, a sense of trust has been shattered, not only for the individual who was abused, but also for the members or adherents of the institution and the belief system that the abuser purported to represent.

Emotional abuse also occurs when an individual is cast out, ridiculed, or humiliated because of a belief, practice, or lifestyle that is inconsistent with dogma. The most glaring example of this abuse is discussed in Chapter 12, Spirituality and Marginalized Groups, which focuses on the experiences of specific groups within organized religion.

In summary, it seems that these concerns have less to do with spirituality and religion in its pure form and more to do with how that form is practiced in reality. If Brigman's (1984) list of the positive outcomes of spiritual and religious practices is to be used as a checklist, then practices that do not cultivate these experiences could be considered harmful or of danger to the individual and the family. Given the immense challenge of objectively weighing that to which one is subjectively committed, the ethical mandate of the professional counselor (to foster the welfare of one's client) requires that questions about each individual's personal experiences within this structure be respectfully raised so that each member can hear "the truth" from each of the other family members.

Although the potential for negative results from religious or spiritual practices has been documented in order to promote awareness on the part of the family-focused mental health services provider, there are also several positive outcomes documented in the professional literature. It is of interest that the negative outcomes focused on the gain of one member at the expense of others, while the more positive outcomes celebrate the systemwide benefits of healthy spiritual and religious beliefs and practices.

Frame (2003, p. 209) stated that "the interface between family life and religion or spirituality is very important," citing Beavers and Hampson (1980) as referring to religion and spirituality as critical aspects of healthy family functioning. Gallup (1996) concluded that "religion [has] been [a] positive strengthening force in family life" (Hodges, 2005b, p. 210). A review of the professional literature offered six themes citing the benefits of religion or spiritual practice on family life:

1. Religion and spirituality offer coping mechanisms to moderate stress. Every creed offers explanations for the presence of pain and suffering in life, why bad things happen to good people, and how to weather the storms of faith or questions of conscience. For those who choose to believe, there is the conviction that the grand design for the universe, and one's place and role in it, may be beyond mortal knowing, but still, one's actions are guided by a faith in the purposefulness of that grand design.

2. Adherence to a spiritual or religious outlook serves as a buffer against anxiety by providing answers to core life questions and a congregation of like-minded persons to support both the individual's struggle and the collective belief system. Emotional healing and development are by-products of spiritual growth and maturity, and, recursively, that growth promotes greater emotional healing and interpersonal and intrapsychic functioning (Griffith & Rotter, 1999).

3. Griffith and Rotter (1999) cited 1996 data which indicated that a higher level of intrinsic faith is positively correlated with higher levels of life satisfaction, personal happiness, social support from friends, and empathy, and negatively correlated with depressive symptoms, high blood pressure, hostility, and the narcissistic exploitation of others.

These data confirms the benefits of religious and spiritual participation for personal and relational dynamics.

4. Wolf and Stevens (2001) detailed the positive effects of religious and spiritual practices on physiological and psychological health, specifically with regard to depression, anxiety, marital adjustment, and marital and sexual functioning. Once again, these outcomes have ramifications for clinicians seeking to promote healthier individual and marital or familial functioning. Clinicians are therefore advised to consider including a discussion of faith-based practices within their counseling service when clients present with any of the aforementioned concerns. This exploration is intended to reveal either how those resources may be of help in addressing the presenting concern or, in contrast, how adherence to such belief systems may exacerbate the presenting concern.

5. Family cohesion can also be built through the observation of ceremonies and traditions associated with holy days. These observances speak not only to the gathering of family, but also to a time of repentance, forgiveness, and new beginnings. The opportunity to lay aside old hurts and commit to a brighter future speaks to the rebirth of dreams for individuals, couples, and families.

6. Hodges (2005) reported lower rates of divorce, greater marital satisfaction, higher levels of marital commitment, and greater use of adaptive communication skills among couples who were religious or spiritual participants over those couples who stated no such participation.

The preponderance of survey and outcome data that confirm the importance of religion and spirituality as guiding forces in the lives of couples and families, as well as the possible negative outcomes, indicate that family clinicians should carefully consider the value of introducing this theme in session. "It seems inevitable that marriage and family counselors will work with clients who wish to share, explore and perhaps draw on their beliefs in the therapeutic process" (Wolf & Stevens, 2001, p. 74). The decision whether or not to pursue such a focus rests solely with the client; the responsibility for choosing to broach the topic rests solely with the mental health services provider. Should the clinician opt to do so, the next sections of this chapter may offer some guidance.

THINKING SYSTEMICALLY ABOUT RELIGION AND SPIRITUALITY

This section outlines the epistemological foundation for approaching family issues from a systemic perspective. It is not within the scope of this book to detail the rich discussions found in family theory texts and writings on a systemic orientation; instead, what follows is intended merely as a foreword to the consideration of differing techniques. However, that said, it is important to clearly articulate what one is trying to do in the provision of mental health services before attempting to do it. The orientation that the clinician brings to the presenting issue and the client will dictate how the client attends to the issue itself and begins to understand what is expected within the therapeutic context. For example, if the clinician applied a medical perspective to a couple, one or both of whom presented with a diagnosis of depression, the focus would probably be directed toward the appropriate choice of medication, the dosage, and benchmarks of physiological improvement. If the clinician applied an individual, cognitive perspective and diagnosis, then the focus might be on the irrational belief systems that underlie the client's interpretation of events. However, a clinician applying a systemic orientation may operate from the principles outlined in the following section.

The locus of concern within systemic approaches would be on what transpires between individuals (Becvar & Becvar, 2006; Goldenberg & Goldenberg, 2008), based on the assumption that problems arise and are maintained interpersonally. This approach asserts that in response to developmental transition struggles, outside stressors, or unresolved conflict, couples and family members develop coping styles in order to self-protect and to try to solve the problem based on an incomplete and nonconsensual viewpoint. Stemming from this lack of teamwork, the individual coping and problem-solving styles seem to be incompatible or in conflict. The focus slips off of the initial issue and is reoriented toward the inability to achieve a resolution and the lack of cooperation among family members. The resulting communication style is ineffective at resolving the initial problem, and it generates a growing atmosphere of distance, distrust, and anxiety.

From a systemic perspective, the clinician must acknowledge that the "whole" of the family is greater than the sum of its parts. Family conflicts, strengths, and interactions can be understood only in their totality, rather than by dealing with each member separately (Goldenberg & Goldenberg, 2008). By maintaining a focus on patterns of reciprocal causality or communication, the recurring family problem and the inability to move beyond repeated attempts at resolving the issue accent the conflicting subjective realities.

Within a relational system, such as a family or couple, there is a tendency for each member to perceive the conflict, tension, or issue differently and, more vitally, separately. Since each member holds a differing view of the issue and the preferred solution, each member expends emotional energy toward that idealized outcome. However, since each family member is working independently, there is no consensus as to family direction or the focusing of family resources, and often the attempts by one member seem to be in opposition to those by another family member, generating even more conflict. One of the tasks of a mental health professional who holds a systemic perspective is to find similarities among the views of the family members. Supported by a professional understanding of the issue, the clinician assists the client in moving toward a conjoint and realistic picture of a future resolution to which each family member can commit and direct personal energies and resources (Becvar & Becvar, 2006).

In utilizing a systemic perspective, there is a greater emphasis placed on a here-and-now focus. Although understanding the past may explain the present communication and belief systems, current interaction styles are serving to maintain the current dysfunction in the family unit. Within this approach are two complementary agendas. The first is to balance the needs of the members and the needs of the system as a whole. Understanding the developmental needs of each family member, the couple subsystem, and the family unit as a whole as it progresses through time and faces life challenges allows attention to be paid to these differing priorities, as well as permitting the experiencing of legitimization. The second agenda deals with balancing family stability and change. As the family members move through life, what they need from the family changes, and the other family members, already seeking to honor their own growth, must also attend to the changing needs of the others, at the same time securing the constancy of family identity that gives the family unit meaning and cohesion.

In order to foster family resilience (Walsh, 2003), clinicians seek to promote a consistent, positive belief system that focuses on shared values without assigning blame and recasts upheaval as a manageable challenge for each family member and for the family as a whole. Under the direction of a clinician whose intent is purposeful and clear, family members can learn how to effectively manage family resources in order to respond to adapt to new situations and remain flexible and open to change while maintaining the cohesion of the family by integrating the family's outside support systems. By promoting family communication and problem-solving processes as exemplified by clear, consistent, and congruent exchanges between family members, it follows that a climate of trust and open expression, a shared range of feelings, shared decision making, and creative brainstorming will emerge that allows the family to move forward with confidence and with the assurance that the needs of every member will be honored and that the previously divisive issue will finally be resolved.

Goldenberg and Goldenberg (2008) described family religion and spirituality as "a central set of organizing beliefs that give their lives meaning and guidance" (p. 22). Aponte (2003) identified religious and spiritual beliefs as forming the values framework of life, which "evolves through the moral and emotional tests of life" (p. 16). These values illustrate the personal signature themes as a function of biology, family history, and social circumstances which foster the peculiar emotional vulnerabilities that color and influence the recurring personal difficulties and that offer guidance toward the resolution of those difficulties. Family religious and spiritual beliefs and practice are "essential to recovery and resilience particularly at times of upheaval and disruption" (Goldenberg & Goldenberg, 2008, p. 22).

Given the recursive nature of patterns of family interaction and the ongoing need for identification of family resources and strengths, the sample interventions presented next may offer a starting point for the mental health professional who is seeking to broach the topics of religion and spirituality. Although each member of the couple or family may refute the relevance of such topics in relation to the presenting issue, it is the mental health professional's responsibility to offer such a potential for exploration, and it is the responsibility of the client to weigh its potential importance. Given the data presented throughout this book on the number of clients who desire the integration of religious and spiritual themes in counseling, it would seem probable that the offer by the therapist would be welcomed.

SAMPLE CLINICAL INTERVENTIONS

This section will offer some examples of spiritual introduction and intervention strategies for mental health professionals who work with couples and families. There is a more detailed description that pertains to specific strategies, such as prayer, in Chapter 13. It is crucial that professionals who wish to incorporate these approaches ensure that they have a basic understanding of systems thinking which goes beyond that summarized in this chapter, as well as of the differing theories of family counseling such as might be covered in a graduate-level course. These techniques can be utilized with couples and families should the clinician determine that their inclusion seems to be warranted and that they are welcomed by the client. The sample interventions presented here are not intended to be an exhaustive listing; rather, they are a starting point for future consideration.

Spiritual or Religious History

In the initial meeting between a client and a mental health clinician, the client shares the presenting issue and perhaps his or her subjective understanding of its origins and maintenance, coupled with the clinician's tentative hypotheses about the same issue. Seen as a confluence of the personal experiences of the client and the professional knowledge of the therapist, what the clinician explores, as well as what is omitted, speaks to the limits of clinical consideration. Furthermore, responding to selected aspects of the client's story and overlooking other aspects begins to focus the client's attention on those dynamics or patterns that are deemed to be important. Likewise, the clinician's addition of subjects that are not presented by the client directs the client's attention toward those previously unconsidered areas of life in terms of generating a better understanding of the current struggles or as a possible resource. Germane to the thesis of this chapter and the objective of this book, it then becomes the clinician's responsibility to broach the topic of religion or spirituality within the initial sessions. Should the clinician not do so, for ethical reasons outlined in another chapter, without owning that reluctance, the client receives a tacit message that the discussion of religious and spiritual concerns is inappropriate in the therapeutic encounter.

Tan (1996) began with a direct, simple question such as "What is your affiliation, if any?" By asking such an open-ended question, the clinician is legitimizing the topic of religion or spirituality, even if the client responds that he or she has no such affiliation. However, given the results of the census and survey data presented in this and other chapters, the likelihood of such a disavowal seems remote. However, in cases where a client responds that he or she has no such affiliation, at least the clinician has broached the topic and now knows that the client sees no relevance or importance in its pursuit.

However, should the clinician receive an affirmative response, the next series of questions carefully skirt the nature of that affiliation in favor of its function within the client's life. Experienced clinicians can appreciate this distinction because these questions are less concerned with beliefs or affiliations and more concerned with the impact of that affiliation on the client's perceptions and functioning. Hodge (2004) offered a brief five-item spiritual assessment:

1. I was wondering if you consider religion or spirituality to be a personal strength.
2. In what ways does your religion or spirituality help you cope with the difficulties you encounter?
3. Are there certain spiritual beliefs or practices that you find particularly helpful in dealing with problems?
4. I was wondering if you attend a church or some other type of spiritual community.
5. Do resources exist within your faith community that might be helpful to you?

The other theme of relevance to the clinician is that the initial three questions are written solely from a strength-oriented perspective. By moving away from the traditional perspective of pathologizing religious participation, this mode of thinking focuses the client's attention on the more positive aspects. Working relationally, the clinician can expect different answers from each family member. The time dedicated to allowing each family member "a voice" is vital in order to confirm that each member may have a different experience of the same event and that all perspectives are welcomed and valued. On a process level, the therapist can observe this exchange to see whether the family needs a consensus around religion or whether each member is allowed to affiliate as he or she chooses. The therapist also can learn how divergence is handled and how individual opinion is honored.

Hoogestraat and Trammel (2003) offered additional intake inquiries in more neutral tones. Although the initial exploration provides vital information about the perceptions of a religious or spiritual experience from each family member, it is the final question that places an evaluative exclamation point on this process. Following are Hoogestraat and Trammel's questions:

- "How has your spirituality or religion influenced your life?
- Tell me about your God.
- What does your spirituality mean to you?

- Help me understand how you learned about spirituality/religion.
- How do you think God views you?
- Tell me about spiritual/religious traditions in your family.
- What spiritual/religious messages were handed down through your family?
- Do you believe [that] spirituality/religion causes more good than harm for you [or] more harm than good?" (pp. 419–420)

In summary, these questions begin to examine "what was," "what is," and "how well." It is of interest that many times family members will be astounded by the comments they hear from other family members, remarking "I never knew that."

Pruyser (1976) clustered intake questions around seven themes:

1. awareness of the holy (What does one hold sacred?),
2. providence (Where is hope and trust in one's life?),
3. grace (For what is one grateful?),
4. faith (To what does one commit oneself?),
5. repentance (How has one dealt with past mistakes?),
6. communion (To whom does one reach out, whom does one care for, and by whom does one feel cared for?), and
7. sense of vocation (What satisfaction and purpose does one find in work and in life?).

Questions such as these assume the presence of all seven areas in the life experiences of each client, whether or not the client has previously reflected on any or all of these issues prior to receiving clinical services. There is also the implication that each of these areas is, in some way, relevant to the presenting family issue.

Spiritual Counseling from a Transgenerational Perspective

In theory, transgenerational counseling offers a historical perspective from which to view one's current level of functioning as it pertains to a specific life challenge or stress. Using an illustrative method of collecting data, which can then be thematically applied, the client can begin to recognize how his or her current functioning around specific issues of conflict or tension mirrors that of the family-of-origin experience that the client has brought to the marriage. This functioning also carries remnants of emotional reactivity that are reminiscent of interactions within the family of origin and that surface in similarly dysfunctional ways within the marriage.

There are three relevant constructs that may be utilized from this perspective in an exploration of religion and spirituality: the spiritual genogram, triangulation, and differentiation:

THE SPIRITUAL GENOGRAM The first construct, the spiritual genogram (Frame, 2000), comprises four stages: (1) creation, (2) reflection, (3) connection with the family of origin in discovery and a deeper understanding, and (4) integration into the therapeutic endeavor. The process is one of illumination, discovery, and then a conscious decision to retain the best of the past and to augment those strengths with present-day interaction styles that strengthen one's contribution to the marriage and/or the family.

Creation. The genogram is a three-generational illustration of family structure and members, events, and relational quality. Frame (2000) suggested color coding religious/spiritual traditions to emphasize continuity, disruption, or the addition of new faiths, including attending to agnostics, atheists, and so forth. Once the religious and spiritual themes are visually portrayed from the perspective of each spouse, themes that became sources of morals, values, and beliefs can be identified. In addition, nodal events that influenced perceptions and attitudes toward spirituality, the leaving and joining of religious or spiritual groups, and religious or spiritual closeness or conflict can be identified.

Reflection. The exercise of reflecting on one's contribution to this two-sided genogram, with each side representing the experiences of one of the spouses, is intended to identify the "role and function" of family-of-origin beliefs and any connection between religious and spiritual beliefs and current therapeutic issues (Frame, 2000, p. 213). The content of the visually displayed representation of this extended family may serve to "externalize religious issues and reduce emotional reactivity in session" (p. 213). The intent of the reflection is not to assign blame, but to analyze one's experiences for their contribution to present attitudes and beliefs and to ascertain how the individual and his or her spouse can begin to identify the strengths that each brings to the current marriage and family, as well as those areas of tension or conflict that need to be renegotiated with the current spouse, removing the influence of the family of origin. Questions such as the following may facilitate this discussion toward both individual insight and conjoint understanding:

- What did/does your religion/spiritual tradition say about gender? About ethnicity? About sexual orientation? How have these beliefs affected you and your extended family?
- How does your religious/spiritual history relate to your current distress or the problem with which you presented for therapy? What new insights or solutions occur to you on the basis of the discoveries that you made through the genogram?

Connection. This step involves retrieving vital information from the past. With regard to moving from a stance of individual insight to one of conjoint discussion and renegotiation of current relationship events and meanings, Frame (2000) offered the following explorative and comparative questions:

- "How did you perceive the importance of religion/spirituality within your family?
- How difficult might it have been for members [of your family] to seek a spiritual or religious path [that was] different from the one in which [you] were raised? Who would have been supportive and why? Who might not have been supportive and why?
- How do you think religion/spirituality has been a source of strength and coping for your family? How do you think it may have interfered with your family relationships?" (p. 214)

Integration. With increased awareness of oneself and knowledge of one's spouse within the religious and spiritual context of family history and the present, plus a reduction in the emotional reactivity that had previously been evidenced by a need to defend one's position, analytical questions may be posed as to how past patterns contribute to the current problem. In addition, spouses can be directed to assess what each has learned that can be used to address current marital or family difficulties.

TRIANGULATION   The second construct of relevance is that of triangles and triangulation (Wolf & Stevens, 2001). In brief, triangles emerge in families in conflict or in tension-filled situations so that the emotional content, which should, ideally, be directed toward the spouse, is "siphoned off" and redirected toward a third party. Although this reduction in emotionality would appear to resolve the issue, the emotions have merely been rerouted to a third party, remaining wholly unaddressed within the family and waiting to return and erupt with even greater force in the next disagreement.

This pattern may appear in two forms in religious or spiritual families; one form is the use of differing interpretations of scripture and the second form includes God or the Higher Power specific to one's faith. These patterns result in ongoing, irresolvable conflict. Spouses may take a respite only to rearm themselves with additional scripture to bring to the fray. Given the scope of scripture in most formal religions, ample text can be found and interpreted in support of almost any position. The notion of the Divine as one's personal confidante may sound appealing; however, when a message better suited for the spouse to hear is directed only to God, then the spouse is left wholly unable to respond in any way, either in terms of explaining him- or herself or attempting to make a change. Such a pattern, while seemingly spiritual, may be seen as building mutual resentment. The spouse who complains to God about his or her partner wonders why change along the desired lines never materializes, and the other spouse knows, on some level, that the partner is disappointed in the marriage, but never knows exactly on what grounds. It is also very difficult in religious families to criticize a member for copious amounts of praying.

DIFFERENTIATION   A third construct of relevance deals with issues of differentiation (Frame, 2003) and the pseudo-self (Hoogestraat & Trammel, 2003). Differentiation of the self is the process of taking self-ownership of values, morals, and standards of conduct, utilizing one's logical capacity, rather than one's emotional reactivity, in instances of conflict or tension and adhering to a solid sense of identity. Questions or puzzlement arises when a spouse seems to constantly renegotiate personal values within the relational system. Poorly differentiated persons shift with the prevailing emotional climate, work from what "feels right" at that moment, are prone to emotional stressors, and feel discomfort and anxiety keenly, even if such unpleasant feelings are those of another family member and not their own.

It would seem that adhering to a personally relevant religious or spiritual belief system, augmented by behaviors that are consistent with those beliefs, may be deemed an indication of healthy differentiation. In addition, the facility to accept the legitimacy of differing belief systems for different persons without feeling the need to defend one's own choice or attack another's choice of spiritual path, or of no spiritual path, speaks to a healthy stance of respect. An individual who can discuss the advantages and disadvantages of personal religious or spiritual choices indicates his or her comfort with the notion that no perfect faith may exist—that one's choice is colored by a careful weighing of the positive and negative factors inherent in that choice.

The final consideration is how religion or spiritual faith is chosen. Although most persons are reared in families with some religious affiliation, at some point questions arise as to its suitability. Those questions are a healthy part of the "spiritual differentiation" process. This questioning means, not that the faith will be abandoned, but rather that the "goodness of fit" between the individual and the faith needs to be confirmed. In some instances, the faith of the family is retained; in other cases, it may be replaced by a process of searching or religious experimentation in order to find a better fit.

Spiritual Counseling from a Structural Orientation

Structural family counseling applies a developmental model of family functioning to the way in which the family members organize themselves around the presenting issue. Issues of religion and spirituality can arise within the theoretically appropriate consideration of family rules, alliances, and expressions of power and control. One of the tensions within the family rule system that governs communication patterns is the need for such rules to be firm and consistent enough to provide feelings of stability and constancy, yet flexible enough to accommodate individual changes over time and adaptive response to external stressors. The question then arises, "Are family rules and the rules about the creation and amendment of those rules based on religion?" and, if so, "How is the need for adaptability built into that structure?" Flexibility seems to be inconsistent with dogma, leaving family members to act on their individual needs even more dramatically than usual in order to escape the shackles of religious or spiritual dogma.

Another area of concern for those families in which God or a Supreme Being plays an active role is the nature of alliances. In healthy families, alliances are generation and subsystem specific. The addition of God to the family system causes an imbalance in the power structure by the inclusion of an insurmountable ally to one individual or subsystem. In such cases, the clinician may wish to "place God within the family structure" and include God within the family enactment system to fully ascertain how that presence influences adaptive change, chaos, or stagnation.

Another structural concern is that of how power and control are exercised in the family. With time, experience, and the demonstration of increased competence, children in healthy families are expected to assume greater self-discipline and responsibility. However, invoking the will of God within a family leaves little room for developmental adjustments between the parent and the child, and no room for negotiation if the parents can make the ultimate reference to God.

Spiritual Counseling from a Narrative Orientation

Narrative theory is categorized as a social constructivist approach which purports that individuals make meaning or "reality" of events and this meaning then becomes imbued and formalized in repeated stories that reflect and define the individual and the values that characterize that person (Wolf & Stevens, 2001). Moreover, the aforesaid meaning is refined through constant interaction with others who share that experience and is amended on the basis of input from others. The result may be the emergence of one dominant, overt narrative of a specific event that occurred in the family system and several covert minor narratives by other participants.

Marriages may be defined by a conjointly created narrative in which both spouses contribute subjective perceptions of an experience and then the spouses agree on certain facets and agree to disagree to allow space for separate realities of the same event. Conversely, often narratives arise from childhood experiences in which the child's cognitive processes dictate an immature interpretation of that event. However, that version never undergoes a revision by which a more mature cognitive process could better understand the event and attach a different, more informed meaning. In this instance, adults are living "life scripts" written when they were children. More important to an understanding of narrative theory is that the individual assumes that the event is the issue, while the clinician assumes that the meaning created by the individual is the issue. Therefore, the main objectives of the narrative approach are to (a) deconstruct the child-based narrative, (b) fit the story to fact, and (c) re-author the same experience utilizing both the adult perspective of the client and the knowledge of the mental health professional.

For those clients who believe in God or a Higher Power, exploration of these clients' narratives around the self in the presenting issue may offer a novel perspective (Anderson & Worthen, 1997). The asking of questions by the counselor would be less a matter of information gathering and more an attempt to open a dialogue in order to better understand how the client came to see him- or herself in this manner. In such cases, obviously, the client cannot "know" the word of God; however, what the client reports carries great weight in terms of personal evaluation and expectations. The following are examples of questions that a mental health professional might ask:

- What would it be like if you could see yourself through God's eyes?
- Do you have a sense that God understands some things that I, as your counselor, cannot?

The value of such questions lies in the client's narrative of how the client believes that he or she is seen by God. The answers are revealing in terms of their indication of the client's perception of God (as judgmental, kind, loving, critical, etc.), his or her relationship with God, how God plays a part in the client's life, to what the client is entitled by his or her faith, and in what ways the client is indebted to God.

Hoogestraat and Trammel (2003) wrote about the process of co-authoring the role and function of religion and spirituality in the marriage or family (pp. 422–423). The responses to these questions about the function and role of religion and spirituality in the marriage, the family, and the presenting concern are less important for the clinician to hear and more important for each family member to hear. Given the sacredness of religious or spiritual beliefs, often family members are astounded by the answers given by the others. Questions posed by the clinician, according to Hoogestraat and Trammel, include the following:

- "In times of need, where do you go or whom do you turn to for comfort?
- In times of need, are you able to find comfort in God or a Higher Power of your understanding?
- How is your religion or spirituality important to you?
- How have the principles of your faith guided you in your past? Now?
- What would your God say about you entering counseling?" (p. 425)

On a more comprehensive level, Hodge (2001) presented an "interpretative anthropological framework" of an individual's religious and spiritual experiences (Hodge, 2005b, p. 345). Covering affect, behavior and cognition, communion, conscience, and intuition, the scope and depth of Hodge's questions would be illuminating for family members. The questions are as follows:

"Affect	What aspects of your spiritual life give you pleasure?
	What role does your spirituality play in handling life's sorrows?
	[In] enhancing life's joys? [In] coping with life's pain?
	How does your spirituality give you hope for the future? What do you wish to accomplish in [the] future?
Behavior	Are there specific practice that help you deal with life's obstacles?
	What is your level of involvement in church, small groups, etc.?
	How are they supportive?
	Are there spiritually encouraging individuals with whom you keep in contact?

Cognition	What are your current religious/spiritual beliefs?
	What are they based on?
	What beliefs do you find particularly meaningful?
	What does your faith say about personal trials?
	How does this belief help you to overcome obstacles? To accept pain in life?
Communion	Describe your relationship with God (or the Transcendent).
	What has been your experience of God?
	How does God communicate with you?
	How have these experiences encouraged you?
	Have there been times of deep spiritual intimacy?
	How does your relationship with God help you face life challenges?
	How would God describe you?
Conscience	How do you determine right and wrong?
	What are your key values?
	How does your spirituality help you deal with sin or guilt?
	What role does forgiveness play in your life?
Intuition	To what extent do you experience intuitive hunches (flashes of creative insight, premonitions, and spiritual insights)?
	Have those insights been [a] strength in your life? If so, how?"
	(pp. 353–354.)

Another postmodern theory is "solution-focused" theory. Solution-focused approaches assume that, at some time in a client's past, the client had utilized his or her resources to deal with similar struggles more successfully than with the current struggle. However, because of the current pain, those past success have been overlooked and the similarity of the current challenge to past challenges has not been considered. In addition, any current exceptions to times of stress, anxiety, and pain are overlooked by the client. Both the past successes and current exceptions provide examples of client-based resources that could be utilized in resolving the current problem.

The clinician's task is to guide the client through a search for such times of success and exception. Identification of these triumphs equips the client to bring those realizations and approaches to the current problem. While perhaps requiring modification, enhancement, or updating, the client then basically provides his or her own solution. For clients who acknowledge a religious or spiritual connection, it may be safe for the clinician to assume that their faith has sustained them in times of previous challenges. That sustenance may have taken the form of accepting what seemed to be intolerable or seeking alternatives. Calling on those previously experienced, yet currently overlooked, faith-based successes may offer insight and a way to cope with the present tension or struggle. In addition, helping family members identify times of cohesion, rather than division, around the presenting issue may reveal episodes of family faith-based practices. In any case, there was probably a time in the family's past when whatever is troubling the family currently either did not exist or was less problematic, and there is the possibility that the family's religious or spiritual practices were of help in those times and could be of even greater help now.

These sample interventions, while far from making up an exhaustive list, were included to offer ways in which differing theoretical approaches could incorporate attention to the spiritual and religious aspects of family life and functioning. Each approach attends to both insight into, and evaluation of, current religious and spiritual practices, because this awareness must be the initial step in revising one's religious or spiritual practices. The intent of such exploration is consistent with the client's hopes for the inclusion of religious and spiritual issues in family counseling and with the anticipated benefits of positive religious and spiritual practices for each member of the family and for the family unit as a whole.

CURRENT AND FUTURE DIRECTIONS

Aponte (2003) indicated that religion and spirituality are "dynamic, ever evolving force[s] that can grow clearer and stronger or languish in the muddy pool of progressive neglect" (p. 17). If mental health professionals accept the postmodern vision of religious and spiritual issues as being at least germane, if not central, to relational counseling, then they must consider how best to address the growing number of requests from current and future clients for the inclusion of religious/spiritual matters in counseling.

One way to become better prepared to address these matters is to develop a keen awareness of one's personal spirituality in the context of everyday struggles and to evaluate how one's present religious or spiritual practices provide health-promoting or health-endangering outcomes both for personal emotional and mental health and for relational harmony and growth. Only through self-discovery can a clinician identify with, and differentiate his or her situation from clients' spiritual struggles.

Hodges (2005) stated that formal training was the surest way to assist clinicians in acknowledging, legitimizing, and working through their own religious and spiritual issues. Aponte (2003) advised that attention to one's own spiritual, religious, and relational struggles allows the clinician to "identify with clients on the basis of our universal flawed humanness" (p. 16).

Case Example Revisited

Tamara accessed the professional literature on marriage and family counseling, as well as that on religion/spirituality. She was amazed at the initial synergy between the two areas of study, then dismayed by their partition, and, finally, reassured by the growing amount of literature integrating the two fields.

Although she was disappointed that her program did not offer courses on the integration of religion/spirituality into marriage and family counseling, she identified workshops on this topic that were to held at upcoming state and national conferences. One of her peers suggested that they both attend as many of these seminars and presentations as possible and share resources after the conferences. Tamara was excited about this opportunity and also offered to contact each presenter to ask whether that individual would speak to the two students about his or her research and writings on the topic.

Conclusion

"Overlooking or ignoring religion and spirituality in working with families diminishes the significance of this influential piece of family life" (Griffith & Rotter, 1999, p. 163). Given this caution and the implied call to action, mental health professionals who offer clinical services to couples and families must determine how they wish to infuse these topics into their therapeutic agendas. Although knowledge of diverse religious and spiritual traditions is important, Aponte (2003) advised that "the most powerful means to learning to empathize with and maneuver within our clients' psychological and spiritual journeys is through an understanding of and groundedness in our own journey" (p. 16).

Self-Understanding Exercises

1. Create a spiritual genogram of your family to illustrate how religious/spiritual themes traveled through the generations. If new themes emerged or if others disappeared, how do you account for those occurrences? What differences have continuity and change made in your life as an individual, as a member of a couple (if applicable), and as a member of a family?

2. In what ways do religious and spiritual practices strengthen or weaken your family rituals and the importance of those rituals?

3. If you chose to be married in a church, mosque, or synagogue (or chose not to be married in such a venue), how was that choice important to you?

Opportunities for Further Learning

1. Interview couples to ascertain how religion and spirituality serve to strengthen their marriages and their families. (Those two experiences are different from one another.)

2. Review different faith traditions to better understand the teachings on men, women, marriage, family, and children as a way to understand how religion and spirituality influence family functioning.

3. Meet with clergy members from different denominations to discuss how they see participation in their specific religious or spiritual institutions as being beneficial to couples and families. What differences did you notice in their responses? What similarities did you notice?

15

. . .

Opportunities for Future Professional and Personal Development

We are always looking to the future; the present does not satisfy us.
Our ideal, whatever that may be, lies further on.

—GEORGE N. GILLETT, JR. (1938)

CASE EXAMPLE

Keandra was excited to read that, among the electives offered in her graduate clinical training program, there was a course on religion, spirituality, and counseling. As a devout member of her faith, Keandra was thrilled to be able to learn how to integrate her religious affiliation into her new profession. However, during the course, she became less and less certain about what she thought she knew and believed at the beginning of the course.

She was puzzled by how other faith traditions addressed some issues in a way that was drastically different from her own. How could all of these ways be equally valid? However, she persevered in the course and took the final exam. Even though she earned an A, her answers had seemed tentative to her, full of uncertainty and less concise than she would have liked. She compared her feelings of dismay after that exam with her feelings of confidence after her exam in research methods, in which she also earned an A. Over the summer break, she took another class with the instructor of her religion, spirituality, and counseling course, who praised her work in that class and her receptivity to new ideas. The instructor then offered to review with her the exam that had given her so much trouble.

. . .

INTRODUCTION

The inclusion of a section entitled "Introduction" within what is obviously intended to be the concluding chapter of a book may seem to be incongruous; however, as in any therapeutic counseling session, it would seem to be beneficial to devote a few moments in closing to reflect on what one has gained from a specific experience. That exercise is as valuable for the clinician as it is for the client—or, in this case, for the author as well as the reader. To merely recap what has already been written and read would be redundant. What may be of importance to remember is that the objective of this book revolved around two central ideas: (a) One cannot be either a genuine clinician or of any appreciable assistance to clients without considering and focusing on the self in session, and (b) one needs to be sensitive to all facets of multicultural identity within clinical services, including those related to religion and spirituality. Given the power of religion and spirituality to shape one's sense of oneself, both as a clinician and as a client, this book was intended to introduce topics and thoughts of relevance to practicing and pre-practicing mental health clinicians.

WHERE DID WE START?

In planning this book, a review of the concluding comments and directions for future research provided by previous authors proved to be of great value. Sperry (2001), writing in the epilogue of his book, predicted that the increased interest in spirituality would be maintained. He forecasted a transition toward positive psychology or strength-focused research, concurrent with a shift toward a focus on wellness. In addition, he projected an expansion of multicultural issues in counseling, incorporating the spiritual dimension into the personal and professional lives of clinicians. These themes became the starting point and, hopefully, the collective thesis of the chapters of this book.

Although I agree with Wiggins (2007) that a basic knowledge of world religions is a foundational aspect of spiritual awareness, I sadly acknowledge that such content remains beyond the scope of this book. However, recognizing the importance of such knowledge, I make two recommendations to the interested reader: First, any local university will offer such a course on comparative religion at the undergraduate level, and that course may meet the reader's needs. Second, it is crucial for the clinical process that one remember that "book knowledge" pales in comparison to the "lived experience" of the client within a faith tradition, so the professional commitment to honor the client's familiarity and adopt a stance of respectful "not knowing," as well as an openness to learn from and with the client, may also be of therapeutic value.

The book began with a plan to provide a series of chapters and topics that were consistent with the purpose of addressing the self of the client as a spiritual being in connection with the self of the mental health services provider. There was less emphasis placed on the goal of becoming a source of answers or authority in this process and more stress placed on the self as a fellow traveler in the process of religious and spiritual maturation. Therefore, the direction of each chapter was to consider how its contents affected both agendas, because it is believed that one cannot be more respectful, supportive, and empathic toward a client's issues than one is toward one's own.

WHAT HAVE WE LEARNED?

As the author of this work, I cannot imagine at this point what the reader has learned; however, I can reflect on personal learning in general. The wealth of professional literature that is being published on this subject is truly astonishing. Not only is this material coming from counselors, but members of the other helping professions, including the field of medicine, are contributing as well. There seems to be consistent growth in the attention being paid to the positive and healthy expression of religion and spirituality in people's lives. This strengthening of a wellness focus increases the depth of understanding of the human experience beyond that of understanding illness or pathology, to include models of optimal functioning and positive growth toward an enhanced way of being rather than simply remedying dysfunction. In addition, there seems to be new evidence of the beneficial outcomes of spiritual and religious practice on all aspects of life, including the biological, the psychological, and the social. Perhaps after the documented history of the distance between religion/spirituality and the helping professions, that gap is now being purposefully narrowed for the betterment of all professions and all peoples.

WHAT HAVE WE YET TO LEARN?

This section is intended to be a conduit or a transition to future editions of this book. As new issues emerge and discussion is generated, subsequent editions of *Counseling and Spirituality* will integrate those topics, as well as their implications for increased counselor self-awareness, knowledge, and skill. In contemplating this final chapter, I decided to offer possible views of emerging issues and topics that are relevant to the broad scope of religion, spirituality, and the mental health services professions.

In accessing the current professional literature, DiClemente and Delaney (2005) offered six recommendations for the evolution of the integration of religion/spirituality and clinical services:

1. Religion and spirituality must be included among those factors that reflect the personal, cultural, and community contexts in the theories of human development, psychological stress and coping, mental health, resiliency, virtues and vices, and social functioning.

2. Newer research methods in psychology and analysis, as well as new conceptual frameworks, are required in order to guide the scientific exploration of religion and spirituality with regard to differing aspects of human functioning.

3. The mental health services professions, both among themselves and between the profession and organized religion, must move beyond polarization and dichotomy toward commonalities, embracing the emergence of a biopsychosocial focus, enhancing the practice of positive psychology (i.e., a salutogenic orientation), and focusing on cultural effects and complex interactive causalities.

4. Mental health services providers must continue to develop cultural awareness and competence and attend to individual and group differences—an approach that is critical to understanding development, health, pathology, and treatment. Although this guideline is applicable to all aspects of cultural diversity, given the recent emergence of attention being paid to religion and spirituality, it is more critical than ever that such an effort be made.

5. "Belief and science are not the same" (DiClemente and Delaney, 2005, p. 285); therefore, both mental health service providers and religious professionals must expect ongoing tension and conflict between religion and science. These boundaries must be respected, with the acknowledgment that some human experiences may never be fully understood or accessible for study, given the methods currently employed.

6. Attention to the previous item

will move [helping professionals] and religious professionals to greater mutual respect, greater realization of personal and perspective limitations, greater tolerance for the ambiguity that dialogue entails, and an increased appreciation for what we do not know as well as what we believe we do know. (p. 285)

Research on actual clients must become a priority (Rose, Westefeld, & Ansley, 2001). This research must be founded on carefully developed constructs that transcend religious/spiritual affiliations and the number of services attended, to include the experience of the participation itself and how transformative it may have been. In addition, researchers must expand their studies beyond the Christian populations. Given the number of different faith practices within American society, it is incumbent upon researchers who are committed to the principles of multiculturalism, as are current clinicians, to explore the ways in which those practices may provide similar or different outcomes for their adherents.

In addition, the insights of previous authors regarding the general subject of religion/spirituality and counseling has provided additional insight into the present and future status of scholarship on spirituality and counseling. All authors acknowledged an increase in professional interest in the issues of spirituality and religion. In particular, Ingersoll (2007) emphasized the continued attention being paid to the interaction of ego development and spirituality, along with questions about the interaction of spiritual/religious variables among other cultural definitions of the self, and Faiver and O'Brien (2007) thought that achieving a better understanding of violence that is perpetrated in the name of religion is important.

In terms of clinical practice, mental health service providers are urged to develop spiritually based responses to disasters such as the events of September 11, 2001, and Hurricane Katrina. Frame (2007) and Sperry (2007) cautioned against conducing research without clearer definitions of spiritual variables and suggested that medical studies were beginning to show a link between the positive effects of religion and spirituality, on the one hand, and physical health and the healing process, on the other. To that end, the emergence of testable models and intervention strategies are greatly needed. However, in the study of spiritual and religious dynamics, a way must be found to move beyond the solely academic focus, to integrate the heart and compassion (Cashwell, 2007).

Implications for Future Research

Several salient ideas were offered for future research within this scope of inquiry. Researchers are asked to weigh the possible limitations in the demand for quantification of spiritual constructs because of the scientific notion that variables must be observable in order to be studied. A more efficacious approach may be an emphasis on more rigorous qualitative study or perhaps on the emergence of new research paradigms (Faiver & O'Brien, 2007; Frame, 2007; Ingersoll, 2007). This question about the observability of variables is reflected in questions about the validity of "counting" the experience without including its meaning, and it is a viable research paradigm for topics infused with the depth and personalization of religion and spirituality (Frame, 2007). For example, counting attendance at religious services without considering its personal meaning or value may diminish the true understanding of one's religious adherence. However, one of the conditions of the utilization of qualitative studies, which may probe for this depth, is the limited ability of such studies to be generalized. Therefore, those who design research methodology may be challenged to envision new models for studying the variables in question in a way that marries the rigor and the advantages of both approaches.

An exploration of the "sense of self as center of spiritual gravity" and as the defining aspect of identity that influences all of the other realms of human experience and functioning has yet to emerge. Given previous comments on the continued and expanded interest in the role of spirituality in ego development, future research may investigate the centrality of spirituality as a defining or linking constituent of identity and esteem. Study in this realm would require concise exploration of the developmental and thinking processes that result in ego growth; oddly enough, those processes may also contribute to ego deficiency.

From a more treatment-focused orientation, future researchers may wonder whether 12-step programs are useful in other contexts, given their relative success in the treatment of addictive behaviors. Practitioners may wish to consider adaptations of the 12-step model to other recovery systems (Faiver & O'Brien, 2007). Although perhaps more well known for recovery from alcoholism, such models have been utilized in the effort to recover from gambling and from codependency, among other issues. Might other aspects of human experience also benefit from the successful application of these programs?

Consistent with this focus on therapeutic effectiveness, one may seek to confirm empirically, not just anecdotally, the positive benefits of religious and spiritual practice as a method for guiding best practices in counseling services. Part of the mandate for efficacious mental health services surrounds the question "How do you know that it works?" So the shift must begin from the artful delivery of the intervention to the assessment of the benefits for the client. Only at that point can helping professionals begin to document the effectiveness of religious and spiritual interventions in the lives of their clients and begin to offer guidance for future clinicians as to which interventions to apply in specific situations with the reasonable expectation of a positive outcome (Frame, 2007).

From a conceptual perspective, might "spirit-deficit disorder" (the lack of spirituality) affect aspects of life functioning? And, if so, how does one describe such a deficiency? If one were to approach spirituality from a developmental perspective, how might the lack of spiritual maturation be described, explained, and addressed? Might individuals achieve physical maturity while lacking spiritual maturity? This phenomenon has already been well established in psychosocial development, where an Eriksonian template proposes that deficiencies in the resolution of early life-stage tasks will reemerge in later-stage development. Might such a pattern apply to spiritual development? In addition, what might it mean to be "spiritually bereft"? How would individuals described as such see themselves differently from others who claim spiritual adequacy or fulfillment?

Another identified focus for the conceptualization of future study tends to be the two central themes of this research: mindfulness and soulfulness. Mindfulness focuses on issues of meaning, and soulfulness is expressed through the recent emergence of the study of positive psychology, such as the study of virtue. The infusion of both topics within clinical service has generated preliminary data—even among lower functioning chronic clients—that indicate increased compliance with treatment and less chance of relapse (Sperry, 2007).

Yet another perspective on relevant spiritual dynamics offers two themes of interest: mindfulness and spiritual bypass. Mindfulness refers to the ability to live differently through one's spiritual orientation—to become more compassionate and empathic. "Spiritual bypass" refers to those who use spirituality as an avoidance mechanism for dealing with anger, grief, and loss; it is a form of spiritual narcissism. The question then changes to "How does one become more open with clients, and what competencies and awareness must a counselor have in order to work toward that goal?" (Cashwell, 2007).

Additionally, future research may wish to adopt a sociological perspective on religion and spirituality to add to the psychological orientation present in the helping professions. The psychological orientation may exaggerate the emphasis placed on the individual without honoring the individual within the various social systems to which he or she belongs. Given the drive toward belonging, affiliation, and relationship, the study of an individual religion or spirituality would seem to be incomplete without consideration of the social context of that connection. What drives individuals to seek spiritual community? What are its benefits? What are its limitations? Might there come a time when one must depart from that community in order to advance on one's spiritual path? To what extent are such communities a commitment for life, and to what extent are they a learning experience that, if successful, prompts each individual to transcend that community for additional personal spiritual growth?

In summary, it is evident that the formal study of religion/spirituality and counseling offers multiple venues for ongoing exploration. The emerging legitimacy of that study within the counseling profession, as well as the intellectual curiosity brought to such study, bodes well for the growth of carefully conceptualized and conducted research, which is the benchmark of any scholarly endeavor and a predictor of the development of valuable new knowledge.

Implications for Standardized Assessment and Diagnosis

Any attention paid to the research protocols and procedures for specific variables must be accompanied by attention to the measurement of those variables. Furthermore, the process of measurement in the mental health services then lends itself to the contemplation of the issue of the optimal, normal, and dysfunctional expression of those aspects of the human experience, resulting in a discussion of mental health diagnoses.

In terms of spiritual assessment and diagnosis, the V-Code, or "adjustment disorder," diagnosis currently in use is sufficient. The question of the emergence of diagnostic categories may lead to the pathologizing of religion and religious practice (Ingersoll, 2007). Currently, our understanding of the influences and effects of religious and spiritual practices on overall functioning is insufficient even to begin to define dysfunction. Might too much religion or spirituality interfere with other facets of life functioning? Hypothetically, one could answer "yes." Might such excesses be currently identifiable or quantifiable? Not at this time.

The ego development of awareness leads to angst regarding the enormity of human pain and suffering (a developmental milestone of spiritual growth), rather than to depression (Cashwell, 2007). There is a tendency, when one is utilizing the *Diagnostic and Statistical Manual of Mental Disorders* (*DSM-IV-TR*), to believe that all human suffering and pain must fit within its descriptions. It must be remembered that such a manual, in its fourth edition, is an ongoing evolution in thinking about pathology. However, each diagnostic category which lists the behaviors that must be observed in order to confirm a diagnosis is prefaced with the caution that such behaviors must exceed those which are developmentally appropriate. Given the relative omission of developmental spirituality within professional training models or practice, might certain behavioral indicators of pathology in fact be developmentally appropriate, considering the context of spiritual development, a context that is *not* being considered? Therefore, before rushing to add spiritual pathology to an ever-growing list of mental illnesses, careful attention must be paid to understanding development; only then can distinctions be made between healthy and unhealthy development (Cashwell, 2007; Faiver & O'Brien, 2007).

Mental health professionals must be concerned with tying the exploration of religion and spirituality to an orientation that is focused more heavily on pathology, especially in light of how the *DSM-IV-TR* requires consideration of cultural mores and norms with no guidance or instruction on how to do so (Frame, 2007). The initial part of this response seems to advocate the strength-focused positive psychology orientation that is currently emerging. Understanding spiritual and religious functioning from this orientation seems to be more consistent and helpful than trying to describe its liabilities. However, adding yet one more caution, one must be concerned not only about the developmental expression of religious and spiritual functioning, but also that such expression lies within the culture of each individual. Once again, the preface to each diagnostic category directs the clinician to weigh the behaviors in light of the culture of each individual client, assuming that the clinician has and uses that knowledge. In cases where that knowledge may be absent, underapplied, or ignored, the validity of the application of the diagnosis must be called into question.

From a more pragmatic perspective, the accuracy and utility of diagnosis in any facet of human functioning must rest on a common definition and use of the term to be defined. Currently, there exists no consensus on the definition and, therefore, no common use of "spirituality." Currently, more than 50 different explanations have appeared within the professional literature. Reaching consensus on such a task must be the primary step toward even considering any type of relevant diagnosis in this field (Sperry, 2007).

However, there is some question as to the relevance or desirability of considering spirituality with a diagnostic framework. The absence of a consensus regarding a definition of spiritual health and pathology exempts spirituality from the possibility of a diagnosis. Although emerging literature discusses spiritual crises and emergencies, the current absence of agreed-upon taxonomies makes such a task impossible at this time. Much akin to the cautions expressed in the designation of variables for research, this caution is applicable to the process of assessment. Construct validation is a critical prerequisite to the creation of any data-gathering instrument, and currently, professional consensus is absent on the terms relevant to the study of spirituality.

The process of assessment goes hand in hand with the process of research, because one cannot study what one cannot define or even study reliably that which lacks a consensual definition. From a conceptual perspective on the function of assessment itself, Faiver and O'Brien (2007) advocated that its practice is more to promote dialogue and self-exploration than diagnosis; that is, assessment is more for the purpose of insight rather than the labeling of pathology. Consistent with the statements made in response to previous questions, there is a reluctance to try to create a diagram of pathological religion or spirituality. The reasons for this stance have been stated. However, there is a valid use for assessment as a method of bringing to consciousness and awareness that which has not been acknowledged. If the current and future assessment instruments designed around religious and spiritual constructs are aimed toward that objective, as a starting point for dialogue, then their continued development would be of benefit to both the client and the clinician.

From another conceptual viewpoint, those invested in assessment may question the value of quantitative assessment as a practice relevant to spirituality and religion. If spirituality is an individual phenomenon, perhaps emerging from the collective experience of religion, how does one quantify or generalize individual growth? And to what end? The very practice of seeking norms may diminish the purpose of spiritual growth, which is an ipsative relationship with the Divine both within and perhaps beyond each individual.

Those cautions having been raised, the practice of assessment in religious and spiritual matters is becoming more legitimized; therefore, students in clinical training programs need to become acquainted with the best of these measures (those based on psychometric properties) and obtain guided practice in their implementation, scoring, and interpretation. In addition, clinicians in practice may wish to explore potential assessment tools, given their current client populations, and begin to identify those assessment procedures which may be of therapeutic value. Although this chapter may be a good reference, the growth in this field demands that practitioners carefully investigate available measures from both a qualitative and a quantitative orientation. Perhaps a true measure of the potential value of any assessment tool is how well the clinician who has self-administered that measure values its results.

Once again, until a working definition of spirituality can be embraced along with descriptions of salient input, process, and output variables, this process may flounder (Sperry, 2007). The challenge becomes more pronounced when one faces the difficulties inherent in articulating a construct definition as distinct as religiosity (Cashwell, 2007). There is encouraging work being done from the perspective of "positive psychology," with the anticipation of a growing clinical utility for this work. Perhaps the union of the two fields will direct those who create assessment tools for identifying positive spiritual and religious virtues as core constructs that require formal measurement.

In summary, although the next section is of greater importance to mental health practitioners, it is the scholarly practice of research and assessment that fosters the dissemination of new knowledge to society. The balance of one's acknowledgment of responsibility to both society in general and the client in particular is what defines the true mental health services provider.

Implications for the Delivery of Clinical Services

The future of the intersection of religion/spirituality and counseling/therapy extends into the interactions between clients and clinicians. Therefore, clinicians who wish to address spiritual issues with clients and who are equally committed to their own spiritual exploration and growth have multiple opportunities for reflection and enhancement. These suggestions are not intended as a complete listing of relevant issues, but merely a sampling of what may be considered a point of embarkation on a lifelong, and career-long, journey of personal exploration.

Clinicians are urged to recognize the diversity within each faith tradition (Ingersoll, 2007). Although simplicity may demand the categorization of individuals according to broad religious affiliations, such minimalization of the experience is disrespectful to the variety in the lived experience. It is critical to recognize, if not understand, the distinctions among denominations within faith traditions (e.g., Orthodox, Conservative, and Reform Judaism); for it is exactly these distinctions that draw certain individuals into the denominations in question. It is also important to infuse a multicultural perspective on the religious and spiritual practices themselves. One must consider the influence of ethnicity, age, and/or gender, for example, on one's experience within a faith tradition. It would again be overly simplistic, and perhaps culturally naïve, to assume that each member feels as if he or she has an equal part in, and a similar experience of that faith.

Immersion in different faith traditions will serve to validate their importance. Clinicians, both present and future, need to visit faith-based services common to their client populations in order to truly appreciate the richness of those practices. Although book learning may touch the mind, only participation in the actual practice can touch the heart. Both growth experiences are critical to understanding the holistic picture of that faith tradition, an admonition echoed by Faiver and O'Brien (2007). Moreover, it is not enough to merely attend and observe; rather it is only the heartfelt appreciation of the power of such participation that can foster a sense of spiritual empathy on the part of the clinician (Cashwell, 2007). Part of this spiritual empathy involves the clinician's understanding of the translative aspects of spirituality and the experiencing the transformative aspects of spirituality. Attendance is incomplete without the integration of the experience into one's sense of the self as a spiritual being and the willingness to embrace of the effects and the meaning of that experience.

Religious or spiritual expression transcends attendance at formal services. Mental health professionals need to understand the value of every level of spiritual development in terms of personal identity and life guides. Rather than epitomize the highest level of spiritual development as being the only optimal level, clinicians must understand how one's spiritual development, at any stage, contributes to a healthy and productive lifestyle. One need not aspire to reach the highest levels in order to be spiritually secure and satisfied. It is then the responsibility of the clinician to legitimize growth to a point that is relevant to the client and to help the client determine how best to use the strengths implicit in that growth in order to direct his or her life course in personally relevant and, hopefully, satisfying ways.

On a conceptual level, practitioners must appreciate the similarities and the differences between religion and spirituality. Once again, providing a working vocabulary for both clinicians and clients can serve to further and deepen these discussions. In addition, such examination may bridge the gap between those who consider themselves to be spiritual, but not religious, and those who find their spirituality within their religious choices. Another aspect of this expanded professional vocabulary deals with gaining a knowledge of the "faith traditions." It is again critical to have a working vocabulary, and clinicians should educate themselves on the mainstream faith traditions found among their client populations. Although the client's lived experience adds the personal perspective, the clinician's ability to "speak that language" conveys a deep respect for that client's choice and creates common ground for discovery.

Mental health service providers are directed to learn about multiple perspectives on religious and spiritual practices by adherents rather than through didactic lecture. In addition to the advocacy for increased knowledge through directed study, the related experiences of religious and spiritual adherents among the different faith traditions offer the learner a perspective that cannot be matched by any text. The opportunity to interact with practitioners—either congregants or clergy—from different faiths may add a real-life point of view to academic learning (Wiggins, 2007). Knowledge regarding the religions of potential and actual clients in relation to one's area of clinical emphasis and the region of the country in which one practices conveys a statement that the clinician respects his or her clients. Perhaps clinical intake forms need to directly ask about one's religious and/or spiritual affiliation, and then the data could be compiled to identify the characteristics of the individuals who are accessing clinical services. The value of such data transcends accounting for this aspect of client diversity if utilized to direct study in those faith traditions that characterize one's client population. This added knowledge on the part of the therapist extends the scope of one's empathic understanding of the client's world and offers one additional venue through which to build a positive therapeutic relationship.

This process of discovery demands an understanding of "peak experience" and its transcendent power. This area of inquiry is critical to honoring such an experience and to begin to grasp the transformative force of such an occurrence. Can such experiences be summoned or self-created? If so, how? If not, under what optimal conditions might they emerge? How is one different as a result of such an experience? How long might such a difference persist? Does it fade with time and subsequent experience, or is it life altering? If one has had a peak experience, is one more open or susceptible to subsequent experiences? Might there be non-spiritual or nonreligious developmental factors that facilitate or hamper such an experience? To my mind, the questions are more numerous than the currently available answers.

For those clinicians working with children and adolescents, an understanding of cult dynamics is important. Given the established dangers of cult participation, children and adolescents need to be educated about such groups, and clinicians and parents need to be aware of the signs of possible cult involvement among children and adolescents in their care.

Dealing with guilt from religious and spiritual perspectives is a natural part of the human condition (Faiver & O'Brien, 2007). Although spoken about widely from an existential perspective, the guilt founded in religious or spiritual mandates is also a critical aspect of self-reflection and self-acceptance. The journey is then based on an acceptance of oneself when one's actions betray one's better judgment and contravene one's spiritual or religious learning. If embraced, the feeling of guilt becomes a motivation for learning; if avoided, due to shame or embarrassment, then guilt becomes a persistent scar on one's esteem and a badge of dishonor. What remains constant and consistent is that, as fallible human beings, no matter how lofty our intent, sometimes (for some, this is often) our actions basely disavow our better nature. The question then becomes "How does one respond in such a circumstance and what does that response say about the individual?" and, finally, "How does that response contribute to that individual's religious and/or spiritual growth?"

A related question is "What constitutes a 'spiritual concern'?" (Sperry, 2007). Identifying or specifying this answer would greatly help clinicians to reliably identify when one should consider the use of spiritual interventions and also would set the stage for the development of coping skills through the planning and delivery of psycho-educational interventions. Another related question is whether spiritual concerns are an exclusive issue or whether they are indeed an inclusive aspect of any presenting problem. If so, then spiritual exploration becomes a common practice. To date, there is no definitive answer to these questions. Instead, it is relegated to each clinician to address the questions in two ways: (a) How does one live one's own life and address one's own issues? and (b) Might client input clarify the client's own narratives or perceptions of the exclusivity or inclusivity of spiritual concerns within the presenting problem?

Yet more questions to be considered revolve around the relative benefits of active or passive spirituality: How active must one be within one's religious or spiritual community in order to derive the maximum benefit from that participation? To what extent might an affiliate of a particular faith be active within that community, and to what extent does living a spiritual life, but not being active within a faith community, earn an individual the right to claim an affiliation. The question may be twofold: (a) Does participation in a religious community compensate for the absence of a life lived outside of that community in accord with one's own spiritual directive? and (b) Can one claim a spiritual or religious identity without an affiliation with a community of worshippers? According to Faiver and O'Brien (2007), the answers to such complex questions help individuals define their place within, or outside of, a formal spiritual or religious community. One's answer is the critical reckoning of an awareness of one's desire for affiliation balanced with the desire for autonomy in the search for that which is holy.

However, clinicians are faced with the task of describing and deciding areas of spiritual/religious competence. Therefore, there is concern about establishing the necessary competencies for responding professionally to clients' religious and spiritual issues. These standards then become the measure and marker for understanding when one's current competencies are less than adequate. The challenge becomes more critical when graduate training programs have yet to include training in this area or supervision within guided clinical practice around the issues of religion and spirituality. Given this status, especially for clinicians who received their training prior to the reemergence of spirituality as a clinical concern, the careful selection of professional development activities, supported by a peer supervisor, would promote attention to the development of one's clinical competence in matters of religion and spirituality (Sperry, 2007).

However, no delivery of clinical services can be viewed as being truly genuine unless those lessons are equally applied to the life of the service provider in a personal way. An understanding of the self on the spiritual journey and then the incorporation of that awareness into one's clinical services would seem to be two vital tasks for all mental health service providers. This point, which forms the crux of this book, remains the most difficult to define. First, one must understand the notion of a spiritual journey and then determine one's place on that journey. Perhaps the surest vehicle toward enlightenment in this quest is the recognition that the answers that one lives daily are of secondary importance to the questions which prompted those specific answers. For it is the awareness of those very questions that can be of help within clinical services in order to assist clients in also identifying a place on that journey and in identifying the next step toward a more fulfilling life.

To guide one's services through the implementation of best practices models, clinicians need access to the results of randomized, controlled trials of clinical interventions, such as the ones currently being conducted on spiritually augmented cognitive-behavioral therapy in order to be appropriately guided in practice. There seem to be two components of such a data-driven study: (a) the development of interventions that are deemed to be effective as a function of the congruence between the desired and the actual affects on the client and (b) measures or benchmarks of desired therapeutic outcomes. Clinicians must guide their choice of technique by asking the question "How well did it [the intervention] do what I hoped it would do?" or perhaps, phrased differently, "To what extent did the client benefit in the way in which I intended the client to benefit?"

Additionally, one of the benchmarks for all of the mental health professions (and one of the chapters in this book) deals with ethical concerns relative to client welfare and the provision of best practices. Given the emergence of spiritual concerns within the scope of the delivery of mental health services, any discussion of issues of treatment must be augmented by paying attention to those guidelines or suggestions which ensure the appropriateness of such treatment and the clinician's responsibilities with regard to the client's welfare.

In summary, it can be readily seen that clinicians who seek spiritual or religious clinical competence are faced with many opportunities for growth and development. Although not offered as a complete list, the issues that are identified are intended to be a starting point in the delivery of clinical services that incorporate religious and spiritual concerns.

Implications for Clinical Training

Given that the delivery of clinical services and its components is a direct reflection of the training provided in graduate programs and ongoing professional development activities, questions can be raised as to how the current attention being paid to religious and spiritual issues can be bolstered to enhance training and competence in this area.

There is some question as to suitability or interest, in that not all mental health service providers have to work with spiritual issues; the choice to immerse oneself in this area of focus as part of one's therapeutic repertoire is a personal one (Cashwell, 2007). Entry into this area requires readiness on the part of the student to "remove [the] personal religious or spiritual blinders" that might interfere with the acceptance of and support for differing values of the faith traditions. One must "[o]pen aspects of [the] self to awareness." Consistent with the previous statement, helping professionals are urged to contemplate themselves as spiritual beings in anticipation of serving as spiritual guides for clients. Once again, any aspects of the self that are overlooked by the clinician will also be overlooked by the client (Ingersoll, 2007). Clinicians embarking on the spiritual journey, both with the self and with clients, must recognize the concept of the legitimacy of the journey versus focusing only on the end product or the goal. In our outcome-focused, results-driven society, it is a challenge to focus instead on the integrity of the process involved in fulfilling any task, seeing such focus on the quality of the doing as a prerequisite to the quality of the outcome. The maxim "the end justifies the means" cannot apply to the human journey. Instead, relative to one's spiritual journey, one may quip that the means dictate the end. Therefore, the necessity of questioning, being open to new learning and new experiences, and achieving comfort with ambiguity and uncertainty becomes apparent.

Students who choose to explore this venue of clinical development must be committed to experiential learning, not just knowledge. The notion of experiential learning involves learning styles that transcend the reading and listening modes and, peculiar to training in the helping professions, demands consideration of how the learned material helps one make better sense of one's life. In such cases, experiential learning involves dialogue not merely with others, but also with the self, around the same topics that one might expect clients to raise (Ingersoll, 2007). Part of this experiential learning may necessitate the preparation of a spiritual autobiography. This exercise is helpful in achieving the reflection required to trace one's spiritual journey and to relate the interplay of one's spiritual growth and other life decisions and directions. In this way, spirituality or religion is not relegated to Sunday services, but rather permeates one's daily life functioning and direction, an opinion also voiced by Faiver and O'Brien (2007) and Sperry (2007). In addition, experiential learning may involve attending and participating in the services of different faiths (Cashwell, 2007). Once again, this type of immersion activity exposes the learner to the full sensory experience of another faith's tradition on a level that a simple reading assignment cannot hope to emulate. For many learners, relinquishing the standard of comparison with their own faith practices is the hardest part of this task. One must come to accept the notion that "different" simply means "not the same," without the need for comparison, and that the practices of every faith tradition make perfect sense and are harmonious within the context in which they are practiced (Wiggins, 2007).

Students may also wish to investigate the value of entering therapy with regard to their own underlying spiritual and religious beliefs. Whether with a professional, a peer, or a group of students, the exploration of one's core religious and spiritual beliefs is an integral part of the identification of those beliefs which may, or may not, facilitate the therapeutic relationship and spiritual empathy. Similar to other exercises that stress self-awareness in multiculturalism, this discovery confirms the centrality of one's religious and spiritual beliefs within one's value system and as direction in one's own life. Such recognition validates the possibility that clients are also building a sense of the self and a life direction by incorporating these values, thereby emphasizing the need for clinicians to at least broach this discussion in therapy (Faiver & O'Brien, 2007).

For students who wish to include clinical competence around religious and spiritual issues in their professional portfolios, adding clinical placements at sites where religious and spiritual concerns are regularly addressed is a programmatic issue. For, as much value as instruction provides, until clinicians-in-training utilize that knowledge in the delivery of mental health services, the exercise of learning remains purely academic when, in reality, it must become both academic and practical. Therefore, the placement of students at sites that encourage addressing religious and spiritual issues, among other clinical concerns, offers the interested student the opportunity to experiment with and hone his or her clinical abilities along this line of clinical services. One may wish to consider how closely postgraduate clinicians replicate their practicum and internship experiences within their new employment in terms of their readiness to see clients with diverse concerns. If there is a positive correlation, then those experiences in their training programs are the first step toward welcoming such clients to their practice. Conversely, the lack of such exposure during the graduate training program may result in therapists who either do not welcome clients with religious or spiritual concerns or overlook the validity of those concerns within the provision of counseling services.

For advanced-level practitioners or doctoral students, training in the supervision of religious and spiritual issues may be the next phase of professional growth. The direct result of expecting clinicians-in-training to recognize and respond to clients' religious and spiritual concerns is an equal demand for supervisors to be prepared to guide the clinicians-in-training in providing such services. If this aspect of practice is omitted from one's own graduate training program, supervisors invested in infusing these issues into clinical services must then seek out professional development opportunities in order to gain the necessary knowledge, awareness, and skills. In addition, such topics may be appropriate for inclusion in doctoral-level classes that address multicultural issues in supervision. Without a directed effort through either venue, if the clinician and the supervisor remain oblivious to the presence of the religious and spiritual issues brought by the client, then the client can only assume that such issues are irrelevant within mental health services, and the client will either repress these concerns, prematurely terminate clinical services, or divide his or her time between seeking a mental health professional and a clergy member.

The vast contributions of the researchers and clinicians mentioned in this book cannot be overestimated. Researchers, scholars, and faculty in professional training programs have provided a wealth of direction for present and future study and teaching of clinical practices. The richness of their guidance will pay enormous dividends in furthering the infusion of religion and spirituality into both professional training programs and the professional literature.

Case Example Revisited

Curious to see what other comments the faculty member had for her, Keandra arranged a meeting to review her program progress to date and to further explore the feedback provided. At some point in the dialogue, her professor remarked, in response to her reactions to research methods and the religion, spirituality, and counseling course, that "it is easier to learn others' truths than your own." Startled by these words, Keandra pondered this notion for a moment and realized that until she began to question her religious tradition, she had been living the "truth of another." She also grasped that questioning did not equal rejection and that the process of generating truth in any area of one's life begins with questioning.

Conclusion

In closing this book, I wanted to add some personal comments. I chose this topic originally on the basis of a personal spiritual quest that I conducted. I later experienced the challenge of integrating that spirituality into my role as a clinician and a faculty member in a counselor education program. As a first-time author of a book, I carefully surveyed existing texts on this subject to determine which topics and themes appeared consistently. I determined that I could not justify omitting topics such as technique and ethics. I also identified topics that were offered in only one text, and I then had to weigh the extent to which I believed that such content was of value for present and future clinicians. I personally evaluated how I made sense of that topic and thought about additional questions that came to mind after having read what other authors had written.

All that said, it was my intent to provoke thought and dialogue around the topics in this book. This text is less about the certainty of answers and more about an appreciation of the ever-emerging questions about areas of growth and challenge in one's religious and/or spiritual life. Although hardly a definitive book on this subject, if the content has spurred such personal and professional inquiry, then its true message has been received.

As the author, I am interested in any feedback that readers may wish to provide. While I acknowledge the peer reviewers, whose encouraging and generous feedback was integrated into chapter revisions, and the editorial staff at Merrill Prentice Hall, who worked so hard to refine and strengthen the book, to me, the true estimate of its worth is in the value ascribed to it by the reader. Much akin to clinical intervention, where the value of the technique lies less in its artful delivery and more in its potential power for client insight, self-exploration, and growth, if this book generates a dialogue with others, or within yourself, around issues of the self as a spiritual traveler preparing to help others on their life journey, then its mission has been modestly accomplished.

Self-Understanding Exercises

1. In the "self-understanding" section after the preface, you were asked to identify three "big spiritual questions" that you have. How well or how poorly do you think this book has answered your questions?

2. Having experienced this book through your course, what are its strengths? What is missing? Are there any weaknesses that need to be revised?

3. What are your next "big spiritual questions"?

Opportunities for Further Learning

1. Given the time lag between the writing of this book and its adoption by your professor, if you are interested, contact the author to ask him how his thinking on specific topics may have evolved.

2. Look at newer books on religion and spirituality in counseling. How do they incorporate or move away from the topics in this book? What do the results of your search reveal about new directions in intellectual inquiry around these topics?

3. Were you to write such a book, what would you include? How do your answers compare with those of your classmates? If there are significant differences, what does that tell you about the scope of this subject?

REFERENCES

Abbot, D. A., Berry, M., & Meredith, W. H. (1990). Religious beliefs and practice: A potential asset in helping families. *Family Relations, 39*, 443–448.

Aiken, L. R. (2003). *Psychological testing and assessment* (11th ed.). Boston: Allyn & Bacon.

Ainsworth, M. D. S. (1985). Attachment across the lifespan. *Bulletin of the New York Academy of Medicine, 61*, 792–812.

Albertsen, E. J., O'Connor, L. E., & Berry, J. W. (2006). Religion and interpersonal guilt: Variations across ethnicity and spirituality. *Mental Health, Religion & Culture, 9*, 67–84.

Allen, D. J., & Oleson, T. (1999). Shame and internalized homophobia in gay men. *Journal of Homosexuality, 37*, 33–43.

Allport, G. W. (1950). *The individual and his religion.* New York: Macmillan.

Ameling, A. (2000). Prayer: An ancient healing practice becomes new again. *Holistic Nursing Practice, 14*(3), 40–48.

American Association of Marriage and Family Therapists (AAMFT). (2001). *Code of Ethics.* Alexandria, VA: Author.

American Counseling Association (ACA). (2005). *Code of ethics.* Alexandria, VA: Author.

American Psychiatric Association (APA). (2000). *Diagnostic and statistical manual of mental disorders* (4th ed.). Text revision. Washington, DC: Author.

American Psychological Association (APA). (1999). Answers to your questions about sexual orientation and homosexuality [Online]. Retrieved December 18, 2008, from www.apa.org. publinfo/orient/html.

American Psychological Association (APA). (2002). Ethical principles of psychologists and code of conduct. *American Psychologist, 57*, 1060–1073.

American Psychological Association (APA). (2002). *Ethical principles of psychologists and code of conduct.* Washington, DC: Author.

American Psychological Association (APA). (2005). *Guidelines and principles for accreditation of programs in professional psychology.* Washington, DC: Author.

Anderson, D. A., & Worthen, D. (1997). Exploring a fourth dimension: Spirituality as a resource for the couple therapist. *Journal of Marital and Family Therapy, 23*, 3–12.

Anthony, E. J. (1971). Folie a deux: A developmental failure of the process of separation–individuation. In J. B. McDevitt & C. F. Settlage (Eds.), *Separation–Individuation* (pp. 234–261). New York: International Universities Press.

Aponte, H. (2003, Sept./Oct.). The soul of the marriage and family therapist. *Family Therapy Networker*, 14–19.

Armstrong, K. (1993). *A history of God: The 4,000-year quest of Judaism, Christianity and Islam.* New York: Ballentine Books.

Ashby, J. S., Moran, W. J., Slaney, R. B., & Cotter, J. M. (1997). Psychologists' labeling of the affective states of shame and guilt. *Psychotherapy, 34*, 58–63.

Association for Spiritual, Ethical, and Religious Values in Counseling (ASERVIC). (2005). Competencies for integrating spirituality in counseling. Retrieved December 19, 2008, from http://www.aservic.org/CompetenciesforIntegratingSpiritualityintoCounseling.pdf.

Astin, J. A., Harkness, E., & Ernst, E. (2000). The efficacy of "distant healing": A systematic review of randomized trials. *Annals of Internal Medicine, 132*, 903–910.

Atwater, E. (1988). *Adolescence.* New Jersey: Prentice-Hall.

Aviles, J. M., Whelan, S. E., Hernke, D. A., Williams, B. A., Kenny, K. E., O'Fallon, W. M., & Kopecky, S. L. (2001). Intercessory prayer and cardiovascular disease progression in a coronary care unit population: A randomized controlled trial. *Mayo Clinical Procedures, 76*, 1192–1198.

Bade, M. B., & Cook, S. W. (1997). Functions and perceived effectiveness of prayer in the coping process. Paper presented at the annual meeting of the American Psychological Association, Chicago, IL.

Baldwin, K. M., Baldwin, J. R., & Ewald, T. (2006). The relationship between shame, guilt and self-efficacy. *American Journal of Psychotherapy, 60*, 1–21.

Barrett, R., & Barzan, R. (1996). Spiritual experiences of gay men and lesbians. *Counseling and Values, 41*, 4–15.

Bart, M. (1998, December). Spirituality in counseling finding believers. *Counseling Today, 41*, 1, 6.

Bartolo, K. (2005). Transforming shame: A pastoral response. *Journal of Family Studies, 11*, 330.

Basham, A., & O'Connor, M. (2005). Use of spiritual and religious beliefs in the pursuit of clients' goals. In C. S. Cashwell & J. S. Young (Eds.), *Integrating spirituality and religion into counseling: A guide to competent practice* (pp. 143–167). Alexandria, VA: American Counseling Association.

Batson, C. D., Schoenrae, P. A., & Ventis, W. L. (1993). *Religion and the individual: A social psychological perspective*. New York: Oxford University Press.

Bauer, J. J., & McAdams, D. P. (2004). Growth goals, maturity and well-being. *Developmental Psychology, 40*, 114–127.

Beck, R. (2006). God as a secure base: Attachment to God and theological exploration. *Journal of Psychology and Theology, 2*, 125–132.

Beck, R., & McDonald, A. (2004). Attachment to God: The Attachment to God Inventory, tests of working model correspondence and an exploration of faith group differences. *Journal of Psychology and Theology, 32*, 92–103.

Beckstead, L. (2001). Cures versus choices: Agenda in sexual reorientation therapy. *Journal of Gay and Lesbian Psychotherapy, 5*, 87–115.

Becvar, D. S., & Becvar, R. J. (2006). *Family therapy: A systemic integration* (6th ed.). Boston: Allyn & Bacon.

Benner, D. G. (1991). *Counseling as a spiritual process*. Grand Rapids, MI: Lingdale Papers.

Bennett, S. B. (2005). Recovering the value of guilt. *Human Development, 26*, 37–43.

Benson, P. L., Roehlkepartain, E. C., & Rude, S. P. (2003). Spiritual development in childhood and adolescence: Toward a field of inquiry. *Applied Developmental Science, 7*, 205–213.

Bergin, A. E. (1983). Religiosity and mental health: A critical re-evaluation and meta-analysis. *Professional Psychology: Research and Practice, 14*, 170–184.

Bergin, A. E. (1991). Values and religious issues in psychotherapy and mental health. *American Psychologist, 46*, 394–403.

Berk, L. (2001). *Development through the lifespan*. Needham Heights, MA: Allyn & Bacon.

Bernard, J. M., & Goodyear, R. K. (2004). *Fundamentals of clinical supervision* (3rd ed). Boston: Allyn & Bacon.

Bilgrave, D. P., & Deluty, R. H. (2002). Religious beliefs and political ideologies as predictors of psychotherapeutic orientations of clinical and counseling psychologists. *Psychotherapy, 39*, 245–260.

Bowen, M. (1978). *Family therapy in clinical practice*. Lanham, MD: Aronson Press.

Bown, J., & Williams, S. (1993). Spirituality in nursing: A review of the literature. *Journal for Advances in Health and Nursing Care, 2*(4), 41–66.

Brawer, P. A., Handal, P. J., Fabricatore, A. N., Roberts, R., & Wajda-Johnston, V. A. (2002). Training and education in religion/spirituality within APA-accredited clinical psychology programs. *Professional Psychology: Research and Practice, 33*, 203–206.

Bretherton, R. (2006). Can existential psychotherapy be good news? Reflections on existential psychotherapy from a Christian perspective. *Mental Health, Religion & Culture, 9*, 265–275.

Briggs, M. K., Apple, K. J., & Aydlett, A. E. (2004). Spirituality and the events of 9/11: A preliminary study. *Counseling and Values, 45*, 145–153.

Briggs, M. K., & Rayle, A. D. (2005). Incorporating spirituality into core counseling classes: Ideas for classroom application. *Counseling and Values, 50*, 63–75.

Briggs, M. K., & Rayle, A. D. (2005). Spiritually and religiously sensitive counselors. In C. S. Cashwell & J. S. Young (Eds.), *Integrating spirituality and religion into counseling: A guide to competent practice* (pp. 85–103). Alexandria, VA: American Counseling Association.

Briggs, M. K., & Shoffner, M. F. (2006). Spiritual wellness and depression: Testing a theoretical model with older adolescents and midlife adults. *Counseling and Values, 51*, 5–20.

Brooke, S. L. (1993). The morality of homosexuality. *Journal of Homosexuality, 25*, 77–99.

Buber, M. (1970). *I and thou*. New York: Charles Scribner & Sons.

Buchanan, M., Dzelme, K., Harris, D., & Hecker, L. (2001). Challenges of being simultaneously gay or lesbian and spiritual and/or religious: A narrative perspective. *The American Journal of Family Therapy, 29*, 435–449.

Bulkeley, K. (2000). Dream interpretation: Practical methods for pastoral care and counseling. *Pastoral Psychology, 49*, 95–104.

Burke, M. T., Hackney, H., Hudson, P., Miranti, J., Watts, G. A., & Epp, L. (1999). Spirituality, religion and CACREP curriculum standards. *Journal of Counseling and Development, 77,* 251–257.

Bush, M. (2005). The role of unconscious guilt in psychopathology and in psychotherapy. In G. Silberschatz (Ed.), *Transformative relationships: The control-mastery theory of psychotherapy* (pp. 43–66). New York: Routledge.

Bynum, E. B. (1994). *Transcending psychoneurotic disturbances: New approaches in psychospirituality and personality development.* New York: Haworth Press.

Byrd, R. C. (1988). Positive therapeutic effects of intercessory prayer in a coronary care unit population. *Southern Medical Journal, 81,* 826–829.

Capuzzi, D., & Gross, D. R. (2007). Achieving and personal and professional identity. In D. Capuzzi & D. R. Gross (Eds.), *Counseling and psychotherapy: Theories and interventions* (4th ed., pp. 26–46). Upper Saddle River, NJ: Merrill Prentice-Hall.

Carlson, T. D. (1996). *Religion, spirituality, and marriage and family therapy.* Unpublished master's thesis, Purdue University, Calumet, IN.

Carlson, T. D., Kirkpatrick, D., Hecker, L., & Killmer, M. (2002). Religion, spirituality and marriage and family therapy: A study of family therapists' beliefs about the appropriateness of addressing religious and spiritual issues in therapy. *The American Journal of Family Therapy, 30,* 157–171.

Carroll, S. (1993). Spirituality and purpose in life in alcoholism recovery. *Journal of Studies in Alcoholism, 54,* 297–301.

Carson, V. (1989). *Spiritual dimensions in nursing practice.* Philadelphia: Saunders.

Cashwell, C. (2007, November). Personal interview from the University of North Carolina at Greensboro.

Cashwell, C. S., & Young, J. S. (2004). Spirituality in counselor training: A content analysis of syllabi from introductory spirituality courses. *Counseling and Values, 48,* 96–109.

Cashwell, C. S., & Young, J. S. (2005). Integrating spirituality and religion into counseling: An introduction. In C. S. Cashwell & J. S. Young (Eds.), *Integrating spirituality and religion into counseling: A guide to competent practice* (pp. 1–10). Alexandria, VA: American Counseling Association.

Cervantes, J. M., & Ramirez, O. (1992). Spirituality and family dynamics in psychotherapy with Latino children. In L. A. Vargas & J. D. Koss-Chiono (Eds.), *Working with culture: Psychotherapeutic interventions with ethnic minority children and adolescents* (pp. 103–128). San Francisco: Jossey-Bass.

Cha, K. Y., Wirth, D. P., & Lobo, R. A. (2001). Does prayer influence the success of *in vitro* fertilization–embryo transfer? Report of a masked, randomized trial. *Journal of Reproductive Medicine, 46,* 781–787.

Chamberlain, T. J., & Hall, C. A. (2000). *Realized religion: Research on the relationship between religion and health.* Philadelphia: Templeton Foundation Press.

Chu, L. & Powers, P. A. (1995). Synchrony in adolescence. *Adolescence, 30,* 453–461.

Clark, M., Madaus, G., Horn, C., & Ramos, M. (2001). The marketplace for educational testing. *National Board in Educational Testing and Public Policy Statements, 2*(3), 1–11.

Cloyd, B. S. (1997). *Children and prayer: A shared pilgrimage.* Nashville, TN: Upper Room Books.

Cohen, C. B., Wheeler, S. E., Scott, D. A., Edwards, B. S., & Lusk, P. (2000). Prayer as therapy: A challenge to both religious belief and professional ethics. *Hastings Center Report, 30,* 40–47.

Cole, B. S. (2005). Spiritually-focused psychotherapy for people diagnosed with cancer: A pilot outcome study. *Mental Health, Religion & Culture, 8,* 217–226.

Cole, B. S., & Pargament, K. I. (1999). Spiritual surrender: A paradoxical path to control. In W. R. Miller (Ed.), *Integrating spirituality into treatment* (pp. 179–198). Washington, DC: American Psychological Association.

Coles, R. (1990). *The spiritual life of children.* Boston: Houghton Mifflin.

Commission on the Accreditation of Marriage and Family Therapy Education (COAMFTE). (2005). Standards of Accreditation (version 11). Washington, DC: Author.

Corey, G. (2005). *Theory and practice of counseling and psychotherapy* (7th ed.). Belmont, CA: Brooks/Cole.

Corright, B. (1997). *Psychotherapy and spirit: Theory and practice in transpersonal psychotherapy.* Albany, NY: State University of New York Press.

Council for the Accreditation of Counseling and Related Educational Programs (CACREP). (2007).

CACREP 2009 Accreditation standards [Draft]. Alexandria, VA: Author.

Crook-Lyon, R. E., & Wimmers, C. L. (2005). Spirituality and dream work in counseling: Clients' experiences. *Pastoral Psychology, 54,* 35–45.

Curtis, R. C., & Glass, J. S. (2002). Spirituality and counseling class: A teaching model. *Counseling and Values, 47,* 3–12.

Davidson, M. G. (2000). Religion and spirituality. In R. M. Perez, K. A. DeBord, & K. J. Biescke (Eds.), *Handbook of counseling and psychotherapy with lesbian, gay and bisexual clients* (pp. 409–433). Washington, DC: American Psychological Association.

Davis, J. (1914). *Moral and vocational guidance.* Boston: Ginn.

Davis, T. L., & Hill, C. E. (2004). Spiritual and non-spiritual approaches to dream work: Effects on client well-being. *Journal of Counseling and Development,* what is missing?

Day, S. X. (2004). *Theory and design in counseling and psychotherapy.* Boston: Houghton Mifflin.

Deci, E. L., & Ryan, R. M. (2000). The "what" and "why" of goal pursuits: Human needs and the self-determination of behavior. *Psychological Inquiry, 11,* 227–268.

Delaney, H. D., & DiClemente, C. C. (2005). Psychology's roots: A brief history of Judeo-Christian perspectives. In W. R. Miller and H. D. Delaney (Eds.), *Judeo-Christian perspectives on psychology: Human nature, motivation and change* (pp. 31–54). Washington, DC: American Psychological Association.

Denzin, N. K. (1974). The methodological implication of symbolic interaction for the study of deviance. *British Journal of Sociology, 25,* 269–282.

DiClemente, C. C. & Delaney, H. D. (2005). Implications of Judeo-Christian views of human nature, motivation and change for the science and practice of psychology. In W. R. Miller & H. D. Delaney (Eds.), *Judeo-Christian perspectives on psychology: Human nature, motivation, and change* (pp. 271–289). Washington, DC: American Psychological Association.

Diener, E. (1984). Subjective well-being. *Psychological Bulletin, 95,* 542–575.

Donnelly, D. (1993). *Spiritual fitness: Everyday exercises for body and soul.* New York: Harper Collins.

Durkeim, E. (1915). *The elementary forms of the religious life.* New York: Free Press.

Dworkin, S. (1997). Female, lesbian, and Jewish: Complex and invisible. In B. Greene (Ed.), *Ethnic and cultural diversity among lesbians and gay men* (pp. 63–87). Thousand Oaks, CA: Sage.

Dyson, J., Cobb, M., & Forman, D. (1997). The meaning of spirituality: A literature review. *Journal of Advanced Nursing, 26,* 1183–1186.

Eck, B. E. (2002). An exploration of the therapeutic use of spiritual disciplines in clinical practice. *Journal of Psychology and Christianity, 21,* 266–280.

Egan, G. (2007). *The skilled helper* (8th ed.). Pacific Grove, CA: Brooks/Cole.

Eliason, G. T., Hanley, C., & Leventis, M. (2001). The role of spirituality in counseling: Four theoretical orientations. *Pastoral Psychology, 30,* 77–91.

Elkind, D. (1984). *All grown up and no place to go.* Reading, MA: Addison-Wesley.

Elkins, D. N., Hedstrom, L. J., Hughes, L. L., Leaf, J. A., & Sanders, C. (1988). Toward a humanistic-phenomenological spirituality. *Journal of Humanistic Psychology, 28,* 21–31.

Ellis, A. (1989). Dangers of transpersonal psychology: A reply to Ken Wilbur. *Journal of Counseling and Development, 67,* 336–337.

Ellis, D. (1980). What happened to the spiritual dimension? *Canadian Nurse, 76*(8), 42–43.

Ellison, C. W. (1983). Spiritual well-being: Conceptualization and measurement. *Journal of Psychology and Theology, 11,* 330–340.

Erikson, E. H. (1959). *Identity and the life cycle.* New York: Norton.

Erikson, E. H. (1968). *Identity: Youth and crisis.* New York: Norton.

Erikson, E. H. (1972). *Young man Luther.* London: Faber.

Erikson, E. H. (1994). *Identity, youth and crisis.* New York: Norton.

Everts, J. F., & Agee, M. N. (1995). Including spirituality in counselor education: Issues for consideration with illustrative reference to a New Zealand example. *Journal for the Advancement of Counselling, 17,* 291–302.

Faiver, C. (2007, October). Personal interview from John Carroll University, Cleveland, OH.

Faiver, C., & Ingersoll, R. E. (2005). Knowing one's limits. In C. S. Cashwell & J. S. Young (Eds.), *Integrating spirituality and religion into counseling: A guide to competent practice* (pp. 169–183). Alexandria, VA; American Counseling Association.

Faiver, C., Ingersoll, R. E., O'Brien, E., & McNally, C. (2001). *Explorations in counseling and spirituality: Philosophical, practical and personal reflections.* Belmont, CA: Wadsworth/Thomson Learning.

Faiver, C. M., O'Brien, E. M., & Ingersoll, R. E. (2000). Religion, guilt and mental health. *Journal of Counseling and Development, 78,* 155–161.

Fenwick, P. (2004). Scientific evidence for the efficacy of prayer.

Finn, M. & Ruin, J. B. (2000). Psychotherapy with Buddhists. In P. S. Richards and A. E. Bergin (Eds.), *Handbook of psychotherapy and religious diversity* (pp. 317–340). Washington, DC: American Psychological Association.

Fowler, J. W. (1981). *Stages of faith: The psychology of human development and the quest for meaning.* San Francisco: Harper & Row.

Fowler, J. W. (1991). Stages in faith consciousness. In F. K. Oser and W. G. Scarlett (Eds), *New directions for child development: Special issue on religious development in childhood and adolescence* (Vol. 52, pp. 27–45). San Francisco: Jossey-Bass.

Fowler, J. W. (1996). *Faithful change: The personal and public challenges of postmodern life.* Nashville, TN: Abingdon Press.

Frame, M. W. (2000). The spiritual genogram in family therapy. *Journal of Marital and Family Therapy, 26,* 211–216.

Frame, M. W. (2003). *Integrating religion and spirituality into counseling: A comprehensive approach.* Pacific Grove, CA: Thomson Brooks/Cole.

Frame, M. (2007, October). Personal interview from the University of Colorado at Denver.

Frank, M. L. B. (2003). Existential theory. In *Psychotherapy: Theories and interventions* (3rd ed., pp. 131–156). Upper Saddle River, NJ: Merrill Prentice-Hall.

Frank, N. C., & Kendall, S. J. (2001). Religion, risk prevention and health promotion in adolescents: A community-based approach. *Mental Health, Religion & Culture, 4,* 133–148.

Frankl, V. E. (1959). *Man's search for meaning.* New York: Washington Square Press.

Frankl, V. E. (1967). *Psychotherapy and existentialism.* New York: Washington Square Press.

Freedman, S. (1998). Forgiveness and reconciliation: The importance of understanding how they differ. *Counseling and Values, 42,* 200–216.

Freud, S. (1927/1961). *The future of an illusion.* New York: Norton.

Freud, S. (1963). *Civilization and its discontents.* New York: Basic Books.

Frey, B. B., Daaleman, T. P., & Peyton, V. (2005). Measuring a dimension of spirituality for health research. *Research on Aging, 27,* 556–577.

Fromm, E. (1950). *Psychology and religion.* New Haven, CT: Yale University Press.

Frost, W. P. (1992). *What is the new age? Defining the third-millennium consciousness.* Lewiston, NY: Mellen Press.

Gall, T. L., Charbonneau, C., Clarke, N. H., Grant, K., Joseph, A., & Shouldice, L. (2005). Understanding the nature and role of spirituality in relation to coping and health: A conceptual framework. *Canadian Psychology, 46*(2), 88–104.

Gallup, G., Jr. (1996). *Religion in America: 1996 report.* Princeton, NJ: Princeton Religion Research Center.

Gallup, G., Jr., & Bezilla, R. (1992). *The religious life of young Americans.* Princeton, NJ: George H. Gallup International Institute.

Gallup, G., Jr., & Lindsay, D. M. (1999). Surveying the religious landscape: Trends in U.S. beliefs. Harrisburg, PA: Morehouse.

Gartner, J. (1996). Religious commitment, mental health and prosocial behavior: A review of the empirical literature. In E. P. Shafranske (Ed.), *Religion and the clinical practice of psychology* (pp. 187–214). Washington, DC: American Psychological Association.

Genia, V. (1995). *Counseling and psychotherapy of religious clients: A developmental approach.* Westport, CT: Praeger.

Genia, V. (2000). Religious issues in secularly based psychotherapy. *Counseling and Values, 44,* 213–221.

Gibson, T. S. (2004). Proposed levels of Christian spiritual maturity. *Journal of Psychology and Theology, 32,* 295–304.

Gilligan, C. (1982). *In a different voice: Psychological theory and women's development.* Cambridge, MA: Harvard University Press.

Gilligan, C. (1993). *In a different voice: Psychological theory and women's development* (2nd ed.). Cambridge, MA: Harvard University Press.

Glasser, W. (1965). *Reality therapy: A new approach to psychiatry.* New York: Harper & Row.

Goldenberg, H., & Goldenberg, I. (2008). *Family therapy: An overview* (7th ed.). Belmont, CA: Thomson.

Goleman, D. (1997). *Emotional intelligence.* New York: Bantam.

Gould, R. L. (1978). *Transformations: Growth and change in adult life.* New York: Simon & Schuster.

Graham, S., Furr, S., Flowers, C., & Burke, M. T. (2001). Religion and spirituality in coping with stress. *Counseling and Values, 46,* 2–13.

Griffith, B. A. (2004). The structure and development of internal working models: An integrated framework for understanding clients and promoting wellness. *Journal of Humanistic Counseling, Education & Development, 43,* 163–177.

Griffith, B. A., & Rotter, J. C. (1999). Families and spirituality: Therapists as facilitators. *The Family Journal, 7,* 161–164.

Guiley, R. E. (1991). *Harper's encyclopedia of mystical and paranormal experience.* San Francisco: Harper.

Hackney, C. H., & Sanders, G. S. (2003). Religiosity and mental health: A meta-analysis of recent studies. *Journal for the Scientific Study of Religion, 42,* 43–55.

Hage, S. M. (2006). A closer look at the role of spirituality in psychology training programs. *Professional Psychology: Research and Practice, 37,* 303–310.

Hage, S. M., Hopson, A., Siegel, M., Payton, G., & DeFanti, E. (2006). Multicultural training in spirituality: An interdisciplinary review. *Counseling and Values, 50,* 217–234.

Hageborn, W. B. (2005). Counselor self-awareness and self-exploration of religious and spiritual beliefs: Know thyself. In C. S. Cashwell & J. S. Young (Eds.), *Integrating spirituality and religion into counseling: A guide to competent practice* (pp. 63–84). Alexandria, VA: American Counseling Association.

Haley, M., Sieber, C., & Maples, M. F. (2003). Gestalt theory. In *Psychotherapy: Theories and interventions* (3rd ed., pp. 181–211). Upper Saddle River, NJ: Merrill Prentice-Hall.

Hall, C. R., Dixon, W. A., & Mauzey, E. D. (2004). Spirituality and religion: Implications for counselors. *Journal of Counseling and Development, 82,* 504–507.

Hall, T. W., Brokaw, B. F., Edwards, K. L., & Pike, P. L. (1998). An empirical exploration of psychoanalysis and religion: Spiritual maturity and object relations development. *Journal for the Scientific Study of Religion, 37,* 305–315.

Hall, T. W., & Gorman, M. (2003, August). Relational spirituality: Implications for the convergence of attachment theory, interpersonal neurobiology, and emotional information processing. *Psychology of Religion Newsletter, 1,* 1–12.

Harris, J. I., Schoneman, S. W., & Carrera, S. R. (2005). Preferred prayer styles and anxiety control. *Journal of Religion and Health, 44,* 403–412.

Hart, T. (2006). Spiritual experiences and capacities of children and youth. In E. C. Roehlkepartain, P. E. King, L. Wagener, & P. L. Benson (Eds.), *The handbook of spiritual development in childhood and adolescence* (pp. 163–177). Thousand Oaks, CA: Sage Publications.

Hartz, P. R. (1993). *Taoism.* New York: Facts on File.

Hartz, P. R. (1997). *Shinto.* New York: Facts on File.

Hassed, C. (2002). Are we approaching mental health in the right spirit? *Ausinetter, 2,* 10–12.

Hattie, J. A., Myers, J. E., & Sweeney, T. (2004). The factor structure of wellness theory: Theory, assessment, analysis, and practice. *Journal of Counseling and Development, 82,* 354–364.

Haug, I. E. (1998). Including a spiritual dimension in family therapy: Ethical considerations. *Contemporary Family Therapy, 20,* 181–194.

Haw, G. W., & Hughes, P. W. (Eds.). (1998). *Education for the 21st century in Asia-Pacific region: Report of the Melbourne UNESCO Conference.* Canberra, Australia: Australian National Commission for UNESCO.

Hay, D. (2000). Spirituality vs. individualism: Why we should nurture relational consciousness. *Journal of Children's Spirituality, 5,* 37–48.

Hayes, M. A., & Cowie, H. (2005). Psychology and religion: Mapping the relationship. *Mental Health, Religion and Culture, 8,* 27–33.

Hazler, R. J. (2003). Person-centered theory. In *Psychotherapy: Theories and interventions* (3rd ed., pp. 157–180). Upper Saddle River, NJ: Merrill Prentice-Hall.

Heath, C. D. (2006). A womanist approach to understanding and assessing the relationship between spirituality and mental health. *Mental Health, Religion & Culture, 9,* 155–170.

Hickson, J., Housley, W., & Wages, D. (2000). Counselors' perceptions of spirituality in the therapeutic process. *Counseling and Values, 45,* 58–66.

Hill, P. C., & Pargament, K. I. (2003). Advances in the conceptualization and measurement of religion and spirituality. *American Psychologist, 58,* 64–74.

Hill, P. C., Pargament, K. I., Hood, R. W., McCullough, M. E., Swyers, J. P., Larson, D. B., & Zinnbauer, B. J. (2000). Conceptualizing religion and spirituality: Points of commonality, points of departure. *Journal for the Theory of Social Behavior, 30,* 51–77.

Hodge, D. R. (2001). Spiritual assessment: A review of major qualitative methods and a new framework for assessing spirituality. *Social Work, 46,* 203–214.

Hodge, D. R. (2004). Spirituality and people with mental illness: Developing spiritual competency in assessment and intervention. *Families in Society, 85,* 36–44.

Hodge, D. R. (2005a). Epistemological frameworks, homosexuality and religion: How people of faith understand the intersection between homosexuality and religion. *Social Work, 50,* 207–218.

Hodge, D. R. (2005b). Spiritual assessment in marital and family therapy: A methodological framework for selecting from among six qualitative assessment tools. *Journal of Marital and Family Therapy, 31,* 341–356.

Hodges, S. (2002). Mental health, depression and dimensions of spirituality and religion. *Journal of Adult Development, 9,* 109–115.

Hollins, S. (2005). Spirituality and religion: Exploring the relationship. *Nursing Management, 12,* 22–26.

Hoogestraat, T., & Trammel, J. (2003). Spiritual and religious discussions in family therapy: Activities to promote dialogue. *The American Journal of Family Therapy, 31,* 413–426.

Howden, J. W. (1982). *Development and psychometric characteristics of the Spirituality Assessment Scale.* Unpublished doctoral dissertation, Texas Women's University, Denton.

Howell, L. C. (2001). Spirituality and women's midlife development. *ADULTSPAN Journal, 3,* 51–60.

Ibrahim, F. A. (1996). A multicultural perspective on principle and value ethics. *Counseling Psychologist, 24,* 78–85.

Inayat, Q. (2005). The Islamic concept of the self. *Counselling Psychology Review,* 20, 2–10.

Ingersoll, E. (2001). The Spiritual Wellness Inventory. In C. Faiver, R. E. Ingersoll, E. O'Brien, & C. McNally (Eds.), *Explorations in counseling and spirituality* (pp. 185–194). Belmont, CA: Brooks/Cole.

Ingersoll, E. (2007, September). Personal interview from Cleveland State University, Cleveland, OH.

Ivey, G. (2005). And what rough beast? Psychoanalytic thoughts on evil states of mind. *British Journal of Psychotherapy, 22,* 199–215.

Jackson, M. A. (2002). Christian womanist spirituality implications for social work practice. *Social Thought, 21,* 63–76.

Jacobs, J. L., & Capps, D. (Eds.). (1997). *Religion, society and psychoanalysis.* Boulder, CO: Westview Press.

Jagers, R. J., & Smith, P. (1996). Further examination of the Spirituality Scale. *Journal of Black Psychology, 23,* 429–442.

James, W. (1902/1961). *The varieties of religious experience.* New York: Collier Macmillan Books.

James, W. (1985). *The varieties of religious experience.* Cambridge, MA: Harvard University Press. (Original work published in 1902).

Jones, W. J. (1991). *Contemporary psychoanalysis and religion.* New Haven, CT: Yale University Press.

Joseph, S., Linley, P. A., & Maltby, J. (2006). Positive psychology, religion and spirituality. *Mental Health, Religion & Culture, 9,* 209–212.

Jung, C. G. (1954/1968). *The archetypes and the collective unconscious* (2nd ed.). London: Routledge and Kegan Paul.

Jung, C. G. (1954/1977). *The practice of psychotherapy.* Princeton, NJ: Princeton University Press.

Jung, C. G. (1958). Psychology and religion. In H. Read, M. Fordham, & G. Adler (Eds.), *The collected works of C. G. Jung* (Vol. 11, pp. 3–106). Princeton, NJ: Princeton University Press.

Jung, C. G. (1960/1981). *The structure and dynamics of the psyche.* Princeton, NJ: Princeton University Press.

Jung, C. G. (1965). *Memories, dreams and reflections.* New York: Vintage Books.

Jung, C. G. (1978). *Psychological reflections.* Princeton, NJ: Bollingen.

Kalodner, C. R. (2003). Cognitive-behavioral theories. In *Psychotherapy: Theories and interventions* (3rd ed., pp. 212–234). Upper Saddle River, NJ: Merrill Prentice-Hall.

Kass, J. D., Friedman, R., Leserman, J., Zuttermeister, P. C., & Benson, H. (1991). Health outcomes and a new index of spiritual experience. *Journal for the Scientific Study of Religion, 30,* 203–211.

Kazdin, A. E. (1989). Developmental psychopathology: Current research, issues and directions. *American Psychologist, 44*(2), 180–187.

Keks, N., & D'Souza, R. (2003). Spirituality and psychosis. *Autralasian Psychiatry, 11,* 170–171.

Kelly, E. W., Jr., & Sandage, S. J. (1995). *Spirituality and religion in counseling and psychotherapy.* Alexandria, VA: American Counseling Association.

King, P. E. (2003). Religion and identity: The role of ideological, social and spiritual contexts. *Applied Developmental Science, 7,* 197–204.

Klenck, M. (2004). The psychological and spiritual efficacy of confession. *Journal of Religion and Health, 43,* 139–150.

Kneezel, T. T., & Emmons, R. A. (2006). Personality and spiritual development. In E. C. Roehlkpartain, P. E. King, L. Wagener, & P. Benson (Eds.), *Handbook of spiritual development in childhood and adolescence* (pp. 266–278). Thousand Oaks, CA: Sage Publications.

Knox, S., Catlin, L., Casper, M., & Schlosser, L. Z. (2005). Addressing religion and spirituality in psychotherapy: Clients' perspectives. *Psychotherapy Research, 15,* 287–303.

Koenig, H. G., McCullough, M. E., & Larson, D. B. (2001). *Handbook of religion and health.* Oxford, England: Oxford University Press.

Koepfer, S. R. (2000). Drawing on the Spirit: Embracing spirituality in pediatrics and pediatric art therapy. *Art Therapy: Journal of the American Art Therapy Association, 17,* 188–194.

Kohlberg, L. (1981). *The philosophy of moral development.* New York: Harper & Row.

Kohlberg, L. (1984). *The psychology of moral development.* San Francisco, CA: Harper & Row.

Konstam, V., Chernoff, M., & Deveney, S. (2001). Toward forgiveness: The role of shame, guilt, anger and empathy. *Counseling and Values, 46,* 26–39.

Kornfield, J. (1993). *A path with heart.* New York: Bantam.

Kroll, J., & Egan, E. (2004). Psychiatry, moral worry and the moral emotions. *Journal of Psychiatric Practice, 10,* 352–360.

Kung, H. (1981). *Does God Exist? An answer for today.* New York: Vintage.

Larson, D. B., Sherrill, K. A., Lyons, J. S., Craigie, F. C., Thielman, S. B., Greenwold, M. A., & Larson, S. S. (1992). Associations between dimensions of religious commitment and mental health reported in the American Journal of Psychiatry and Archives of General Psychiatry: 1978–1989. *American Journal of Psychiatry, 149,* 557–559.

Larson, D. B., Swyers, J. P., & McCullough, M. E. (Eds.). (1998). *Scientific research on spirituality and health: A consensus report.* Rockville, MD: National Institute for Healthcare Research.

La Torre, M. A. (2004). Prayer in psychotherapy: An important consideration. *Perspectives in Psychiatric Care, 40,* 37–40.

Lauver, D. R. (2000). Commonalities in women's spirituality and women's health. *Advances in Nursing Science, 22,* 76–88.

Lease, S. H., Horne, S. G., & Noffsinger, F. (2005). Affirming faith experiences and psychological health for Caucasian lesbian, gay and bisexual individuals. *Journal of Counseling Psychology, 52,* 378–388.

Ledbetter, M. F., Smith, L. A., Vosler-Hunter, W. L., & Fischer, J. D. (1991). An evaluation of the research and clinical uses of the Spiritual Well-Being Scale. *Journal of Psychology and Theology, 19,* 49–55.

Liu, W. C. (1993). Confucianism. In Encarta.msn.com/encyclopedia-Confucianism.

Loevinger, J. (1976). *Ego development: Conception and theory.* San Francisco: Jossey-Bass.

Lonborg, S. D., & Bowen, N. (2004). Counselors, communities and spirituality: Ethical and multicultural considerations. *Professional School Counseling, 7,* 318–323.

Lottes, L., & Kuriloff, P. J. (1994). Sexual socialization differences by gender, Greek membership, ethnicity and religious background. *Psychology of Women Quarterly, 18,* 203–219.

Lownsdale, S. (1997). Faith development across the lifespan: Fowler's integrative work. *Journal of Psychology and Theology, 25,* 49–63.

Lukoff, D., Lu, F., & Turner, R. (1992). Transpersonal psychology research review: Psycho-religious dimensions of healing. *The Journal of Transpersonal Psychology, 24,* 41–60.

Lynch, B. (1996). Religious and spirituality conflicts. In D. Davies & C. Neal (Eds.), *Pink therapy: A guide for counselors and therapists working with gay, lesbian and bisexual clients* (pp. 199–207). Buckingham, England: Open University Press.

MacDonald, D. (2004). Collaborating with students' spirituality. *Professional School Counseling, 7,* 293–300.

Malloy, E. A. (1981). *Homosexuality and the Christian way of life.* Washington, DC: University Press of America.

Marcia, J. E. (1987). The identity status approach to the study of ego identity development. In T. Honess & K. Yardley (Eds.), *Self and identity: Perspectives across the lifespan* (pp. 161–171). Boston: Routledge and Kegan Paul.

Marcia, J. E., Waterman, A., Matteson, D., Archer, S., & Orlofsky, J. (1993). *Ego identity: A handbook for psychosocial research.* New York: Springer-Verlag.

Markstrom, C. A. (1999). Religious involvement and adolescent psychosocial development. *Journal of Adolescence, 22,* 205–221.

Maslow, A. H. (1968/1980). *Religion, values and peak experiences.* Harmondsworth, UK: Penguin.

Maslow, A. H. (1971). *Farther reaches of human nature.* New York: Viking.

Maslow, A. H. (1986). *Religions, Values and Peak-Experiences* (4th ed.). New York: Penguin Books.

Maslow, A. H. (1998). *Toward a Psychology of Being* (3rd ed.). New York: Wiley.

Mattis, J. S. (2002). Religion and spirituality in the meaning-making and coping experiences of African American women: A qualitative analysis. *Psychology of Women Quarterly, 26,* 309–321.

May, R. (1972). *Power and innocence: A search for the sources of violence.* New York: Dell Publishing.

Mayer, J. D., & Geher, G. (1996). Emotional intelligence and the identification of emotion. *Intelligence, 22,* 89–113.

McColl, M. (Ed.). (2003). *Spirituality and occupational therapy.* Ottawa: Canadian Association of Occupational Therapists.

McDermott, J. P. (1993). Buddhism. In Encarta.msn.com/encyclopedia-Buddhism.

McLean, K. C., & Thorne, A. (2003). Adolescents' self-defining memories about relationships. *Developmental Psychology, 39,* 635–645.

McLennan, N. A., Rochow, S., & Arthur, N. (2001). Religious and spiritual diversity in counselling. *Guidance and Counselling, 16,* 132–138.

McNish, J. L. (2004). *Transforming shame: A pastoral response.* New York: Haworth.

Mercer, J. A. (2006). Children as mystics, activists, sages and holy fools: Understanding the spirituality of children and its significance for clinical work. *Pastoral Psychology, 54,* 497–515.

Miller, G. (1999). The development of the spiritual focus in counseling and counselor education. *Journal of Counseling and Development, 77,* 498–501.

Miller, G. (2003). *Incorporating spirituality in counseling and psychotherapy: Theory and techniques.* Hoboken, NJ: Wiley.

Miller, W. R., & Delaney, H. D. (2005). Psychology as the science of human nature: Reflections and research directions. In W. R. Miller & H. D. Delaney (Eds), *Judeo-Christian perspectives on psychology* (pp. 291–308). Washington, DC: American Psychological Association.

Miller, W. R., & Thoresen, C. E. (2003). Spirituality, religion and health: An emerging research field. *American Psychologist, 58,* 24–35.

Milliren, A. P., Evans, T. D., & Newbauer, J. F. (2003). Adlerian counseling and psychotherapy. In *Psychotherapy: Theories and interventions* (3rd ed., pp. 91–130). Upper Saddle River, NJ: Merrill Prentice-Hall.

Miner, M. H. (2007). Back to the basics in attachment to God: Revisiting theory in light of theology. *Journal of Psychology and Theology, 35,* 112–122.

Mitroff, I. I. (2003). Spiritual I.Q.: The farthest reaches of human development. *World Futures, 59,* 485–494.

Moore, T. (1985). *Care of the soul: A guide for cultivating depth and sacredness in everyday life.* New York: Harper Collins.

Moser, R. S. (2006). Handbook of the psychology of religion and spirituality. *Archives of Clinical Neuropsychology, 21,* 368–369.

Murgatroyd, W. (2001). The Buddhist spiritual path: A counselor's reflection on meditation, spirituality, and the nature of life. *Counseling and Values, 45,* 94–102.

Myers, J. E. (1990, May). Wellness throughout the lifespan. *Guidepost,* 11.

Myers, J. E., Hattie, J. A., & Sweeney, T. J. (1999). *A multidisciplinary model of wellness: The development of the Wellness Evaluation of Lifestyle.* Unpublished manuscript, University of North Carolina at Greensboro.

Myers, J. E., & Williard, K. (2003). Integrating spirituality into counselor preparation: A developmental, wellness approach. *Counseling and Values, 47,* 142–155.

Narramore, S. B. (1974a). Guilt: Where psychology and theology meet. *Journal of Psychology and Theology, 2,* 18–25.

Narramore, S. B. (1974b). Guilt: Christian motivation or neurotic masochism? *Journal of Psychology and Theology, 2,* 182–189.

Nash. G. (1997). Researchers, health professionals and the "S" word. *DATA, 16,* 2–3.

National Association of Social Workers (NASW) (1999). *Code of Ethics.* Washington, DC: Author.

National Association of Social Workers, Committee on Racial and Ethnic Diversity. (2001). *NASW Standards for cultural competence in social work practice.* Washington, DC: Author.

Nelson, P. L., & Hart, T. (2003). *A survey of recalled childhood spiritual and non-ordinary experiences: Age, rate and psychological factors associated with their occurrence.* Retrieved April 15, 2007, from http://www.childspirit.org.

Novie, G. J. (2003). Psychoanalytic theory. In D. Capuzzi & D. R. Gross (Eds.), *Counseling and psychotherapy: Theories and interventions* (3rd ed., pp. 47–67). Upper Saddle River, NJ: Merrill Prentice-Hall.

Nugent, F. A., & Jones, K. D. (2005). *Introduction to the profession of counseling* (4th ed). Upper Saddle River, NJ: Merrill Prentice-Hall.

Nye, R., & Hay, D. (1996, Summer). Identifying children's spirituality: How do you start without a starting point? *British Journal of Religious Education, 9,* 144–154.

Nystul, M. S. (2006). *Introduction to counseling: An art and science perspective* (3rd ed.). Boston: Pearson.

O'Connor, M. (2004). A course in spiritual dimensions of counseling: Continuing the discussion. *Counseling and Values, 48,* 224–240.

Odell, M. (2003, September/October). Intersecting worldviews: Including vs. imposing spirituality in therapy. *Family Therapy Networker,* 26–30.

Olive, K. E. (2004). Religion and spirituality: Important psychosocial variables frequently ignored in clinical research. *Southern Medical Journal, 97,* 1152–1153.

Opatz, J. (Ed.). *Wellness promotion strategies: Selected proceedings of the eighth annual National Wellness Conference.* Dubuque, IA: Kendall/Hunt.

Oser, F. K. (1991). The development of religious judgment. In F. K. Oser & W. G. Scarlett (Eds.), Religious development in childhood and adolescence [Special issue]. *New Directions for Child Development, 52,* 5–25.

Pals, J. L., & McAdams, D. P. (2004). The transformed self: A narrative understanding of posttraumatic growth. *Psychological Inquiry, 15,* 65–69.

Pardeck, J. T., & Pardeck, J. A. (1993). *Bibliotherapy: A clinical approach for helping children.* Landhorne, PA: Gordon & Breach.

Pargament, K. I. (1997). *The psychology of religion and coping: Theory, research, and practice.* New York: Guilford Press.

Pargament, K. I., Magyar-Russell, G. M., & Murray-Swank, N. A. (2005). The sacred and the search for significance: Religion as a unique process. *Journal of Social Issues, 61,* 665–687.

Pargament, K. I., & Mahoney, A. (2005). Sacred matters: Sanctification as a vital topic for the psychology of religion. *The International Journal for the Psychology of Religion, 15,* 179–198.

Parker, M. S. (1985). Identity and the development of religious thinking. In A. S. Waterman (Ed.), *Identity in Adolescence: Processes and Content* (pp. 43–60).

Parker, W. E. (1988). *Consciousness-raising: A primer for multicultural counseling.* Springfield, IL: Thomas.

Parsons, F. (1909). *Choosing a vocation.* Boston: Houghton Mifflin.

Parsons, F. (1911). *Legal doctrine and social progress.* New York: B. W. Huebsch.

Parsons, W. B., & Jonte-Pace, D. (2001). Mapping religion and psychology. In D. Jonte-Pace & W. B. Parsons (Eds.), *Religion and psychology: Mapping this terrain* (pp. 1–101). London: Routledge.

Pate, R. H., & High, H. J. (1995). The importance of client religious beliefs and practices in the education of counselors in CACREP-accredited programs. *Counseling and Values, 40,* 2–5.

Pate, R. H., Jr., & Hall, M. P. (2005). One approach to a counseling and spirituality course. *Counseling and Values, 49,* 155–160.

Patterson, C. H. (1985). *The therapeutic relationship: Foundations for an eclectic psychotherapy.* Pacific Grove, CA: Brooks/Cole.

Patterson, C. H. (1989). Values in counseling and psychotherapy. *Counseling and Values, 33,* 164–176.

Patterson, J., Hayworth, M., Turner, C., & Raskin, M. (2000). Spiritual issues in family therapy: A graduate-level course. *Journal of Marital and Family Therapy, 26,* 199–210.

Peck, M. S. (1993). *A world waiting to be born: Civility rediscovered.* New York: Bantam Books.

Peck, M. S. (1978). *The road less traveled.* New York: Simon & Shuster.

Pergament, K. I., Murray-Swank, N. A., & Tarakeshwar, N. (2005). An empirically-based rationale for a spiritually-integrated psychotherapy. *Mental Health, Religion & Culture, 8,* 155–165.

Peterson, J. V. & Nisenholz, B. (1999). *Orientation to counseling* (4th ed.). Needham Heights, MA: Allyn & Bacon.

Piaget, J. (1932/1965). *The moral judgment of the child.* New York: Free Press.

Piaget, J. (1952). *The origins of intelligence in children* (M. Cook, Trans.). New York: Norton.

Pieper, J. Z. T. (2004). Religious coping in highly religious psychiatric inpatients. *Mental Health, Religion & Culture, 7,* 349–363.

Pineles, S. L., Street, A. E., & Koenen, K. C. (2006). The differential relationships of shame-proneness and guilt-proneness to psychological and somatization symptoms. *Journal of Social and Clinical Psychology, 25,* 688–704.

Poll, J. B., & Smith, T. B. (2003). The spiritual self: Toward a conceptualization of spiritual identity development. *Journal of Psychology and Theology, 31,* 129–142.

Powers, R. (2005). Counseling and spirituality: A historical review. *Counseling and Values, 49,* 217–225.

Pruyser, P. W. (1968). *A dynamic psychology of religion.* New York: Harper & Row.

Pruyser, P. W. (1976). *The minister as diagnostician.* Philadelphia, PA: Westminster Press.

Purdy, M., & Dupey, P. (2005). Holistic flow model of spiritual wellness. *Counseling and Values, 49,* 95–106.

Rak, C. F., & Patterson, L. E. (1996). Promoting resilience in at-risk children. *Journal of Counseling and Development, 74,* 368–373.

Rayburn, C. A. (2004). Religion, spirituality and health. *American Psychologist, 59,* 52–53.

Rayle, A. D., & Myers, J. E. (2004). Counseling adolescents toward wellness: The roles of ethnic identity, acculturation and mattering. *Professional School Counseling, 8,* 81–90.

Reed, P. (1992). An emerging paradigm for the investigation of spirituality in nursing. *Research in Nursing and Health, 15,* 349–357.

Richards, P. S., & Bergin, A. E. (1997). *A spiritual strategy for counseling and psychotherapy.* Washington, DC: American Psychological Association.

Richards, P. S., & Bergin, A. E. (1999). Toward religious and spiritual competency for mental health professionals. In P. S. Richards & A. E. Bergin (Eds.). *Handbook of psychotherapy and religious diversity* (pp. 1–39). Washington, DC: American Psychological Association.

Richards, P. S., & Bergin, A. E. (2000). Toward religious and spiritual competency for mental health professionals. In P. S. Richards & A. E. Bergin (Eds.). *Handbook of psychotherapy and religious diversity* (pp. 3–26). Washington, DC: American Psychological Association.

Richards, P. S. & Bergin, A. E. (2005). Ethical issues and guidelines. In P. S. Richards & A. E. Bergin (Eds.), *A spiritual strategy for counseling and psychotherapy* (2nd ed., pp. 143–169). Washington, DC: American Psychological Association.

Richards, P. S., Keller, R. R., & Smith, T. B. (2004). Religious and spiritual diversity in counseling and psychotherapy. In T. B. Smith (Ed.), *Practicing multiculturalism: Affirming diversity in counseling and psychotherapy* (pp. 276–293). Boston: Pearson Education.

Richmond, L. (2004). When spirituality goes awry: Students in cults. *Professional School Counseling, 7*(5), 367–375.

Riemer-Reiss, M. (2003). A counseling and human services course in spirituality. *Human Services Education, 23,* 67–74.

Ritter, K. Y., & Terndrup, A. I. (2002). *Handbook of affirmative psychotherapy with lesbians and gay men.* New York: Guilford Press.

Rizzuto, A.-M. (1979). *The birth of the living God.* Chicago: University of Chicago Press.

Rizzuto, A.-M. (1991). Religious development: A psychoanalytic point of view. In F. K. Oser & W. G. Scarlett (Eds.), Religious development in childhood and adolescence [Special issue]. *New Directions for Child Development, 52,* 47–60.

Roberts, L., Ahmed, I., & Hall, S. (2000). Intercessory prayer for the alleviation of ill health. Cochrane Database System Retrieval, CD 000368.

Robinson, B., Frye, E. M., & Bradley, L. J. (1997). Cult affiliation and disaffiliation: Implications for counseling. *Counseling and Values, 41,* 166–173.

Rodriguez, E. M., & Oullette, S. C. (2000). Gay and lesbian Christians: Homosexual and religious identity integration in the members and participants of a gay-positive church. *Journal for the Scientific Study of Religion, 39,* 333–347.

Rogers, C. R. (1957). The necessary and sufficient conditions of therapeutic personality change. *Journal of Consulting Psychology, 21,* 93–103.

Rogers, C. R. (1980). *A way of being.* Boston, MA: Houghton Mifflin.

Roof, W. C. (1999). *Spiritual marketplace: Baby-boomers and the remaking of American religion.* Princeton, NJ: Princeton University Press.

Rose, E. M., Westefeld, J. S., & Ansley, T. N. (2001). Spiritual issues in counseling: Clients' beliefs and preferences. *Journal of Counseling Psychology, 48*, 61–71.

Ruether, R. (1992). Mother Earth and the megamachine. In C. Christ & J. Plaskow (Eds.), *Womanspirit rising: A feminist reader in religion* (pp. 43–52). San Francisco: Harper San Francisco.

Ruether, R. (1995). Feminist metanois and soul-making. In J. Oschschorn & E. Cole (Eds.), *Women's spirituality, women's lives*. New York: Haworth Press.

Russell, S., & Yarhouse, M. A. (2006). Training in religion/spirituality with APA-accredited psychology predoctoral internships. *Professional Psychology: Research and Practice, 37*, 430–436.

Ryan, R. M., & Deci, E. L. (2000). Self-determination theory and the facilitation of intrinsic motivation, social development and well-being. *American Psychologist, 55*, 68–78.

Ryan, R. M., & Deci, E. L. (2002). Overview of self-determination theory: An organismic dialectical perspective. In E. L. Deci & R. M. Ryan (Eds.), *Handbook of self-determination research* (pp. 3–33). Rochester, NY: University of Rochester Press.

Ryff, C. D. (1989). Happiness is everything, or is it? Explorations on the meaning of psychological well-being. *Journal of Personality and Social Psychology, 57*, 1069–1081.

Ryff, C. D., & Keyes, C. L. M. (1995). The structure of psychological well-being revisited. *Journal of Personality and Social Psychology, 69*, 719–727.

Ryff, C. D., & Singer, B. (1998). The contours of positive human health. *Psychological Inquiry, 9*, 1–28.

Salsman, J. M., & Carlson, C. R. (2005). Religious orientation, mature faith, and psychological distress: Elements of positive and negative associations. *Journal for the Scientific Study of Religion, 44*, 201–209.

Savolaine, J., & Granello, P. F. (2002). The function of meaning and purpose for individual wellness. *Journal of Humanistic Counseling, Education & Development, 41*, 178–189.

Scharf, R. S. (2004). *Theories of psychotherapy and counseling: Concepts and cases* (3rd ed.). Pacific Grove, CA: Brooks/Cole-Thomson Learning.

Schlosser, L. Z. (2003). Christian privilege: Breaking a sacred taboo. *Journal of Multicultural Counseling and Development, 31*, 44–51.

Schmader, T., & Lickel, B. (2006). The approach and avoidance function of guilt and shame emotions: Comparing reactions to self-caused and other-caused wrongdoing. *Motivation and Emotion, 30*, 43–56.

Schopen, A., & Freeman, B. (1992). Meditation: The forgotten Western tradition. *Counseling and Values, 36*, 123–134.

Schuck, K. D. & Liddle, B. (2001). Religious conflicts experienced by lesbian, gay and bisexual individuals. *Journal of Gay and Lesbian Psychotherapy, 5*, 63–82.

Schulte, D. L., Skinner, T. A., & Claiborn, C. D. (2002). Religious and spiritual issues in counseling psychology training. *The Counseling Psychologist, 30*, 118–134.

Schwartz, S. E. (2003). Jungian analytical theory. In D. Capuzzi & D. R. Gross (Eds.). *Counseling and psychotherapy: Theories and interventions* (3rd ed., pp. 68–90). Upper Saddle River, NJ: Merrill Prentice-Hall.

Sealts, M. M. (1992). *Emerson on the scholar.* Columbia, MO: University of Missouri Press.

Seligman, L. (2006). *Theories of counseling and psychotherapy: Systems, strategies and skills* (2nd ed). Upper Saddle River, NJ: Pearson Merrill Prentice Hall.

Seligman, M., & Csikszentmihalyi, M. (2000). Positive psychology: An introduction. *American Psychologist, 55*, 5–14.

Seybold, K. S., & Hill, P. C. (2001). The role of religion and spirituality in mental and physical health. *Current Directions in Psychological Science, 10*, 21–24.

Sharma, A. R. (2000). Psychotherapy with Hindus. In P. S. Richards and A. E. Bergin (Eds.), *Handbook of psychotherapy and religious diversity* (pp. 341–365). Washington, DC: American Psychological Association.

Sheldon, K. M., & Kasser, T. (2001). Getting older, getting better? Personal strivings and psychosocial maturity across the life span. *Developmental Psychology, 34*, 491–501.

Shrafanske, E. P. (2000). Religious involvement and professional practices of psychiatrists and other mental health professionals. *Psychiatric Annals, 30*, 525–532.

Shrafanske, E. P., & Malony, H. N. (1996). Religion and the clinical practice of psychology: A case for inclusion. In E. P. Shrafanske (Ed.), *Religion and the clinical practice of psychology* (pp. 561–586). Washington, DC: American Psychological Association.

Silberman, I. (2003). Spiritual role modeling: The teaching of meaning systems. *The International Journal for the Psychology of Religion, 13*, 175–195.

Simmons, J. G. (2005). Other than "the set pattern": Developing one's own thoughts about spirituality and religion. *Mental Health, Religion & Culture, 8*, 239–251.

Sink, C. A., & Richmond, L. J. (2004). Introducing spirituality to professional school counseling. *Professional School Counseling, 7*, 291–294.

Sirkin, M. I. (1990). Cult involvement: A systems approach to assessment and treatment. *Psychotherapy, 27*, 116–123.

Smith, D. P., & Orlinsky, D. E. (2004). Religious and spiritual experience among psychotherapists. *Psychotherapy, 4*, 144–151.

Smith, E. J. (2006). The strength-focused counseling model: A paradigm shift in psychology. *The Counseling Psychologist, 34*, 134–144.

Smith, H. (1958). *The religions of man.* New York: Harper & Row.

Smith, S. G. (1988). *The concept of the spiritual: An essay in first philosophy.* Philadelphia, PA: Temple University Press.

Souza, K. Z. (2002). Spirituality in counseling: What do counseling students think about it? *Counseling and Values, 46*, 213–217.

Spero, M. H. (1992). *Religious objects as psychological structures.* Chicago: University of Chicago Press.

Sperry, L. (2001). *Spirituality in clinical practice: Incorporating the spiritual dimension in psychotherapy and counseling.* Philadelphia, PA: Brunner-Routledge/Taylor & Francis.

Sperry, L. (2007, November). Personal interview from Florida Atlantic University, Boca Raton.

Sperry, L. (2007). *The ethical and professional practice of counseling and psychotherapy.* Boston: Pearson.

Stanard, R. P., Sandhu, D. S., & Painter, L. C. (2000). Assessment of spirituality in counseling. *Journal of Counseling and Development, 78*, 204–210.

Steen, R. L., Engels, D., & Thweatt, W. T., III. (2006). Ethical aspects of spirituality in counseling. *Counseling and Values, 50*, 108–118.

Steere, D. A. (1997). *Spiritual presence in psychotherapy: A guide for caregivers.* New York: Brunner/Mazel.

Sterling, R. C., Weinstein, S., Hill, P, Gottheil, E., Gordon, S. M., & Shorie, K. (2006). Levels of spirituality and treatment outcome: A preliminary examination. *Journal of Studies on Alcohol, 67*, 600–606.

St. John, I. (2000). *Creative spirituality for women.* Springfield, IL: Charles C. Thomas.

Stonehouse, C. (1998). The power of Kohlberg. In J. Wilhoit and J. Dettoni (Eds.), *Development that is Christian: Developmental perspectives on Christian education.* Grand Rapids, MI: Baker Books.

Sue, D. W., Bingham, R., Porche-Burke, L., & Vasquez, M. (1999). The diversification of psychology: A multicultural revolution. *American Psychologist, 54*, 1061–1069.

Sue, D. W., & Sue, D. (2003). *Counseling the culturally diverse* (4th ed.). New York: John W. Wiley.

Summit on spirituality: Counselor competencies (1996, May, Rev.; 1997, Spring). *ACES Spectrum, 57*, 16.

Tan, S. (1996). Religion in clinical practice: Implicit and explicit integration. In E. P. Shafranske (Ed.), *Religion and the clinical practice of psychology* (pp. 365–387). Washington, DC: American Psychological Association.

Tan, S. Y. (2003). Integrating spiritual direction into psychotherapy: Ethical issues and guidelines. *Journal of Psychology and Theology, 31*, 14–23.

Tangey, J. P., & Fischer, K. W. (1995). *Self-conscious emotions: The psychology of shame, guilt, embarrassment and pride.* New York: Guilford.

Taylor, B. B. (2004). Bibliotherapy. *The Christian Century, 121*(5), 40–41.

Teyber, E. (2006). *Interpersonal Process in Therapy: An Integrative Model* (5th ed.). Pacific Grove, CA: Brooks/Cole.

Thoresen, C. E. (1999). Spirituality and health: Is there a relationship? *Journal of Health Psychology, 4*, 291–300.

Thoresen, C. E., & Harris, A. H. S. (2002). Spirituality and health: What's the evidence and what's needed? *Annals of Behavioral Medicine, 34*, 3–13.

Thoresen, C. E., Oman, D., & Harris, A. H. S. (2005). The effects of religious practices: A focus on health. In W. R. Miller & H. D. Delaney (Eds.), *Judeo-Christian perspectives on psychology* (pp. 205–226). Washington, DC: American Psychological Association.

Thorne, A., McLean, K. C., & Lawrence, A. (2004). When remembering is not enough: Reflecting on self-defining events in late adolescence. *Journal of Personality, 72*, 513–542.

Thurston, N. S. (2000). Psychotherapy with evangelical and fundamentalist Protestants. In P. S. Richards and A. E. Bergin (Eds.), *Handbook of psychotherapy and religious diversity* (pp. 131–153). Washington, DC: American Psychological Association.

Townes, E. M. (1995). *In a blaze of glory: Womanist spirituality as social witness*. Nashville, TN: Abingdon Press.

Townsend, M., Kladder, V., Ayele, H., & Mulligan, T. (2002). Systematic review of clinical trials examining the effects of religion on health. *Southern Medical Journal, 95*, 1429–1434.

Tse, S., Lloyd, C., Petchkovsky, L., & Manaia, W. (2005). Exploration of Australian and New Zealand indigenous people's spirituality and mental health. *Australian Occupational Therapy Journal, 52*, 181–187.

Turner, T. E., Center, H., & Kiser, J. D. (2004). Uniting spirituality and sexual counseling. *The Family Journal, 12*, 419–422.

Vaillant, G. E. (1993). *The wisdom of the ego*. Cambridge, MA: Harvard University Press.

Van Dierendonck, D., & Mohan, K. (2006). Some thoughts on spirituality and eudaimonic well-being. *Mental Health, Religion & Culture, 9*, 227–238.

Van Kleef, G. A., De Dreu, C. K. W., & Manstead, A. S. R. (2006). Supplication and appeasement in conflict and negotiation: The interpersonal effects of disappointment, worry, guilt and regret. *Journal of Personality and Social Psychology, 91*, 124–142.

Van Soest, D. (1996). The influence of competing ideologies about homosexuality on nondiscrimination policy: Implications for social work education. *Journal of Social Work Education, 32*, 53–64.

Veach, T. L., & Chappel, J. N. (1992). Measuring spiritual health: A preliminary study. *Substance Abuse, 13*, 139–147.

Vera, E. M., & Speight, S. L. (2003). Multicultural competence, social justice and counseling psychology: Expanding our roles. *The Counseling Psychologist, 31*, 253–272.

Vernon, A. (2003). Rational emotive behavior therapy. In *Psychotherapy: Theories and interventions* (3rd ed., pp. 47–67). Upper Saddle River, NJ: Merrill Prentice-Hall.

Wagner, G., Serafini, J., Rabkin, J., Remien, R., & Williams, J. (1994). Integration of one's religion and homosexuality: A weapon against internalized homophobia. *Journal of Homosexuality, 26*, 91–110.

Wagner, W. G. (1996). Optimal development in adolescence: What it is and how it can be encouraged. *The Counseling Psychologist, 24*, 360–369.

Walker, D. F., Gorsuch, R. L., & Tan, S. Y. (2004). Therapists' integration of religion and spirituality in counseling: A meta-analysis. *Counseling and Values, 49*, 69–80.

Wallace, J. M., & Williams, D. R. (1997). Religion and adolescent health-compromising behavior. In J. Schulenberg, J. L. Maggs, & K. Hurrelmann (Eds.), *Health risks and developmental transitions during adolescence* (pp. 444–468). Cambridge, UK: Cambridge University Press.

Wangu, M. B. (1991). *Hinduism*. New York: Facts on File.

Wangu, M. B. (1993). *Buddhism*. New York: Facts on File.

Watts, F., Dutton, K., & Gulliford, L. (2006). Human spiritual qualities: Integrating psychology and religion. *Mental Health, Religion & Culture, 9*, 277–289.

Weaver, A. J., Samford, J. A., Morgan, V. J., Larson, D. B., Koenig, H. G., & Flannelly, K. J. (2002). A systemic review of research on religion in six primary marriage and family journals: 1995–1999. *American Journal of Family Therapy, 30*, 293–309.

Weinstein, C. M., Parker, J., & Archer, J. (2002). College counselor attitudes toward spiritual and religious issues and practices in counseling. *Journal of College Counseling, 5*, 164–174.

Weld, C., & Eriksen, K. (2007). The ethics of prayer in counseling. *Counseling and Values, 51*, 125–138.

Westgate, C. E. (1996). Spiritual wellness and depression. *Journal of Counseling and Development, 75*, 26–35.

Wiggins Frame, M. (2000). Spiritual and religious issues in counseling: Ethical considerations. *The Family Journal, 8*, 72–74.

Wiggins Frame, M. (2003). *Integrating religion and spirituality into counseling: A comprehensive approach*. Pacific Grove, CA: Brooks/Cole-Thomson Learning.

Wiggins Frame, M. (2005). Spirituality and religion: Similarities and differences. In C. S. Cashwell & J. S. Young (Eds.), *Integrating spirituality and religion into counseling: A guide to competent practice* (pp. 11–30). Alexandria, VA: American Counseling Association.

Wiggins, M. (2007, October). Personal interview from the University of Colorado at Denver.

Wilber, K. (1999). *Integral psychology: Consciousness, spirit, psychology, therapy (A synthesis of premodern, modern and postmodern approaches).* Boston, MA: Shambala.

Wilber, K. (2000). Waves, streams, states and self. *Journal of Consciousness Studies, 7,* 11–37.

Wilson, A. (1996). How we find ourselves: Identity development and two-spirit people. *Harvard Educational Review, 66,* 303–317.

Wittmer, J. M., & Sweeney, T. J. (1992). A holistic model for wellness and prevention over the lifespan. *Journal of Counseling and Development, 71,* 140–148.

Wittmer, J. M., & Sweeney, T. J. (1998). Toward wellness: The goal of counseling. In T. J. Sweeney, *Adlerian counseling: A practitioner's approach* (pp. 43–99). Philadelphia: Accelerated Development Press.

Wolf, C. T., & Stevens, P. (2001). Integrating religion and spirituality in marriage and family counseling. *Counseling and Values, 46,* 66–75.

Wolf, J. T. (2004). Teach, but don't preach: Practical guidelines for addressing spiritual concerns of students. *Professional School Counseling, 7,* 363–366.

Wong, Y. J., Rew, L., & Slaikeu, K. D. (2006). A systemic review of recent research on adolescent religiosity/spirituality and mental health. *Issues in Mental Health Nursing, 27,* 161–183.

World Health Organization (WHO). (1958). Annex 1: In the first ten years of the World Health Organization. In *Constitution of the World Health Organization.* Geneva, Switzerland: Author.

Worthington, E. L., Jr. (1989). Religious faith across the lifespan: Implications for counseling and research. *The Counseling Psychologist, 17,* 555–612.

Worthington, E. L., Jr. (2001). Religion and spirituality. *Psychotherapy, 38,* 473–478.

Worthington, E. L., Jr., Kurusu, A. T., McCullough, E. M., & Sandage, J. S. (1996). Empirical research on religion and psychotherapeutic processes and outcomes: A 10-year review and research project. *Psychological Bulletin, 119,* 448–487.

Worthington, E. L., Jr., O'Connor, L. E., & Berry, J. W. (2005). Compassion and forgiveness: Implications for psychotherapy. In G. Paul (Ed.), *Compassion: Conceptualizations, research, and use in psychotherapy* (pp. 168–192). New York: Routledge.

Wubbolding, R. E. (2003). Reality therapy theory. In *Psychotherapy: Theories and interventions* (3rd ed., pp. 47–67). Upper Saddle River, NJ: Merrill Prentice-Hall.

Yalom, I. D. (1980). *Existential guilt.* New York: Basic Books.

Yamey, G., & Greenwood, R. (2004). Religious views of the "medical" rehabilitation model: A pilot qualitative study. *Disability and Rehabilitation, 26,* 455–462.

Yathouse, M. A., & Fisher, W. (2002). Levels of training to address religion in clinical practice. *Psychotherapy, 39,* 171–176.

Young, J. S., & Cashwell, C. S. (2005). Epilogue: Where do you go from here? In C. S. Caashwell & J. S. Young (Eds.), *Integrating spirituality and religion into counseling: A guide to competent practice* (pp. 185–190). Alexandria, VA: American Counseling Association.

Young, J. S., Cashwell, C., Wiggins Frame, M., & Belaire, C. (2002). Spiritual and religious competencies: A national survey of CACREP-accredited programs. *Counseling and Values, 47,* 22–33.

Zimpfer, D. G. (1992). Psychosocial treatment of life-threatening disease: A wellness model. *Journal of Counseling and Development, 71,* 203–209.

Zinnbauer, B. J., & Pargament, K. I. (2000). Working with the sacred: Four approaches to religious and spiritual issues in counseling. *Journal of Counseling and Development, 78,* 162–171.

Zinnbauer, B. J., Pargament, K. L., & Scott, A. B. (1999). The emerging meanings of religiousness and spirituality: Problems and prospects. *Journal of Personality, 67,* 889–920.

INDEX

Becvar, R. J., 247
Behavioral theory, wellness and, 199–200
Bell Object Relations Inventory, 98
Benner, D. G., 96
Bennett, S. B., 114, 125–126
Benson, H., 98
Benson, P. L., 188
Bergin, A. E., 20, 95, 97, 166, 175, 177, 178, 180, 230
Berk, L., 110
Bernard, J. M., 19
Berry, J. W., 118
Berry, M., 243
Bibliotherapy, 228–230
Bilgrave, D. P., 30
Bowen, M., 79
Bowen, N., 213
Bown, J., 38
Bowring, J., 239
Bradley, L. J., 110
Brawer, P. A., 30
Briggs, M. K., 20, 25, 26, 33, 188, 189, 220
Brokaw, B. F., 159
Brooke, S. L., 209
Buber, M., 157, 161
Buchanan, M., 207, 208
Buddhism, 42–43
  evil and, 137–138
Bulkeley, K., 227
Burber, M., 51
Burke, M. T., 52, 53
Buros Mental Measurement Yearbook series, 97
Bush, M., 115, 127–128
Bynum, E. B., 120
Byrd, R. C., 222

C

Campbell, D., 12
Capps, D., 46
Capuzzi, D., 22
Carlson, T. D., 29, 96, 224, 240
Carrera, S. R., 221
Carroll, S., 233
Carson, V., 38
Cashwell, C. S., 5, 15, 27, 33, 261, 263, 264, 265, 266, 269
Center, H., 203
Centrality, period of, 7–8
Cervantes, J. M., 6, 96
Cha, K. Y., 222
Chappel, J. N., 99–100
Chernoff, M., 126–127

Children
  cognitive development, 66–67
  Fowler's faith development model, 58–59, 64
  Genia's faith development model, 60–61, 64
  moral development, 69–71
  Oser's religious judgment development model, 59–60, 65
  psychosocial, 67–69
  religion/spirituality and, 210–215
  Rizzuto's development of representations of God model, 61–62, 65
  Spero's religious transformations model, 62–64
Christianity
  description of beliefs, 39–40
  early, 7–8
Chu, L., 71
Claiborn, C. D., 32
Clark, M., 96
Clients
  role of, 162–163
  types of, 220
  welfare and ethics, 167–169
Clinical services, recommendations for future work on, 260–270
Clinical view
  of evil, 138–147
  of guilt, 124–127
  spiritual wellness and, 189–200
Cloyd, B. S., 211, 215
Cobb, M., 38
Cognitive development, 66–67
Cognitive theory, wellness and, 196–199
Cohen, C. B., 222–223
Cohen, H., 214
Cole, B. S., 234, 235
Coles, R., 211
Compassion, 88
Competence
  ethics and, 172–173
  spiritual wellness and, 188
Confucianism, 43
Constructivist stance, 91–92
Consultations
  ethics and, 180–182
  use of, 235–236
Cook, S. W., 221
Corey, G., 185, 190, 193, 194, 197, 198, 199, 200
Corright, B., 93
Council for the Accreditation of Counseling and Related Educational Programs (CACREP), 20
  standards, 28–29